C0-CCO-136

HONG KONG

HONG KONG

Economic, Social and Political Studies in Development

with a comprehensive bibliography

TZONG-BIAU LIN
RANCE P. L. LEE
UDO-ERNST SIMONIS
Editors

A PUBLICATION OF THE INSTITUTE OF ASIAN AFFAIRS IN HAMBURG

M.E. SHARPE, INC.

DAWSON

A publication of the Institute of Asian Affairs, Hamburg

The Institute of Asian Affairs pursues and promotes research on contemporary Asian affairs. It cooperates with other Institutes of regional studies in Hamburg which together form the Foundation German Overseas Institute.

Opinions expressed in the publications of the Institute of Asian Affairs are the authors'. They do not necessarily reflect those of the Institute.

First published in 1979 by M. E. Sharpe, Inc.
901 North Broadway, White Plains, New York 10603, U.S.A., and
Wm Dawson & Sons Ltd, Cannon House, Folkstone, Kent, England

Library of Congress Catalog Card Number: 79-88894
M.E. Sharpe ISBN: 0-87332-151-0
Dawson ISBN: 0-7129-0942-7

Printed in the United States of America

CONTENTS

PREFACE

Hong Kong's successful transformation from a traditional entrepôt economy into a major industrial city-state and an important financial centre in the Far East has often been acclaimed as one of the "economic miracles" in the history of the modern world. Within less than three decades, the per capita income in Hong Kong has increased about 13 times (reaching nearly US $ 3,000 in 1978) and ranks third in the entire Far East region, second only to Japan and Singapore, while Hong Kong's total exports multiplied 11 times, ranking 20th in the whole world. Furthermore, Hong Kong is probably the third city in the world, after London and New York, in terms of foreign banking and quasi-banking institutions.

These few figures already indicate the tremendous economic success Hong Kong has achieved in the past 30 years. What is more surprising, however, is that all this has been done in a colonial city-state with a total land area of only 400 square miles, in which approximately 4.6 million people live.

Although numerous publications about Hong Kong's economic success have appeared in the past, the majority of them touched on a specific aspect, either political, social or economic, in the dramatic transformation process. Since the appearance of the book "Hong Kong: The Industrial Colony" in 1971, there has not been a single book which covers the whole field of political, economic and social development in Hong Kong. The aim of this publication is to fill that gap.

Politically Hong Kong is still, de facto, a colony of Great Britain, although since 1972 Hong Kong and Macau have been removed from the United Nations' list of colonies at the request of the People's Republic of China - and despite the fact that even the Government now prefers to ignore its colonial appellation and has ordered its information services to avoid the word "colony" when talking about Britain's last possession in the Far East. In 1997, however, the lease for the New Territories, which make up the largest part of Hong Kong's overall territory, will expire. If the tenure of the running lease is not renegotiated and renewed, the New Territories will be returned to China within less than 20 years. Without the New Territories it is inconceivable that Hong Kong could survive. As long as this political cloud (this "question mark") is not dispersed from the time horizon Hong Kong is still a "borrowed place living on borrowed time" (and as such long-run investments are bound to be adversely affected sooner or later). Notwithstanding the uncertain political future, Hong Kong has been remarkably stable in the past three decades. The political stability coupled with the long cherished economic policy formed an institutional environment attractive to industrialists, local and overseas alike, and conducive to rapid economic growth.

The stable political situation since the second world war was marred by two social up-risings, first in 1966 and then more pronounced in 1967. Although the unrest in 1967, which was spawned by the cultural revolution in China, diminished after a few months, it precipitated a series of social and political reforms adopted by the Hong Kong Government. The Government's previous preoccupation with the socio-economic elite has given way to a grass-roots approach, showing increasing concern for the "man on the street". This is also due to the emergence of a new young generation in the last ten years who identify themselves more closely with the fate of Hong Kong. This change of political attitude has been reflected in the strengthening of the social services and in the introduction of labour legislation. Consequently, the idea of a "minimal government" whose prima facie task is to provide an infrastructure for economic growth has been supplemented by the idea of a more active government which shows more interest in the improvement of the quality of life for all. The traditional policy of laissez-faire has been skillfully changed and is now more pragmatically "guided".

The changes on the socio-political level in Hong Kong are discussed in seven papers in this book. H.C. Kuan and L. Nthenda give an excellent analysis of the political framework and the subtle changes in policy making which have taken place since 1967 and resulted in a rapid growth of "realpolitik". While socialist China has discovered that this capitalist doormat at its southern gateway could be a distinct help in a new policy of detente and international cooperation (even though Hong Kong remains for her an example of detestable capitalism), the colony has begun to stand up to its social responsibilities. Long-range plans have been developed to provide for improvements in the various fields of society and economy. The role of public bodies and the kind of government controls are analysed with some detail in L. Nthenda's paper.

The pressing population and housing problems which attract a great deal of the Government's attention are discussed and analysed in C.Y. Choi and Y.K. Chan's paper on public housing development. Using the new satellite industrial town of Kwun Tong as an example, the paper shows the Government's approach towards solving the thorny problems of public housing which in 1978 accommodates about 1.8 million people, roughly 40 per cent of the total population.

F.M. Wong attempts to analyse the features of the Chinese family structure and its process of change and stabilization over the past twenty years. The political situation exerts an unquestionable influence on the youth. As a result, their sense of belonging to Hong Kong as a whole is still rather weak and adolescents seem to be "socially malnourished" and detached. The details of the issue are discussed in T.S. Cheung's paper.

Hong Kong has experienced a tremendous increase in prosperity in the past 30 years. Whether the material gains reached will also mean a higher degree of life-satisfaction, is the subject matter of the paper by R.P.L. Lee, T.S. Cheung and Y.W. Cheung.

As Hong Kong develops economically and socially, human behaviour will inevitably change, though with differing intensity in the various areas. One particular aspect of this is the change in the managerial attitudes towards employees. Traditionally, the indigenous employers emphasized the kinship-friendship connections. The question as to whether or how these old-fashioned attitudes have been changed in the course of industrialization is empirically examined in the paper by S.K. Lau.

In development economics it is commonly said that in order to attain rapid industrialization it is necessary to develop large-scale industries. In fact, in most industrialization programmes too little attention has been paid to the development of small industries. Contrary to this general belief, the Hong Kong economy is characterized by a fairly small number of big enterprises surrounded by a very large number of small size factories. The contribution of the small factories to the Hong Kong economic growth therefore is carefully examined in the paper by A.Y.C. King and P.J.L. Man.

The changing political and social situation has repercussions for economic development. Within three decades Hong Kong has developed from the stage of labour-intensive industries to the current stage of skill- and technology-intensive industries. The traditional textile industry, which still occupies some 50 per cent of the total visible exports from Hong Kong, has encountered double difficulties: growing competition from neighboring countries, notably South Korea and Taiwan, on the international markets, and the quota restrictions imposed on Hong Kong's exports by the Western industrialized countries - especially the European Economic Community, with British encouragement, which dealt a blow to Hong Kong's vital textile export quotas. As the Hong Kong economy is essentially export-propelled, the export barriers will definitely hamper further economic growth. To emphasize Hong Kong's dependence on undisturbed economic relations, we have selected five papers which cover the various aspects of the recent economic developments.

The paper by K.C. Mun and S.C. Ho on foreign investment investigates Hong Kong's attraction to and the motivation of foreign investors. The questions of trade barriers and trade promotion activities are dealt with in V. Mok's paper, while in the paper by T.B. Lin and M.C. Lin the relationship between exports and employment are discussed in detail.

As mentioned earlier, the Hong Kong economy as a free port is to a large extent unique among the developing countries; its highly successful transformation was achieved without strong governmental intervention or special incentives. The development pattern is indeed a process of continued adjustment made spontaneously by the entreprises to changing world market conditions. This rather unique development is formulated in T.T. Hsueh's paper. By and large, the Hong Kong economy can best be depicted as a type of belonging to the classical laissez-faire model in the contemporary world. In such a model the fiscal conservatism has constituted the rule of law for the operation of the Hong Kong economy, and the main task for the public sector until recently was to maintain law and order so that the residents could pursue their self-interest under the mechanism of the "invisible hand", and to create an environment which is conducive to investment and attractive to industrialists and capitalists from all over the world. Neutral budgetary and fiscal policy was adopted and the size of the government sector was kept to a minimum. But in more recent years, due to changing political attitudes and the emphasis of the education and social programmes, the role of the government has significantly increased and has been structurally changed. This development is specifically examined in the paper written by T.T. Hsueh and K.L. Shea.

Finally, the bibliographical stock of the Economic and the Social Research Center of the Chinese University of Hong Kong and of the Institute of World Economy in Kiel have been put together to produce the most comprehensive bibliography extant on Hong Kong.

Summing up, Hong Kong is marching ahead with unchanged assurance, continuing production and trade expansion, improving housing, traffic and social welfare programmes - and with the best relations ever with China. The topics discussed in the present book have been carefully chosen so as to cover all the important political, social and economic aspects of the highly successful transformation which Hong Kong has undergone in the last three decades, and also to give some clues as to what might possibly happen in the future.

Hong Kong and Berlin, December 1978

Tzong-Biau Lin
Rance P.L. Lee
Udo E. Simonis

I. ECONOMIC GROWTH AND STRUCTURAL CHANGE

HONG KONG'S MODEL OF ECONOMIC DEVELOPMENT

Tien-tung Hsueh

I. The Structure and Operation of the Hong Kong Economy[+]

Hong Kong is one of the most exciting and ex ante one of the most improbable cases of rapid economic growth in history. Endowed with only few raw materials all inputs, except labor and land, must be imported from abroad. Exports and the inflow of foreign capital are the only two possible ways of effectively ensuring the smooth flow of imports. Thus the rest of the world constitutes not only a supply of available resources but also a necessary outlet for Hong Kong's products. Hong Kong, a tiny land with a tremendously high population density, is destined to have an outward-looking feature during the course of economic development. The first circuit of the Hong Kong economy goes to foreign trade, rather than to the domestic production sector.

Throughout the recorded history of Hong Kong, laissez-faire doctrine and free-port policy have been adopted and followed by the authorities; the free flow of information, making the dissemination of international technical know-how possible, as well as the attraction of foreign investors and tourists, have been considered the most important tactics for achieving a rapidly growing economy. Hong Kong has been developed as one of the great financial centres of the world. The excellent financial facilities play an indispensable role in absorbing domestic savings and foreign capital and transforming them into fixed capital formation.

Hong Kong has followed the classical liberal model as the mainstay of economic policy. It is believed that the mechanism of free competition will lead to the best allocation of productive resources

[+] This paper was written when I was affiliated with the Harvard-Yenching Institute at Harvard University as a research fellow for the academic year 1977-78. Special appreciation goes to Mrs. Kate Field of the Institute, who made the paper more readable.

from the viewpoint of efficiency, given income distribution determined by the competitive market forces. Therefore, the size of the public sector has been reduced as small as possible, so that distortion of the private sector is avoided. The public sector is at most subordinate to the private sector.

There is no central bank in Hong Kong. The issue of money was authorized to three private commercial banks[1], based on 100 % sterling backing. By this is meant that money can only be issued against an equal amount of certificates of indebtedness bought with sterling from the Exchange Fund of the British Government. As a matter of fact, the currency issue in Hong Kong has been more than 100 % backed by sterling assets. This monetary policy maintains the strong ties with the available foreign exchanges stemming from the foreign trade sector.[2]

Given this sketch of the contour of the Hong Kong economy, we are now able to have an overall view of the actual performance during the period of 1961-1976, the only period for which official data are available.

The outward-looking feature of the economy of Hong Kong can be clearly seen from the fact that throughout the period under review, more than half of the current fixed capital formation was financed by foreign capital. The capability of domestic saving was maintained by approximately 10 % of the Gross Domestic Product (GDP), which was lower than those of other countries, selected for comparison (Table 1).

In general, the industrial sector of Hong Kong adopted relatively labor-intensive production techniques, ranging from simple assembly to more sophisticated manufacturing. The marginal capital-output ratio was inclined to be lower when compared with the selected countries in the specific periods.

The service sector has been well established since the early development of Hong Kong as an entrepôt.[3] The recent growth of the

---

[1] Namely the Hong Kong and Shanghai Banking Corp., the Chartered Bank and the Mercantile Bank. Cf.Y.C. JAO: Banking and Currency in Hong Kong, London: Macmillan, 1974.

[2] See T.T. HSUEH, Y.C. WONG: Growth and Liquidity in a Small Open Economy, Hong Kong, The Chinese University of Hong Kong, mimeo.

[3] See G.B. ENDACOTT: An Eastern Entrepôt, London: Her Majesty's Stationery Office, 1964.

Table 1: Indicators of the Hong Kong Economy

	1961-63	64-66	67-69	70-72	73-75	Average
Δ GDP/GDP %	10.95	10.94	9.13	5.40	6.59	8.43
F/GDP %	15.65	14.33	4.20	11.51	12.93	11.72
F/I %	62.23	54.97	23.36	54.08	59.34	51.00
$\sum_{\tau=1962}^{t} I_{\tau}$ $GDP_t - GDP_{1961}$	2.68	2.71	2.60	2.72	2.86	2.72

Other selected countries	United Kingdom 1930/38 - 52/58	Italy 1921/39 - 52/58	Denmark 1931/39 - 52/58	United States 1939/48 - 48/57	Japan 1935/39 - 52/58
	6.6	5.6	6.4	4.7	4.2

	1961-63	64-66	67-69	70-72	73-75	Average
S/GDP %	9.10	11.63	13.78	9.41	8.84	10.55

Other selected countries S/GNP	Canada 1926-30	Canada 50-59	Japan 1927-36	Japan 50-59	Denmark 1921-30	Denmark 50-59	Germany 1928	Germany 50-59
	19.5	22.4	15.3	30.2	12.2	18.9	16.7	26.8

	1961-63	64-66	67-69	70-72	73-75	Average
G/GDP %	7.15	6.82	6.90	6.61	6.91	6.88

Other selected countries G/GNP	United Kingdom 1950-58	Germany (1950 - 59)	Italy (1950 - 59)	Denmark (1950 - 59)	USA (1950 - 59)	Australia (1950 - 59)	Japan (1950 - 59)
	16.9	14.4	12.0	12.5	17.9	9.9	10.3

Sources: (1) Hong Kong: Estimates of Gross Domestic Product 1961-1975, Census and Statistics Department, Hong Kong, 1977, p. 23.

(2) Other selected countries: Simon Kuznets, Modern Economic Growth, New Haven: Yale University Press, 1973, pp. 236-239, 252-256.

Notes: 1. 1966 constant prices for Hong Kong. Data for other countries are in current prices.

2. Data for Hong Kong in the period before 1961 back to 1952 can be obtained from Tien-tung Hsueh (a): "The Transforming Economy of Hong Kong 1952-1973", Hong Kong Economic Papers, No. 10, 1976, pp. 62-63.

manufacturing sector further accelerated the expansion of the service sector because of the huge inflow of foreign capital. As shown in Table 2, the service sector has long since taken a dominant GDP share, more than 60 %, for both Hong Kong and Singapore, and contributed the greatest part of the growth of the national economy in the period under review.

Since the domestic market is still fairly small, Hong Kong has made every effort in the promotion of exports, rather than by substitution of imports, because of the economies of scale. Exports are confined to a narrow range of industries, and their markets depend heavily upon a few developed countries, such as the U.S.A., U.K., Germany, Japan, Australia and Canada.[4] As a result, the Hong Kong economy is destined to be unstable. Some information is given in Table 2, from which one can perceive that the manufacturing sector grew by only 2 % and contributed to the growth of GDP merely 0.5 % in the period of 1970-1974.

Of the four functions of the public sector,[5] i.e. allocation, stabilization, distribution and economic growth, the Hong Kong government occasionally takes the fourth one into account and leaves the other three to be fulfilled by the private sector through the market mechanism.[5] It is noted that among the few specifically economic regulations set up by the government, the following are perhaps the important ones: reduction of hours of work for women and young children, measures of wage protection, maternity leave, four rest-days per month, worker's compensation, etc., set up in the late '60's;[6] 25 % reserve ratio requirement, in 1964; and small-scale firms loan scheme, in 1972.

Given the narrow scope of the public sector whose main function is to provide the requirements of social overhead capital and social services for the private sector, the tax base has long been limited. Accordingly, government consumption shared merely a small percentage of GDP compared with the other countries.

---

[4] See Tien-tung HSUEH (b): "Growth Pattern and Structure Change of Hong Kong 1959-1970", <u>United College Journal</u>, Vols. 12-13, 1975, p. 315.

[5] About Hong Kong's public sector, see also Tien-tung HSUEH and Koon-lam SHEA: "Analysis and Projection of Hong Kong Public Finance", in this Volume.

[6] See Joe ENGLAND: "Industrial Relations in Hong Kong", in: Keith HOPKINS (ed.): <u>Hong Kong: The Industrial Colony</u>, Hong Kong: University Press, 1971, pp. 215-221.

Table 2: Sectoral Contribution to the Growth of GDP at Factor Cost, Hong Kong (1970-74), and Singapore (1960-72)

		Agriculture & fishing	Manufacturing & quarrying	Construction	Electricity, gas & water	Commerce	Service	$\frac{\Delta GDP}{GDP_{t-1}}$
Size factor	Hong Kong	1.91	29.07	3.81	1.74	21.24	42.23	
	Singapore	4.39	15.25	4.27	2.26	29.10	44.63	
Growth factor	Hong Kong	-0.70	1.79	16.67	1.37	6.94	10.70	
	Singapore	3.06	19.58	23.71	10.51	8.90	7.47	
Consolidation factor	Hong Kong	-0.02	0.50	0.64	0.017	1.40	4.51	7.05
	Singapore	0.11	3.01	0.93	0.23	2.50	3.31	10.10

Sources: (1) Hong Kong: Estimates of Gross Domestic Product 1961-1975, p. 33.

(2) Singapore: Tien-tung HSUEH (c): "Development Features of a Mini Open Economy: The Cases of Singapore and Hong Kong", Journal of the Chinese University of Hong Kong, Vol. III, No. 1, 1975, p. 261.

Notes: 1. Formula for measurement:

$$\frac{\Delta GDP}{GDP_{t-1}} = \sum_{\tau=1}^{6} \underbrace{\underbrace{\frac{V_{i,t-1}}{GDP_{t-1}}}_{\text{size factor}} \cdot \underbrace{\frac{\Delta V_i}{V_{i,t-1}}}_{\text{growth factor}}}_{\text{consolidation factor}}$$

where V_i: the components of GDP by industry

2. Data for GDP by industrial origin have been adjusted to be consistent with the expenditure approach by an even distribution of the statistical discrepancy.

3. Hong Kong 1970-74, 1970 constant prices; Singapore 1960-72, current prices.

II. A General Model for Hong Kong: A Mini Open Economy

By mini open economy we mean a tiny land with an outward-looking feature: Hong Kong and Singapore belong to this type of economy. The model constructed below is designed to portray such a growth pattern.

A. Production, Investment and Savings

$$Y = \Psi [K, L, A(t)] \qquad (1)$$

$$\frac{\partial Y}{\partial K}, \quad \frac{\partial Y}{\partial L}, \quad \frac{\partial Y}{\partial A(t)} \geq 0$$

$$\frac{K}{L} = k \qquad (2)$$

$$I = \phi (E, \check{r}) \qquad (3)$$

$$\frac{\partial I}{\partial E} \geq 0, \quad \frac{\partial I}{\partial \check{r}} \geq 0$$

$$S = \Delta (Y, \dot{P}) \qquad (4)$$

$$\frac{\partial S}{\partial Y} \geq 0, \quad \frac{\partial S}{\partial \dot{P}} \leq 0$$

$$I = S + F \qquad (5)$$

where Y: national income or product
K: capital stock which can also be partitioned as $I_t + \sum_{r=0}^{t-1} I_r$
L: labor force
A(t): technological change
k: capital-labor ratio, a technical factor
I: gross investment
E: exports of goods and services
$\check{r}$: rate of return in equilibrium state
S: domestic savings
$\dot{P}$: change in price level
F: inflow of foreign capital

B. Foreign Trade

$$M = \eta (Y) \qquad (6)$$

$$\frac{dM}{dY} \geq 0$$

$$F = f (\check{r}) \qquad (7)$$

$$\frac{dF}{d\check{r}} \geq 0$$

$$M = E + F \qquad (8)$$

where M = imports of goods and services

C. Financial Activity

$$r - \dot{P} + U = \bar{r} \qquad (9)$$

where r: interest rate

U: net marginal non-interest utility[7]

D. Factor Distribution

$$Y = wL + \bar{r}K \qquad (10)$$

where W: wage rate

Given the exogenous variables E, k, P, the remaining ten endogenous variables, Y, I, L, S, U, r, w, $\bar{r}$, M, F can be simultaneously determined by the ten equations at any time horizon t.

The most important characteristic of a mini open economy is that apart from the domestic inputs L, S and part of I (or K), the external elements, namely a great portion of A(t), F, and part of I (or K), constitute significant forces for creating the output Y /see Eqs. (1), (7), (5), (8) and (3)/.

Figure 1 shows two vital factors stimulating the growth of a mini open economy, i.e. the absorption of international technology because the domestic economy is incapable of affording the cost of research, and the inflow of foreign capital which plays a complementary part in making up the domestic capital formation on the financing side /Eq. (5)/, and to remedy the trade deficits on the expenditure side /Eq. (8)/.

Attention should be paid to the financial market of Hong Kong which has been developed as an international center. Among the many reasons for the development such as serving the trade affairs, commerce and tourist industry, the most important one is to attract foreign investment and capital inflow. Policies adopted by the Hong Kong government are conducive to the inflow of foreign resources. These include the low tax system, no customs duties except for a few items,[8] few impediments to the entry of firms, little restriction on the remittance of profit, and few wage regulations. As expressed in Eq. (9), the mini open economy attempts to make U high enough to compensate for the deficiency of $(r - \dot{P})$ and to make $\bar{r}$ attractive enough to absorb foreign capital.

---

[7] In the case of Hong Kong, U can be reckoned as the marginal utility of the safety of deposit, fluctuation of exchange rate and the "convenience" of holding money.

[8] See also Tien-tung HSUEH and Koon-lam SHEA, op. cit.

Figure 1: Output, Technology and Financing Capital Formation

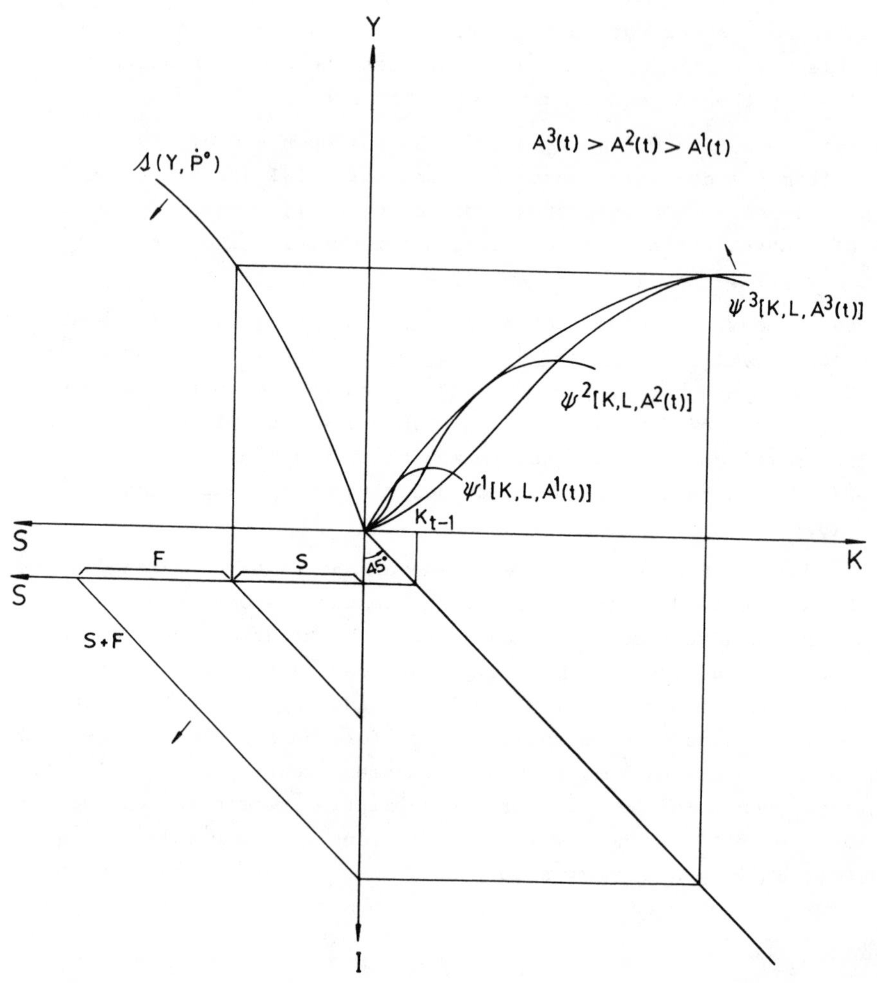

Since a mini open economy has to take special consideration of keen competition from other countries in the world market, in Hong Kong economic growth rather than full employment has always been placed as the first priority. Consequently, investment activity in the manufacturing, commerce and service sectors are treated as a matter of the utmost concern. Given the profit rate as an indicator for measuring the possibility of investment, there is some trade-off between wage rate (w) and rate of return ($\bar{r}$) in a static sense[9], as shown in quadrant III of Figure 2. However, in the dynamic sense, as the income goes up in the time horizontal, the wage rate is inclined to rise. Whether income distribution tends to be in favour of the labor force depends upon the bargaining power of the employers and employees [reflected by Eq. (10)] on the one hand, and the social welfare function [W ($\bar{r}$, w)] commonly shared by both sides on the other. The scanty data[10] show that the growth of wage rates did not lag too far behind that of labor productivity in the period under review. Consequently, the labor share probably did not tend to decline (or if it did, the degree would not be so serious as to fall to a critical level).[11]

---

[9] $Y^o = wL + \bar{r}K$, Y^o: given; differentiating, we have

$$0 = dw \cdot L + d\bar{r} \cdot K, \text{ i.e. } -\frac{dw}{dr} = \frac{K}{L} = k$$

[10] A comparison of the growth index of labor productivity with that of daily wage rates is shown as follows:

	1966	1971	1975
Labor productivity	100.00	167.93	
	(7,094)[1]	100.00	152.33
Daily rates	100.00	170.37	
	(10.16)[2]	100.00	134.89

Sources: As for Table 4 sources (1) & (4), and Table 1 source (1) in the text.

Notes: 1. Actual figure in HK$: GDP (f.c.)/Labor force
2. Actual figure in HK$.

[11] Cf. James RIEDEL: The Industrialization of Hong Kong, Tübingen: J.C.B. Mohr, 1974, pp. 91, 114-115, 128; N.C. OWEN: "Economic Policy in Hong Kong", in: Keith HOPKINS (ed.), op. cit., pp. 187-190.

Figure 2: Economic Growth and Income Distribution

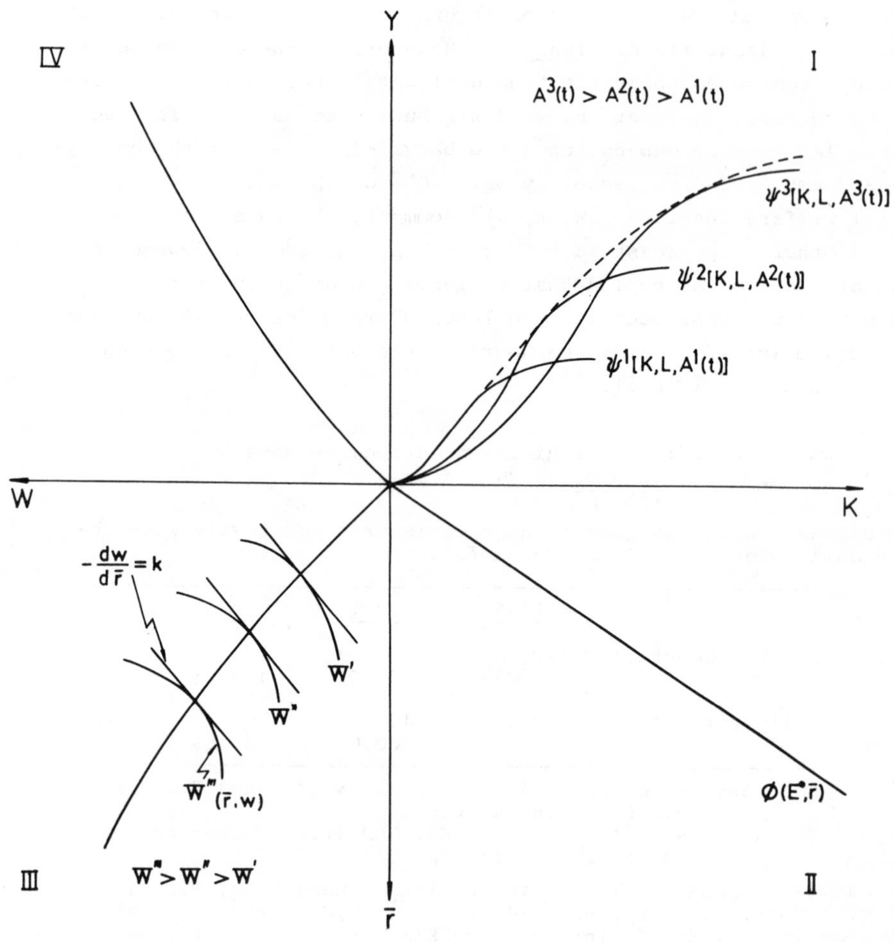

III. Features of Hong Kong's Economic Development

Based on the model set up in section II, it is now convenient for us to search for the features of Hong Kong's economic development. In doing so, the major issues concerning foreign trade, the manufacturing sector and the financial market will be elaborated in some detail.

A. Imports and the Inflow of Foreign Capital

Because of Hong Kong's excellent harbor and its geographical position as a gate for the Far East, Southeast Asia and Europe to enter Southern China, the entrepôt trade played a predominant role in the economy for over a century, since Hong Kong was ceded in 1841. It was not until 1959, following the end of the embargo on strategic exports to China, that the domestic commodity exports were able to take a dominant position in the trade structure (see Table 3).

Hong Kong's trade structure can be best viewed by the following simple dynamic model.[12] Let

$\Delta Y_t = \gamma I_t$ (1a)

$I_t = \theta \Delta E^+_{t-1}$ (3a) where E^+: exports of goods

$\Delta E_t^+ = \varepsilon \Delta M_t^+$ (11)[13] where M^+: imports of goods

$\Delta M_t^+ = m \Delta Y_t$ (6a)

where $\gamma, \theta, \varepsilon, m \geq o$ are parameters.

By substitution, we can easily obtain

$$\Delta M_t = m\gamma\theta\varepsilon \Delta M_{t-1}, \quad (12)$$

i.e. $M_t - (1 + m\gamma\theta\varepsilon)\, M_{t-1} + m\gamma\theta\varepsilon\, M_{t-2} = 0$ (13)

---

[12] Such a simplified specification is partly subject to data limitation and partly for illustration purposes.

[13] This is something different from the specification in Section II. For simplicity, we assume that exports are exogenous in the general model.

Table 3: Hong Kong's Foreign Trade, 1871-1973

	Shipping Tonnage[1] (link index)	China's imports[1] & exports via Hong Kong (link index)	Ratio of China's[1] imports & exports via Hong Kong	Ratio of domestic commodity exports to total commodity exports
1871-80	100,00 (41,695)+	100.00 (406,311)+	27.12 %	
1881-90	190.83	171.06	39.13 %	
1891-1900	148.65	204.99	43.08 %	
1901-10	161.03	164.36	35.48 %	
1911-20	103.51	115.81	26.35 %	
1921-30	161.60	136.39	19.36 %	
1933-40			10.64 %	
1948-51				12.32 % [2]
1952-58				30.45 % [3]
1959				69.63 % [3]
1959-73				76.76 % [3]

Sources: 1. G.B. ENDACOTT, op. cit., pp. 133-34, 191-92.

2. S.Y. CHUNG: "The Role of Manufacturing Industry in the Economy of Hong Kong", in: J.W. ENGLAND (ed.), The Hong Kong Economic Scene, Hong Kong: University of Hong Kong, 1969, p. 8.

3. T.T. HSUEH (a), op. cit., p. 52.

Notes: + Actual figure in '000 tonnage. + Actual figure in '000 HK taels

The solution[14] of Eq. (13) turns out to be three interesting cases:

(i) if $m\gamma\theta\varepsilon > 1$, imports grow on an explosive path

(ii) if $m\gamma\theta\varepsilon = 1$, imports are maintained at a constant level

(iii) if $m\gamma\theta\varepsilon < 1$, imports damped to a certain amount.

In checking up Hong Kong's data[15] we have $m\gamma\theta\varepsilon = 1.2576$. The growth path of Hong Kong's imports thus appears to be

$$M_{(t)} = 2{,}756\ (1.2576)^{t} + 15{,}074 \qquad (14)$$

where $M_{(t=1974=0)} = 17{,}830$ (H.K. million dollars at 1966 constant prices)

$M_{(t=1975=1)} = 18{,}540$

(14) indicates that Hong Kong's imports move explosively upward.

It is conceivable that Hong Kong has devoted its best efforts to the promotion of exports. However, throughout the trade statistics recorded, Hong Kong constantly encountered a situation of trade deficits. Nevertheless, Hong Kong has been lucky to be free from balance-of-payments and overvalued exchange rate problems, which is obviously due to the laissez-faire and free-port policy.[16] Under the non-discrimination and non-restriction principles, there is no divergence between the opportunity cost of domestic and foreign supplies. The comparative advantage rule can be applied fairly well in the production sphere. A favourable climate has therefore been created for attracting foreign investors and foreign capital.

B. Dissemination of Technology and Transformation of the Manufacturing Sector

By and large, the development of the Hong Kong manufacturing sector can be divided into three stages. As a centre of entrepôt trade

---

14 See W.J. BAUMOL: Economic Dynamics, London: Macmillan, 1970, Chapter 10, pp. 169-178.

15 $\gamma = 0.342$, the average of 1962-1975; $\theta = 3.26$ the average of 1962-1973; $\varepsilon = 0.94$, the average of 1962-1972, except 1967 when the change was too drastic to be treated as a normal figure; m = 1.20 average of 1962-1975, except 1971 and 1974. All data come from Estimates of Gross Domestic Product 1961-1975, p. 23.

in the first stage of development (up to 1949)[17] ship-repairing, ship-chandling and shipbuilding were developed. Other industries, which were inclined to be simple manufactured export goods with high labor content, such as rope making, sugar refining, cement works, and textile manufacturing were also established, particularly during World War I when the European countries were deeply involved in their warfare and could not trade in industrial products with China. This provided a stimulus to Hong Kong to develop knitting, weaving, spinning, metal goods and rubber goods, printing, tobacco, engineering, simple electrical products, medicines, plastics, cosmetics etc. to be exported to China.

The second stage of industrial development arose from the period around 1949. Hong Kong was able to absorb a massive influx of industrialists, skilled labor, administrative staff and other labor force, with the bulk injection of flight capital from China, in particular the southern provinces. Machinery equipment and facilities originally imported into China from the advanced countries were diverted to Hong Kong.[18] As a result, a number of industries with more precise production techniques, still labor-intensive, were set up. These included clothing, textile other than clothing, plastic manufacturing, toys, dolls, artificial flowers, footwear, rubber shoes, some electrical appliances and transistor radios, etc. Hong Kong experienced a drastic shock with the imposition of the United Nations embargo upon strategic exports to China during the Korean War. Apart from a small number of businessmen who were able to gain windfalls from smuggling via Hong Kong, most business activities had to make the transfer of internal capital from entrepôt trade to domestic commodity exports. It was not until 1959, several years after the end of the embargo, that Hong Kong's domestic exports by far exceeded re-exports.

---

16 See H.G. JOHNSON: "Fiscal Policy and the Balance of Payments in a Growing Economy", Malayan Economic Review, Vol. IX, No. 1, 1964, pp. 1-13.

17 See also S.G. DAVIS: Hong Kong in its Geographical Setting, London: Collins, 1949, Chapter 11, pp. 150-163.

18 See also Edvard HAMBRO: The Problem of Chinese Refugees in Hong Kong, Leiden: A.W. Sijthoff, 1955, pp. 176, 200-202.

The third stage of industrial development began in the 70's; since then Hong Kong has been facing the difficult situation of import quotas, restrictions, and high tariffs on clothing & textile products from the importing countries on the one hand, and strong competition from Taiwan, South Korea, Singapore etc., which are at a lower wage rate, on the other (see Table 4). Thus an impetus has been given to Hong Kong to develop higher quality, more skillful and sophisticated, products.

Table 4: Daily Earnings in the Manufacturing Sector - Selected Countries (US$, current prices)

	1966-'67	'68-'69	'70-'71	'72-'73	'74-'75
Hong Kong	2.15	2.39	3.33	4.55	5.52
Philippines	1.76	1.85	1.46	1.67	1.80
Korea	0.87	1.35	1.87	2.09	2.99
Taiwan	1.36	1.63	na	na	na
Singapore	2.46	2.46	2.38	3.16	4.54
Japan	4.66	6.19	8.35	14.22	20.50
Germany	9.02	10.20	14.14	21.08	29.55
U.S.A.	22.20	24.80	27.72	31.56	36.88

Sources: (1) International Labor Office, Year Book of Labour Statistics, Geneva, 1976.

(2) International Monetary Fund, International Financial Statistics, Washington, D.C., Jan. 1974 & Sept. 1976 issues.

(3) United Nations, Monthly Bulletin of Statistics, New York, Dec. 1971.

(4) Asian Development Bank, Key Indicators of Developing Member Countries of ADB, Vol. III, No. 1, Jan. 1972 & Vol. VIII, No. 1, April 1977.

As shown in Table 4, by comparison with other advanced countries, Hong Kong has had a relative advantage of lower labor costs. Hence the important thing that Hong Kong has to do is to transfer production technology from the advanced countries, through either imported setup, multinational corporations, or foreign investment.[19]

19 See also R. HSIA: "Technological Change in the Industrial Growth in Hong Kong", in: B.R. WILLIAMS (ed.), Science and Technology in Economic Growth, London: Macmillan, 1973, pp. 335-353 and the Discussions, pp. 354-359.

Many new products have been innovated and introduced in the markets by now, as e.g. calculators, small computers, cameras, watches, television sets, electronic tubes and valves, various scientific instruments, etc. (A general picture of Hong Kong's industrial production is shown in Table 5).

Summing up the process of industrialization, the strategies taken by Hong Kong can be listed as follows:

(1) The free port enables Hong Kong to receive the injection of new technology from the external world and keeps Hong Kong in a well-informed position, which raises the productivity of domestic labor to a higher level. The products are labor-intensive in content.

(2) As the domestic market is small, Hong Kong's main products are orientated towards the export market in order to gain the economies of scale and optimum size of production. It is further due to the principle of comparative advantage that Hong Kong's industrialists concentrate on a rather narrow range of most efficient industries. The fluctuation of industrial growth is attributed to the instability of the international market.

(3) Foreign investments were always welcomed and cover a wide range of manufacuring industries.[20] Foreign investors perform a complementary role to that of the domestic economy by introducing new technology and absorbing the labor force.

C. Financial Market and Capital Formation

Hong Kong was developed to be an international financial center, starting far back in the middle of the 19th century. A large and well-organized bank, the Hong Kong and Shanghai Banking Corporation, was formed in 1864 and soon became the leading financial institution. It then followed that quite a number of the foreign countries and the Chinese established their banks in Hong Kong for dealing with trade affairs and related business. Banking activities since then

---

[20] See Tien-tung HSUEH (b): op. cit., pp. 308-312; James RIEDEL: op. cit., pp. 112-113, 125-126.

Table 5: Hong Kong's Industrial Production, 1973

	Intermediate input / Gross output (%)	Labor cost / Value-added (%)	% share Value-added+	% share Gross output
1. Food, Beverage, & Tobacco	64.47	35.59	4.74	4.32
2. Textiles, wearing, apparel, leather and footwear	69.45	59.27	49.42	52.43
3. Wood, clock, furniture & fixtures	61.09	59.22	1.75	1.46
4. Printing & publishing	60.35	53.03	4.94	4.03
5. Chemicals, rubber & plastic	63.02	67.85	11.27	9.88
6. Non-metallic mineral	68.24	57.84	0.69	0.70
7. Basic metal	74.28	30.06	1.40	1.76
8. Fabricated metal, machinery, electrical machinery, transport equipment, professional and scientific instruments	64.82	67.01	22.61	20.82
9. Other manufacturing	77.54	63.13	3.18	4.59
Total+)	67.60	59.93	100,00 (9,071)"	100.00 (27,994)"
Industries employed 20 or more persons	67.84	60.30	83.19	85.65
10 - 19	64.24	62.76	7.99	7.40
1 - 9	57.97	51.69	8.82	6.95
Total	66.89	59.74	100.00 (10,583)"	100.00 (31,961)"

Source: Census and Statistics Department, Hong Kong, July 1975.

Notes: + Value-added has been redefined as gross output minus intermediate input, which is slightly different from the original source.

+) 20 or more employees for tobacco manufactures, 10 or more for the rest of the industries.

" Actual figure in million H.K. dollars.

have been rapidly expanded, to such an extent that Hong Kong is counted as having one of the highest densities of banking services in the world.[21]

Hong Kong has had no problem in siphoning both the permanent investment fund and the "hot money" from both the domestic economy and the rest of the world. It has been the oversupply of capital funds in the financial market that has caused the banks to reduce the interest rate for 6 months savings deposits to 3 % or less since the middle of 1977. The reasons for this supply of financial capital can be explained at least in three ways:[22]

(1) As a result of economic growth, the desire ratio of money to national income tends to be higher, the higher the growth of income is; this is the "portfolio effect" of growth on saving.

(2) The idle hoarding of money will further be reduced because of the efficient services of the banking system in Hong Kong. The transaction cost between savings deposits and spendable funds tends to be negligible in the Hong Kong financial market.

(3) It is due to its distinct characteristics, free exchange market and open port facilities, that Hong Kong has been capable of creating a higher net marginal non-interest utility than elsewhere in the world. This, in effect, attracts many funds from other countries especially from Southeast Asia and the Middle East.

As shown in Table 6, the highly developed financial structure of Hong Kong is partly evidenced by the higher ratio of money supply to GDP in comparison to other countries.

IV. Concluding Remarks

An extremely outward-looking feature has been adopted by both the mini open economies in Asia, Hong Kong and Singapore. Both of them placed strong emphasis on efficiency and achieved great success in

---

[21] See Y.C. JAO: op. cit., Chapters 2, 6 and 8.

[22] Cf. also R.I. McKINNON: Money and Capital in Economic Development, Washington, D.C.: The Brookings Institution, 1973, pp. 48, 123-129.

Table 6: Financial Structure of Hong Kong and Selected Countries

	Money Supply (MS)			MS/GDP (%)	MS/GNP (%)					
	Demand deposit plus currency	Time & savings deposits	MS	Hong Kong	Japan	Germany	USA	Taiwan	S. Korea	Indonesia
1961	100 (2,383)+	100 (1,897)+	100 (4,280)+	71	89	37	66	25	14	
62	110	140	123	77	87	38	67	27	15	
63	127	181	156	81	95	40	69	31	11	
64	143	228	181	87	93	41	70	34	10	
65	170	249	205	83	98	42	71	36	12	
66	180	302	234	90	99	44	68	40	15	
67	189	290	234	81	97	49	71	43	20	
68	202	381	281	90	95	53	70	41	26	
69	236	452	329	89	98	53	66	42	33	
70	208	560	397	91	97	52	70	45	35	10
71	323	710	495	101	107	53	73	50	34	13
72	479	849	643	114	117	56	76	56	38	16
73	494	926	685	95	113	56	75	57	40	16
74	477	1,204	799	97	108	57	75	53	36	15
75	569 (13,563)+	1,393 (26,432)+	934 (39,995)+	107	114	62	77	64	34	18

Sources: (1) *Hong Kong Monthly Digest of Statistics*, Census & Statistics Department, Hong Kong, various issues; *Hong Kong Annual Report*, Hong Kong Government, various issues.

(2) Other selected countries: International Monetary Fund, *International Financial Statistics*, various issues.

Notes: + Actual figures in million H.K. dollars.

their economic growth.

Since economic growth is of the utmost importance for the Hong Kong economy, it seems not inappropriate here to give some remarks on the possible obstacles to future development, following the discussion of the operation and development features of the Hong Kong economy.

First of all, obstacles may come from the restrictions or fluctuations of the export markets. As to past experience, Hong Kong suffered from the agreements on tariffs and trade between the advanced countries, such as the European Economic Community, U.S.A., and Hong Kong. These covered finished fabrics and made-ups, apparel, cotton textiles, wool and man-made fiber textiles, etc. to agreed limits. In addition, various kinds of quotas, tariffs and other import restrictions from other international markets, plus the strong competition from other Asian countries, Taiwan, S. Korea, Singapore etc., impeded the export expansion in one way or another. In a mini open economy, the first repercussion of the retardation of growth is to spill the cutdown over the production of the firms and then over employment. The slow-down in production also directly or indirectly affects the growth of the service sector.

Secondly, obstacles may come from the People's Republic of China and other raw material exporting countries. Since Hong Kong has been endowed with few material resources, foodstuffs and industrial raw materials have to be imported from other countries at the cheapest possible price, so that exports can be placed in a favourable position. For example, rising prices of the daily necessities imported from China will promptly affect the living standard of the low income people, and so produce social tensions; rising prices of industrial raw materials from Japan immediately created a difficult situation in the plastics industry in the 70's; the same happened to the cotton textile industry from the bidding up of the cotton price by Pakistan.

Thirdly, obstacles may come from external non-economic factors. If the free-port policy could not be maintained, it would be quite certain that the foreign investment, entrepôt trade, and the financial system would shrink. The same might be true for the tourist industry. Furthermore, Hong Kong is quite sensitive to changes of the political climate in China; in the past, political changes in China produced a thermometer effect on the Hong Kong stock market.

Last but not least, an acceptable working and living environment for the people has to be provided and sustained. Any special social tensions and disturbances will create a scare not only among foreign investors and visitors, but also the indigenous industrialists. One prominent issue in this regard is, for instance, that public housing in Hong Kong has to be improved.[23] Others, such as better public safety, more welfare services, minimum wage regulation, and social infrastructure, are all necessary conditions to create an acceptable environment for further economic development.

---

[23] See H. SMITH: John Stuart Mill's Other Island: A Study of the Economic Development of Hong Kong, London: The Institute of Economic Affairs, 1966; L.F. GOODSTADT; "Urban Housing in Hong Kong 1945-1963", in I.C. JARVIE and J. AGASSI (eds.): Hong Kong: A Society in Transition, London: Routledge & Kegan, Paul, 1969, pp. 257-298; Keith HOPKINS, "Housing the Poor", in: Keith HOPKINS (ed.), op. cit., pp. 271-335.

SMALL FACTORY IN ECONOMIC DEVELOPMENT: THE CASE OF HONG KONG

Ambrose Y. C. King and Peter J. L. Man

I. Introduction

Industrialization has been universally envisaged both as a goal value in itself and as a means to attain national wealth and power. And not uncommon among laymen, policy-makers and practitioners alike, there is an opinion that to attain industrialization is to develop large-scale, capital-intensive industries. Indeed, large-scale industries have been regarded as the trademark of highly-industrialized societies. Most economists, as Aubrey points out, are believers in the "iron law" of history, i.e., that the eventual application of large-scale urban industries is regarded as inevitable.[1]

In our view, in most industrialization programmes, too little attention has been paid to the benefits to be gained by helping develop the small industry sector. Students of industrialization tend to think that although small industry does have a place in the process of industrialization it will only "occupy a position betwen peasant agriculture and modern large industry."[2] In other words, small industry is regarded as a passing phenomenon, appearing only at the initial or early stage of industrialization.

As a report has pointed out, such an illusion might arise from an acceptance of any one or combination of the following erroneous propositions:[3]

---

[1] H. AUBREY, "Small Industry in Economic Development," _Social Research_, 18 (1951): 273-274; cited in Th. HERMAN, "The Role of Cottage and Small-Scale Industries in Asian Economic Development," _Economic Development and Cultural Change_, 4 (1955-56): 359.

[2] B.F. HOSELITZ, "Small Industry in Underdeveloped Countries," _Journal of Economic History_, 19 (1959): 618.

[3] Stanford Research Institute, _The Role of Small-Scale Manufacturing in Economic Development_. Report prepared for Office of Industrial Resources, International Cooperation Administration, Washington, D.C., 1957, p. 12.

- That manufacturing industries in advanced industrial countries, particularly the United States, are composed almost wholly of large establishments.
- That modern technology is incompatible with small and medium-sized establishments.
- That existing small-scale enterprises in underdeveloped areas should not be encouraged because they are doomed in the long run.

At this juncture, we are not going to debate these contentions, though we are not ready to accept them. We shall return to this point later. What interests us is the fact that in recent years some attention has been given to the examination of the role and function of small industry in the economic development of both developed and developing countries, in capitalistic as well as in socialistic societies.[4]

More and more countries have shown interest in small industry development activities and a few have developed well-planned and comprehensive programmes. India is an example in this regard. Other countries have developed sporadic and isolated measures responding to some single aspect of the needs of small industry, such as financial assistance, technological and managerial training, product design and marketing.

It is not the purpose of this paper to discuss what is the best strategy for industrialization.[5] Rather, it aims at a moderate attempt, based on empirical data on small factories in Hong Kong, and especially in the industrial town of Kwun Tong, to give an account of the role and function of small factories in this "industrial colony". In so doing we will hopefully shed some light on the issues and problems of small factories in the process of industrialization. It is our belief that more empirical studies are needed in substantiating the theoretical arguments for or against the employment of small factories in industrialization.

---

[4] Consult: St. WOSZCZOWSKI, Small Industry in Economic Development of Contemporary Countries, Research Program on Small Industry Development, Misc. Paper No. 5, Stanford Research Institute, 1960; E. STALEY and R. MORSE, Modern Small Industry for Developing Countries, New York: McGraw-Hill, 1965; E.D. HOLLANDER, et.al. The Future of Small Business, New York: Praeger, 1967; and B.F. HOSELITZ (ed), The Role of Small Industry in the Process of Economic Growth, The Hague and Paris: Mouton, 1968.

[5] Consult: B.H. HIGGINS, Economic Development: Principles, Problems and Policies, New York: W.W. Norton, 1959.

II. The Small Factory Defined

It is by no means an easy job to arrive at an agreed upon definition of the small industry. It is because of the confusion over what exactly a small industry is that has impeded us from having a clear understanding of the role of the small industry in economic development. Different countries have different legal definitions to suit their particular situations, and different writers on small industry offer their own definitions for their particular purpose. Under such circumstances, any definition of small industry is apt to be arbitrary.

There are generally two approaches to the problem. The first approach is to differentiate small industry from large on the basis of some quantitative measures; the second approach attempts to define small industry in terms of some functional criteria.[6] Functional criteria primarily refer to the degree of specialization and bureaucratization internal to the industrial organization, and degree of strength with respect to its position in dealing with the market and community of which it is a part, which are external to the industrial organization.

Eugene Staley is a major advocate of the functional approach to the problem of definition. He defines small industry in terms of certain functional characteristics which make its problems and its opportunities somewhat different from those of medium or large industry. His list includes: relatively little specialization in management ("one-man" management), lack of access to capital, close personal contact of top management with production workers, no special bargaining strength in buying and selling, often relatively close integration with the local community, and dependence on nearby markets and sources of supply.[7]

---

[6] Consult: D. FISHER, "A Survey of the Literature on Small-Sized Industrial Undertakings in India," in: HOSELITZ (ed), The Role of Small Industry, pp. 124-129; E. STALEY, Development of Small Industry Programs, Stanford Research Institute, Stanford University, 1961, pp. 3-7; S. WOSZCZOWSKI, op. cit., pp. 5-8; and H. SUTU and others: "A Study of Government Financial Assistance to Small Industries, With Special Reference to Hong Kong," The Lignan Institute of Business Administration, The Chinese University of Hong Kong, May 1973.

Staley's list is rather inclusive and places special emphasis on the problems of small industry, notably the lack of access to capital and bargaining power. However, it seems to us that using functional criteria raises not only the question of measurement, but also leads to the risk of confusing size with performance, the latter of which being what we are attempting to investigate. To put it differently: we would rather regard the functional characteristics of an industrial organization as dependent variables.

The use of distinctively measurable statistical criteria, on the other hand, satisfies the more expedient desires of government and research workers. However, there is no really satisfactory way of measuring the size of an industrial establishment. Measures suggested include the number of employees, fixed assets or capital investment, output, amount of energy used, and relative position in the industry generally. Among these statistical criteria, the number of employees has been most commonly used, not only because these data are more readily available but also because such data are most likely rendered for international comparison.

Again, the criterion of number of employees which constitutes a small industry or factory is by no means uniform. A working party of the Economic Commission for Asia and the Far East in the early fifties suggested that a small-scale industry be defined as those with 50 workers or less on hand power, or not over 20 workers using motive power.[8] In fact, what is officially defined as small industry in terms of number of employees varies from one country to another: the upper limit ranges from 50 for Malaysia, Singapore, and Thailand, 100 for the Republic of China, and Philippines, 200 for Hong Kong and South Korea, and up to 300 for Japan, in the Asian countries.[9] In the United States, a manufacturing firm is officially a small business if it is not dominant in its field of operation and has less than 500 employees, or if it is certified as small by the Small Business Administration.[10]

---

[7] STALEY, ibid., p. 5.

[8] STALEY and MORSE, op. cit., pp. 12-13.

[9] SUTU et. al., op. cit..

[10] STALEY and MORSE, op. cit., p. 12.

Among students of industrialization, it has been common to define a small industry or factory as an industrial establishment employing fewer than 50 workers[11] or fewer than 100 workers.[12] In our present study we adopt the former definition and define small factories as those employing less than 50 workers. Furthermore, we shall divide them into three subgroups:

(1) "The Mini-small factory": 1-9 employees;
(2) "The Midi-small factory": 10-19 employees; and
(3) "The Maxi-small factory": 20-49 employees.

The rationale for subgrouping small industry into three categories are manifold, but the primary reasons are that we assume that the role and function of these three subgroups in economic development will be different among themselves as small industry is different from large industry, and also because we further assume that the structural characteristics, such as division of labour, hierarchy of authority, and level of professionalization, will vary as widely among themselves as small industry varies from large industry.

In addition, we are more and more led to believe that another criterion, namely, level of technology, may be vital in dividing small industry into two types: (1) technology- or capital-intensive small industry and (2) non-technology- or labour-intensive small industry. The technology criterion includes both the physical technology of production as well as the social technology of management. Staley refers to the labour-intensive small industry as the "traditional" establishment and the technology-intensive small industry as the "modern" establishment, in which reasonably good application is made of the best science and technology currently available.[13] It is the labour-intensive type that is often identified as the trademark of small industry. The justification of using "level of technology" as a criterion in the classification of industrial organization has

---

[11] HOSELITZ, "Small Industry in Underdeveloped Countries," op. cit., pp. 600-618; D.J. DWYER and LAI, C.Y., The Small Industrial Units in Hong Kong: Patterns and Policies, University of Hull, 1967; and V. MOK, "The Nature of Kwun Tong as an Industrial Community," Social Research Centre, The Chinese University of Hong Kong, 1972.

[12] STALEY, op. cit.; STALEY and MORSE, op. cit.; and WOSZCZOWSKI, op. cit.

[13] STALEY, ibid., p. 6.

been well documented by students of organization known as the technological school.[14] Moreover, employing technology as a criterion will enable us to have a more sophisticated account for the performance of small industry in the process of industrialization.

III. The Role and Function of the Small Factory in Hong Kong's Economy

It is now a well-known fact that Hong Kong has been rapidly transformed in the last two decades from a colonial entrepôt dominated by its trade with mainland China to a modern cosmopolitan industrial city-state, with a population of over 4.5 million. Hong Kong as a fast growing industrial city-state can be described by various economic indices: the estimated Gross Domestic Product at market prices has increased eight times between 1948 and 1968, reached HK$ 13,350 in 1968 and HK$ 54,400 million in 1977. The per capita Gross Domestic Product has increased 4 times for the same period, reaching HK$ 3,510 by 1968, and HK$ 12,070 by 1977. The consumption of electricity has also increased, from 150 million kilowatt-hours in 1948 to 3,338 million in 1968, an increase of more than 22 times. In addition, among the working population of about 1.85 million, nearly 46 % are engaged in manufacturing, 15.5 % in services, 23 % in commerce, 7.3 % in communications, 5.6 % in construction, and only 2.8 % in farming and fishing.[15]

Another phenomenal aspect of Hong Kong's economy is its fast-increasing capacity for export: it has increased more than six times between 1948 and 1968; by 1968 it was HK$ 10,570 million. Although Hong Kong has a population of slightly over 4.5 million, the value of its exports is greater than India's.[16] In terms of income per capita, Hong Kong is the third highest in Asia, after Japan and Singapore.

[14] See J. WOODWARD, Industrial Organization Theory and Practice Oxford: Clarendon Press, 1965; R. INFIN, The Sociology of Industrial Relations, Englewood Cliffs, N.J.: Prentice-Hall, 1959; and Ch. PERROW, Organizational Analysis, London: Tavistock, 1970, esp. pp. 75-91.

[15] D. PODMORE, "The Population of Hong Kong," in: K. HOPKINS (ed): Hong Kong: The Industrial Colony, Hong Kong: Oxford University Press, 1971, pp. 21-54.

[16] HOPKINS, ibid., Preface, p. xi.

The miraculous performance of Hong Kong's economy bemuses and intrigues students of economic development. Certainly it warrants a systematic study in understanding the structure and behaviour of the economy of this industrial city-state. It seems to us that among others, E.H. Phelps Brown and Nicholas Owen have given us a fairly realistic account for the phenomenal growth of the economy of Hong Kong.[17] Both of them seem to share the view that Hong Kong's economic growth originated primarily in the fast developing export-oriented manufacturing sector of industry. And both of them have attributed the achievement of Hong Kong's economy, more or less, to the role and functions played by the small industry. Indeed, the following statement is probably very much shared by those who are familiar with the operation of Hong Kong's economy in the last 20 years:[18]

"The most remarkable feature of the Hong Kong economy is the proportion - often estimated to be over 90 per cent - of manufacturing output which is exported. Also remarkable is the volume of trade per capita. In total volume of trade, Hong Kong lies ninth in the world, an amazing achievement considering its size. The achievement is the result of a profilerating multitude of small and primitive firms, exporting to markets which are separated by distance, culture, and language."

Recognizing their share in Hong Kong's economy, we have, however, to ask: exactly in what way and to what extent have these "small and primitive" firms contributed to the amazing achievement of the Hong Kong economy? And more specifically, how many small firms are active, what are their internal structural traits, and how do they relate to the large economic systems? Moreover, how small and how primitive are these firms?

To our knowledge, these questions have neither been fully examined nor answered until now.[19] It is our belief that these questions are too important to be ignored if we are to have near-complete

---

17 See BROWN's "The Hong Kong Economy: Achievements and Prospects," and OWEN's "Economic Policy in Hong Kong," both in: HOPKINS (ed), ibid., pp. 1-20, and 141-206, respectively.

18 OWEN, in: HOPKINS (ed), ibid., p. 160.

19 To date the publications on small industry in Hong Kong are few and scarce. D.J. DWYER and LAI C.Y., op. cit.; and D.J. DWYER,

knowledge of the miraculous performance of the Hong Kong economy. Furthermore, an attempt to answer these questions will not only further enhance our knowledge about the economic development of Hong Kong, but will also shed some light on the role and functions of small industry in the process of industrialization, which more than half of the nations in the world are now pursuing.

In the pages that follow, we shall attempt to answer the questions just raised.[20] To begin with, we want to know how many small industrial units are active in the new industrial town of Kwun Tong and in Hong Kong as a whole, and what proportion does the small industry occupy in the industrial system of Hong Kong?

Table 1: Size and Number of Factories in Kwun Tong and Hong Kong, 1971

Size \ No. of Factories	KWUN TONG			HONG KONG		
	Number	%	Cum. %	Number	%	Cum. %
1 - 9	623	38.9	38.9	16,391	62.7	62.7
10 - 19	236	14.7	53.6	4,520	17.3	80.0
20 - 49	272	17.0	70.6	2,854	10.9	90.9
50 - 99	235	14.7	85.3	1,228	4.7	95.6
100 - 499	203	12.7	98.0	1,007	3.9	99.5
500+	34	2.1	100.1	149	0.5	100.0
TOTAL	1,603	100.1		26,149	100.0	

Source: Computed from Census of Manufacturing Establishments, Hong Kong Government, 1973

From Table 1, we find that among the 1,603 factories in Kwun Tong (in 1971), 1,131 (or 70.6 %) employed less than 50 workers. If we regroup them according to the criteria set up earlier, then 623, or 38.9 % were mini-factories employing 1 to 9 workers; 236, or 14.7 % were midi-factories with 10 to 19 employees; and 272, or 17 % were maxi-factories employing 20 to 49 persons.

"Problems of the Small Industrial Unit," in: D.J. DWYER (ed): Asian Urbanization: A Hong Kong Casebook, Hong Kong: University of Hong Kong Press, 1971, pp. 123-136.

20 The data on Hong Kong come from two sources: firstly, data on Kwun Tong, based primarily on an empirical study conducted by

Looking at the picture for the whole of Hong Kong, we find that among the 26,149 factories (in 1971) there were as many as 23,765 (or 90.9 %) that fell into our classification of small factory; furthermore, amazingly or not, there were 16,391 (62.7 %) that belonged to the mini-factory category; 4,520 (17.3 %) midi-factories and 2,854 (10.9 %) maxi-factories. According to the Factories and Industrial Undertakings Ordinance, only establishments employing twenty or more workers must be registered with the Department of Labour. Although the Department also maintains a record of smaller establishments, there is reason to believe that a substantial number of small industries, paeticularly the cottage industries, have not been registered with the Department. Therefore, the above number of small factories, especially the mini- and midi-factories, might be too low.

Judging from the absolute numbers and percentages in Table 1, it would not be wrong to say that Kwun Tong is predominantly an industrial town of small factories (more than 70 % of its factories having less than 50 workers), and Hong Kong as a whole is overwhelmingly an industrial city of small factories, especially midi- and mini-factories. However, when the average size of the factory (see Table 2) is taken into account, we find that the average size of the Kwun Tong factory (65.79 persons) is much larger than the Hong Kong average (25.67 persons).

In fact, the Kwun Tong figure is the highest among all the CME districts. This is not difficult to understand when we realize that Kwun Tong, unlike most other districts of Hong Kong, is an industrial community that started from the ground up in the late 50's. In Kwun Tong, there is a certain physical segregation of the industrial sector from the residential/commercial sector and most of the factories are to be found in flat industrial buildings where the traditional cottage type industries do not have a place. To start a new business under such circumstances where rent is high and equipment expensive, it may not be economical to begin an industry

---

the Social Research Centre, The Chinese University of Hong Kong, in the summer of 1971, as part of the Centre's Kwun Tong Industrial Community Research Programme. Stratified random sampling was used and subsequently 346 factories were surveyed. Our second source of data comes from the Government Census of Manufacturing Establishments. It was the first big-scale industrial census to be carried out in Hong Kong, and was conducted by the Department of Census and Statistics in the summer of 1971.

Table 2: Average Size of Factories in Various Districts of Hong Kong, 1971

CME Districts	No. of Establishments	No. of Employees	Average Size/ Factory
H.K. Island West	2,308	39,894	17.29
H.K. Island, Central	1,044	12,944	12.40
H.K. Island, East	1,318	53,203	40.37
Yaumati, Tsim Sha Tsui	2,937	23,582	8.03
Mongkok	2,997	49,884	16.64
Hung Hom, Ho Man Tin	2,368	66,662	28.15
Cheung Sha Wan	5,772	114,381	19.82
San Po Kong	2,865	102,478	35.77
Kwun Tong	1,603	105,467	65.79
Tsuen Wan	1,357	71,240	52.72
NT, except Tsuen Wan	1,580	31,573	19.98
TOTAL	26,149	671,308	25.67

Source: Computed from Census of Manufacturing Establishments, Hong Kong Government, 1973

of less than, say, 5 persons. As a result, the average size of a factory in Kwun Tong is considerably higher than in most other areas in Hong Kong.

The next question we would like to ask is: What is the share of the labour force in small industry?

Table 3: Size and Employees of Kwun Tong and Hong Kong Factories, in 1971

No. of Factories / Size	KWUN TONG			HONG KONG		
	Employees	%	Cum. %	Employees	%	Cum. %
1 - 9	3,404	3.2	3.2	77,709	11.6	11.6
10 - 19	3,235	3.1	6.3	59,796	8.9	20.5
20 - 49	8,767	8.3	14.6	87,110	13.0	33.5
50 - 99	16,589	15.7	30.3	84,383	12.6	46.1
100 - 499	42,405	40.2	70.5	201,474	30.0	76.1
500+	31,067	29.5	100.0	160,836	24.0	100.1
TOTAL	105,467	100.0		671,308	100.1	

Source: Computed from Census of Manufacturing Establishments, Hong Kong Government, 1973

Table 3 shows that among the 105,467 industrial workers in the community of Kwun Tong, 15,406 (14.6 %) were working in small factories employing less than 50 workers. Furthermore, among the 105,467 workers, 3,404 (3.2 %) were working in mini-factories, 3,235 (3.1 %) in midi-factories, and 8,767 (8.3 %) in maxi-factories. From these figures, the share of the industrial force in ini-factories and in idi-factories is not too significant in itself alone, though the total share of industrial force in all small factories (14.6 %) is quite substantial.

However, when we take Hong Kong industry as a whole for our unit of analysis, the picture looks quite different. Table 3 indicates that among the 671,308 industrial workers in 1971, as many as 224,615 (33.5 %) of them worked in small factories employing less than 50 workers. Furthermore, among them, 77,709 (or 11.6 %) are to be found in the mini-factory type, 59,796 (or 8.9 %) in the midi-type, and 87,110 (or 13 %) in the maxi-type of small factories. From these figures, we find that the share of labour force in small factories does occupy a very high proportion in Hong Kong's manufacturing labour force, and that the share of labour force in each of these three subgroups of small factories is very significant.

The third question we want to ask concerns the performance of small factories vis-à-vis large factories in both Kwun Tong and Hong Kong. Regarding the performance of small factories, we would like to make two kinds of assessments: (1) the overall output value, and (2) the productivity per worker of small factories. (See Tables 4 and 5, respectively).

Table 4 shows that the total output value of all industrial enterprises in Kwun Tong was HK$ 3,294,194,000 (in 1971) of which 13.3 % came from the small factories. By further breakdown, we find that 1.6 % were from mini-factories, 2.7 % from midi-factories, and 9 % from maxi-factories. When we look at these figures alone, we might be led to conclude that the share of the output value of small factories in Kwun Tong is rather low. But when we compare them with the corresponding figures in the share of employment (see Table 3), we discover that the share of output value of small factories in Kwun Tong (13.3 %) is, in fact, very high considering its share of employment (14.6 %).

Table 4: Size and Output Value of Factories in Kwun Tong, 1971

OUTPUT / INPUT	VALUE OF EXPORTS		VALUE OF LOCAL SALES		TOTAL SALES	
	HK$ '000	%	HK$ '000	%	HK$ '000	%
1 - 9	16,842	.8	37,306	3.0	54,148	1.6
10 - 19	41,296	2.0	49,062	3.9	90,358	2.7
20 - 49	113,894	5.6	181,373	14.4	295,267	9.0
50 - 99	289,546	14.2	226,385	18.0	515,931	15.7
100 - 499	971,525	47.8	377,145	29.9	1,348,670	40.9
500+	600,897	29.5	388,923	30.9	989,820	30.0
TOTAL	2,034,000	99.9	1,260,194	100.1	3,294,194	99.9

Source: Computed from Census of Manufacturing Establishments, Hong Kong Government, 1973

When we look at the breakdown of the total sales of the Kwun Tong factories into exports and local sales, we find that the small factories, especially the mini-factories, have low export-orientation. In other words, the products of small factories in Kwun Tong are more for domestic consumption.

Table 5: Size and Output Value of Factories in Hong Kong, 1971

OUTPUT / INPUT	VALUE OF EXPORTS		VALUE OF LOCAL SALES		TOTAL SALES	
	HK$ '000	%	HK$ '000	%	HK$ '000	%
1 - 9	372,069	3.2	988,637	15.6	1,360,706	7.5
10 - 19	589,053	5.0	665,765	10.5	1,254,818	7.0
20 - 49	1,260,948	10.8	932,595	14.7	2,193,543	12.2
50 - 99	1,602,936	13.7	682,185	10.8	2,285,121	12.7
100 - 499	4,605,916	39.3	1,533,169	24.2	6,139,085	34.0
500+	3,291,896	28.1	1,523,551	24.1	4,915,447	26.7
TOTAL	11,722,818	100.1	6,325,902	99.9	18,048,720	100.1

Source: Computed from Census of Manufacturing Establishments, Hong Kong Government, 1973

Table 5, which shows the situation for Hong Kong as a whole, seems in general to confirm our findings on Kwun Tong, with some differences. The total output of the industrial system of Hong Kong was HK$ 18,048,720,000 (in 1971) of which 26.7 % came from the small factories. Further breakdown shows that 7.5 % came from the mini-factories, 7 % from midi-factories, and 12.2 % from maxi-factories.

Again, when we consider that the share of employment in small factories in Hong Kong is only 33.5 % (see Table 3), we find that the difference between its share of employment and that of its output is not too large.

Breaking down the total sales into exports and local sales, we find that the small factories in Hong Kong, particularly the mini-factories, have a relatively low export-orientation: the output value of small factories for export occupies about 19 % of the total value of export, which implies that the output value of small factories for local sales is proportionally very high; this is especially true of the Mini-factories. From Tables 4 and 5, we also find that the larger the factories, the higher is their export orientation, or the lower is their domestic-consumption orientation.

Now let us take a closer look at the performance of small factories in terms of the productivity per worker.

Table 6: Productivity per Employee of Kwun Tong Factories, 1971

SIZE	NO. OF EMPLOYEES	TOTAL SALES (HK$ '000)	PRODUCTIVITY PER EMPLOYEE (HK$)	
1 - 9	3,404	54,148	15,907	
10 - 19	3,235	90,358	27,931	28,546
20 - 49	8,767	295,267	33,679	
50 - 99	16,589	515,931	31,101	
100 - 499	42,405	1,348,670	31,805	31,694
500+	31,067	989,820	31,861	
TOTAL	105,467	3,294,194	31,234	

Source: Computed from Census of Manufacturing Establishments, Hong Kong Government, 1973

Table 6 shows the productivity per employee of factories of all sizes in Kwun Tong (in 1971). The average productivity per employee of all small factories was HK$ 28,546, while the average figure for all large factories (employing 50 persons or more) was HK$ 31,694.

Some aspects of those figures are particularly noteworthy: First, there are great variations in the productivity per employee among different types of small factories: from HK$ 15,907 for the mini- to HK$ 33,679 for the maxi-factories. Second, there is very little difference in the productivity per employee among the large factories. Third, the productivity per employee of mini-factories is very low whilst that of maxi-factories is extremely high, in fact the highest among all types of factories. Finally, the average productivity per employee of all small factories is about 90 per cent of that of large factories.

Table 7: Productivity per Employee of Hong Kong Factories, 1971

SIZE	NO. OF EMPLOYEES	TOTAL SALES (HK$ '000)	PRODUCTIVITY PER EMPLOYEE	(HK$)
1 - 9	77,709	1,360,706	17,510	
10 - 19	59,796	1,254,818	20,985	21,410
20 - 49	87,110	2,193,543	25,181	
50 - 99	84,383	2,285,121	27,080	
100 - 499	201,474	6,139,085	30,470	29,639
500+	160,836	4,815,447	29,940	
TOTAL	671,308	18,048,720	26,886	

Source: Computed from Census of Manufacturing Establishments, Hong Kong Government, 1973

Table 7 illustrates the situation for Hong Kong as a whole. The average productivity per employee for all small factories was HK$ 21,410, whilst that for all the large factories was HK$ 29,639.

Taking Hong Kong industry as a whole as a unit of analysis, we find the following features: First, the productivity of factories of all sizes, with the exception of the mini-factories, in Hong Kong is lower than the corresponding figure for the factories in the new industrial town of Kwun Tong. Second, with the exception of the factories employing 500 persons or more, the productivity per employee increases with the size of the factory: that is, the larger the size, the higher the productivity. Third, the average productivity of all small factories in Hong Kong is slightly more than 72 % of the productivity of large factories, and about 80 % of the industrial average. Fourth, whilst the productivity of the mini-factories is only about 60 % of that of large factories (and about 65 % of the industrial average), the productivity of the maxi-factories is about 85 % of that of large factories (and about 93.7 % of the industrial average).

What we can learn from these figures is that if we want to talk about the economic performance of small factories more intelligently, we must first of all bear in mind what type of small factory we are referring to, mini-, midi-, or maxi-factories. In Hong Kong a relative poor performance of small factories in terms of productivity per employee is confined to only one type of small factory, that is, mini-factories. The other two types perform rather well when compared with either the large factories or with the overall industrial average.

From the above analysis, one could summarize the role of small factories in the Hong Kong economy as follows: (1) The Hong Kong industrial system is predominantly a system of small factories: over 90 % of the entire industrial enterprises are factories employing less than 50 persons, and over 62 % are mini-factories, employing one to nine persons. (2) A very significant proportion, or about one third, of the total industrial labour force work in small factories, (of which the mini-factories are responsible for 11 %). (3) A significant share of the total output value, or nearly 27 %, comes from the small factories (of which more than 7 % come from the mini-factories). (4) The productivity per employee of all the small factories is more than 71 % of that of the productivity of the large factories (and about 80 % of the industrial average); the productivity per employee of mini-factories, however, is less than 60 % of the productivity of large factories (and about 65 % of the industrial average).

IV. Some International Comparisons

Comparable statistical data on small industry are few and scanty on the international level; this being partly a result of different definitions of small industry used by different governments and researchers, and partly because of the relative lack of interest in small industry. Consequently, it is hardly possible to make any systematic comparative study on the role of small industry at various stages of economic development in different countries. However, some scattered data do allow us to make a few comparisons, thus placing the case of Hong Kong in a broader perspective.

First, we shall look at the trend of development in Hong Kong. The following table will give us some idea of how fast small industry has developed since 1962.

Table 8: Size and Distribution of Industrial Undertakings in Hong Kong 1962, 1964, 1968, 1971

SIZE	December 1962		March 1964		March 1968		August 1971	
	No. of under-takings	%	No. of under-takings	%	No. of under-takings	%	No. of under-takings	%
1- 9	4,455	64.1	5,063	62.9	5,204	47.7	16,391	62.7
10- 19					2,179	20.0	4,520	17.3
20- 49	1,353	19.5	1,576	19.6	1,779	16.3	2,854	10.9
50- 99	548	7.9	681	8.5	832	7.6	1,228	4.7
100-499	511	7.4	654	8.1	794	7.3	1,007	3.9
500+	80	1.2	75	0.9	120	1.1	149	.5
TOTAL	6,947	100.1	8,049	100.0	10,908	100.0	26,149	100.0

Sources: (1) 1962, by private communication with Labour Department, Summer, 1973.
(2) 1964, Commissioner of Labour, Annual Report.
(3) 1968, Commissioner of Labour, Annual Report.
(4) 1971, Census of Manufacturing Establishments, 1973.

Table 8 shows the size of industrial establishments in Hong Kong in various years. Let us first take a look at the share of small firms in the entire industrial system. In 1962, there were 5,808 factories in Hong Kong employing less than 50 workers, occupying 83.6 % of the total number of factories. This number rose to 6,639 in 1964, or about 82.5 % of all factories. By 1968, the number of small factories had reached 9,162, or 84 % of all factories. The rise was even steeper for the following 3 years, as by 1971, the number of small factories reached the amazing figure of 23,765, or 90.9 % of the total number of economic establishments in Hong Kong.

Table 9: Size and Distribution of Industrial Employment in Hong Kong, 1962, 1968, 1971

Size of Establishment	December 1962		March 1968		August 1971	
	Employment	%	Employment	%	Employment	%
1 - 9	37,572	12.6	24,856	5.4	77,709	11.6
10 - 19			29,622	6.5	59,796	8.9
20 - 49	41,228	13.8	54,801	11.9	87,110	13.0
50 - 99	37,904	12.7	57,802	12.6	84,383	12.6
100 - 499	103,878	34.9	161,600	35.2	201,474	30.0
500+	77,315	26.0	130,259	28.4	160,836	24.0
TOTAL	297,897	100.0	458,940	100.0	671,308	100.1

Sources: (1) 1962, by private communication with Labour Department, Summer 1973.
(2) 1968, Commissioner of Labour, Annual Report.
(3) Computed from Census of Manufacturing Establishments, Hong Kong Government, 1973.

As far as industrial employment is concerned, small factories in 1962 employed some 78,800 workers, or 26.4 % of total industrial employment. The figure reached to 224,615 workers in 1971, or more than one third of the total industrial work force. These figures show that between 1962 and 1971, the number of employees in small factories has increased by 2.85 times.

In comparing Hong Kong with other countries, we shall first give some attention to selected Asian countries. An ECAFE report of 1953 showed that in Japan, the industries employing less than 3 people made up 57 % of the total, and industries employing 4 to 49 people comprised 39 % of all factories, i.e. factories with less than 50 people made up 96 % of all factories in Japan in 1953.[21] This is even higher than the Hong Kong figure in 1971 (90.9 %). Of course, one might tend to explain such a high percentage of small factories in the Japanese economy in the early fifties as an effort in their post-war recovery. However, another source[22] reveals that the proportion of small industry did not decline in later years. In 1955, small industries employing less than 50 persons still made up about 96 % of all factories in Japan and more than 50 % of total industrial employment. These figures have shown only a slight decrease since 1960, largely due to the decline of handicraft and cottage industries, and also because of the general shift in the composition of industrial output. However, the discussion shows how significant a role the small industry has played in the economic development of Japan, the most industrialized country in Asia.

As for India, small industries seem to be ideally suited to Indian economic resources and needs and indeed form the industrial backbone of the country. It is estimated that in 1956 there were as many as 5,191,000 small establishments in India (employing less than 50 people) which together occupied some 99.8 % of the total factories. In terms of employment, these small factories employed about 12,270,000 people, or 81.8 % of the total industrial employment. Obviously India relies more heavily on small industry than Hong Kong does.[23]

South Korea, another fast developing country in Asia, has also been dominated by small manufacturing firms. According to the mining and manufacturing census of 1963, 98.7 % of the total manufacturing establishments were operating on a small scale, employing from 5 to 199 workers,[24] the greatest portion being concentrated in the smallest bracket of 5 to 9 workers. This bracket of establishments occupied 15 % of the total manufacturing workers, while the establishments employing 5 to 49 workers accounted for about 45 % of the total employment. Doubtlessly, small industries in South Korea have contributed greatly toward the development and stabilization

---

21 ECAFE, Economic Survey of Asia and the Far East 1953, New York: United Nations, p. 14.

22 M. SHINOHARA, "A Survey of the Japanese Literature on Small Industry," in: HOSELITZ (ed.), The Role of Small Industry, op. cit., p. 21.

of the country's economy. Like India, the shares of both the number of establishments and employees in South Korea were larger than in Hong Kong.

What about some of the more industrialized countries outside Asia? Hoselitz finds that the share of workers in dwarf (which he refers to establishments employing not more than 5 persons) and small (referring to factories employing 6 to 49 persons) industries in various post-war years in several European countries was as follows:[25] "In general betwen 12 and 15 % of the labor force was engaged in handicrafts establishments and around 25 to 35 % in small industry. All establishments with a labor force below 50 workers employed roughly between 40 and 50 % of the total labor force in industry." But by the mid-fifties, the proportion of the labour force in small industries, especially in dwarf industries, had declined. Germany's 1956 industrial census showed that 12.3 % of the industrial labor force was employed in establishments with less than 50 persons. However, these figures do not include handicraft establishments. According to Hoselitz's estimate, with handicraft establishments, "approximately 20 %, or perhaps a little less, of the total industrial labor force were engaged in establishments with 6 to 49 workers."[26]

In 1958 in the United Kingdom, there were 63,889 manufacturing establishments employing less than 50 persons, making up 73 % of the total manufacturing firms; together they employed 896,000 persons, or 11.7 % of the total industrial labor force; their total sales amounted to 10 % of the total sales in manufacturing industries.[27]

In the United States in 1947, there were about 197,600 establishments employing less than 50 employees each, and making up more than 82 % of the total number of firms.[28] In 1958, both the absolute number and relative percentage of small establishments increased to 248,928 or 83.6 %, respectively. Though we see a slight

---

23 FISHER, in: HOSELITZ (ed.), The Role of Small Industry, op. cit., p. 122.

24 The Medium Industrial Bank, An Introduction to Small Industries in Korea, Seoul, 1966, p. 10-11.

25 HOSELITZ, "Small Industry in Underdeveloped Countries," op. cit., p. 603.

26 Ibid., p. 605.

drop in 1967, the number of small factories in 1967 remained very stable at 247,483, or nearly 81 % of the total. In both 1958 and 1967, mini-establishments accounted for more than 50 % of the total establishments. As far as employment in the United States is concerned, the share of small establishments is far from negligible. In 1947, the small establishments employed 2,277,600 persons, or nearly 16 % of the total industrial labour force; the share in 1958 rose to 17.2 %, while the 1967 figure showed a slight drop, with 2,578,300 persons or 13.9 % of the total industrial employment in the small establishment sector.

Compared with the 1968 Hong Kong figures, the 1967 United States' share of small establishments was only slightly lower than that of Hong Kong (81 versus 84 %); however, the United States' share of employment was substantially lower than that of Hong Kong for the same period (13.9 % versus 23.8 %).

When comparing Hong Kong with other countries, the other important question to be answered on the role and performance of small industry is that of its productivity. Here again, difficulties are present in international comparison, and further complicated by the different methods employed in measuring small industry and productivity. In comparing labour productivity, we shall adopt a method originally developed by Simon Kuznets, in which the share of employment and output are the two main variables used[29].

Table 10 gives us some ideas of how well the small factories of Hong Kong perform vis-à-vis the small establishments in other countries. It reveals that the small factories of Hong Kong perform considerably better than those in both Japan and South Korea in terms of productivity.

---

27 H.J. GRAY, "Some Aspects of the Role of Small Industry in the United Kingdom," Small Industry Bulletin for Asia and the Far East, No. 10. New York: United Nations, 1973, p. 27.

28 U.S. Bureau of the Census, Census of Manufactures 1967, Vol. 1, Washington, D.C.: Government Printing Office, 1971.

29 For KUZNETS' method, see his "Quantitative Aspects of the Economic Growth of Nations: II, Industrial Distribution of National Product and Labour Force." Economic Development and Cultural Change, 5 (1957), Supplement, pp. 32ff; and HOSELITZ, "Small Industry in Underdeveloped Countries", op. cit., pp. 608-9.

Table 10: Labour Productivity of Small Manufacturing Establishments

Country & Year	% of all Industrial Employment	% of all Industrial Output	Productivity Index of Small Industry (1 - 49 workers)	Productivity Index of Large Industry (50+ workers)	Small Industry/Large Industry
Hong Kong (1971)	33.2	26.6	.79	1.10	.72
Japan (1960)	43.4	22.4 (1)	.52	1.37	.38
Korea (1963)	45.1	31.5 (2)	.70	1.25	.56
United Kingdom (1958)	11.7	10.0	.86	1.02	.84
USA (1967)	13.9	12.1 (3)	.87	1.02	.85

N.B.: Productivity index of industrial average taken as 1.

(1) Value added, 4-49 employees

(2) Value added, 5-49 employees

(3) Value added, 1-49 employees

Sources: Hong Kong - Census of Manufacturing Establishments, Hong Kong Government, 1973.

Japan - M. SHINOHARA, "A Survey of the Japanese Literature on Small Industry," in: B. HOSELITZ (ed.), The Role of Small Industry in the Process of Economic Growth, The Hague and Paris: Mouton, 1968, p. 39.

Korea - The Medium Industrial Bank, An Introduction to Small Industries in Korea. Seoul, 1966, p. 26.

U.K. - H.J. GRAY, "Some Aspects of the Role of Small Industry in the United Kingdom," Small Industry Bulletin for Asia and the Far East, No. 10, New York: United Nations, 1973, p. 27.

U.S.A. - U.S. Bureau of the Census, Census of Manufactures, 1967, Vol. 1, Washington, D.C.: Government Printing Office, 1971, pp. 2.4-2.5.

Compared with the United States and United Kingdom, the productivity figures of small factories in Hong Kong do not perform as well, in fact, the productivity of small establishments in the U.S.A. and the U.K. is not much lower than that of the industrial average of the large establishments. Such results are not surprising, however, for one expects small establishments in the United States and United Kingdom to be more modern in nature, a condition which helps boost productivity.

In conclusion, when we compare the labour productivity of small factories on the basis of the data available, the small factories of Hong Kong perform better than their counterparts in South Korea, Japan (and India), and not much worse than the performance of small establishments in the United States and United Kingdom.

V. The Main Characteristics of Small Factories in Hong Kong

As was pointed out in section III, the Kwun Tong and Hong Kong industrial systems are predominantly composed of small factories employing less than 50 workers. In our own investigation of 346 Kwun Tong factories, 252 or nearly 73 % of them employ less then 50 people; most of these small factories had a capital value of less than HK$ 200,000 and a total plant space of less than 2,000 square feet. They are primarily of the paper, food, plastic, basic metal, rubber, chemical and non-metallic categories. Of the 252 small factories in our Kwun Tong sample, 236 are Chinese-owned. In terms of capital, 56.8 % of these small factories are of single proprietorship, and another 20.4 % of family proprietorship. In large measure, these small Chinese enterprises tend to be family businesses. Although we are not attempting in this study to analyse the organizational and management structure and ideology of the small factories as such, suffice it to make a few comments:[30]

The owners of these small factories, in general, have a low level of formal education: more than half of them have only had a

---

[30] A detailed analysis of these aspects can be found in A.Y.C. KING and D. LEUNG, The Chinese Touch in Small Industrial Organizations, Social Research Centre, The Chinese University of Hong Kong, 1975.

primary education and a large number of them were "self-educated". The Chinese small-factory owner can, for the most part, probably be called a modernized "traditionalist" who, in urbanized and industrialized Hong Kong, with its mixed culture of the East and the West, remains fairly faithful to traditional Chinese values yet seems to appreciate some modern and/or Western values as well. More concretely, these owners believe in hard-work, honesty and responsibility, which we assume to be traditional values, together with other qualities, such as organization and management ability, which we assume to be modern/Western values, as well as profit-mindedness, which we assume to be a value for both the Western and traditional Chinese merchant class. They are rather conservative and consider risk-taking the least important quality for a successful entrepreneur; however, when asked what the reasons are for hiring relatives or kinsmen for important positions in their factories, they almost unanimously answer that "being a relative" is not the determining factor, but rather because they are "trustworthy", "capable" and "responsible".

In light of these observations, it is then not incorrect to say that these small entrepreneurs are more universalistic- than particularistic-oriented. Or, we may say that they are no longer kinship-oriented as such.[31] Compared with the large establishments, the small factories in our sample are less bureaucratic; more than 64 % of them have an average of less than 2 horizontal departments and 2 vertical levels. Moreover, 54 % of the small factories have no managerial staff; and clerical work is done by the owner/manager himself. Only 11 % of the small factories have a promotion scheme and 35 % a salary-revision scheme. In terms of the decision-making structure of the 252 small factories, in 180 of them the major decisions are made solely by the owner himself. Occasionally when the owner is absent or away decisions are made by either his "kinfolks" or his "appointees".

In the small factories of our sample, the communication pattern is predominantly informal; 86 % of them use verbal communication,

---

[31] J.L. ESPY, The Strategies of Chinese Industrial Enterprises in Hong Kong. Dissertation, School of Business Administration, Harvard University, 1970.

and 56 % of the owners "always" or "often" give direct instructions to the workers on the production line. All these phenomena combined seem to amount to what Harbison and Myers call the "patrimonial management", which is "business management in which ownership, major policy-making positions, and a significant proportion of the jobs in the hierarchy are held by members of an extended family".[32] It is true that the owners/managers of the small factories are in large measure traditionalistic, paternalistic and conservative, but it is far from being true that they are persons with an inevitable and almost built-in disposition for depotistic inclination which is often the mental characteristic of the so-called "patrimonial manager." On the contrary, what strikes us most is that the Chinese owners/managers are pragmatic, practical and serious. The above-mentioned fact of hiring relatives should not be interpreted as an indication that kinship relationship is cherished as a goal value in itself; instead it is more or less used as an instrumental mechanism to secure one whom they feel they can trust. It is indeed our contention that the Chinese traditional familistic system has been modified by Western business ideology and practical necessity, or by the functional prerequisites, if you so wish to call it, of the industrial system. As such, it may have enhanced rather than undermined the economic performance of the small factories.[33]

However, the reasons attributing to the relative strong performance of the small factories in Hong Kong may lie elsewhere too and therefore we shall further attempt to present some plausible accounts for it, in addition to entrepreneurship discussed above.

First, labour: It is often said that one of the reasons why small industry should be promoted in developing countries is because there is an ample supply of cheap surplus labour. While this may be true in many developing countries, this is not the case in Hong Kong, at least no longer true since the late 50's, despite the

---

[32] F. HARBISON and Ch.A. MYERS, Management in the Industrial World: An International Analysis. New York: McGraw-Hill, 1959, p. 69.

[33] A similar argument can be found in studies of Lebanon and Japan. See S. KHALAF and E. SHWAYRI, "Family Firms and Industrial Development: The Lebanese Case", Economic Development and Cultural Change, 15 (1966-67): 59-69; J. PELZEL, "The Small Industrialist in Japan", Explorations in Entrepreneurial History 7 (1954): 79-93; and L. OLSON, "A Japanese Small Industry: A Letter from

fact that Hong Kong shares with the Third World the common characteristic of high population density. The overall population density of Hong Kong, including the rural areas of the New Territories, is above 4,000 persons per square kilometre, which doubtlessly makes Hong Kong one of the most densely populated areas in the world. It is however not labour abundance, but rather labour shortage, that has become a major problem in Hong Kong's economy since the early 60's. By the end of the 50's, full employment had been attained; the Census of 1961 found only 1.7 % of the economically active persons to be unemployed. The corresponding figure in the 1966 By-census was somewhat higher, at 3.7 %, but with three-fifths of them looking for their first job. The 1971 Census showed that of all the economically active persons, the unemployment rate was 4.4 %, but again with more than one-third of them looking for their first job. More than once between these years the Commissioners of Labour reported that "many industrialists were forced to defer plans for extension of their factories, while others found difficulty in maintaining their establishments at the levels reached", by reason of labour shortages.[34]

Not surprisingly, the wages in Hong Kong are much higher than in many developing or even semi-developed countries. Between 1958 and 1966, the average increase in wages in a dozen industries was about 80 %, and by 1969 it was believed that, of Asian countries, only Japan had higher wages.

According to the study of the Kwun Tong factories, the mean monthly wage for production workers in 1971 for factories of all sizes was about HK$ 650,[35] whereby the mean wage of the small factory workers was 85 % of the mean wage of the large factory workers.

What should be noted here too is that the workers in Hong Kong are in general industrious and intelligent, which seem to be characteristics of Chinese workers everywhere; this is only more true in Hong Kong. In another study, Owen uses the average number of hours

Kyoto", <u>Explorations in Entrepreneurial History</u>, 8 (1956): 233-244.

34 E.H. PHELPS BROWN, in: HOPKINS (ed.), op. cit., p. 3.

35 MOK, op. cit., p. 70.

per loom as an index to quantify the high productive nature of Hong Kong's labour force. He shows that no other country in Asia approaches within 75 % of the Hong Kong figure of 8,160 hours per loom, which, incidentally, is the highest possible annual maximum, entailing 24-hour operation for 360 days in the year.[36] Such a mode of operation suggests a strong economically-motivated labour force.

Second, capital: Hong Kong has no shortage of capital which is as unique as its no abundance of labour. After 1949, the Hong Kong economy has been on the path of fast industrialization resulting from mass inflow of enterpreneurial skills and capital brought in by merchants from mainland China, particularly those from Shanghai, and from other countries. Our survey shows that among the 233 small factories which reported their sources of capital, 81.4 % have their own capital. Although there is a need for (Government and Industrial Bank) loans, no sign of urgent dependence has been detected.[37]

In Hong Kong, the factories have well passed the stage where labour is the main input; they gradually increased their capital intensity: "... we cannot state whether these industries are capital or labour intensive. But there is one thing we are sure ..., capital (in the form of machinery and equipment) is a very important input in most industries."[38] It is our belief that the factories in Hong Kong are relatively capital- or technology-intensive. In our study of Kwun Tong factories, there are as many as 60 % of the small factories reporting that their machinery and equipment were purchased within the last three years.[39]

It is probably not far from the truth to say that one of the basic factors attributing to the strong performance of small factories in the Hong Kong economy is that they are technology- capital-intensive. The case of Hong Kong seems to support the view made by Staley and Morse that the average labour productivity in small plants is not very far below that in large plants; but this is

---

36 OWEN, in: HOPKINS (ed.), op. cit., pp. 149-150.

37 SUTU and others, op. cit.

38 MOK, op. cit., pp. 76 and 69, respectively.

39 DWYER, "Problems of the Small Industrial Unit", in: DWYER (ed.), op. cit., p. 17.

because the majority of the small units use modern processes and techniques and, in addition, are usually power based.[40] In other words, the small factories are modern in nature. The significant advances made in the exports of electronics and telecommunications apparatus, which require a fairly advanced technology, is an adequate indicator in this regard.

Third, industrial integration: It has been observed that the expansion of small industry in the Asian countries lends itself to a large extent to industrial subcontracting, an arrangement by which certain manufacturing processes are decentralized and carried out by small industrial units which are capable of producing them on an economic scale.[41] In fact, the finished output of many large plants is based to a high degree upon subcontracting arrangements with small firms for the supply of constituant parts.[42]

In Japan, for instance, it has long been known that the role of its small factories strongly resulted from what may be called the "interorganizational or intersystem feature" of the Japanese small factories. John Pelzel has vividly shown that small factories in Japan were highly dependent upon the large industrialists or wholesalers for capital supply. And it is through the latter that the small industries were integrated into the entire economic system. Their relationship is one of powerful patron-client, which is both diffused and quasi-kinship in nature.[43] This feature which has become adjusted to modern industrial society is the oyabun-kobun, or as it has also been called, the boss-henchman system. Hoselitz, in his comparative study of small industry, has the following to say about Japan:[44]

"Ultimately the integration of small industry into the overall process of industrial production of Japan depends upon subcontracting. The middlemen who boss the small industrialists are, in turn, dependent upon large enterprises who often maintain the same boss-henchmen relationship with regard to these middlemen as the latter

---

40 STALEY and MORSE, op. cit., p. 17.

41 S. AWANOHARA, "A Break in the Lifetime," Far Eastern Economic Review, 83, No. 12, 1974, p. 18.

42 U. NYUN, "Preface", in: Small Industry Bulletin for Asia and the Far East, No. 10, p. iii.

vis-à-vis their "clients". Thus the survival of small industry in Japan is the outcome of a highly complex and hierarchical social structure within industrial production, and presents a feature of industrial organization which is probably not approximated in any western country. We must bear in mind this socio-structural peculiarity of Japanese industrial organization, which appears to be unique not only with reference to other Asian countries."

It is our view that Japan's system is indeed unique and is not shared by the Hong Kong industrial system. However, there is ample evidence to believe that the small factories in Hong Kong are well, if not fully, integrated into the overall process of production. In Hong Kong, the small factories, and indeed, also large plants, have fairly heavily depended upon the merchants. The merchants, serving the role of sub-contractors, have provided managerial services to small factories thus permitting the latter to integrate themselves into the overall system in two directions, successful designing and marketing. It is worth to mention that Hong Kong is not only a thriving manufacturing centre but also a mature and sophisticated commercial centre. In 1977, there were as many as 23 % of the working population employed in the commercial sector, a clear reflection of a highly developed commercial infrastructure resulting from Hong Kong's traditional role as an entrepôt. This mature and cosmopolitan commercial structure has in large measure helped to make Hong Kong's rapid industrialization possible.

The kind of managerial help rendered to small factories by merchants has been that an order provides them with the security on which to negotiate loans to provide the working capital they need to carry the order out. It is observed that "to a considerable extent, Hong Kong industry is manufacturing goods to designs and specifications dictated by the purchaser, and, where it is not, the initiative in any transaction comes more frequently from

[43] PELZEL, op. cit., pp. 79-93.

[44] HOSELITZ, "Small Industry in Underdeveloped Countries", op. cit., p. 607.

outside than from within the producing firm ... At least three-quarters and perhaps more of the manufactures exported are thought to be handled by the export houses."[45] There were reckoned to be at least 1,000 of such export houses.

In our study on the industrial community of Kwun Tong, we find some illuminating data bearing on the subject under discussion. Among the 252 small factories surveyed, about two-thirds of them depend heavily upon merchant-business connections as their source of information from which they obtain input and market their output. Furthermore, among the important industries in Kwun Tong, rubber, plastics, fabricated-metal are the ones having low proportions in direct exportation and high proportions in indirect exportation. In short, we can say that the small factories in Kwun Tong, and in Hong Kong as a whole, depend to a significant degree, like their Japanese counterparts, on sub-contracting with larger firms or upon marketing their products through wholesalers, merchants or export houses. But unlike Japan, this relationship is not based on a diffused, quasi father-child relation; instead it is rather similar to the European "putting-out" system which is more characterized by specific, contractual relations. We have good reasons to believe that this intersystem characteristic of the small factories has a great deal to do with their impressive economic performance.

At this juncture, it is worthwhile to mention two other factors which help the successful integration of small factories into the large economic system, namely, geographic compactness and relative high level of technology of small factories. In Japan, Lockwood has observed that geographic compactness is another factor in facilitating industrial integration. He notes that when Japan began its industrialization in 1868, existing small industry was quickly drawn into the production system by virtue of Japan's "geographic compactness...(for) it was far easier (here) than in continental India or China to diffuse new ideas and skills through the countryside", to attract nearby labour and to "create easy, efficient

---

45 Report on Industry in Hong Kong, p. 8b; quoted in BROWN, in: HOPKINS (ed.), op. cit., p. 12.

ties ... with factories, banks, and merchants."[46] Lockwood's argument rings even more truth in Hong Kong than in Japan. With the exception of Singapore, Hong Kong is probably the most geographically compact society in Asia, if not in the world, Hong Kong is in fact a city-state. New ideas and skills are much easier to be diffused here and its physical compactness has provided a most convenient social place congenial to the development of various ties between factories, banks, and merchants. Face-to-face talks and telephone conversations have become common channels of communication for business transactions.

A fourth factor is the level of technology: In many developing countries, small industry is inefficient and low in productivity by modern standards of manufacturing efficiency. Traditional goods are thus unable to compete in quality or price. To successfully integrate small industry into the overall production system, a minimum degree of technological development must be attained. It has been observed that in the course of economic growth of Western countries small establishments could fit themselves into the interstices which were left unexploited by larger enterprises, either by intention or default; the bulk of small enterprises in the poor countries of Asia, however, are much less capable of doing so.[47] We believe that it is precisely because of this fact, among others, that the small industry in these developing countries is technologically too primitive. The Indian situation seems to be a case in point: "In most of the small-scale industries, both specialization and technology are frozen at a relatively simple level. There is widespread obsolescence even in such an important trade as engineering... Any process or phenomenon in the chemical or electrical fields must be transformed into the ultimate working proposition through the application of available engineering techniques. The willingness of this sector to accept and adapt to changing conditions is a prerequisite for its integration with the large-scale sector."[48]

---

[46] W.W. LOCKWOOD, The Economic Development of Japan, Princeton: Princeton University Press, 1954, pp. 213-214.

[47] HOSELITZ, "Small Industry in Underdeveloped Countries", op. cit., p. 617.

[48] L.R. UPASANI, "Problems and Difficulties Faced by Small Industries in India," Small Industry Bulletin for Asia and the Far East, No. 8, United Nations, 1971, pp. 128-129.

In Hong Kong the fast adoption of and adaptation to changing technological development by the small industries is surely accountable for their fitness to the large production system. The small industry in Hong Kong, unlike most of its Asian counterparts, has taken a modern form.

VI. The Small Factory and Industrialization

The Hong Kong economy has thus far enjoyed a continuous prosperity. Despite this remarkable performance, new challenges and difficulties should not be ignored. The strong exporting capacity of the Hong Kong economy is being challenged mainly by two factors: the increasing competition from similar economies in this region, notably Taiwan and South Korea, and the rapid rise in production costs. With the oil crisis and other energy shortages on the scene, oil and oil-based raw materials will cost more, and Japan in particular will no longer be a source of cheap raw materials and components.

In light of the present situation, the Governor of Hong Kong recognizes that "the rapid growth of our light industries has created sufficient demand for materials and services to favour the establishment of carefully selected medium and heavy industries. As low-wage competitors erode the cheap end of our markets, the redevelopment of Hong Kong industry into higher technology is inevitable as it is desirable."[49] The need for higher technology and larger industries was also specifically noted by E.H. Phelps Brown:[50]

"The one evident way to prevent an imposed rise of money wages from raising unit labour costs is to make productivity rise at the same rate ... At the present stage of its industrial development, two main ways of doing this are to achieve more economies of scale by forming bigger units of production, and (often at the

---

[49] M. MACLEHOSE, "'Introduction' to Hong Kong '74 Focus", Far Eastern Economic Review, 83, No. 12, 1974, p. 4.

[50] BROWN, in: HOPKINS (ed.), op. cit., p. 15.

same time) to increase the amount of equipment per worker. But in the difficult terrain of Hong Kong bigger factories raise a special problem of siting, worker housing, and communications; and both they and the increased equipment per worker will raise the cost of varying the output of the firm, and tie it more closely to particular processes and products. There will thus be some loss of the flexibility that the smaller firm and the simpler equipment afforded, and that helped to keep exports up as opportunities varied from day to day."

Brown's diagnosis of the Hong Kong economy and his answers to the problems are basically sound. The first and foremost thing for Hong Kong to do is to strengthen its competitive exporting capacity by increasing its productivity. However, as Brown points out, there is a built-in nature of inflexibility with the larger factories; thus it still seems sensible to further develop smaller industries to adapt to the ever-changing market situation by virtue of its flexibility.

Based on our previous comparative analysis of the economic performance of small factories of various sizes, it is desirable to pay special attention to the midi- and the maxi- types, especially the latter, both because of their strong performance in productivity vis-à-vis mini-factories and of their simpler technology vis-à-vis large factories. Needless to say, this does not mean that we are in favour of other types of factories larger than the maxi-factories. What we are trying to say is that the midi- and maxi-categories, which constitute the bulk of Hong Kong's factories are the types with good economic strength among the small factories. Hong Kong has, thus far, a very short history of industrial development, of approximately two-decades' time, a history of rapid development in terms of both quantity and quality of small factories. It is not easy to predict with a high degree of certainty what the role of the small factory is going to be in Hong Kong's future. But one thing certain is that the small factory will continue to occupy a very strong and significant position.

We are very skeptical about the so-called "iron-law" of history; we do not believe without reservation that the eventual application of large-scale urbanized industries is inevitable; nor do we think that the small industry is only a passing phenomenon occupying a position between peasant agriculture and modern large industry. True, the overall tendency of industrialization is towards bureaucratization and large-scale industry; however, there will be, and probably always will be, room for a small factory in even a highly industrialized economy. Germany, the United Kingdom, the United States and Japan are cases in point. It is precisely the type of small factory, modern and technology-intensive, which we believe is probably going to have a permanent place in even what some would call the post-industrial society. And it is this type of small factory which will prove to hold out great promise for Hong Kong (and other developing countries as well).

EMPLOYMENT RELATIONS IN HONG KONG: TRADITIONAL OR MODERN ?

Siu-kai Lau

I. Introduction[+]

Managerial ideologies, as concomitant constituents of the process of industrialization, are used to being fabricated and articulated, deliberately or otherwise, to legitimatize the differential distribution of rewards and authority within economic institutions.[1] Though a number of common themes can be discerned from the ideologies originating from a variety of industrial settings, the historical pre-conditions for industrialization in a given society, its developmental trajectory as well as its relationships with other societies will structure the formation of managerial ideologies to a considerable extent. Among the components of a managerial ideology, the managerial attitudes toward employees are of particular significance, since the ascertainment of these attitudes tells much about the 'proper' employer-employee relationships as envisaged by the employers concerned. Differences in the conception of an 'employee' not only have enormous practical implications for industrial relations in economic institutions, they also have serious overtones for the larger social structure as well. In fact, as an integral part of the societal value system pertaining to the distribution of authority and rewards and its rationalization, managerial attitudes toward employees are part of the so-called 'class structure in the social consciousness'.[2]

The primary goal of this study is to discover the managerial attitudes toward employees among the Hong Kong employers, who are

---

[+] This paper is based on the data collected in a survey of Hong Kong employers conducted in the summer of 1976 jointly by the Committee on Vocational Training, Hong Kong Training Council, and the Social Research Centre of the Chinese University of Hong Kong.

[1] See R. BENDIX: Work and Authority in Industry: Ideologies of Management in the Course of Industrialization, Berkeley and Los Angeles: Univ. of California Press, 1974, pp. 1-21.

predominantly Chinese. Even though our main interest lies in the unearthing of psychological dispositions, a brief discourse on the relevant structural and historical contextual features of the Hong Kong economy would provide the background for the interpretation of the findings reported here.

II. The Setting of Hong Kong

Hong Kong has witnessed a rather rapid rate of industrial progress since 1949, and, more precisely, since the outbreak of the Korean War. Transformation of the Hong Kong society of such a magnitude and at such a fast pace would lead us to expect that a cohesive and 'class-conscious' managerial and entrepreneurial group is still in the formative stages; a popular and internally consistent managerial attitudinal syndrome toward employees should therefore be only partially congealed and institutionalized in Hong Kong.

The economic structure of Hong Kong manifests a dualistic character in the sense that a small number of large-scale economic establishments co-exists with a large number of medium- and small-size establishments. A census of manufacturing establishments conducted in 1971 revealed that 62.8 % of the manufacturing establishments in Hong Kong employed less than 10 persons; and these small establishments accounted for only 11.6 % of the total number of manufacturing employees, 11.9 % of the total floor area, and 7.6 % of the total sales.[3] With minor modifications, these characteristics apply also to the commercial enterprises.

Most of the medium- and small-size firms in Hong Kong are family businesses with resources and, in many cases, personnel, pooled from the family and other close relatives.[4] In large-scale establishments, heavily dominated by foreign (and Shanghainese)

---

[2] St. OSSOWSKI: Class Structure in the Social Consciousness. New York: Free Press, 1963.

[3] Census and Statistics Department, 1971 Census of Manufacturing Establishments, Hong Kong: Government Printer, 1971, p. 17.

[4] See E.H. PHELPS BROWN: "The Hong Kong Economy: Achievements and Prospects," in: K. HOPKINS (ed.): Hong Kong: The Industrial Colony, Hong Kong: Oxford Univ. Press, 1971, pp. 1-20 and J. ENGLAND: "Industrial Relations in Hong Kong," in: HOPKINS, op. cit., pp. 207-260.

capital, relatively modern and formalized personnel management doctrines and practices hold sway. On the other hand, in the medium- and small-size establishments, mostly under Cantonese ownership, employer-employee relationships reflect, to a certain degree, the superior-subordinate relationships which characterize the government bureaucracy and the craft guilds in traditional China, where paternalism and authoritarianism loomed large.[5] Nevertheless, being under the shadow of the large-scale enterprises and in face of the endemic need to struggle for survival in the heavy competition for foreign markets, the adoption of some rational personnel policies and attitudes is essential to stay afloat for most of these small establishments. Under such circumstances, the managerial attitudes towards employees are expected to combine both modern and traditional elements into a mix which might not necessarily be logical, but would at least be practical.

III. Research Design

A sample of 255 employers were asked the following general question: "if you are looking for an employee, how important do you think are the following characteristics?" Eight such characteristics were listed: aggressiveness, ability to do the job, related to me through kinship or other ties, obedient to superiors, loyalty to the company, loyalty to the boss, male, and show respect towards elders. For each characteristic, the respondent was asked to indicate whether it is, to him, extremely unimportant, not important, neutral in importance, important, or extremely important.

The employers who answered this question were the personnel managers, the owners, the general managers or other responsible personages in the 255 companies surveyed, and they were overwhelmingly Chinese in origin. These companies reflect quite well the variety of industrial and commercial establishments in Hong Kong, even though they do not constitute a representative sample of all the establishments (see Table 1).

5 See W. BRUGGER: Democracy and Organization in the Chinese Industrial Enterprise (1948-1953), Cambridge: Cambridge Univ. Press, 1976, pp. 3-4.

Table 1: Establishments studied, by Type of Industry

Type of Industry	N	% of Total
Automobile	10	3.9
Construction	19	7.5
Clothing	32	12.5
Electrical	12	4.7
Electronic	24	9.4
Mechanical Engineering	16	6.3
Plastics	19	7.5
Printing	22	8.6
Shipbuilding	2	0.8
Textiles	17	6.7
Commerce and Services	46	18.0
Others	35	13.7
Unidentified	1	0.4
TOTAL	255	100.0

Among our respondents, a large proportion were male (86.3 %), were below 40 years in age (61.6 %), and had received a secondary education or more (86.3 %); hence most of our respondents were young, male, and well-educated employers.

The distribution of the size of the responding establishments is, however, not a realistic reflection of the economic structure of Hong Kong. 56.9 % of the 255 establishments have more than 101 employees, 14.9 % between 51 and 100, and therefore could even be classified as large-scale organizations in view of Hong Kong average. If the observation is valid that traditionalistic managerial attitudes towards employees tend to be more frequent in the small- and medium-size establishments under primarily family ownership, the conclusions drawn from our findings should have an upward bias in favor of modern managerial attitudes, and hence extraordinary care should be exercised in the interpretation of the data.

IV. Employers' Ratings of the Importance of Employee Characteristics

The employers' evaluations of the importance of each of the employee characteristics are summarized in Table 2.

Most of the respondents (85.1 %) considered that 'aggressiveness' was either important or very important for an employee to possess. In traditional China, on the other hand, the ideal employee would rather be one who was meek, compliant, amicable and complacent with the status quo. Moreover, he should be constantly group-conscious in that he would withdraw from disturbing group harmony for the sake of his own self-advancement. If change was contemplated, it should be initiated gradually and with the rapport among the group members preserved along the process. Our respondents' reaction to the characteristic 'aggressiveness' hence indicates an abandonment of traditionalistic attitudes in this respect. In many ways, not only is 'aggressiveness' approvingly tolerated by the Hong Kong employers, but is deliberately and meticulously nurtured by them. In the competitive economy of Hong Kong where originality of ideas and actions initiated at the most opportune moments means success and their absence spells failure, 'aggressive' employees seem to be an asset to most of the employers in the colony.

Not surprisingly, the 'ability to do the job' was rated very high by our respondents, as 57.3 % of them considered it important and 32.9 % of them considered it very important. However, this characteristic does not serve as a distinct demarcation line between traditionalistic and modern managerial attitudes toward employees since it certainly was also considered to be of importance by employers in traditional China. The traditional relationship between employers and employees was, ideally speaking, a diffuse one. In such a relationship, employees were expected not only to perform well in the job, but were also required, among other things, to serve families, to be involved sentimentally in the employers' firms, to safeguard the 'face' and 'name' of their employers, and to regard themselves as members of a larger family in which the employer was the family head. In such a situation, 'ability to

Table 2: Importance of Employee Characteristics to Employers

Employee Characteristics	Degree of Importance						
	Extremely unimportant	Not important	Neutral	Important	Extremely important	Missing values	Total
Aggressiveness	0.0 (0)	1.6 (4)	6.7(17)	57.3(146)	27.8(71)	6.7(17)	100.0(255)
Ability to do the job	0.0 (0)	0.4 (1)	4.3(11)	57.3(146)	32.9(84)	5.1(13)	100.0(255)
Related to me through kinship or other ties	34.5(88)	32.5(83)	15.7(40)	11.8(30)	0.0 (0)	5.5(14)	100.0(255)
Obedient to superiors	0.0 (0)	0.0 (0)	12.2(31)	59.6(152)	22.7(58)	5.5(14)	100.0(255)
Loyalty to the company	0.0 (0)	0.8 (2)	12.2(31)	58.4(149)	23.1(59)	5.5(14)	100.0(255)
Loyalty to the boss	0.4 (1)	3.5 (9)	20.0(51)	57.6(147)	11.8(30)	6.7(17)	100.0(255)
Male	4.7(12)	11.4(29)	46.7(119)	25.5(65)	1.2 (3)	10.6(27)	100.0(255)
Show respect towards elders	3.1 (8)	7.8(20)	30.6(78)	45.9(117)	5.9(15)	6.7(17)	100.0(255)

Note: in percentage, number of cases in parentheses.

do the job' would be a valuable trait to the employers, but it might not be the most important one in the employers' priority list, particularly when the expansion of the operations of the firms was not perennially in the mind of the employers. In Hong Kong, where profit-making is the leitmotif in the business ideology of the employers in both large and small establishments, the employees' ability to do the job enters weightily into their cost-benefit calculations. As the employer-employee relationship in Hong Kong becomes more and more specific, 'ability to do the job' will increasingly become the key criterion in employee recruitment. With regard to this characteristic, our data seem to report the receding importance of traditionalism.

The responses given to the characteristic 'related to me through kinship or other ties' also depict unmistakenly an overwhelming dominance of modernism. More than two-thirds of our respondents deemed it as not important (32.5 %) and extremely unimportant (34.5 %). As familism was the ethos that permeated almost all arenas in the culture and society of traditional China, the gradation of one's relationships with other people based on familial principles was a common phenomenon. Under these principles, as applied to the recruitment of employees, familial members, kinsmen, clansmen and fellow-natives would be preferred to outsiders. The responses given by our respondents with regard to this characteristic signify that, as an ideal, 'relationship with the employer through kinship or other ties' has already lost favour among the Hong Kong employers. Nevertheless, as actual practice, whether relatives, kinsmen and fellow-natives are actively sought after as employees is far from clear. In large-scale establishments, it can safely be said that achievement criteria are the norms for employee recruitment. In small establishments, however, it is still fairly common for employers to deliberately rely on relatives, kinsmen and fellow-natives as their major source of employees. This practice of recruitment is and can be justified on rational grounds, and is definitely not simply the result of sentimental attachments. In a survey of 346 factories in Kwun Tong, most of them small in scale, Victor Mok concluded:[6]

[6] V. MOK, The Organization and Management of Factories in Kwun Tong, Social Research Centre, The Chinese University of Hong Kong, 1973, p. 48.

"It is rather customary for a Chinese proprietor to put a trusted man in each department as some kind of supervisor to safeguard his own interests. Beyond direct kinfolks and clansmen, a person who comes from the same place of origin, speaking the same dialect and probably being a remote relative would be next in line of reliability. Thus the employment of these people does have its rationale (though it may not be directly economic) beyond just taking care of one's fellow-natives, and the need increases as a factory gets larger. These people, then, constitute the nucleus in a factory whose loyalty the proprietor can count on."

Two other researchers on the small factories in Hong Kong have argued along the same line:[7]

"It is true that the owners/managers of small factories in Kwun Tong are in large measure traditionalistic, paternalistic and conservative, but it is far from being true that they are persons with an inevitable and almost built-in disposition for nepotistic inclination which is often the mental characteristic of the so-called patrimonial manager. On the contrary, what strikes us most is that the Chinese owners/managers are pragmatic, practical and absolute no-nonsense. The above-mentioned fact of hiring relatives should not be interpreted as an indication that kinship relationship is cherished as a goal value in itself; instead it is more or less being used as an instrumental mechanism to secure somebody whom they really can trust. It is indeed our contention that the Chinese traditional familistic system has been modified by Western business ideology and practical necessity, or functional prerequisite, if you wish to call it, of the industrial system. As such, it may have enhanced rather than undermined the economic performance of the small factories."

In short, emphasis on the kinship and other ascriptive aspects in the employer-employee relationship is frowned upon by most of the employers in Hong Kong, unless it can be rationalized on other non-ascriptive grounds. The denial of any intrinsic good in nepotism denotes another step towards modernism in the managerial attitudes towards employees.

---

[7] A.Y.C. KING and P.J.L. MAN, The Role of Small Factory in Economic Development: The Case of Hong Kong, Social Research Centre, The Chinese University of Hong Kong, 1974, pp. 41-42.

The reactions to the characteristic 'obedient to superiors' by the respondents are more difficult to interpret, as are the ratings of the characteristic 'loyalty to the company'. In the first instance, an overwhelming majority of our respondents considered the characteristic as either important or extremely important (82.3 %). The same applies to the second instance (with 81.5 %). Although it might be reasonable to expect that both modern and traditionalistic employers would stress the importance of the two characteristics, there are some differences in degree as well as in kind. Traditionalistic employers would be inclined to demand more 'obedience' and 'loyalty' from their employees than their modern counterparts. Moreover, they would tend to prefer that the 'obedience' and 'loyalty' be total, lifelong, and absolute, rather than specific, temporally circumscribed, and situationally determined. The responses given to the two characteristics by the Hong Kong employers, in view of the heavy emphasis laid on their importance, seem to betray some traditionalism in their managerial attitudes. However, the strong emphasis might also be a rational response to an increasing labor shortage and to the need to retain their employees, who might have upgraded their skills through on-the-job experiences. Alternatively speaking, even if these attitudes do not serve any manifest functions, at least they are not dysfunctional to the operation of the enterprises.

It has been profusely documented in the literature that modern managerial ideology stipulates the organization as the proper target with which the employees should identify, while in traditionalistic managerial ideology the owner or the proprietor is the target. In their ratings of the importance of the characteristic of 'loyalty to the boss', a large majority of the respondents regarded it as important or extremely important (69.4 %). To a certain extent, this phenomenon may reflect the lingering influence of family ownership in the economic structure of Hong Kong. Nonetheless, it is more likely to be a legacy of the past as well as a reaction to the labor market in Hong Kong. As most employers would attribute the high rate of economic growth in Hong Kong to the weakness of trade union organizations and the relative absence of collective bargaining in industrial and commercial institutions, the stress on the vertical tie between employers and employees would serve to impress on the employees the 'common interests' notion, and to prevent the emergence of 'class-consciousness' among the employees.

The reactions to the characteristic 'male' demonstrate some shift toward modernism among the Hong Kong employers. More than half of them had rated it as extremely unimportant, not important or neutral in importance. This means that, in the eyes of the employers, being a 'male' does not confer an intrinsic good to a prospective employee. Therefore, compared to the situation in traditional societies, where predominantly males are employed in economic organizations, the Hong Kong employers seem able to adopt a pragmatic approach to employee recruitment. At the present moment, employees are selected largely on the basis of merit, even though the substantial minority of respondents (26.7 %) who still claimed importance for 'maleness' indicates that the process of modernization is far from completed.

The last characteristic listed, 'show respect toward elders' does not seem to have serious implications for the operation of economic institutions, though it is connected, to a certain degree, to the structure of interpersonal relationships in these organizations. Approximately half of the respondents had rated it as important and extremely important, but it is significant that 30.6 % of them expressed an indifferent attitude towards it. Traditionalism is evident here, though its influence is gradually diminishing.

V. Employers' Ratings and Other Correlates

It may be surmised that the size of the establishments with which our respondents were affiliated, as well as their sex, age and education will affect their ratings of the importance of the various employee characteristics. In the form of hypotheses, we may expect to find employers from large-scale establishments who are male, young and better educated to evince modern managerial attitudes towards employees, while employers from small-scale establishments and who are female, advanced in age and less educated to be more traditionalistic.

Table 3 gives all the chi-square relationships between the employee characteristics evaluated and the hypothetical causal variables of 'number of employees in the establishment', 'sex of respondent', 'age of respondent' and 'education of respondent'. There is only one statistically significant correlation between number of employees and the employee characteristics, namely, that with 'related to me through kinship and other ties'. Hence, the larger the establishment, the more likely the employer will de-emphasize kinship ties.

The sex and age of the respondents, on the other hand, are totally useless in accounting for the differences in the employers' ratings of employee characteristics. This finding seems rather surprising as it shows that the females and the elderly are not necessarily more traditionalistic than the males and the young.

The differentiating capacity of education of respondents has significant correlations with 'aggressiveness', 'ability to do the job', 'related to me through kinship or other ties' and 'show respect towards elders', meaning that the better educated are more prone to demand aggressiveness and ability to do the job from their employees, and are less inclined to lay emphasis on kinship ties. Surprisingly enough, the better educated are also more desirous of employees who 'show respect towards elders'. The interpretation we can make here is that, in view of the fact that education of the respondent is significantly correlated with only one half of the employee characteristics, it can only be considered to be a moderately good explanatory factor rather than the determinant of managerial attitudes among employers.

VI. Conclusions

Thus far our findings have demonstrated that in general, the Hong Kong employers seem able to adopt a fairly modern orientation in their managerial attitudes towards employees. Irrespective of the size of their establishments, their sex, age and education, they are to a large extent rational and pragmatic. Though there are still traditionalistic elements of various sorts embedded in the

Table 3: Chi-square Relationship between Employee Characteristics and Other Variables

Employee characteristics	Number of employees	Other Variables		
		Sex of respondent	Age of respondent	Education of respondent
Aggressiveness	28.09 (18)	6.13 (3)	16.33 (12)	36.60 (18)++
Ability to do the job	27.20 (18)	2.71 (3)	10.65 (12)	35.15 (18)++
Related to me through kinship or other ties	31.14 (18)+	1.27 (3)	11.60 (12)	30.41 (18)+
Obedient to superiors	19.01 (12)	3.28 (2)	10.81 (8)	10.41 (12)
Loyalty to the company	18.56 (18)	5.92 (3)	6.50 (12)	17.92 (18)
Loyalty to the boss	32.45 (24)	0.90 (4)	15.87 (16)	33.06 (24)
Male	20.56 (24)	1.90 (4)	10.65 (16)	17.75 (24)
Show respect towards elders	17.23 (24)	0.99 (4)	12.92 (16)	36.91 (24)+

Notes: + $p < .05$
++ $p < .01$

Degrees of freedom enclosed in parentheses.

managerial attitudes, they can in many cases be justified on rational and pragmatic grounds, in view of the specific economic and labor conditions in Hong Kong. For those traditionalistic elements which do not have a direct impact on the operation of economic organizations, the continued adherence to them by a majority of the employers can be explained either as cultural legacy or as the result of a process of insulation, whereby traditional values that affect the survival or development of economic organizations are only marginally protected from the attack by the process of modernization. The more or less mutually insulated co-existence of both modern and traditionalistic elements in the managerial attitudes of employers in Hong Kong has resulted in a relatively inconsistent managerial ideology, which, nonetheless, is highly practical for the Hong Kong situation.[8]

[8] The co-existence of both modern and traditionalistic elements in the managerial ideology of the Chinese employers and managers had also been found in a research utilizing the laboratory method: "Modern Chinese realize the necessity of changing their own behavior and that of organizations in order to meet the challenge of the West, but in some contexts they also value Chinese ways (much modified, of course) of doing things. Often these two elements co-exist in the same person, perhaps one or the other aspect becoming more dominant according to circumstances." A.L.S. Chin: *Hong Kong Managerial Styles: Chinese and Western Approaches to Conflict Management*, Social Research Centre, The Chinese University of Hong Kong, 1972, p. 34.

References:

Census of Manufacturing Establishments. Department of Census and Statistics, Hong Kong Government, 1973.

Commissioner of Labour, Annual Reports. Hong Kong Government.

DWYER, D.J. "Problems of the Small Industrial Unit," in D.J. DWYER (ed.), Asian Urbanization: A Hong Kong Casebook. Hong Kong: Hong Kong University Press, 1971.

DWYER, D.J. and Lai CHUEN-YAN, The Small Industrial Units in Hong Kong: Patterns and Policies, University of Hull, 1967.

ECAFE, Economic Survey of Asia and the Far East, New York: United Nations, 1953.

ESPY, J.L., The Strategies of Chinese Industrial Enterprises in Hong Kong, Dissertation, School of Business Administration, Harvard University, 1970.

GRAY, H.J., "Some Aspects of the Role of Small Industry in the United Kingdom," Small Industry Bulletin for Asia and the Far East, No. 10. New York: United Nations, 1973.

HARBISON, F. and Ch.A. MYERS, Management in the Industrial World: An International Analysis, New York: McGraw-Hill, 1959.

HERMAN, Th., "The Role of Cottage and Small-Scale Industries in Asian Economic Development", Economic Development and Cultural Change, 4, (1955-56): 356-370.

HIGGINS, B.H., Economic Development: Principles, Problems and Policies, New York: W.W. Norton, 1959.

HOLLANDER, E.D. and others, The Future of Small Business, New York: Praeger, 1967.

Hong Kong Population and Housing Census 1971: Main Report, Census and Statistics Department, Hong Kong Government Press, 1973.

"Hong Kong '74 Focus," Far Eastern Economic Review, 83, No. 12, 1974: 1-20.

HOPKINS, K. (ed.), Hong Kong: The Industrial Colony, Hong Kong: Oxford Univ. Press, 1971.

HOSELITZ, B.F., "Small Industry in Underdeveloped Countries," Journal of Economic History, 19 (1959): 600-618.

HOSELITZ, B.F., (ed.), The Role of Small Industry in the Process of Economic Growth, The Hague and Paris: Mouton, 1968.

INFIN, R., The Sociology of Industrial Relations, Englewood Cliffs, N.J.: Prentice-Hall, 1959.

KHALAF, S. and E. SHWAYRI, "Family Firms and Industrial Development: The Lebanese Case," Economic Development and Cultural Change 15, (1966-67): 59-69.

KUZNETS, S., "Quantative Aspects of the Economic Growth of Nations: II, Industrial Distribution of National Product and Labor Force," Economic Development and Cultural Change 5, (1957), Supplement, pp. 32ff.

LOCKWOOD, W.W., The Economic Development of Japan, Princeton: University Press, 1954.

The Medium Industrial Bank, An Introduction to Small Industries in Korea, Seoul, 1966.

MOK, V., "The Nature of Kwun Tong as an Industrial Community," Social Research Centre, The Chinese University of Hong Kong, 1972.

OLSON, L., "A Japanese Small Industry: A Letter from Kyoto," Explorations in Entrepreneurial History 8 (1956): 233-244.

PELZEL, J., "The Small Industrialist in Japan," Explorations in Entrepreneurial History 7 (1954): 79-93.

PERROW, Ch., Organizational Analysis. London: Tavistock, 1970.

Report on Small Industries in India. Prepared by the International Planning Team, the Ford Foundation, Ministry of Commerce and Industry, Delhi, Manager of Publications, 1954.

STALEY, E., Development of Small Industry Programs. Stanford Research Institute, 1961.

STALEY, E. and R. MORSE, Modern Small Industry for Developing Countries. New York: McGraw-Hill, 1965.

Stanford Research Institute, The Role of Small-Scale Manufacturing in Economic Development, Report prepared for Office of Industrial Resources, International Cooperation Administration. Washington, D.C.: 1957.

SUTU, H. and others, "A Study of Government Financial Assistance to Small Industries, With Special Reference to Hong Kong," The Lignan Institute of Business Administration, The Chinese University of Hong Kong, 1973.

UPASSANI, L.R. "Problems and Difficulties Faced by Small Industries in India," Small Industry Bulletin for Asia and the Far East, No. 8, New York: United Nations, 1971, pp. 126-129.

U.S. Bureau of the Census, Census of Manufacturers, 1967. Vol. 1, Summary and Subject Statistics, U.S. Government Printing Office, Washington, D.C.: 1971.

WOSZCZOWSKI, S., Small Industry in Economic Development of Contemporary Countries. Research Program on Small Industry Development, Misc. Paper No. 5, Stanford Research Institute, 1960.

WOODWARD, J., Industrial Organization Theory and Practice, Oxford: Clarendon Press, 1965.

II. SOCIAL DYNAMICS

MATERIAL AND NON-MATERIAL CONDITIONS AND LIFE SATISFACTION OF URBAN RESIDENTS IN HONG KONG

Rance P. L. Lee, Tak-sing Cheung and Yuet-wah Cheung

I. Introduction

The relationship between material well being and life satisfaction has perennially been a focus of investigation in recent years. The interest in this area, as McCall (1975) stated, represents a feeling on the part of many people that industrial society, despite impressive gains in affluence, ease of communication and increased leisure, has not made significant overall progress in improving man's quality of life.

Research findings in this area, however, are not as consistent as we would expect. Although many studies have shown that life satisfaction is positively associated with material well being (cf., Gurin, Veroff and Feld, 1960; Inkeles, 1960; Wessman, 1959; Bradburn and Caplovitz, 1965; Rogers and Converse, 1975), some studies have found no such relationship (Easterlin, 1973; Duncan, 1975 ; Schneider, 1975).

Part of the inconsistencies, in our opinion, stem from confusing the level of analysis. It is important to note that the correlation between material well being and life satisfaction can be established at two different levels, namely, the individual level, at which an individual's material condition is correlated with his own state of satisfaction, and the regional level, at which the material standard of a region is correlated with the summary state of satisfaction of all the individuals in that region. Methodologically, findings established at one level cannot be inferred to the other. It seems that most, if not all, of the studies that do not lend support to a positive relationship between material well being and life satisfaction are established at the regional level. The relationships between material well being and life satisfaction at both the individual and the regional levels have succinctly been summarized by Easterlin's statement (1973) that "in all societies, more money for the individual typically means more individual happiness. However, raising the income of all does not increase the happiness of all."

Studies on the relationship between material well being and life satisfaction in Asia are relatively few, although there are numerous such studies in the United States and other countries (Easterlin, 1974). A study that is worth mentioning is the one directed by Robert E. Mitchell (1969) in the urban areas of five Southeast Asian countries in 1967-68. It was found that 33 % of the urban residents in Hong Kong were unhappy, whereas comparable figures were 15 % in Taipei, 11 % in the six major cities of Western Malaysia, 8 % in Singapore, and 8 % in urban Bangkok-Thonburi. According to Mitchell's study, Hong Kong had a significantly higher rate of personal unhappiness than had other Asian cities. This finding is quite surprising because by the time this research was conducted, Hong Kong had a higher level of economic development than most of the other countries under study. Hence, the economically more advanced society turned out to have a higher rate of unhappiness.

However, it should be noted that Mitchell collected the data during the summer of 1967, when residents in Hong Kong were suffering from a serious political turmoil, with widespread bomb threats, strikes, shortage of food supplies and the shadows of a communist takeover. These events might have had an adverse effect on the psychological well being of its people although the extent of this effect cannot be precisely determined. Moreover, Mitchell did not correlate material well being and happiness at the individual level. Consequently, there is no way to tell what kinds of people are the most happy as well as the most unhappy. From a policy point of view, such information is very important because if we want to convert the unhappy citizens into happy ones, we need to know what makes them unhappy.

The objective of this paper is to analyse and elaborate the relationship between material well being and life satisfaction on the basis of the data collected from a sample of individuals in the urban areas of Hong Kong in 1974. In light of similar studies conducted in other countries, we hypothesized that among urban residents in Hong Kong, material well being would lead to greater satisfaction with life, and that the relationship would be independent of social background factors such as sex, age, and education. In the latter part of this paper, attempts will be made to elaborate the relationship for the purpose of identifying some of the ways in which material conditions may interact with non-material factors in their effects on life satisfaction. As will be explained later, it is our proposition that individuals in relatively good material conditions will be more concerned with their super-material pursuits than those in poorer material conditions. Some of the implications will be discussed below.

II. Survey and Sampling Method

Data were drawn from the Biosocial Survey conducted jointly by the Social Research Center of the Chinese University of Hong Kong and the Human Ecology Group of Australian National University in 1974. A proportionate stratified sample of 3,983 household heads between the ages of 20 and 59 were selected from the urban areas of Hong Kong. Census districts and housing types were used as criteria for stratification, and the sampling fraction for each stratum was .62 % (for details of the sample design, see Chan and Lau, 1974). Information from respondents was collected through personal interviews with a standardized questionnaire. The response rate was about 71 %. Unsuccessful interviews were replaced by cases randomly selected from a supplementary list.

Life satisfaction was measured by the questionnaire item: "Generally speaking, are you satisfied with your daily life (your status, things you do, and the situation around you, etc)?" This item was often used in previous studies on life satisfaction (cf., Gurin, et al., 1960; and Bradburn, 1969). Responses to the question were grouped into three categories: low (very or quite dissatisfied), medium (in-between), and high (very or quite satisfied).

Material well being was measured by four indicators; they were (1) total income of the household, (2) type of housing, (3) total size of the household's living space, and (4) facilities and appliances inside the household as observed by the interviewer. Scores on these four indicators were summed for each respondent and then grouped into four levels to form a scale of material well being. Analysing the internal consistency of the scale, we found that the total scale was strongly correlated with each of its indicators.

The gamma coefficients were .93 for total income, .92 for housing type, .96 for living space, and .94 for household facilities. The scale, therefore, appears to have a high degree of reliability.

Sex, age and educational status were introduced as control variables. Age was divided into four categories: 20-29, 30-39, 40-49, and 50-59. Educational status was also divided into four levels: no schooling, primary school or private tutoring, secondary school, and post-secondary school.

III. Results: Satisfaction and Material Conditions

Of the respondents under study 63.7 % reported that they were very or quite satisfied with their lives, whereas 24.5 % gave a neutral response, and only 11.9 % were reportedly quite or very dissatisfied. Apparently, the proportion of dissatisfied individuals was much smaller than that of the satisfied individuals.

As previously reported, Mitchell (1969) found that 33 % of his Hong Kong respondents were unhappy in 1967-68; while according to our study only about 12 % of the individuals were dissatisfied with their lives in 1974. Comparing the findings of these two studies, it may appear that the urban residents in Hong Kong have become happier over these years. But, it should be remembered that the difference might be a result of the massive civil disorders at the time of Mitchell's survey.

Table 1 shows the relationship between life satisfaction and material well being. The gamma coefficient was .36, and the relationship was statistically significant at the .001 level. Our hypothesis was thus confirmed. In other words, the higher the level of material well being, the higher the degree of life satisfaction among the urban population in Hong Kong.

According to our study, life satisfaction was also related to sex and education, but not to age. The gamma coefficients were .14 for sex, and .13 for education, both significant at .01 level. In general, the female and the better educated tended to express a higher degree of life satisfaction. In view of these findings, we should ask: is the relationship between life satisfaction and material well

Table 1: Life Satisfaction by Material Well Being

Satisfaction	Material Well Being			
	IV (Low)	III	II	I (High)
Low	17.6 %	10.8 %	7.6 %	6.6 %
Medium	34.0 %	24.3 %	19.3 %	9.3 %
High	48.4 %	64.9 %	73.1 %	84.1 %
(N)	(1213)	(1396)	(662)	(517)

Gamma = .36; $p<.001$.

Table 2: The Relationship between Life Satisfaction and Material Well Being among Various Sex, Age, and Educational Subgroups

	Gamma	Significance	N
Sex			
Male	.37	.001	1626
Female	.36	.001	2162
Age			
20-29	.27	.001	1052
30-39	.39	.001	814
40-49	.35	.001	1109
50-59	.48	.001	813
Education			
No schooling	.37	.001	732
Primary/tutoring	.34	.001	1728
Secondary	.34	.001	1026
Post-secondary	.38	.05	301

being affected by sex and educational status? In addition, although age is not related to life satisfaction, we would also like to know whether the relationships between material well being and life satisfaction are equally strong in the different age-groups.

The control analyses revealed that the original positive relationship between life satisfaction and material conditions persisted.

The partial gammas for the separate control on age, sex, and education were .36, .36, and .35, respectively; they were almost the same as the original zero-order gamma (.36). Furthermore, Table 2 shows that the relationship between life satisfaciton and material conditions remained positive and statistically significant in various age, sex, and educational subgroups.

It was observed, however, that the relationship became relatively weak among the youngest group of individuals (gamma = .27), but stronger among the oldest (gamma = .48). These findings seem to be consistent with the observation made by Davis (1940) and others. It was argued that unlike the later stage of life, young adulthood is a time for hope and exploration. At the starting point of a life career, the young adult usually attaches greater importance to the opportunity for development rather than to immediate material rewards, or he may be more idealistic and so tend to glorify lofty ideals rather than material achievements. Accordingly, we would expect that the older people would attach greater importance to immediate material success than future opportunities.

In short, it can be demonstrated that in Hong Kong there was a positive relationship between life satisfaction and material well being, and that the relationship was independent of age, sex, and educational status. This finding is consistent with Cantril's fourteen nation survey (Cantril, 1965), in which economic matters stand out as the most conspicuous human concern. It should not be misunderstood, however, that life satisfaction is simply a matter of material well being.

IV. Beyond Material Considerations: Sense of Personal Fulfillment

Maslow (1954) has called our attention to the "hierarchy of human needs". It was postulated that human needs are organized into a hierarchy of relative prepotency and that higher needs cannot be aroused until the more basic ones are gratified. The basic needs are physiological and safety needs, while the higher ones are those of belongingness, esteem, and self-actualization. It is noted that gratification of the basic needs primarily depends on material conditions.

In view of Maslow's postulate that the basic needs, if they are not met, dominate the individual's behavior, we would expect that people in poor material conditions are more concerned with the meeting of the basic rather than the higher needs. On the contrary, since people in better material conditions have no difficulty in meeting their basic needs, they come to be concerned with their higher needs. The needs that occupy Maslow's hierarchy, be they belongingness, esteem, or self-actualization, are in fact the needs for a sense of personal fulfillment. In other words, once an individual has reached a certain level of material well being, what he strives for in his life is a sense of being able to fulfill his psychosocial or non-economic needs such as being accepted by friends and relatives, being recognized as a person of worth, and living in a meaningful way.

Based on Maslow's postulate, we scanned the questionnaire to identify the following three items which are closest in meaning to the sense of personal fulfillment: (1) Do you feel somewhat lonely even among friends? (2) Would you say that nothing ever turns out for you the way you want it to? (3) Do you sometimes wonder if anything is worthwhile anymore? Responses to each item were dichotomized and then the scores on the three items were summed for each individual to form a scale of sense of personal fulfillment. It should be reported that intercorrelations among the three items were all statistically significant at the .001 level. The gamma coefficients were .61 for the relationship between the first and second item, .67 between first and third, and .68 between second and third. The scale, therefore, appears to have an acceptable degree of internal consistency.

<u>Table 3</u> shows that life satisfaction was positively associated with the sense of personal fulfillment. In other words, individuals who had greater sense of personal fulfillment were more satisfied with their lives as a whole. The relationship was found to be independent of sex, age, and education. The partial gammas for the separate control on sex, age, and education were also about the same as the zero-order gamma (.24). Besides material conditions, therefore, non-material considerations such as the sense of personal fulfillment were also an important source of life satisfaction. It should be noted that similar findings were found in previous studies (cf., Fellows, 1965; Phillips, 1967; and Breiser, 1974).

Table 3: Life Satisfaction by Sense of Personal Fulfillment

Satisfaction	Fulfillment			
	0 (Low)	1	2	3 (High)
Low	36.5 %	24.9 %	14.6 %	9.0 %
Medium	17.6 %	27.8 %	23.2 %	23.4 %
High	45.9 %	47.3 %	62.3 %	67.6 %
(N)	(74)	(334)	(824)	(2540)

Gamma = .24; p<.001;

Table 4: The Relationship Between Sense of Personal Fulfillment and Life Satisfaction among Various Material Well Being Subgroups

Material Well Being	Gamma	Significance level	N
IV (Low)	.19	.001	1147
III	.16	.01	1327
II	.34	.05	636
I (High)	.52	.001	503

Let us now examine whether or not the sense of personal fulfillment would have differential effects on life satisfaction among individuals in different levels of material conditions. Table 4 shows that in every level of material well being, the relationship between material well being and the sense of personal fulfillment remained positive and statistically significant. It was, however, observed that in general the higher the level of material well being, the greater was the gamma coefficient of their relationship. These findings lend support to the hypothesis derived from Maslow's postulate. In other words, the sense of personal fulfillment was more conducive to satisfaction with life among individuals in better rather than poorer material conditions.

V. Conclusions

In this paper, we analysed and elaborated the relationship between life satisfaction and material well being on the basis of the data collected from a probability sample of 3,983 urban residents in Hong Kong. It was found that most respondents (nearly two-thirds) were satisfied with life as a whole. Only a small portion (approx. one-tenth) reported dissatisfaction.

The degree of life satisfaction was found to be positively associated with the level of material well being. The relationship was independent of sex, age, and educational status. It was suggested that material well being permits an individual to meet his personal needs and therefore leads to satisfaction with life.

To elaborate on the relationship between satisfaction and material conditions, we took into account non-material conditions. In view of Maslow's postulate on the hierarchy of human needs, we proposed that non-material conditions would produce differential effects on the life satisfaction of individuals with different levels of material well being. We maintained that the so called higher needs in Maslow's hierarchy were largely the search for personal fulfillment. It was found that the sense of personal fulfillment was positively associated with life satisfaction, and that the relationship was independent of sex, age, and education. More important was the finding that the effect of the sense of personal fulfillment on life satisfaction was stronger among individuals in better material conditions.

The proposition about the positive relationship between life satisfaction and material well being has been repeatedly confirmed by empirical studies in various countries. The present study confirmed the proposition in the context of Hong Kong, and hence contributes an additional item of evidence to the cross-cultural validity of the proposition.

A more important implication of the present study relates to the interaction effects of material and non-material conditions. Using three empirical items as indicators of non-material conditions, this study shows that non-material conditions tend to have a stronger impact on the life satisfaction of individuals with a higher level of material well being. These findings lend support to Maslow's theory on the hierarchy of human needs.

The present study also has a practical implication. The findings suggest that if we wish to make the relatively poor people happier, efforts should be directed to improving their material conditions, such as better housing and more adequate facilities inside and outside the household. Their personal happiness is mainly dependent upon the extent to which their basic physiological and safety needs are satisfied. For those individuals in better material conditions, however, emphasis should be placed on improving their sense of personal fulfillment such as relationships with friends and relatives, and participation in community affairs as well as the pursuit of meaningful life goals. As they have managed to meet their basic needs, they come to be concerned with higher needs, such as the needs for affection, acceptance, and self-actualization.

Before ending, some notes of caution are needed. First, the conclusions in this paper were based on the analysis of individual, rather than aggregate, data. What is true for the individuals may not be true for the aggregates. Second, this study dealt with the "global" life satisfaction rather than the satisfaction with specific domains of life. Although the global assessment is of interest in itself, further studies are needed to analyse the impact of material and/or non-material conditions upon the satisfaction with different aspects of life in Hong Kong (see, for instance, Breiser, 1974; Levy and Guttman, 1975; Rogers and Converse, 1975; and Schneider, 1975). Third, this paper has adopted the social causation approach, which assumes that better material or non-material conditions cause a greater satisfaction with life. As suggested by Easterlin (1973), the converse may be true, i.e., the more satisfied individuals are more productive and dynamic and are thus likely to achieve a higher level of material or non-material well being. In view of our theoretical rationale concerning human needs, it makes sense to assume the direction of relation from material or non-material conditions to satisfaction. Quite probably, however, there is a circular causation. The causal priority between these two sets of variables apparently constitutes meaningful areas for further research (Pelz and Andrews, 1964, Lee, 1976).

References:

Bradburn, N. (1969), The Structure of Psychological Well-Being, Chicago: Aldine.

Bradburn, N. and D. Caplovitz (1965), Reports on Happiness, Chicago: Aldine.

Breiser, M. (1974), "Components and Correlates of Material Well-Being", Journal of Health and Social Behavior, Vol. 15:320-327.

Cantril, H. (1965), The Pattern of Human Concerns, New Brunswick, N.J.: Rutgers University Press.

Chan, Y.K., and R. Lau (1974), "Biosocial Survey: Report on Sampling". Social Research Centre, The Chinese University of Hong Kong, Hong Kong.

Clemente, F. and W.J. Sauer (1976), "Life Satisfaction in the United States", Social Forces, Vol. 54: 621-631.

Davis, J.A. (1971), Elementary Survey Analysis, New Jersey: Prentice-Hall.

Davis, K. (1940), "The Sociology of Parent-child Conflict", American Sociological Review, Vol. 5: 523-535.

Duncan, O.D. (1975), "Does Money Buy Satisfaction?" Social Indicators Research, Vol. 2: 267-274.

Easterlin, R.A. (1973), "Does Money Buy Happiness?", The Public Interest, Vol. 30: 3-10.

Easterlin, R.A. (1974), "Does Economic Growth Improve Human Lot? Some Evidence," in: Paul A. David and Melvin W. Reder (ed.), Nations and Households in Economic Growth, Stanford University Press.

Endacott, G.B. and A. Hinton (1968), Fragrant Harbour: A Short History of Hong Kong, London: Oxford University Press.

Fellows, E. (1965), "A Study of Factors Related to Happiness," Journal of Educational Research, Vol. 50: 231-234.

Gurin, G., J. Veroff, and S. Feld (1960), Americans View Their Mental Health, New York: Basic Books.

Hopkins, K. (ed.), (1971), Hong Kong: The Industrial Colony, London: Oxford University Press.

Inkeles, A. (1960), "Industrial Man: The Relation of Status to Experience, Perception, and Value," American Journal of Sociology, Vol.66: 1-31.

Lee, R.P.L. (1976), "The Causal Priority Betwen Socioeconomic Status and Psychiatric Disorder: A Prospective Study", The International Journal of Social Psychiatry, Vol. 22: 1-8.

Levy, S. and L. Guttman (1975), "On the Multivariate Structure of Wellbeing," Social Indicators Research, Vol. 2: 361-388.

Maslow, A.H. (1954), Motivation and Personality, New York: Harper and Row.

McCall, S. (1975), "Quality of Life", Social Indicators Research, Vol. 2: 229-248.

Mitchell, R.E. (1969), Levels of Emotional Strain in Southeast Asian Cities, Vol. 1 and 2. A Project of the Urban Family Life Survey, The Chinese University of Hong Kong, Hong Kong.

Pelz, D.C. and Andrews, F.M. (1964), "Detecting Causal Priorities in Panel Study Data", American Sociological Review, Vol. 39: 836-854.

Phillips, D.L. (1967), "Social Participation and Happiness", American Journal of Sociology, Vol. 72: 479-488.

Robinson, W.S. (1950), "Ecological Correlation and the Behavior of Individuals," American Sociological Review, Vol. 15: 351-357.

Rogers, W.L. and P.E. Converse (1975), "Measures of the Perceived Overall Quality of Life," Social Indicators Research, Vol 2: 127-152.

Schneider, M. (1975), "The Quality of Life in Large American Cities: Objective and Subjective Social Indicators," Social Indicators Research, Vol. 1: 495-509.

Wessman, A.E.A. (1956), A Psychological Inquiry into Satisfaction and Happiness, Unpublished doctoral dissertation, Princeton University.

Wilson, W. (1967), "Correlates of Avowed Happiness", Psychological Bulletin, Vol. 67: 297-306.

FAMILY STRUCTURE AND PROCESSES IN HONG KONG

Fai-ming Wong

I. Introduction

The family system in Hong Kong has undergone a process of change and stabilization over the past twenty years. It developed a structure of its own and operated through a set of functional processes in order to maintain itself as well as to contribute toward the functioning of other social systems and the society as a whole. It is therefore of great significance to study its structure and processes and to analyse them along certain lines of questioning.

Conceptually, the family is to be viewed as a social system and analysed in terms of its structure and functional processes. With regard to its structure, it will be examined in its location and regional origin, family type, family size and composition, rules of lineality, and the pattern of marriage. Its internal functional processes will be analysed in terms of its power and decision-making, role differentiation and performance, and other family interactions. Lastly, its relations with external systems will be analysed, covering such areas as educational attainment and mobility, economic involvement and occupational mobility, and social and religious participation.

The data for the present study are drawn mainly from two recent empirical studies. The first is a general survey of the family life of the people in Kwun Tong (Ng, 1975). It was conducted on a net representative sample of 818 households which were randomly selected from a total of some 100,000 households living in five types of housing in this district of Hong Kong. Its data were collected through the form of a structured interview, and both the household heads and their spouses as well as two of their eldest children were interviewed. The second study is a more specific research project which focuses on the patterns of the differentiation of marital power and household tasks inside the family (Wong, 1972).

It was done on a representative sample of 637 Chinese families which were randomly drawn from a total population of about 450,000 in the Kwun Tong district. It also made use of a structured interview, but only the wives of the family heads were interviewed.

II. Family Structure and Composition

The families under study live in the industrial town of Kwun Tong which is located on the southern region of East Kowloon and has at present a population of about half a million spread over an area of about five square miles. Fifty-eight percent of these families resided in the Government resettlement blocks, one-third of them in low-cost housing estates, eight percent in private housing and a very small fraction in squatter huts. These dwellings were distributed over various parts of the Great Kwun Tong District, and many of the housing units provided only minimum living facilities sufficient for a small household at a relatively low rent. The families originally lived in various districts throughout the Colony, and they moved into this district mainly because they were assigned to these housing units as part of the Government resettlement plan, with some seeking better living conditions, and the rest cheaper rent or proximity to their working place. Most of these families relocated during the past ten years, and they were in general satisfied with the living environment of the district.

The majority of the heads of these families immigrated from the China mainland and came to the Colony immediately after the Second World War or after the revolution in China in 1949. Their age distribution ranged primarily from 30 to 59 years old, with the median age of the husbands being 44 and that of the wives 39. The regional origin of about one third of these people was Canton, Macau and nearby areas; next in importance were the areas of Chiu Chau, Sze Yap, Wai Yeung and others, while only 18 percent of them were actually born in Hong Kong. Being born and brought up in their native towns and villages in China, they were endowed with different tratitions, customs and dialects, and they brought along these regional differences to their newly settled place. As a result, like Hong

Kong as a whole, Kwun Tong became a town composed of people with multi-regional origins, dialects, and styles of living.

The structure and composition of these families varies greatly, and in order to study them properly, it is necessary to classify them in accordance with certain criteria. The type of family structure here therefore is defined in terms of the number of generations existing in a family, and the nature of relationships among its family members. Accordingly, the following family typology has been formed:

(1) Nuclear: consists of one married couple with or without unmarried children, and with or without unmarried relatives.

(2) Stem: consists of one married couple with unmarried children and the parents of the husband, and with or without unmarried relatives.

(3) Joint: consists of one married couple with or without unmarried children, and with at least one married brother/sister of the husband and his/her family.

(4) Stem-joint: consists of one married couple with unmarried children and the parents of the husband, and with at least one married brother/sister of the husband and his/her family.

(5) Other extended: consists of a miscellaneous group of relatives who are related to one another either consanguineously or by marriage.

Table 1 shows that, among the general types of families, the nuclear family was the most prevalent one, comprising 73.2 % of all the families under study. The next most common type was the stem family, with 25.2 % of the total number of families. Taking these two types of families together, they accounted for 98.4 % or almost all of the families, whereas only a very small fraction of them spread among the joint, stem-joint and other extended types. Of the nuclear variants, the most popular unit was the family which consisted of the husband and wife and their unmarried children. Next was the family of a couple with their unmarried children and one or more relatives on the husband's side. Close to this unit was the single couple which would only in some time become a typical nuclear family, after having given birth to their children. The

Table 1: Distribution of the Families by Family Type

Family Type	Number		Percent	
Nuclear		599		73.2
Single couple	13		1.6	
Couple with husband's relatives	4		0.5	
Couple with wife's relatives	1		0.1	
Couple with unmarried children	550		67.2	
Couple with unmarried children and husband's relatives	24		2.9	
Couple with unmarried children and wife's relatives	7		0.9	
Stem		206		25.2
Couple with unmarried children and husband's father/mother	137		16.7	
Couple with unmarried children and husband's parents	39		4.8	
Couple with unmarried children and wife's father/mother	24		2.9	
Couple with unmarried children and wife's parents	6		0.1	
Joint		1		0.1
Couple with unmarried children and husband's brother's family	1		0.1	
Stem-Joint		8		1.0
Couple with unmarried children, husband's parents and his brother's/sister's family	8		1.0	
Other Extended		4		0.5
Total		818		100.0

unpopular nuclear units were those which were composed of a couple with their unmarried children and the wife's relatives, or a single couple with either the husband's relatives or the wife's kinsmen.

Among the stem types of family, the most common ones were the families which consisted of the spouses, their unmarried children, and one or both of the parents of the husband. The less common stem units were families which included a married couple with their unmarried children and one or both of the parents of the wife. In regard to the large extended types, the stem-joint unit was more numerous than either the joint or the other extended ones. All in all, the distribution pattern of family types among the families of the Kwun Tong sample was very similar to that of the families in the Colony as a whole, with only a slightly greater preference for the stem type than for the other extended ones (Cf. Wong, 1975:992).

The size of the families under study ranged widely, from two to sixteen persons (with one exceptional case of a family of twenty-one persons). The model family size tended to cluster on those families with five to eight persons, and the overall average family size was 6.57 persons, as compared to 6.45 persons of an earlier Kwun Tong study (Wong, 1972:7). As family type is defined in terms of its lineal and lateral extensions, the size of a family is expected to correlate with its type. So, as it was found, the nuclear families generally had a smaller number of members than the extended ones. The typical nuclear family accommodated about five-and-a-half persons under its roof (husband, wife and three to four children), whereas the stem unit usually had a little over seven members (including the married couple, three to four children, and one or both of the husband's parents). The large extended families often consisted of more than nine persons, and varied rather widely in their forms of composition. (Occasionally one or more relatives, often on the husband's side, were accommodated in these families either temporarily or on a more permanent basis.)

The rules of lineality and locality as practised in these families also varied with the types of families. On the whole, these rules had been slackened and deemphasized with the increasing trend toward the nuclear family structure, and were therefore modified in both their nature and form when adopted by the studied families.

Thus, the prevalent nuclear families tended to practise the patterns of bilineality and neolocality. This means that, by the former pattern, descent and inheritance were passed on to both sons and daughters even though sons were often more favored and might receive a larger share of it. Likewise, both the father's and the mother's relatives were accepted equally as kin, but relations with paternal kinsmen were usually stronger and more extensive. By the latter pattern, the newlyweds were expected to set up their own independent family, but they might, and often did, stay with the husband's parents for some time before doing so. In fact, when they married, almost half of these couples set up their own home, slightly over one-third of them lived with the husband's parents for a while or permanently, and the remaining portion stayed either with the wife's parents or with other relatives.

In contrast, the large extended families were more likely to adopt the rules of patrilineality and patrilocality. Both descent and inheritance were determined by the father's line and interaction with paternal kin was much honored and closely maintained. The married couple was also expected to join and function as part of the husband's parents' household. This practice applied, however, only to a very small number of the families and therefore signified a greatly diminishing tendency. With the substantially practised stem families, the patterns of lineality and locality were basically mixed. They were mainly patrilineal and patrilocal. The father's line was usually emphasized in considering matters concerning descent and inheritance, but the status and rights of daughters were respected and relations with a limited number of maternal relatives were also maintained. Regarding their residence pattern, instead of joining their parents' families, most of these men invited their parents, or, increasingly, the parents of their wife, to stay with them, or they alternated among the siblings in accommodating the parents and giving them money when not staying with them.

The marriage pattern as adopted by these couples was monogamous, as is required by law. In Hong Kong, the practice of plural wives or concubinage has not only lost its legal status but its normative support as well. It was basically homogamous in terms of the matched socio-economic characteristics of the marital partners, even though the husband was preferred to have a slightly higher social status. This means that the women often wished to and did marry up the social ladder, with their husbands being a bit older in age, better educated, higher in occupational position, and with a larger income, whereas the men were expected to marry either only their social equals or down the status scale a little but not too far. Thus, the age of the husbands at marriage was somewhat older, ranging from 23 to 30 years, with an average age of 27, and that of the wives was between 18 and 24 years, with an average age of 22. Furthermore, these marital couples were very similar in their regional origin and religious belief. Homogamy in terms of their place of birth was overwhelmingly practised by those couples coming from Hong Kong, Canton and Chiu Chau, and only a little less so among the groupings of Sze Yap, Wai Yeung and other districts. Likewise, both of the spouses either identified themselves as having no religion, or claimed to share the same belief, mostly in traditional deities, Buddhism and Catholicism, and slightly less so in Protestantism.

III. Internal Processes of the Family

Having analysed their structure and composition, it is time to examine the functional aspects of the families under study. The functions of these families may be viewed in two ways: as processes which take place inside the family and help it to operate and maintain as a social system of interacting individuals, and, as a series of functional interchanges which occur between the family and other social systems. In this section we will concentrate on the internal processes of the family.

A. Power and Decision-Making Process

The family fulfills a wide variety of household activities or tasks which must be carried out in order to maintain it as a viable, operating unit. To do so, it involves the power to make decisions as to what tasks should be done and when and how they should be done. Power is here defined as the potential ability of one member of the family to influence the behavior of other members. It is acquired in the process of negotiating, mainly between the spouses over family matters, and is manifested in their ability to make decisions affecting the life of the family. It may derive basically from either cultural prescription or individual competence or both (Blood and Wolfe, 1960: 12-15), but in fact these two sources of power often work together or complement each other in deciding on the balance of power between the marital partners. In other words, a patriarchal system may favor the husband in the distribution of marital power, but it still depends on his ability to manipulate and actualize such power in the decision-making process. Both of these perspectives are, therefore, important and helpful in analysing the division of power between the spouses.

As defined, family power is reflected in decision-making regarding household tasks. In order to measure the balance of power between husbands and wives in the families studied, the range of household tasks was classified into four areas: economic activities, social activities, child care and control and household duties; and each of these task areas was in turn composed of several specific tasks.

Thus, the area of economic activities was defined to include such tasks as choosing an occupation, purchasing various household items (from more expensive ones, such as an apartment, to some less valuable ones, such as a television set, or an electric fan), and planning the family budget. The components of the social activities area consisted of various participations in religious and welfare programmes; forms of interaction among kinsmen (such as mutual visits, exchange of gifts and financial assistance); kinds of family celebration (i.e. birthday parties, social festivals and wedding feasts); and social entertainment events (i.e. dining out, going to movies and attending functional feasts). The area of child care and control included such forms of physical care as feeding, clothing and consulting the doctor; behavioral controls such as supervising school work, giving pocket money and handling general discipline; and career controls such as selecting school, making educational plans and helping to choose an occupation. The last task area was household duties which covered various routine household chores (i.e. grocery shopping, cooking, dish-washing, washing clothes, ironing, mending, and house cleaning, decorating and maintaining).

To compute the power score for the spouses, several steps were followed. First, the respondents (only the wives in this case) were questioned as to who was usually the one to make decisions concerning a particular household task and their responses were recorded on a five-point descending scale from 'husband always', 'husband more than wife', 'husband and wife equally', 'wife more than husband', to 'wife always'. Secondly, each point on this scale was given a numerical weight so that a precise power score could be obtained. Thirdly, a mean power score was calculated for each specific task by summing up all the points on its scale and dividing them up by the number of respondents. Finally, an overall mean power score was acquired for each task area by adding up all the power scores for its constituent tasks and dividing them by the number of tasks.

As a result, the distribution of the husband's mean power scores for the various household tasks and task areas were obtained and tabulated.

Table 2 shows that, on the one hand, in terms of the overall mean power over the various task areas, it was basically an equalitarian pattern being practised by the spouses in the areas of economic activities (Husband's Mean Power = 3.17) and social activities (HMP = 2.85). With regard to the other areas of child care and control (HMP = 2.25) and household duties (HMP = 1.70), a wife-dominant pattern was found among these families.

On the other hand, in terms of the mean power on specific tasks within each task area, the husbands were much more likely than their spouses to make decisions regarding occupational activities, slightly more so regarding the purchase of household items, but much less so in the budgeting of family expenditures, within the area of economic activities.

In the social activities area, the husbands were more likely to initiate decisions about taking the family out for dinner, participating in social welfare programmes, going to a movie or attending a functional feast; less so in participating in the celebration of weddings and birthdays, giving financial assistance and gifts, and visits with relatives; and much less so in taking part in church and social festival activities.

Concerning the area of child care and control, the wives played a much more active role. As compared with their husbands, they were

Table 2: Distribution of Husband's Mean Power on Household Tasks

Household Tasks	Husband's Mean Power	
Economic Activities		3.17
Occupational activities	4.20	
Purchase of electric fan	3.13	
Purchase of apartment	3.10	
Purchase of television set	3.08	
Family budgeting	2.32	
Social Activities		2.85
Dining out	3.29	
Participation in welfare programmes	3.26	
Going to movie	3.18	
Attending feast	3.15	
Celebration of wedding	2.93	
Giving financial assistance	2.82	
Gift-giving	2.66	
Celebration of birthday	2.66	
Visiting relatives	2.65	
Participation in church activities	2.48	
Celebration of social festivals	2.27	
Child Care and Control		2.25
Making educational plan	2.76	
Choosing occupation	2.68	
Selecting school	2.47	
Handling discipline	2.36	
Supervising homework	2.28	
Giving pocket money	2.09	
Consulting doctor	1,90	
Clothing	1.86	
Feeding	1.82	
Household Duties		1.70
House maintaining	2.63	
House decorating	2.06	
House cleaning	1.66	
Shopping	1.56	
Cooking	1.50	
Dish-washing	1.50	
Ironing	1.48	
Washing	1.47	
Mending clothes	1.46	

much more likely to decide about what their children should eat and wear and when they should see a doctor; and slightly more so in those matters regarding pocket money, supervising their homework and handling their discipline; but they tended to consult their husbands in making educational plans and selecting schools and occupations, for their children.

Finally, the wives enjoyed much autonomy in the area of household duties. Except for the tasks of maintaining and decorating the household which required the assistance of their husbands, they made almost all the decisions regarding the other household duties.

B. Task Performance and Role Differentiation

In order to maintain the viability of a family, decisions about household tasks must not only be made but actually carried out. This section is concerned with the routine daily tasks which have to be performed in every family in order to keep the home going. Two key questions are: (1) how do husband and wife divide the house work, and (2) what kinds of roles do they assume in the family? The question of relative task performance between the husband and wife was first dealt with and could be seen in the distribution of the husband's mean performance on household tasks as tabulated in Table 3.

As shown in Table 3, the husband's overall mean performance scores for the four task areas were: economic activities 3.29, social activities 2.78, child care and control 2.14, and household duties 1.71. This indicates that, in general, the husbands participated jointly and more or less equally with their wives in those household tasks concerning economic and social activities, but the latter were found to be more responsible than the former for the performance of those tasks relating to child care and control and household duties.

As to their actual participation in a specific task area such as economic activities, the husbands were almost solely engaged in their occupational activities, but tended to consult their spouses in making major household purchases, as well as in the budgeting of family expenditures.

In the area of social activities, the husbands were more likely to be the ones to take their spouses or their families out for dinner,

Table 3: Distribution of Husband's Mean Performance on Household Tasks

Household Tasks	Husband's Mean Performance	
Economic Activities		3.29
Occupational activities	4.10	
Purchase of electric fan	3.26	
Purchase of television set	3.24	
Purchase of apartment	3.17	
Family budgeting	2.66	
Social Activities		2.78
Dining out	3.22	
Going to movie	3.19	
Participation in welfare programmes	3.19	
Attending feast	3.14	
Celebration of wedding	2.87	
Giving financial assistance	2.76	
Visiting relatives	2.61	
Gift-giving	2.59	
Participation in church activities	2.55	
Celebration of birthday	2.40	
Celebration of social festivals	2.05	
Child Care and Control		2.14
Making educational plan	2.67	
Choosing occupation	2.64	
Handling discipline	2.31	
Selecting school	2.28	
Supervising homework	2.24	
Giving pocket money	2.00	
Consulting doctor	1.75	
Clothing	1.73	
Feeding	1.68	
Household Duties		1.71
House maintaining	2.84	
House decorating	2.12	
House cleaning	1.69	
Shopping	1.51	
Cooking	1.48	
Dish-washing	1.47	
Ironing	1.43	
Washing	1.43	
Mending clothes	1.43	

go to a movie, attend a functional feast, or engage in welfare programmes, whereas the wives were more involved in kinship activities, and especially so in attending church functions and preparing for the celebration of birthdays and social festivals.

With respect to the area of child care and control, the wives played a much more active role and were more likely to be responsible for such matters as feeding, clothing, consulting the doctor, giving pocket money, supervising homework, selecting school and handling discipline, even though they would ask for the advice of their husbands in carrying out long-term matters such as making educational plans and advising on the choice of occupation for their children.

Finally, the performance of household duties was primarily in the hands of the wives. While they tended to request the help of their husbands in maintaining and decorating the house, they did almost all the household work themselves.

The second question, of role differentiation between the marital partners, was examined in terms of both the patterns of the division of power and that of labor. A spousal role can be defined as a pattern of behavior which is structured around specific rights and duties and associated with one's particular status within the family. This pattern of behavior consists of both the dimensions of the decision-making about and the performance of household tasks, which taken together, may reflect the nature of a specific role. Furthermore, the substance of this behavior pattern provides the content of this role which may then be classified and interpreted.

In comparing Table 2 with Table 3, it was found that the two distributions of the husband's mean power, on the one hand, and mean performance, on the other hand, were very much similar to each other in terms of the rank order of these various tasks and their respective scores. This means, as far as participation in household tasks is concerned, that the making of decisions about them was mostly consistent with their performance. In other words, the same person who made decisions about a specific task also carried them out.

This can be explained by the fact that the family is usually a small arena with only two major partners and the tasks they are to undertake are mostly routine, so that there is no need for a clear differentiation of their decision-making and performance. This had a significant effect upon the role-playing of the marital partners, so much so that they were able to avoid role conflicts existing between the making of decisions and their actualization.

C. Other Patterns of Family Interaction

In addition to those patterns of decision-making which are concerned with the family as a whole, there are other patterns of interaction among family members on an individual basis. These interactions were analysed along two major dimensions: husband-wife and parent-child. These dimensions were in fact fundamental, as most of the families under study were found to be nuclear in structure and consisting of two generations only.

Husband-wife: The relationship between the husbands and wives was basically determined by their relative participation in the making of decisions about and the performance of the household tasks. As already shown, the husband is no longer the irrefutable master of his family, being dominant in all family relations and making all major decisions about family life. Instead, he now tends to consult his wife concerning major family matters and they reach joint decisions about them. With respect to their participation in household tasks, they begin to practise a collaborative pattern. While they usually shared with each other in the undertaking of family affairs, the husband was mainly concerned with the economic and social tasks of the family, whereas the wife was predominantly engaged in household duties, child care and control, and social activities (Cf. Wong, 1972: 17-18). On the basis of this finding it can be said that the husband-wife relationship is moving toward a companionship pattern (Burgess, et al., 1963:3-5).

They were found to have increased their communication in both frequency and depth. A large number of these couples said they had developed personal hobbies in common and enjoyed these hobbies, either together or individually, such as, in preferential order, going to films and Chinese opera, playing mah-jong, visiting the teahouse, watching television, shopping, listening to music, and others.

The marital partners also shared with each other some common family values and the emphasis on family planning in general. Hence, they were both in favor of such values as small family size, fewer children, little sex preference of children, obedience of children toward parents, neolocal residence, independence of children after marriage, and children's responsibility for the support of aged parents. They concurred in emphasizing the importance of general family planning such as budgeting their family expenses, planning their children, and designing their life style in general. When marital disagreements occurred, usually concerning the discipline of children or family expenditures, they tended to discuss openly about the problems in question and try to solve them peacefully and rationally, rather than resort to outright conflict or quarrels.

Parent-child: The parent-child relationship is basically related to the structure of the family as well as the value and meaning in having children. On the one hand, as it was found, the overwhelming majority of the studied families were adopting the nuclear type of family. As such, they became structurally isolated from external social systems, and tended to evolve into an independent, closely knitted system of their own. Their members were interdependent among one another not only for economic support and protection, but also for emotional sustenance. Hence in most cases, the relations between the parents and their children were strong, capable of being transformed into a pure or mixed pattern of love, trust and suspicion, as they interacted and imposed upon one another constantly with their role expectations and personal needs. Furthermore, the gap of understanding between them seemed to have widened as they were found to differ more and more in their family values, general outlooks and personal styles of living. For example, as compared with their children, the parents were much more likely to endorse the traditional family values, accept a conservative outlook, and follow a practical and comfort-oriented style of living.

On the other hand, the value and meaning in having children as perceived by the parents had a significant bearing on their relations with the children. Despite their endorsement of the traditional value of having children, over 84 % of the parents considered child-raising a very laborious job. They identified the major disadvantages of having children as causing emotional burdens on the parents, increased financial expenses in running the family, and disturbing inconveniences to family members. However, they also believed children brought along such major advantages as adding fun to the family, being sources of emotional satisfaction, providing for security against old age, and perpetuating the family line. In addition, some parents confessed having children improved their marital relations as well as those between themselves and their kinsmen.

In raising their children, the parents were most concerned about their studies, as a result of the cultural value on education and the highly competitive nature of the local education system. Next, they were most concerned about their childrens' conduct, making sure they would not be led astray, then about their physical safety, and lastly about their career prospects. Regarding the education of their children, the parents showed some slight sexual preference in favor of the boys. Almost two-thirds of them expected their sons to complete a university or secondary education, and a small fraction even ventured to think of sending their children abroad for further studies. Girls were primarily expected to finish secondary school, perhaps even the university, and then further studies abroad. However, these parents stated that, in spite of their ideal goals for their children's education, three-fourths of them found themselves unable to provide sufficient financial support for the realization of such goals; only a small portion claimed to be able to do so. Thus, in allocating their limited financial resources, they attempted to provide for the education of their children, but they were somewhat more willing to support their sons than their daughters.

About three-fourths of the parents interviewed, considered it a filial duty of the children to support them and expected them to do so even when they were employed themselves and had regular income, or even when the latter were married and had their own families to maintain. Others were quite lenient in this regard and said it would depend on the actual situation. Both boys and girls were expected to help the family financially as early as possible. They were expected to first complete their secondary or university education which was regarded as the basic qualification for entering the labor market, and contribute toward the family budget from then on.

The relations between parents and children were shown in three ways: children's assistance in household work, their communication with the parents, and their responsibility toward the parents. Firstly, the children claimed to have actively participated in all kinds of household tasks. In fact, this had become necessary if not indispensable for the daily functioning of the household as domestic help from outside sources, e.g. house-maids or relatives, had dwindled drastically and become very difficult or expensive to obtain in recent years. Consequently, they were expected to lend a hand in whatever tasks they were able and ready to do.

Secondly, both the parents and their children reported to have shared with one another a wide variety of family and other matters. They either communicated mutually on various subjects for the exchange of information and the fun of interaction, or consulted one another for opinions and suggestions as to what and how major forms of family action should be carried out. In fact, most of the children said to have made use of such chance and given their opinions prior to major family decisions. Also most of these opinions were taken into consideration before such decisions were enforced.

Lastly, the parents' expectation of their children's responsibility, i.e. financial support of the parents in old age, tended to come true in both the views and conduct of their children. An overwhelming majority of the children, especially the first child, deemed it their duty to give money to their parents when they were gainfully employed. This was considered so even when they were married and had to support their own families or even if they happened to live away from their parents. In actual practice, of those who had started working, almost all claimed to have given money to their parents in one form or another. Most of them did it regularly once every month, whereas others did so only during social festivals, on their parents' birthdays, when they needed money, or at any time irregularly. The amount of money they contributed ranged widely but clustered mainly around $ 100 to $ 400 (the latter amounting to about one-third of total monthly income). This money indeed contributed significantly toward the physical subsistence of most of the parents as in Hong Kong there are still far insufficient welfare provisions for the aged.

IV. Family Relations with External Systems

As a system the family not only operates through its internal processes, but also maintains a set of relations with external social systems. The relations of the family with external systems will be analysed with regard to educational attainment and mobility, occupational engagement and mobility, and social and religious participation.

A. Educational Attainment and Mobility

In Hong Kong there is increasingly a trend toward universal education for the local population. Most of the people under study had gone to school and had received modern formalized education rather than the traditional, private-tutorial one. On the whole, they had attained a relatively low level of education, mainly the primary level, and only a small proportion of them had been able to complete the secondary school. The men were usually better educated than their spouses; over 50 % of them were able to complete some form of primary education, 22 % went to the secondary school, 4 % attended the post-secondary school or above, and 15 % received no schooling at all, as compared to 47 %, 11 %, 2 % and 40 % of the women, respectively.

With respect to educational mobility, the level of these men's education can be compared to that of their fathers' education, and the distribution of the levels of education for both the generations is given in Table 4.

Table 4 shows that, first of all, there was a very strong correlation between the level of education of the family heads and that of their fathers. This was found especially in the categories of no schooling and primary school, which indicated over two-thirds of the family heads had completed the same level of education as that of their fathers, having either been deprived of the opportunity to go to school or gone as far as only the primary school. Secondly, looking at the columns of Total Cases, it is shown that, even though both the generations had had for the most part only a relatively low

Table 4: Comparison of Intergenerational Levels of Education

Family Head's Level of Education	Father's Level of Education				
	No Schooling	Primary School	Secondary School	Post-Secondary School	Total Cases
No Schooling	69.9 %	28.9 %	1.2 %	0.0 %	83 (16.3 %)
Primary School	23.6 %	70.8 %	4.2 %	1.4 %	288 (56.7 %)
Secondary School	14.4 %	66.7 %	11.7 %	7.2 %	111 (21.9 %)
Post-secondary School	7.7 %	46.2 %	19.2 %	26.9 %	26 (5.1 %)
Total Cases	144 (28.3 %)	314 (61.8 %)	31 (6.1 %)	19 (3.7 %)	508 (100.0 %)

$X^2 = 150.47$; $p < .001$.

level of education, the heads of these families were generally better educated than their fathers. In other words, they had obviously enjoyed some upward mobility in education. Lastly, upward educational mobility occurred in favor of the family heads as well as their fathers, even though the latter had less such mobility than the former.

B. Occupational Engagement and Mobility

As to the occupational engagement of the families under study, while the men, as a rule, were employed in some gainful activities, the women had also participated in various forms of economic enterprise, with about 41 % of them being fully or partially employed. Work in manufacturing and service industries was most common and less so in transport and communication, commerce and construction. The couples were more likely to be employed in blue-collar or clerical posts than in highly technical and administrative positions. Being the major bread-winner of the family, the husband usually worked full-time, with a better job, and away from home, whereas a substantial number of the wives were engaged only in part-time work, with a lower job, and more at home. Consequently, the husband was able to earn a much larger income, ranging from $ 500 to $ 1,250 per month and with a monthly average of $ 870, as compared to a range of $ 200 to $ 750 and a monthly average of $ 372, earned by the wives.

With increasing participation of the wife and grown-up children in economic activities, the families were often able to increase the sources of their family income. While the husband's income still constituted the major income of the family, the wages of the wife and the other family members contributed substantially to the family coffer. Consequently, total family income was increased by one-third over the husband's salary and ranged from $ 500 to $ 1,750 per month, amounting to an average monthly total of $ 1,192. This enlarged income, in turn, made it possible for them to improve their living conditions and to enjoy a relatively decent standard of living. Most of the families were equipped with modern home appliances, including electric fan, radio, television, refrigerator and sewing machine, one-third of them with camera and washing machine, and a small portion even with such items as private car and air-conditioner.

In order to measure the intergenerational occupational mobility, an analytical scheme was followed. First, occupations were classified into three types in terms of the nature of the work, such as administrative or clerical, production, and service work. Secondly, each type of occupation was differentiated into four levels of position, on the basis of several factors including the amount of training, degree of autonomy, social prestige, and size of income involved. Hence, for the administrative or clerical type of occupation, there are the positions of directors and managers, supervisory staff, clerks, and office boys; for the occupation in production work, the positions are engineers and systems analysts, technicians and skilled workers, semi-skilled workers, and unskilled workers; for service occupations, the positions include higher professionals such as physicians and lawyers, lower professionals such as school teachers and nurses, semi-skilled service workers, and unskilled service workers. Lastly, the three types of occupations were combined into a single category of occupational position and their respective levels of positions were incorporated into a four-point vertical scale with positions ranging from upper, upper-middle, lower-middle, to lower level. The actual distribution of the intergenerational occupational positions of the studied sample is given in Table 5.

Table 5: Comparison of Intergenerational Occupational Positions

Family Head's Occupational Position	Father's Occupational Position				
	Upper	Upper-Middle	Lower-Middle	Lower	Total Cases
Upper	19.0 %	52.4 %	19.0 %	9.5 %	21 (3.5 %)
Upper-Middle	4.0 %	26.4 %	52.0 %	17.6 %	125 (21.0 %)
Lower-Middle	5.2 %	28.0 %	51.1 %	15.7 %	325 (54.6 %)
Lower	0.0 %	17.7 %	61.3 %	21.0 %	124 (20.8 %)
Total Cases	26 (4.4 %)	157 (26.4 %)	311 (52.3 %)	101 (17.0 %)	595 (100.0 %)

$X^2 = 34.22$; $p < .001$.

As shown in Table 5, there was a strong correlation of the occupational positions of the family heads with those of their fathers. This means that, by and large, one's occupational position was very likely to follow that of one's father. This was especially true in the category of lower-middle positions where slightly over half of the family heads occupied similar occupational positions as their parents, whereas between one-fourth and one-fifth of them did so among the upper, upper-middle and lower categories. Furthermore, looking at the columns of Total Cases, it is shown that around three-fourths of both the family heads and their fathers had occupied merely lower-middle and lower occupational positions, with only about one-fourth of them being able to enjoy upper-middle and upper positions. There were also slightly larger proportions of the fathers having upper-middle and upper positions, as compared with their sons, which might be explained as an effect of the more advanced position of the former in their occupational careers. Lastly, as demonstrated in the specific figures of Table 5, there was found a slightly upward occupational mobility in favor of the heads of these families. In the upper and upper-middle categories of the family head's occupational position, 81 % and 70 % of the fathers, respectively, had lower positions than their sons, whereas only 79 % and 33 % of the former in the lower and lower-middle categories, respectively, occupied higher positions than the latter.

C. Social and Religious Participation

Hong Kong's residents as a whole have often been criticized for lack of social consciousness and participation. They are said to be selfish and self-centered, looking often for their own affairs and not caring about others' business. Consequently, they tend to isolate themselves and lead their own lives, and seldom participate in community activities. However, as reflected by the present data, the Kwun Tong residents demonstrated a moderate and reasonable amount of social awareness and participation. While most of them knew exactly where the community playgrounds, post offices and the City Hall were, and had often visited these places, they were not able to locate the City District Office, Kaifong (Neighborhood) Associations and other community services, and therefore did not fully utilize these facilities and services. Many of them had contributed to the welfare fund-raising campaigns, such as various Flag's Days and the Community Chest, and had actively participated in their community action programmes like the Clean-Hong-Kong-Campaign.

Most of the residents believed in the freedom of speech as a right of every citizen, even though they had some doubt in the effectiveness of the opinions of individuals. As a result, they were prepared and ready to take up social issues with the authorities concerned, either by forming sit-in petitions or by making direct individual complaints. For example, they had voiced a strong disapproval of the legalization of off-course betting and made complaints by telephone or writing to the Department concerned regarding the unattended rubbish piled up in their neighborhood. In general, they were supportive of the Government and would like their children to work in its various departments. However, if the Government enforced certain public policies which had adverse effects upon them, they would complain first to the Government, next to the local City

District Office, and then to their 'Kaifong' Associations and the Press for help; even though a substantial proportion of them would not react. Many of them would even think of putting up group sit-in petitions at the Governor's House, a method which was believed to be effective for solving such issues. Lastly, most of them clearly expressed a sense of belonging to Hong Kong, as they said they would live there even after having made a great deal of money or if they could make a choice about the place of their residence.

As far as spiritual life is concerned, over half of the heads of the families were adherents of one form of religion or another, while the rest claimed to have no religious belief at all. About 38 % of the population worshipped traditional Chinese deities like Tu Ti (Earth God), Tsao Tsun (Kitchen God), and Kwan Ti (God of Loyalty), and many of them kept miniature shrines for them at home, burned incense and prayed to them regularly. The other less practised religions include Buddhism (8.4 %), Catholicism (4.8 %), Protestantism (4.5 %), Taoism and others (0.2 %). As their major religion was of the "diffused religion" type whose "theology, rituals, and organization (are) intimately merged with the concepts and structure of secular institutions and other aspects of the social order" (Yang, 1961: 20), only a small number of them claimed to have affiliated with any church or religious association. In addition, the majority of these people still worshipped their ancestors, which might be deemed as a semi-religious practice with mixed beliefs, ranging from treating ancestors as gods and asking for their supernatural blessings to accepting them only as senior family members and paying filial respect to them. As compared with the family heads, the wives were as a rule even more religious, being particularly devoted to the traditional deities. On the other hand, the young people were much less religious than their parents, and those who had a religious faith tended to identify less with the traditional deities and more with the modern sects of Christianity.

V. The Family in A Nutshell

In conclusion, the family in Kwun Tong could be defined as a unique form of the modern Chinese family with its distinctive structure and functional processes. Regarding its structure and composition, the family is primarily a first-generation immigrant Chinese family which came to Hong Kong from the various nearby districts of the province of Kwantung, China, and moved into Kwun Tong within the past ten years. It is predominantly nuclear in structure, and composed of about six persons, typically including the husband, his wife and three to four children. It practises, for the most part, the rules of bilineality and neolocality, which means its descent and inheritance are usually passed on to both sons and daughters and the newly-wed tend to set up their own home. The marriage pattern is both monogamous and homogamous, as the practice of plural wives or concubinage has lost its legal status as well as its normative support, and the marital partners are basically similar in their socio-economic background, region of origin and religious belief.

The functional aspects of the Kwun Tong family were examined in terms of its internal processes, on the one hand, and its relations with other social systems, on the other. The internal processes of the family focused mainly on the power and decision-making of its members, their role differentiation and performance, and other forms of interaction inside the family. First, in its daily operation, family power is generated through the decision-making of the marital partners over family matters and usually manifested in the potential ability of one partner to influence the other's attitude and behavior. Thus, in general, the pattern of power differentiation practised among these couples is a relatively equalitarian one as decisions about major family matters are usually made through a process of mutual consultation and agreement between the spouses. Specifically, while the husband is more dominant in making decisions over the areas of economic and social activities of the family, the wife demonstrates her power mainly in those areas of child care and control and household duties.

Secondly, as it was found, there is a high degree of consistency between the pattern of marital task performance and that of their decision-making; this means that the same spouse who made decisions about certain household tasks also tends to carry them out. In particular, the husband is more responsible for managing the economic activities and taking his family out for social events, whereas the wife is more involved in taking care of routine household tasks and supervising her children's studies and conduct.

Lastly, the other patterns of family interaction were analysed along the dimensions husband-wife and parent-child. The relationship between the husband and the wife has been moving toward a companionship type. They claimed to hold many family values in common, communicate with each other frequently and participate jointly in social and recreational activities. When marital disagreements occur, they are tackled and solved rationally and peacefully. The parent-child relations have become closer and more intense as the family moves to the smaller nuclear type. They consist of a mixed yet balanced set of feelings, including mutual love and trust as well as some mutual suspicion, but this balance is liable of being tipped off by a lack of mutual understanding, due to their differences in family values, general outlooks and personal styles of living.

The relations of the family with external social systems were seen to include primarily the processes of educational attainment, occupational engagement, and social and religious participation. First, educational attainment is widespread, particularly among the male heads of the families, who were generally better educated than their fathers. Second, regarding their occupational engagement, the men as a rule are employed in an economic enterprise, but the women also participate in some gainful activities. Both of them work mainly in manufacturing and service industries and are employed mostly in blue-collar and clerical posts. Hence, the husband's role as the sole bread-winner of the family has now been challenged, his income is considerably supplemented by that of the wife and their grown-up children. In terms of intergenerational occupational mobility, the heads of the families in both the upper and lower categories of position still have rather limited mobility as their positions are very close to those of their fathers, whereas those in the upper-middle stratum enjoy much upward mobility, being, for the most part, one or two levels of position higher than their fathers.

And, finally, as far as social and religious activities are concerned, the families were found to have demonstrated a reasonable amount of social awareness and participation. They take part in various social campaigns and community events, and voice their views or even take various forms of action regarding controversial social issues. The majority of these people still worship their ancestors in one form or another and many of them believe in some god, especially traditional Chinese deities, and participate regularly in related religious activities.

References:

BLOOD, Jr., R.O. and D.M. WOLFE (1960): Husbands and Wives, New York: The Free Press.

BURGESS, E.W., H.J. LOCKE and M.M. THOMES (1963): The Family: From Institution to Companionship, 3rd ed. New York: American Book.

CENTERS, R., B.H. RAVEN and A. RODRIGUES (1971): "Conjugal power structure: a re-examination." American Sociological Review, 36: 264-278.

GOODE, W.J. (1963): World Revolution and Family Patterns, New York: The Free Press.

HONG, L.K. (1970): The Chinese Family in a Modern Industrial Setting: Its Structure and Functions (Unpublished Ph.D. Dissertation, University of Notre Dame).

LANG, O. (1946): Chinese Family and Society, New Haven: Yale University Press.

MISHER, E.G. and N.E. WAXLER (1968): Interaction in Families. New York: John Wiley and Sons.

MITCHELL, R.E. (1969): Family Life in Urban Hong Kong, Vols. 1-11 (Unpublished Project Report of the Urban Family Life Survey).

MOWRER, E.R. (1969): "The differentiation of husband and wife roles." Journal of Marriage and the Family, 31: 534-540.

NG, P. (1975): The Family and Family Planning in Kwun Tong: An Overview of Findings, Social Research Centre, The Chinese University of Hong Kong.

PARSONS, T. and R.F. BALES (1955): Family, Socialization and Interaction Process, Glencoe: The Free Press.

ROSOW, I. (1965): "Intergenerational relationships: problems and proposals." in: E. SHANAS and G.F. STREIB (eds.): Social Structure and the Family: Generational Relations, Englewood Cliffs: Prentice-Hall, pp. 341-378.

SAFILIOS-ROTHSCHILD, C. (1970): "The study of family power structure: a review 1960-1969." Journal of Marriage and the Family, 32: 539-552.

WONG, F.M. (1972a): "Modern ideology, industrialization, and conjugalism: the Hong Kong case." International Journal of Sociology of the Family, 2: 139-150.

(1972b): Maternal Employment and Family Task-Power Differentiation among Lower Income Chinese Families, Social Research Centre, The Chinese University of Hong Kong.

(1975): "Industrialization and Family Structure in Hong Kong." Journal of Marriage and the Family, 37: 985-1000.

YANG, C.K. (1967): Religion in Chinese Society, Berkeley and Los Angeles: University of California Press.

ZELDITCH, Jr., (1955): "Role differentiation in the nuclear family: a comparative study." in: T. PARSONS and R.F. BALES (eds.): Family, Socialization and Interaction Process, Glencoe: The Free Press, pp. 307-351.

(1964): "Cross-cultural analyses of family structure." in: H.T. CHRISTENSEN (ed.), Handbook of Marriage and the Family, Chicago: Rand McNally, pp. 462-500.

"THE SOCIALLY MALNOURISHED GENERATION": AN ANATOMY OF THE SELF-IMAGE OF A STUDENT POPULATION IN HONG KONG

Tak-sing Cheung

I. Introductory Remarks

If role is the individual in society, then the self is society in the individual. From one point of view, as Newcomb (1951) suggested, nothing is so private, so strictly intra-individual, as one's own self which is the individual as known to the individual. From another perspective, however, nothing can be more social than the self because if one squeezes the self of all its social contents, what remains, perhaps, is the "I" - the self as the knower or the synthesizer, the existence of which is rather much in doubt upon further deliberation (see James, 1890; Kolb, 1944). In fact, the self originates from nowhere but society. It is the miniature of society in the individual (Mead, 1965). The significance of the self-concept, therefore, goes beyond the individual himself, for it mirrors the reality of the society of which he is a member.

This paper attempts to study the society of Hong Kong as reflected in the self-concept of a group of 588 students, who come from one primary and two secondary schools. Their ages range from 5 to 19, with 326 males and 262 females. These subjects do not constitute a probability sample of any kind. Strictly speaking, therefore, the findings generated cannot be generalized to the entire student population of Hong Kong. The study is intended as an exploratory study, hoping to shed light on the possibility of studying a kaleidoscopic society with a simple measuring instrument known as the Twenty Statements Test, designed by Kuhn and McPartland (1954).

The instrument is very simple. It is a sheet of paper with twenty blanks, preceded by the following instruction:

There are twenty numbered blanks on the page below. Please write twenty answers to the simple question "Who am I?" in the blanks. Just give twenty different answers to this question. Answer as if you were giving the answers to yourself, not to somebody else. Write the answers in the order that they occur to you. Don't worry about logic or "importance". Go along fairly fast, for time is limited.

Needless to say, Primary 1 and Primary 2 students would have difficulty in comprehending this long and somewhat complicated passage, so oral explanation was necessary. All the subjects were given twelve minutes to finish this part. Afterwards, they were requested to turn to another page to provide some background information such as age, religious affiliation, place of origin, place of birth, father's occupation, etc. The entire test took about twenty minutes.

Despite its simplicity, the Twenty Statements Test is a very promising instrument for eliciting an individual's conceptions of himself. According to a recent assessment (Spitzer and Parker, 1976), it has the highest perceived validity, among other measures of the self-concept, in the eyes of the subjects. One of its obvious advantages is that it allows the respondent to volunteer statements about himself. As Newcomb said (1950:151), "if we present ready-made statements to a respondent we can never know whether he would have ever made such statements about himself without such suggestion; it is a reasonable conjecture on the other hand that if he volunteers statements about himself with a minimum of stimulation, then these statements may be taken to be significant ones."

Whether that social fact has to be explained at its own level, as Durkheim so vehemently sanctioned, or that the ultimate explanation of all social behavior has to be sought in psychology, as Homans so confidently contended, is an endless controversy. Let us for the moment forget about the traditional feuds between these two levels of analysis and see how much of a complicated society like Hong Kong can be reflected from a psychological mirror. Contrary to Cooley's metaphor that society is the looking glass of an individual's self, the author takes the position that the self can in turn serve as a mirror from which we can view society. Needless to say, the present approach is not, and never can be, a substitute for others. It serves its own purpose so long as it succeeds in yielding insights on certain aspects of the society of Hong Kong which could not have been otherwise obtained.

II. The Uni-Model Distribution of Locus Scores

According to Kuhn (Schwirian, 1964:51), all statements given by the respondents can be classified into five categories, as follows:

- Consensual: "... all statements about social position of the respondent and his roles attendant thereupon. These include statements of social category such as name, age, religious membership, political affiliation, kin relations, race, national origin, other formal and informal group memberships,...."

- Preferences: "... all statements of the general order of 'I am interested in ....,' 'I avoid....,' 'I prefer..., ..."

- Beliefs: ".... all statements of a cosmic sort, all those having to do with religious beliefs, philosophical assumptions or on the general nature of morals and ethics."

- Aspirations: "all statements indicating what the respondent expects to do or be in the future...."

- Self-evaluations: ".... all evaluation statements - statements assessing one's own mental, physical and other abilities, physique and appearance, relatedness to others,...."

Kuhn and McPartland gave particular attention to the consensual statements (all other statements are called subconsensual statements). The number of consensual statements made by a respondent is called the locus score, which is taken as a measure of the extent of an individual's social anchorage, or the extent to which he sees himself as a member of social systems (Kuhn and McPartland, 1954).

Figure 1 shows the mean locus scores of the respondents in different age-groups. On the whole, the locus score of our respondents is quite low, with a grand mean of 5.5, as compared to 10 in Kuhn and McPartland's study. From a developmental point of view, the locus scores increase steadily from the age-group of 5-6 to that of 11-12 and starts to level off at that stage. Since the total statements given by respondents in each age-group vary, Figure 2 presents the proportion of each type of statement in different age-groups. Now to compare the curve of consensual statements with that in Figure 1: although the peak has shifted from the age-group of 11-12 to

Figure 1: Mean Consensual Statements made by Different Age-Groups

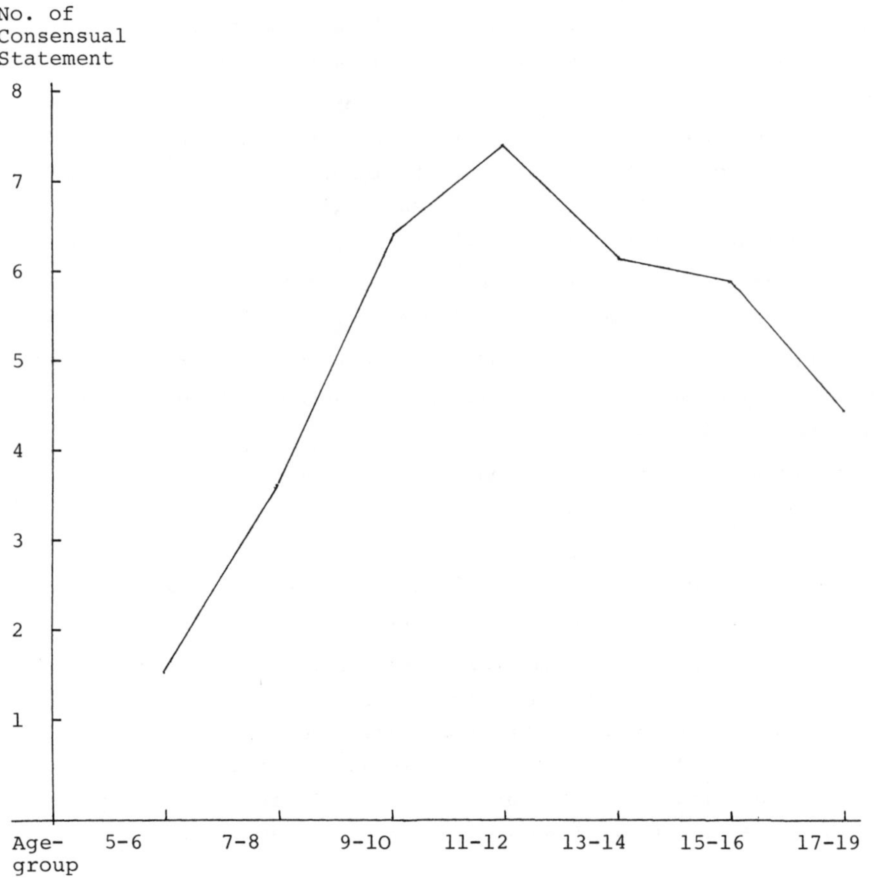

that of 9-10, the pattern is largely similar - both exhibit a unimodel pattern, climbing up at first and, to a certain point, moving downward thereafter.

This pattern is in contradistinction to that observed by McPartland (1953) and Kuhn (1960), in their respective studies. In Kuhn's research, which dealt with a greater age range, it was found that "locus scores steadily increase from those of seven-year-olds (the youngest thus far tested) with an average locus score of 5.79, through

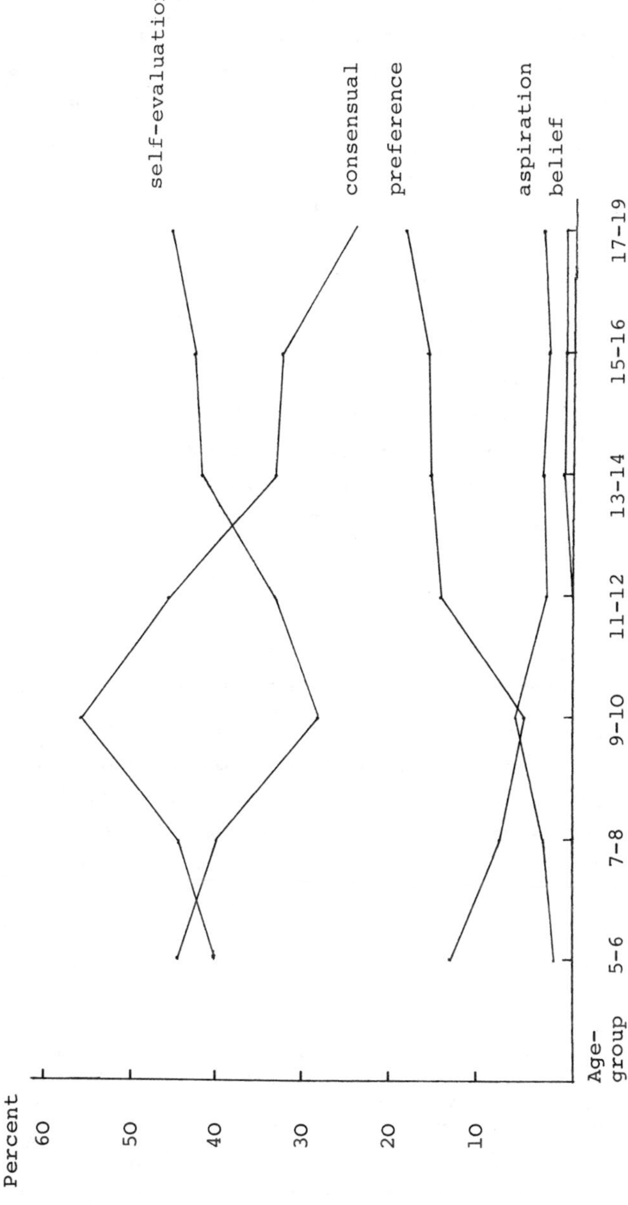

Figure 2: Proportions of Types of Statements in Different Age-Groups

twenty-four-year-olds with an average locus score of 11.03". He added that "this association is what we would expect from the orientation. As the average individual grows from the age of seven to that of twenty-four, he becomes - or so we would suppose - a member of more groups, and his roles are differentiated on the basis of divergent categories. As a consequence he will internalize as a significant part of his self-definition a larger volume of these identifying statuses" (pp. 44-45).

If the positive association between age and the locus score is "what we would expect," as Kuhn maintained, then the pattern of movement as observed among our subjects is something peculiar. And, if the locus score reflects the extent of an individual's social anchorage, as mentioned earlier, then the curve in Figure 1 suggests that our subjects have begun to retreat to individualism from the ages of 13-14 onwards.[1] For a more detailed analysis, let us now turn to the substantive aspect of our subject's self-image, as shown in Table 1.

III. The Three Stages of Self-Development

Table 1 further analyses the consensual statements given by our respondents. All the consensual statements were content-analysed and classified. The social categories listed in the table are not exhaustive; a few of the subjects mentioned they were Asians, men in the sub-tropical zone, etc. These categories were not entered here because of the extremely small number of individuals mentioning them. However, the social categories listed there represent at least 98 % of all the consensual responses. They were cross-tabulated with

---

[1] Dr. Rance P.L. LEE, in his critique of the first draft of this paper, voiced the concern that because the older subjects are intellectually more mature, they are more capable of writing down non-consensual statements and, as a result, there will be lesser space for making consensual statements. This concern can be clarified by two points: 1) If intelligence, which is assumed to be positively related to age, is positively related to the locus score, then the pattern of movement in Figure 1 should be linear rather than unimodal. 2) According to Kuhn and McPartland (1954:115), "respondents tended to exhaust all of the consensual references they would make before they made (if at all) any subconsensual ones." This finding was confirmed in all subsequent replication studies that I know of, including the present research.

Table 1: Percentages of Subjects Mentioning Particular Social Categories in Different Age-Groups

Age-Groups	Name[+]	Age	Sex	Family	School	Human Being	Hong Kong	China	Religion	Resi-dence	Place of Origin	Society	Associa-tion	Race	Social Class
5-6 (N=39)	92.3	7.7	7.7	15.4	33.3	5.1	0.0	0.0	0.0	0.0	0.0	0.0	0.0	0.0	0.0
7-8 (N=83)	84.3	28.9	30.1	30.1	36.1	44.6	4.8	12.0	7.2	3.6	3.6	0.0	0.0	0.0	0.0
9-10 (N=78)	70.5	35.9	34.6	51.2	67.9	46.2	6.4	5.1	17.9	11.5	2.6	2.6	9.0	0.0	0.0
11-12 (N=87)	55.2	40.2	47.1	58.6	85.1	42.5	14.8	18.4	12.6	24.1	3.4	11.5	3.4	1.1	1.1
13-14 (N=112)	46.2	36.6	56.3	52.7	76.8	37.5	24.1	25.0	12.5	22.3	7.1	18.8	6.3	2.7	8.0
15-16 (N=103)	44.7	35.9	52.4	44.7	71.8	35.0	25.2	37.9	21.4	11.7	6.8	15.5	3.9	8.7	6.8
17-18 (N=84)	36.9	27.4	52.4	36.9	83.3	17.9	17.9	33.3	25.0	3.6	4.8	7.1	1.2	4.8	5.6
Total	57.5	32.5	44.0	43.9	67.7	34.9	15.1	20.6	15.0	12.6	5.1	9.4	3.7	2.9	3.7

[+] Including references to oneself without indicating the name such as "I am XXX," "I am myself". In most instances, however, the name was written down.

age-groups so that we can follow the development of the self from early childhood to the later stage of adolescence.

We know from Mead (1965:199) that "the self has a character which is different from that of the physiological organism proper .... It is not initially there, at birth, but arises in the process of social experience and activity."[2] However, when the self begins to emerge is not certain. Theoretically, since the self is a conscious experience, it could not have existed before a child has a certain degree of consciousness. And, since language is primarily responsible for creating consciousness, it could not have arisen before the acquisition of language. Generally, there are indications that the self has already emerged for a two-year-old child (Cooley, 1964; Piaget, 1968; Denzin, 1972). Between this and the time when the simplest kind of measuring instrument is assessible to the child, the interim development is still a matter of speculation.

But this does not matter, for the self-concept of our youngest subjects (aged 5 and 6) is not much different from that as it first came into existence. It is still in a primordial state, remaining largely as an undifferentiated entity. The name is the major tag of identification[3] around which lie some dim and vague reflections of the child's own characteristics. The average total statements given by this age group is three. Most of them just write down their names. Some add one or two statements, such as "I am a student", "Mama loves me", etc. Beyond these, they have difficulty in describing themselves. According to the observation of our research assistant who administered questionnaires to the students, they were caught in perplexity when asked to answer the question "Who Am I?". It seemed that they did not know who they were except by giving out their names.

---

[2] In his presidential address to the 14th Annual Meeting of the Eastern Psychological Association, ALLPORT (1943) said that, "Infants, all writers concur, do not recognize themselves as individuals; they behave in what PIAGET calls an 'undifferentiated absolute' composed of self and environment. Only gradually and with difficulty does a segregated ego evolve."

[3] The child succeeds in differentiating himself from the rest of the surrounding environment largely through the recognition of his own name, given to him by his parents, and its association with his organic body. This explains why the name usually serves as the major tag of self-identification at the early stage of self-development.

For those in the age-group of 7-8, the self-image becomes more variegated. In addition to that more students locate themselves in the categories of age, sex, school, the family, and human being; such social axes as religion and residence sprout at the age of 7, while Hong Kong, China, and place of origin at the age of 8. We see, therefore, differentiation of the self is in process. If the emergence of the self begins with the differentiation of the organic body from its surrounding environment, i.e., an external differentiation, then the second stage of development begins when differentiation occurs within one's own self, i.e., an internal differentiation.

For the children in the age-group of 9-10, internal differentiation continues. The percentage of self-reference in name, though still the largest, keeps on declining. Their self-image is more solidly grounded in age, sex, the family, school, and human being. Besides, some students at the age of 10 begin to identify themselves as members of society and associations.

In the age-group of 11-12, it is for the first time that the percentage of self-reference in name is surpassed by those in the family and school. This signals that the internal differentiation of the self has developed to the extent where an individual's name is no longer the most important tag of self-identification. On the other hand, both at the age of 12, one student mentioned race and the other social class in their responses. With the emergence of these two objects of self-identification, we can say that the internal differentiation of the self has been completed, in the sense that all the major social groupings have already been incorporated in the individual's mind.

At the ages of 13-14, approximately the time when an individual enters secondary school, the percentages of subjects mentioning the family, school[4], age and residence categories begin to decline. This signals the gradual transition of the self-development into its third stage, despite the fact that, in other social axes, their percentages continue to increase. The major characteristic of this stage is the individual's disengagement from the social axes upon

[4] The upsurge of percentage in the age-group of 17-19 may be attributed to the fact that students of this age-group are facing the Education Certificate Examination which heightens their self-consciousness of being a student.

which he anchored at the previous stage. This stage covers the entire population of our subjects in the secondary school. Further disengagement can be observed in the age-group of 15-16, where the categories of sex, society, social class and place of origin begin to level off and, among our oldest subjects, even the categories of Hong Kong, China, and race decline.

However, unlike the first stage when an individual's self is primarily anchored in his name, the individualistic orientation at this stage is no longer expressed in name but in more frequent references to personal characteristics and preferences. If we return to Figure 2, we can see that at the third stage, as the proportion of consensual statements decreases, the proportions of preferential and self-evaluative statements increase. In the same figure, we can also observe that among all age-groups, aspirational statements are very few and ideological (belief) responses are conspicuously absent. This suggests that our subjects' consciousness is preoccupied with a present-tense and a this-worldly orientation.

To recapitulate, the self-image of our subjects, whose ages range from 5 to 19, has undergone three stages of development. The first stage, to which the 5 and 6 year old children belong, is continuous with early development when the child succeeds in differentiating himself from the surrounding environment and hence acquires a primitive self-image. At this stage, the self is quite homogeneous and egocentric, with the name as its major tag of identification. Roughly beginning from the seven year old child, the development of the self enters the second phase, when it undergoes an internal differentiation, adding to it, gradually and successively, more social components. All the major social axes have already emerged in the self around the age of twelve and by now the self can be taken as mature and its development largely completed. From thirteen years old onwards, although most social components continue to grow, the percentages of subjects mentioning the family, school, age and residence show signs of decrease. This signals the development of the self into its third phase, when the individual gradually disengages himself from the social axes upon which he anchored at the previous stage and returns to an individualistic orientation.

Just as the stream of historical evolution is inseparable in reality, the division of the development of our subjects' self-image into three stages is purely analytical. There is no clear demarcation line between one stage and another. Nonetheless, as our data indicate, the trend discussed above does exist and is visible. More important is that it is consistent with the pattern shown in Figure 1, suggesting the declining importance of social participation in shaping our subjects' self-image from the age of 13 onwards.

IV. The Socially Malnourished Generation

We see, therefore, that the analyses of both the frequency and the substantive content of the consensual statements given by our subjects consistently reveal that they retreat to individualism at a very early stage of life, especially in comparison with findings established by Kuhn (1960). It is, of course, unjustifiable to label the self-development of our subjects abnormal merely by a comparison with similar findings generated from another sample. Theories abound to show, however, that man has a deep-rooted psychological propensity for ego-extension. Contrary to the common notion that man is inherently selfish, many psychologists and sociologists have noted the tenacious tendency of extending the boundary of one's self far beyond the organic body (James, 1890; McDougall, 1908; Allport, 1955; Durkheim, 1963; etc.). For some obscure reasons, man is in fear of being alone, which we sometimes refer to as the gregarious instinct. The individual's precarious existence gives rise to psychological vulnerability which, in turn, propells him to affiliate with a larger entity.[5] So, as Allport (1968:28-29) said:

"(The early developments of the self) have a heavily biological quality and seem to be contained <u>within the organism</u> itself. But soon the process of learning brings with it a high regard for possessions, for loved objects, and later, ideal causes and loyalties ..... A child, however, who identifies with his parents is definitely <u>extending his sense of self</u>, as he does likewise through his love for pets, dolls, or other possessions, animate or inanimate.

As we grow older we identify with groups, neighborhood, and nation as well as with possessions, clothes, home.... Later in life the

---

[5] Eric FROMM's observation of the German and Italian massive escape from freedom is a classic revelation of this underlying psychological propensity.

process of extension may go to great lengths, through the development of loyalties and of interests focused on abstractions and on moral and religious values. Indeed, a mark of maturity seems to be the range and extent of one's feeling of self-involvement in abstract ideals". (Underlining not in original).

This quotation well summarizes the normal course for a child's self-development. It is a transition from the organismically-centered orientation to the socially-extended orientation. As he grows older and becomes a member of more groups and categories, his self will take lodging in a wider spectrum of social bases. We do not know even roughly at what age this social extension of the self reaches its peak. We do know, however, that this trend continues until at least the age of twenty-four, in adults from the U.S.

The question is: what are the factors that prevent the continued social anchorage of our subjects' self-image? Before answering this question, let us return to Table 1 and look at the Total row. We can see that, generally, our subjects' self is anchored primarily in such categories as school[6], name (or similar reference to oneself without name), sex, family, human being, and age, in that order. These are the major social axes in which they locate themselves. Among them, human being is the only category that goes beyond the individual's immediate social environment. What makes it such a prominant axis of self-identification is quite perplexing. But one thing is certain: it is only a very general universe and does not constitute a potential threat to other major social groupings in competing for an individual's loyalty. For those that may pose a threat, such as one's resident country (Hong Kong), national origin (China), race, religion, social class, and place of origin, etc., their percentages are quite small, none of them succeeds in claiming more than one-fourth of our subjects.

---

[6] The exceptional high percentage of self-identification in terms of school roles can be taken as somewhat biased by the testing situation. TUCKER (1966) has already pointed out that one of the inherent limitations of the Twenty Statements Test is that the responses it elicited can be susceptible to situational influences. Since our subjects responded to the questionnaire in classroom, dressed in school uniform, it is quite possible that the exceptional high percentage of self-identifications in terms of school roles is caused by such situational factors, although the extent of their influence cannot be precisely determined.

Of particular interest is the obscure impact of Hong Kong on our subjects' self-identification. If the column of "Hong Kong" is compared with that of "China", we can see that except for the age-group of 9-10, the percentage of subjects mentioning Hong Kong is consistently lower than that mentioning China. Moreover, whereas nearly all the entries that go into the China category are statements like "I am a Chinese", those that are classified under the heading of Hong Kong are more heterogeneous in content, including statements such as "I am a Hong Kong citizen", "I live in Hong Kong", and "I was born in Hong Kong", etc.

On the whole, our subjects rarely described themselves as a "Hongkongese". Usually, a resident country, with a clear geographical boundary and political sovereignty, is a very favorable candidate for claiming an individual's loyalty and hence constituting a major axis of self-identification. It is especially true when we know that, among our subjects, 91.7 % were born in Hong Kong. In a traditional Chinese expression, they "were born here, and were brought up here". Why their sense of belonging to Hong Kong is so weak is indeed an enigma, which deserves a little more elaboration. Far from exhaustive, the following remarks should be enough to make this enigma more comprehensible.

First, although Hong Kong was ceded to Britain in 1842, for many years it remained as an entrepôt. The population is very unstable, composed mainly of immigrants from mainland China who only planned for a temporary settlement and aimed at short-term economic goals. Their social and psychological roots were tied to their hometowns. It was not until the Korean War when the so called "bamboo curtain" was laid between Hong Kong and China that the constant flux of population came virtually to a halt. However, for various reasons, the psychological mentality of the people in Hong Kong had never been fully stabilized. In the 50's when the Kuomintang's yearning to recover the mainland was received as more than being a slogan, many longed to go back to their place of origin some day. As soon as they realized that this would never come true, the shadow of a communist takeover surged through. Especially after the political turmoil in 1967, emigration routes, leading mostly to North America, were packed with people at each other's heels. For the lower class majority emigration is unimaginable and they may consider staying in Hong Kong permanently.[7] However, trapped in a paradox of fearing the communist takeover,[8] on the one hand, and having no other alternative but to stay in Hong Kong permanently, on the other, these people console themselves, perhaps quite unconsciously, by burying their heads in a limited time horizon, looking forward to no more than, say, five years ahead. Under these circumstances, they share with the economically-better-off citizens what may be called a "tourist mentality" which, by definition, is highly incompatible with the formation of a sense of belonging to the community.

Second, the government usually plays a decisive role in instilling a sense of belonging to its citizens (e.g., Singapore). But in Hong Kong, the tourist mentality mentioned above exists in the minds not only of the people but the British government as well. Consequently, most policies have been designed and implemented in an ad hoc manner. Needless to say, the cultivation of a sense of belonging among its people, which is of fundamental importance from a long-term perspective, is not its primary concern. In the last decade, there have been isolated efforts aiming at this goal (e.g. the Hong Kong Festival). But, given the absence of a whole-hearted patronage from the government and the constraint of financial resources, little has been accomplished over the years.

Third, the identity of being a Chinese is a suppressing factor for the emergence of a sense of belonging to Hong Kong. Because of the British government's indifference to cultivate a sense of identification with the Hong Kong community (unlike Singapore), it has never launched any systematic campaign deliberately designed to dismantle the Chinese identity of its people. On the contrary, Chinese history and geography, the temporal and spatial axes for sustaining the Chinese identity, are taught in school, though somewhat outdated in content and interpretation. Although the Chinese language has been discriminated against in favor of English, Chinese traditions and

---

[7] According to LAU (1977), 68.8 % of the respondents in his study indicated that, either mostly probably or definitely, they will stay in Hong Kong permanently.

[8] Also in LAU's study (1977), he established that 81.6 % of the respondents do not prefer a communist takeover of Hong Kong, while only 0.7 % of them expressed that preference.

customs have been largely respected. (This can be illustrated by the fact that government officials, including the Governor himself, participate in the celebration of major Chinese festivals, e.g., the Dragon Boat Festival. Even on such occasions as a visit by the Queen, Chinese traditional arts, e.g., Dragon dance, lead the celebration procession).

Despite all these factors, the Chinese identity does seem not strong enough to constitute a major axis of self-identification. Only 20.6 % of our subjects indicated they were Chinese in their responses. As a colonial government, if the British authorities are not enthusiastic in cultivating a sense of belonging to Hong Kong, there is no reason to expect them to do anything to encourage the formation of a Chinese identity through political socialization in school. It is, for example, well understood that the national anthem and flag are important symbols in articulating one's national consciousness. With the absence of these and other symbols, the Chinese identity of the Hong Kong people can only be a diffused one, sustained mainly through historical and cultural linkages. The situation is further influenced by the existence of two rival governments, one in Peking the other in Taipei, each claiming political legitimacy over its people. The divided loyalty inevitably weakens the sense of belonging.

Race, a major social identity in many societies, is barely preceptible among our subjects, with 2.9 % describing themselves in racial or ethnic terms. Consciousness of one's own race becomes acute only in societies where racial conflicts pose a serious problem, such as the U.S. In Hong Kong, so far no major social conflict has originated from racial or ethnic differences. The white minority lives on top of the society. But because of their small number, their existence is barely perceptible in the eyes of the Chinese majority in their daily encounters. Also because of their number, they cannot afford to discriminate against local Chinese, at least explicitly, on racial grounds. Up until the present time, in Hong Kong no voluntary club or association has closed its doors to other races. Although the white minority tend to concentrate on certain residential areas, they share neighborhoods with upper-class or upper-middle-class Chinese. Therefore, we can say that social and cultural segregations exist between different socio-economic strata rather than between different races.[9] In the past, the local Cantonese used to discriminate against other Chinese ethnic minorities (e.g., Chiu Chow). However, partly because of the absence of a physical basis for differentiation and partly through the assimilation process that is going on in school, mass media, and other social avenues, the boundary between the Cantonese and other Chinese ethnic minorities has virtually been wiped out in the younger generation.

Religion is not a dominant facet of life in Hong Kong either. Traditional religious rituals and practices are constantly observed by the Chinese majority, but their orientation is a diffused one, as so aptly characterised by C.K. Yang (1961). Under the influence of the Western missionaries, who nearly monopolized the secondary education in Hong Kong, 59.4 % of our respondents are religious believers, mostly Protestants and Catholics. However, as shown in Table 1, only 15 % of our subjects identified themselves with religious categories, including non-religious indications, such as "I am not a religious believer". The reason is that religious indoctrination, though ubiquitous in schools run by religious organizations, is far from intensive. Hong Kong is a highly competitive society. Whatever values dominate society also dominate school. While the competition for a good result in the School Certificate Education Examination is keen, religious practices in many schools have been reduced to the minimum and remain largely as protocol and decoration.

Despite Marx's contention that the history of all hitherto existing society is the history of class struggles, social class does not constitute a major component in our subjects' self-image. Only 3.7 % identified themselves in terms of social class background. All of these statements, however, look like "I was born in a poor family", or "I belong to a middle-upper family". Strictly speaking, these are but expressions of socio-economic status, the substitute for social class in Western sociology. This is, of course, not to deny the existence of social classes in the society of Hong Kong. But, as Marx pointed out, they exist at two levels, i.e., the subjective and the objective. Whatever the objective conditions, our data indicate that subjective class consciousness has not been formed among our respondents.

---

[9] For a more detailed analysis, see LAU (1977), especially p. 31.

The small percentage of self-identification with place of origin (5.1 %) signals the passing away of the traditional agrarian mentality. As Fei (1970) observed, rural society is characterised by an earth-bound value orientation. The phrase "All fallen leaves of a tree come back to its roots" is a familiar expression. For business or for livelihood, an individual may spend most of his life time in foreign places, but his social and psychological roots are tied to his homeland. He even hopes that after death his body will be sent back there for burial. This is a social solidarity based on geographical territory. Traces of this type of solidarity are still discernible in Hong Kong, as can be evidenced by the existence of so many hometown organizations. But most of them fell into oblivion as soon as they came into existence, remaining more as living fossils than as functioning organisms. On the other hand, a new type of earth-bound mentality has emerged, as indicated by 12.6 % of our subjects who mentioned the place they live in their self-identification. But in a highly modernized city like Hong Kong where physical and social mobility are frequent, geographical location can hardly serve as a solid ground for personal identity.

While participation in voluntary associations is a major characteristic of modern life, only 3.7 % of our subjects identified themselves in terms of memberships in voluntary associations, most of which revolve around extra-curricular activities in school. It is true that, as students, our subjects are preoccupied with studying and hence their participation in voluntary associations may not be as important in their lives as in the lives of adults. However, there are indications that the apathy surrounding participation in voluntary organizations is a reflection of the whole society, instead of being restricted to the student population. In Lau's study (1977:133-136) mentioned above, it was found that only 19.6 % of the adults in Hong Kong have joined voluntary associations of any kind, as compared to 84 % in a Midwestern state in the U.S.; and that those who join two voluntary associations or less represent 89.4 % of all the joiners. Lau also indicated that among the voluntary organizations joined, many are closely connected with familistic relationship (such as clan and locality association), or with the requirement of one's job (e.g., trade unions). These figures clearly show that participation in voluntary associations is not a major facet of the daily life of the Hong Kong people.

I have just shown, in a sketchy way, the non-existence of any viable social group that lies beyond the purview of our subjects' immediate daily activities. Because of this, the ego-extension tendency of our subjects cannot continue to flourish in a proper environment. In other words, they are socially malnourished. Gradually and inevitably, the social base of our subjects' self-concept shrinks back to their immediate environment, i.e., the nuclear family and school. School, however, is only a transient stage in life. Once he graduates, I am afraid, the only major social axis in the individual's self is the nuclear family. But our data show that even the frequency of mentioning family roles in our subjects' responses begins to decline at age thirteen. I am afraid that the trend is to recede to the individual himself. This is by no means a morally healthy state, as Durkheim made it clear that "the domain of the moral begins where the domain of the social begins" (1963:60), and that "there is no truly moral force save that involved in attachment to a group" (1963:82). Unless systematic efforts are directed to avert this trend, one of the foremost crises in this society will be a moral crisis - the non-attachment of its citizens to any social group, resulting in a state of massive demoralization whereby the maintenance of social order will more heavily rely on law enforcement than ever before.

V. Concluding Remarks

Like any study, the present research suffers from many limitations. To expose the major ones will help to chart the course of future investigations in this area. First, because the different age groups are comprised of different individuals, this is not a longitudinal study in the strict sense. Therefore, the present research harbors the assumption that background characteristics other than age are either randomly distributed or not responsible for accounting for the pattern of self-development as previously reported. The acceptability of my interpretations of the research results is, therefore, contingent upon whether this assumption is true. Second, as previously mentioned, the sample of this study is not a probability sample. Although sometimes a nonprobability sample may turn out to be very representative, there is no way to determine the degree of confidence over such a sample. Therefore, a replication of the present study with a probability sample would be desirable if practically possible. Third, I have made some value judgements in the latter part of this article, i.e., the retreat to individualism is given a deprecatory evaluation. However, this is not a violation of the value-free principle in science. This principle should and can be upheld only in the process of research design and data collection. In interpreting research findings, the author is free to bring forth his own value judgements. Indeed, serious doubts have been raised as to whether biases can be avoided at all in the whole process of conducting social science research. The most we can do, therefore, is to expose one's own biases.

References:

ALLPORT, G., 1943, "The ego in contemporary psychology", Psychological Review, 50:451-478.

ALLPORT, G., 1955, Becoming, New Haven: Yale University Press.

COOLEY, Ch., 1964, Human Nature and Social Order, New York: Schocken.

DENZIN, N., 1972, "The genesis of self in early childhood", The Sociological Quarterly, 13: 291-314.

DURKHEIM, E., 1963, Moral Education, New York: Free Press.

FEI, H.T., 1970, Hsiang-tu-chung-kuo (Rural China), Hong Kong: Phonix Press.

JAMES, W., 1890, Principles of Psychology, New York: Holt.

KOLB, W., 1944, "A critical evaluation of Mead's 'I' and 'Me' concepts", Social Forces, 22:291-296.

KUHN, M., 1960, "Self-attitudes by age, sex and professional training", The Sociological Quarterly, 1:39-56.

KUHN, M. and MCPARTLAND, Th., 1954, "An empirical investigation of self-attitudes", American Sociological Review, 19:68-76.

LAU, S.K., 1977, Utilitarianistic Familism: An Inquiring into the Political Stability in Hong Kong, Social Research Centre, The Chinese University of Hong Kong.

MCDOUGALL, W., 1908, An Introduction to Social Psychology, London: Methuen.

MCPARTLAND, Th., 1953, "The self and social structure: an empirical approach", Ph.D. thesis, University of Iowa.

MEAD, G., 1965, George Herbert Mead in Social Psychology, Chicago: Univ. of Chicago Press.

NEWCOMB, Th., 1950, Social Psychology, New York.

NEWCOMB, Th., 1951, "Social psychological theory: integrating individual and social approaches", in: J.H. ROHRER and S. SHERIF (eds.), Social Psychology at the Crossroads, New York: Harper.

PIAGET, J., 1968, Six Psychological Studies, New York: Random.

SCHWIRIAN, K., 1964, "Variation in structure of the Kuhn - McPartland Twenty Statements Test and Related Response Differences", The Sociological Quarterly, 5: 47-60.

SPITZER, St., and PARKER, J., 1976, "Perceived validity and assessment of the self: a decade later", The Sociological Quarterly, 17: 236-246.

TUCKER, Ch., 1966, "Some methodological problems of Kuhn's self-theory", The Sociological Quarterly, 3: 345-358.

YANG, C.K., 1961, Religion in Chinese Society, Berkeley: Univ. of California Press.

III. POLITICAL DEVELOPMENTS

POLITICAL STABILITY AND CHANGE IN HONG KONG

Hsin-chi Kuan

I. Raison d'être of the Colony

The fundamental question to be raised about Hong Kong's political status is whether it is still a colony. The word "still" should not obscure the fact that from the very beginning the colony of Hong Kong represented a case apart from the other British colonies. Hong Kong was not acquired as a settlement for the British, but rather as a diplomatic, commercial and military post in order to secure trade with China.[1] Such a raison d'être of the colony had two important consequences; one economic and the other social. Economically, Hong Kong became an entrepôt port for all, instead of an exploitative market for Britain alone.[2] Socially, Hong Kong became an immigrant society, in which the local Chinese residents were pretty much left in peace and their customs and laws largely respected by the British government.[3]

Today, the political situation in Hong Kong is still unique. In the midst of a universal tide of de-colonization, the colonial constitution of Hong Kong set up almost a century ago has remained surprisingly durable. The governmental structure of Hong Kong follows the typical pattern of a Crown Colony with the supreme power vested in the Governor who as the representative of the Crown is assisted by an Executive Council and advised by a Legislative Council.[4] Such an institutional arrangement should strongly secure a constitutional

---

1 The island of Hong Kong and the Kowloon peninsula were ceded in 1842 and 1860 respectively, while the New Territories were leased in 1898 for 99 years. For the British motivation, see G.B. ENDACOTT, Government and People in Hong Kong 1841-1962: A Constitutional History, Hong Kong Univ. Press, Hong Kong, 1964, Ch. 2.

2 T.N. CHIU, The Port of Hong Kong: A Survey of Its Development, Hong Kong Univ. Press, Hong Kong, 1973, Ch. 2.

3 J.W. NORTON-KYSHE, History of the Laws and Courts of Hong Kong, Reprinted Version, Vetch & Lee, Hong Kong, 1971, passim.

4 For details, see John REAR, "The Law of the Constitution", in: K. HOPKINS (ed.), Hong Kong. The Industrial Colony, Oxford Univ. Press, Hong Kong, 1971, pp. 339-415.

relationship of colonial dependency, in which the imperial motherland retains ultimate control over the Colony through the selective appointment of the Governor and his senior advisers as well as through the issue of royal instructions.

The persistence of the colonial constitutional order has been accompanied by remarkable political stability. Hong Kong has never experienced any large-scale revolt or revolution. On the contrary, it is reputed for its lack of serious disputes.[5] Various explanations have been advanced to account for this situation. One line of argument centers upon the functional utility of the Colony to Britain and China, primarily in terms of financial rewards. While Britain has received strong backing of her devaluating sterling by Hong Kong's external reserves which make up about a quarter of the assets of the Bank of England,[6] China earns from and through Hong Kong between 40 to 50 percent of her foreign exchange.[7] Another approach emphasises the willingness and ability of the Government to "timely change and enlarge the elite circle by co-opting the ever-emerging leadership groups" in a society in which "the masses remain primarily in the apolitical strata".[8] In addition to the above, a new line of inquiry has recently been undertaken that seeks to uncover the endogeneous forces of political stability. It is argued that Hong Kong can be conceptualized as a hierarchical dyad with a power elite at the top and a mass of familial groups on the botton which, however, lacks the mediating influence of an intermediate level of organizations. In such a society, the family "represents the major reference group with which an individual identifies and for whose material well-being an individual strives." Therefore, to the extent that families are able to cater for the needs of individuals,

---

5 Joe ENGLAND and John REAR, Chinese Labour Under British Rule, Oxford Univ. Press, Hong Kong, 1975, pp. 278-287.

6 Hong Kong: A Case to Answer, Hong Kong Research Project, Spokesman Books, London, 1974, pp. 103-106.

7 T. GEIGER and F.M. GEIGER, Tales of Two City-States, National Planning Association, Washington D.C., 1973, pp. 135ff.

8 Ambrose Y.C. KING, The Administrative Absorption of Politics in Hong Kong, Social Research Centre, Chinese University of Hong Kong, May 1973; compare with S.N.G. DAVIS, "One Brand of Politics Rekindled", in: Hong Kong Law Journal, Vol. 7, No. 1, pp. 44-80.

politics is absorbed by utilitarianistic familism with individuals possessing only the most meagre expectations in regard to the provision of government services. Thus, in this situation, even assuming the existence of potentially exploitable political discontent, the task of mobilizing families is exceedingly difficult.[9]

Apart from these theories, a neglected area that can be opened up for discussion is the question as to what extent public policy in Hong Kong can be regarded as "colonial". The relevance of the topic to political stability is obvious. If Hong Kong were really administered as a colony in the true sense of the word, i.e. sheer exploitation of the local residents for the benefit of the motherland, neither China nor the local residents could afford to stand aloof for any prolonged period.

It is the intention of this paper to suggest that a combination of factors has made it possible for Hong Kong to embark on a rather indigenous path of political development in which a new pattern of working relationships between the Government and the people is emerging, despite the persistence of the colonial order.

II. Freedom for Internal Development

The notion of national autonomy has thus far received comparatively little attention in the study of political development.[10] However, autonomy must be regarded as a very important indicator in the study of political development of a colony, a satellite country or a "penetrated political system".[11] In Hong Kong, the external setting that is primarily structured by Sino-British relations has offered both constraints and opportunities for endogeneous political development.

A. The China Factor

The fundamental political problem of Hong Kong is its relationship

---

9 LAU Siu-Kai, Utilitarianistic Familism: An Inquiry Into the Basis of Political Stability in Hong Kong, Social Research Centre, Chinese University of Hong Kong, September 1977.

10 For an exception, see J.F. TRISKA and P.M. JOHNSON, "Political Development and Political Change", in:C. MESA-LAGO and C. BECK (eds.), Comparative Socialist Systems, Univ. of Pittsburgh Press, Pittsburgh, 1975, pp. 249-285.

with Britain on the one hand and with China on the other. The old pattern of an adversary power relationship between an expanding Britain and a weakening China, which is the context in which the Colony of Hong Kong was born and developed, has given way (since the Korean War) to a new one of compatible policy relationships between an aspiring China which is asserting itself at the global level in general and in Asia in particular, and a withdrawing Britain which has relinquished its commitments east of Suez and turned itself increasingly to regional politics in Europe. This fundamental change in Hong Kong's political situation cannot but affect the political development of Hong Kong.[12]

The implications of the China factor have been subtle and twofold. On the one hand, China definitely has a stake in Anti-colonialism. In March 1972, it requested the United Nations to delete Hong Kong and Macau from the list of colonial territories. The move was nothing more than a reinforcement of its traditional claim of sovereign right over the colonies and a reservation of its freedom to determine the timing and method of the final settlement when conditions are ripe. By making its actual anti-colonial intention clear as a matter of principle and ambiguous as a matter of practical policy, China has imposed upon Hong Kong a temporal perspective, conducive to the development of defeatist attitudes by many people. The uncertain future of Hong Kong has been interpreted in a fatalistic way, as captured by the subtitle of a well-known book, i.e. "Borrowed Place - Borrowed Time".[13] It was believed that such fatalism, together with a gambler's mentality, could well account for the surface indifference of Hong Kong to change and the rewards of change. The impact of the time constraint on government was no less decisive. The Hong Kong Government could never dream of becoming an active agent in social-economic change. Its public policy was laissez-faire at best and conservative at worst. Quite often,

---

[11] The concept of autonomy is central to the "dependency theory" in Latin American literature and to the notion of the "penetrated political system" in international politics.

[12] For a recent reference by the Governor to the impact of Anglo-Chinese relations on the development in Hong Kong consult his address before the Legislative Council on 8th Oct. 1975, in: Hong Kong Hansard, 1975-76, p. 26.

public policy was much a matter of expediency and of pragmatism. The rapid expansion of the bureaucracy and of the governmental services was largely a reaction to previous crises.[14]

On the other hand, China also has a stake in a stable and prosperous Hong Kong to serve it as a diplomatic, commercial and military post for the maintenance of contact with the outside world, and for the acquisition of foreign exchange and the securement of logistic support in times of national defense. While the policy of the Hong Kong Government has continuously been one of consideration and attempted constraint from acts deemed provocative or detrimental to the Chinese interest,[15] China has become increasingly appreciative of the usefulness of Hong Kong to its national development and has changed from a policy of outright hostility in the early days to the present one of cooperation. In practical terms, the Chinese tolerance of the jurisdiction of the British over Hong Kong is ample in scope, and the Hong Kong Government actually possesses substantial room for freedom in its pursuit of public policy, provided that it is not provocatively colonialistic.

B. The Britain Factor

Apparently, Britain never entertained the idea of giving up Hong Kong, either immediately after the Second World War, as her American ally urged, or in October 1949 when the Chinese communists were approaching the border. Several lines of argument, strategic, economic and moral, have been advanced to account for the continuity of the British rule over Hong Kong.[16]

---

[13] Richard HUGHES, Hong Kong. Borrowed Place - Borrowed Time, Andre Deutsch, London, 1968, p. 112.

[14] For example, consult Andrew W.F. WONG, "The Implementation of the Resettlement Program," in: G.U. IGLESIAS (ed.), Implementation. The Problem of Achieving Results, EROPA, Manila, 1976, pp. 267-308.

[15] Alexander GRANTHAM, Via Port. From Hong Kong to Hong Kong, Hong Kong University Press, Hong Kong, 1965, pp. 139, 169, 179-180.

[16] See N.J. MINERS, The Government and Politics of Hong Kong, Oxford Univ. Press, Hong Kong, 1975, pp. 3-13; for a good statement of the moral argument see David TRENCH, "Hong Kong and Its Position in the Southeast Asian Region", Nov. 3, 1971, East West Centre, Honolulu, Hawaii, p. 8.

Whatever merits these arguments might have, the essential fact is that the actual exercise of British rule has become increasingly minimal in recent decades.

The British proposal of local self-government, which was genuine but buried by local notables and political transformation in the Far East in the late 40s and early 50s, has become a legend.[17] But the British commitment to the idea of self-government for colonial people did survive those critical years. As early as the 50s, the colonial dependency of Hong Kong on Britain was already confined to issues of foreign policy, on which London had to be consulted.[18] Currently in the sphere of local affairs, Hong Kong has become largely autonomous. A journalist familiar with the Hong Kong situation claimed in the 60s that "one can list examples of any London intervention in local affairs on the fingers of one hand."[19]

The most significant development in local autonomy was, of course, the granting to Hong Kong of a wide measure of financial autonomy in 1958. Since then, Hong Kong has no longer been required to submit for approval annual estimates and supplementary provisions to the Secretary of State.[20] The then Financial Secretary of Hong Kong, Mr. John Cowperthwaite, skilfully availed himself of this autonomy to strike an independent path for Hong Kong.

Local autonomy was interrupted shortly after the 1966-67 riots when the British interest in Hong Kong was revived and British labour experts were sent in to advise the Government on the improvement of labour conditions in Hong Kong. This reverse trend could not but invite strong criticism, as when Dr. S.Y. Chung, a leading unofficial member of the Legislative Council categorically demanded full authority for Hong Kong: "It appears, then, that we are neither fish, flesh nor fowl in so far as our relations with the United Kingdom are concerned. This is highly unsatisfactory. I firmly believe that our Government in Hong Kong must be given full authority to

---

17 G.B. ENDACOTT, op. cit., pp. 182-195.

18 A. GRANTHAM, op. cit., p. 105.

19 Derek DAVIES, Shepherd, Tend Thy Sheep, in: Far Eastern Economic Review, Oct. 26, 1967, p. 208.

20 Alvin RABUSHKA, Value for Money. The Hong Kong Budgetary Process, Hoover Institution Press, Stanford, Calif., 1976, Ch. 2.

make decisions on internal matters so that we can adopt measures which, in our own opinion, are in the overall interests of our community."[21]

Gradually, the Hong Kong Government regained its leverage and again became able to champion local interests. In 1973, a contract for the construction of a mass transit system worth HK$ 5,000 million was given to a Japanese consortium instead of to a competing British firm. In January 1975, Hong Kong became completely free to diversify its foreign reserves, an issue which had long been taken as evidence of colonial exploitation.[22]

The extent to which Hong Kong has become autonomous can probably best be summarised in the words of N.J. Miners as follows: "In constitutional law the administration of Hong Kong is completely subordinate to the Crown - that is, to the government at present holding office in Britain; but in practice the Colony is very largely autonomous, particularly in internal matters, and discussions between London and Hong Kong are sometimes much more like diplomatic negotiations between two sovereign states than the compliant obedience by an inferior to orders from above."[23]

III. Endogeneous Forces for Change

The previous section has demonstrated the development of conditions under which the Government of Hong Kong has attained a substantial measure of freedom from external pressures in its pursuit of internal policies. It may be argued that, in comparison with other governments in the world, the Hong Kong Government seems to be the one which actually faces the least constraints. It could very well have become an active agent of development, but it did not. Undoubtedly, the Hong Kong Government's inertia in this respect may be traced to deep-seated, but as yet unresearched causes. Among them, two factors appear to be suggestive.

---

21 Hong Kong Hansard, 1969-70, p. 344.

22 By the end of 1976, only 20 % of the Hong Kong reserves were deposited in sterling. Hong Kong 1977. Report for the Year 1976, Hong Kong Government Press, 1977, Chinese Version, p. 31.

First, the Hong Kong Government, working under a temporal perspective of uncertainty, has been unable to eradicate the cognitive conception of Hong Kong as a colony, which has become entrenched since the Korean War. No research has been carried out to date on the temporal perspective of the political culture of government officials which of course must have a serious impact on the determination of public policy. But a case exists which can highlight the significance of the time perspective for policy making in Hong Kong. In the instance of the China Light & Power Co. Ltd. in Hong Kong, it is worthwhile to investigate at some length the contents of its Combined Report for 1957-1963. In that report the chairman of the company quoted representative opinions of the day on the delicate uncertainty of Hong Kong's future in noting that: "Had these views governed the Board, there would have been no expansion; .... In the opinion of the Directors, all of whom are persons who have made Hong Kong their home, the security of the Colony can be measured in terms of its usefulness to the world in general, and to China in particular."[24]

The remainder of the report as well indicates the company's concern for the future. Yet in recognizing not only the difficulties of planning for the future but also the fact that freedom for expansion constitutes an essential ingredient for success, the company decided to adopt a "policy of optimism". This was a case of successful transcendence of the trauma of "borrowed place - borrowed time".

The second reason for the Government's refusal to opt for an active role in development was largely due to its complacency with laissez-faire policy as determined by Hong Kong's position as a free port. Laissez-faire had its great utility in economic transformation and expansion in the '50s and '60s, but it became increasingly repugnant when urbanization and industrialization brought forth important social changes and massive social problems.[25] It required the riots of 1966-67 to strike home in the mind of the Government that things must change. In this sense, the riots proved to be a watershed in the political development in Hong Kong, although they were of small

---

[23] N.J. MINERS, op. cit., p. 203.

[24] China Light & Power Co. Ltd., Combined Report, 1957-1963, p. 6.

[25] I.C. JARVIE, Hong Kong Society in Transition, R. & K. Paul, London, 1969, passim.

magnitude in terms of the number of participants involved.

In April 1966, a riot spontaneously broke out as a result of a peaceful demonstration against an increase in ferry fare. Before the dust could settle, wage disputes in a textile industry in May 1967 escalated into riots of much more violence, encouraged by the Cultural Revolution in China and organized by local communists.

The implications of the events in 1966-67 are manifold. Among them, three are particularly important to the present paper. The events demonstrated that (1) a potentially unruly younger generation was arising; (2) a tiny social issue was sufficient to ignite a social outburst and (3) colonialism was no longer salient to practical politics in Hong Kong.

In as much as the participants in the disturbances were comparatively poorly educated, poorly housed and poorly employed youth, the protest was believed to be a manifestation of an undercurrent of suppressed frustrations and resentment and in this sense not a protest against the increase of ferry fares so much as a protest of the Government's handling of public affairs generally.[26] It seems however paradoxical that the protest had formally little to do with anti-colonialism. Neither communist ideology nor anti-colonialism played any significant role in the 1966-67 events. Furthermore, the feeling of impermanance and rootlessness, as derived from an uncertain colonial status, was not prominent among the young people involved in the disturbances. Rather it is believed that the majority of the Hong Kong people have accepted Hong Kong as a home and that they would not welcome any fundamental change in the constitutional form of the Government.[27] Nor did the communist agitation of anti-colonial feeling in the disturbances evoke any response from the majority of the members of the community. In other words, the events in 1966-67 were neither a constitutional crisis, nor an identification crisis, which are both related to an entrenched but uncertain colonial status.

---

[26] Kowloon Disturbances 1966, Report of Commission of Inquiry, Acting Government Printer, Hong Kong, 1967, pp. 109, 136.

[27] Ibid, pp. 125-127, 141.

Nor was the 1966-67 crisis a participation crisis in theoretical terms. Apart from the conceptual ambiguity, a participation crisis must presuppose a significant proportion of the population becoming increasingly oriented towards a participant culture while being denied appropriate avenues for externalization. It is true that there was in the '60s a general lack of structure for political participation, it is however equally true that existing channels were insufficiently used if not unknown. The assumption of an increase in participant culture can not be borne out by survey findings of the day or later periods.[28] The political culture of the younger generation is particularly relevant to the present discussion, for in end effect they were the dominant participants in the 1966 riot. A survey of university students in the spring of 1967 reports: "Unless they follow the example of radical students abroad, their demands on the system will be small and satisfied by decent jobs, relative status, and a nominal opportunity to participate if they choose."[29]

As to the notion of an integration crisis, the concept suffers an even greater degree of ambiguity. Even if one can agree that the meaning of integration primarily denotes value consensus, concerted actions and a sense of solidarity, there is still much room left for debate on matters of scope, degree, and substance. In the present context, the burden of proof lies with the theorists of integration crisis, who must first account for the fact that the people in Hong Kong commonly share with each other stability and prosperity as their highest values, generally cooperate with the government not because of the threat of punishment for non-compliance, and feel that all are equal in the face of crisis.[30]

---

28 J.S. HOADLEY, "Hong Kong is the Life Boat. Notes on Political Culture and Socialization", in: Journal of Oriental Studies, Vol. VIII, 1970, pp. 206-218; Ambrose Y.C. KING, The Political Culture of Kwun Tong, A Chinese Community in Hong Kong, Social Research Centre, Chinese University of Hong Kong, 1972.

29 J.S. HOADLEY, ibid., p. 218.

30 Regrettably, the 1966 riot has never been subject to closer scrutiny, despite its significance to the political development in Hong Kong. Interpretations have been quite often presented as by-products of research works designed for totally different purposes.

The 1966-67 crisis was, certainly, a trust crisis. With due allowance for the inadequacy of communication structures, it has been submitted that they existed but were barely utilized.[31] Apparently, what matters as a rule in politics is not so much what the structures are but rather the political mind which determines the introduction and utilization of structures. The colonial status has given rise to a political mind which has separated the people from the Government. The public could not believe that a foreign Government, i.e. a Crown Colony with appointed expatriates using English as the official language in governing, could genuinely care about the common Chinese on the street. The Government apparently did not care to tell the people what it thought and what it did knowing that the Chinese, living as they were under a colonial rule, would in any case remain skeptical or unthankful vis-à-vis the Government. Trust in Government is indeed an anomaly to colonialism. To the extent, however, that colonialism has become less salient in the practical politics of Hong Kong, youths can stand up to demand from the Government positive evidence of care, while the Government can respond more positively to the needs and aspirations of the man on the street.

The stake was thus neither democracy, nor participation. Every brand of politics has some essential factors for its effective functioning. For democracy there is the informed and educated citizenry that is given the right to participate in politics but which chooses not to exercise it often so as not to impair the efficient operation of the Government.[32] For communist politics, there is the integrity and dedication of the cadres who strive towards the utopian millenium. The Hong Kong brand of politics has relied in the past on a certain measure of confidence and understanding between a benevolent Government and cooperative social-economic elites. But since 1966-67, the stability and prosperity of Hong Kong must depend on universal trust in which the Government and the people cooperate to make it possible and desirable to improve life in Hong Kong.

---

31 Kowloon Disturbances 1966, Report of Commission of Inquiry, op. cit., p. 128.

32 G.A. ALMOND and S. VERBA, The Civil Culture, Princeton University Press, Princeton, 1963, concluding chapter.

IV. New Departures in Politics

The events of 1966-67 had a profound impact on Hong Kong politics in every aspect. The immediate response of the Government was to introduce a number of legal-institutional reforms, but more important changes occurred in the form of an overall policy re-orientation.

A. Legal-institutional Reforms

The legal-institutional reforms were designed to bring the Government and the people closer to each other by a greater degree of decentralization of administration and by an improvement in communication structures.

The decentralization of administration was to be accomplished by the establishment of the City District Officer (C.D.O.) scheme. Beginning in February 1968, Hong Kong was divided into ten districts with an administrative grade officer responsible for the welfare of the locality as affected by the overall policy of the central government. These officers have a wide range of duties. They are (1) to supplement with personal explanation Government's output of information through the mass communication media; (2) to advise on public opinion and local needs; (3) to arouse the interest and the participation of residents in the affairs of their district; and (4) to help individuals with their personal problems. In the words of the Secretary for Chinese Affairs, the aim of the scheme is "to superimpose on the functionally orientated executive departments a geographically based advisory and co-ordinating organization in order to strengthen the ability of the Government to give everyone a fair hearing and a fair share of the services which the community can afford."[33]

The scheme, as it is practised in the Kwun Tong District, has been evaluated as "fairly successful" in playing the boundary role between

---

33 The City District Officer Scheme, Report by the Secretary for Chinese Affairs, 24th January, 1969, p. 3.

the Government and the Society, although more so in spreading information from the Government to the people than in articulating and transmitting interests from the people to the Government.[34]

In the process of improving communication structures, the existing Government Information Service (G.I.S.) has gained increasing importance since 1967. The new emphasis on information and public relations can be seen from the rocketing increase in expenditures for this purpose[35] as well as from the installation of a new public relations division within the Government Information Service in 1969 and the establishment of an Information Branch in the Colonial Secretariat and of similar units in individual departments. The Public Relations Division of the G.I.S. was established to improve understanding between the public and the Government by all possible means.[36] In practice, this unit is devoted to collecting and transmitting to the Government public attitudes expressed in the mass media. It undertakes periodic reviews of the press, especially those in Chinese, and distributes them to senior officers in the Government.[37] It also monitors citizens' complaints and demands in the correspondence columns of newspapers and passes them on to the individual departments concerned with reply.[38]

Apart from the introduction and expansion of communication channels in the Government, a traditional barrier between the Government and the people was to a certain degree removed in early 1968 by the Government's policy of "as near equality of use and status as is practically possible" for the two languages, i.e. English and Chinese

---

[34] Ambrose Y.C. KING, The Administrative Absorption of Politics in Hong Kong, With Special Emphasis on City District Officer Scheme, Social Research Centre, Chinese University of Hong Kong, May 1973, pp. 29-30.

[35] The expenditure rose from 4.6 millions in 1967-68 to 27.1 millions in 1976-77; Hong Kong 1969, Report for the Year 1968, Appendix VII, item No. 39 and Hong Kong 1977, Report for the Year 1976, Chinese Version, Appendix 8, item on public relations.

[36] Annual Departmental Report, 1969, Director of Information Services, Hong Kong Government Printer, 1969, p. 5.

[37] Distribution figures are 120 officers in 1969-70, 160 in 1970-71, 180 in 1971-72, no data for 1972-73, 200 in 1973-74; Annual Departmental Reports, Director of Information Services; The Government Information Service ceased to publish its Annual Departmental Report as from 1973-74 on.

in official business. The policy of replying in Chinese to letters received in Chinese was emphasized with the added instruction that "all public notices, forms, warnings, and other documents requiring attention by people who may not understand English should be treated in the same way".[39] In 1974, the Government responded to public demand by legalizing Chinese as an official language.

The Government's efforts at improving its relationship with the public was soon rivaled by the unofficial members of the Executive and Legislative Councils. After 1967 an old office of the unofficials, which had been set up in August 1963 to link the unofficials with the general public[40] but with little administrative success, became the subject of re-organization for the purpose of political communication. The Office (known as UMELCO) was not, however, significantly strengthened until May 1970 when a staff grade administrative officer was seconded by the Government. Since then, there is evidence that indicates the greater willingness of the public to bring their complaints to the Office as well as the increasing effectiveness of the Office in assisting the public.[41]

---

[38]The reply figures are 1,225 in 1969-70, 1,071 in 1970-71, 1,000 in 1971-72 respectively; Annual Departmental Reports, op. cit., see the remark in the above note.

[39]General Circular of the Colonial Secretariat of 30th March, 1968, as quoted in The Second Report of the Chinese Language Committee by the Chinese Language Committee, April 1971, Hong Kong Government Printer, 1971, p. 2.

[40]It received only 14 cases of citizen's complaints on average per month in 1966.

[41]Figures of complaints dealt with by UMELCO are tabled as follows:

	New Cases	No Further Action	Completed Cases
1970/71	834	158	492
1971/72	1,208	347	825
1972/73	1,689	382	1,249
1973/74	2,812	604	2,064
1974/75	3,115	819	2,358
1975/76	3,304	797	2,514

Source: Annual Report of the UMELCO, Hong Kong, 25/1976, Appendix 4.

B. Policy Re-orientation

It becomes apparent from the preceding section on legal-institutional reforms that the Hong Kong Government has changed substantially in its policy orientation. To cite a few alterations, one can note the adoption of a grass roots approach to supplement elitist politics, a greater awareness of individual welfare, the active pursuit of community involvement and finally the attempt to implement an active role in social change.

The events of 1966-67 have encouraged the emergence of an attitude within the administration that is oriented towards the public. This iniative was provided by the Governor himself who, in the summer of 1967, instructed the departments to take "proper account of the present situation and further, in re-examining their duties, to place prime importance on their contact with the public at large."[42]

Such a public-oriented attitude is particularly significant when it is evaluated in the context of past Government attitudes towards unofficial members as representatives of the public as well as Government perceptions as to the nature of public opinion. The nature and the scope of the public certainly remain ambiguous and even mystical to the Government. It is clear, however, that the Hong Kong Government will no longer depend on the elites alone for policy making but will endeavour to go to the grass roots by taking as many individuals into consideration as possible. Traditional contacts with elites and established organizations (such as the Tung Wah Hospital Group) definitely remain indispensable, for no government can maintain contact with everyone in the public. Of significance, however, was the recognition that these traditional contacts do not necessarily reach the poorer people or those well-to-do people who are not interested in public activities or public life, and the Government has made a start to reach these people, too.[43]

As a result of the grass roots approach in public policy, the Government has realized the importance of welfare care for the individual

---

[42] Hong Kong Hansard, 1967, p. 377.

[43] City District Officer Scheme, op. cit., pp. 12-13.

member of public. Such a new departure is evident in an address before the Legislative Council by the then Governor Sir David Trench on the 1st of October 1971, in which he underlined: "For many years since the war, we have had to concern ourselves primarily with meeting needs of an urgent, basic nature: mass problems, which had to be met with massive solutions, and which left few resources available for anything else. I believe that we can now turn our attention increasingly to rather more specialized and personal problems, and pay more attention to individual rather than to mass needs".[44]

Personalized care given to the public has been reflected not only in the above mentioned activities of the Public Relations Division of the G.I.S. and those of UMELCO, which are targeted towards individual complaints and problems; but it has also been reflected in the increase of Government expenditure on social services and in active planning for the future. In 1976-77 the Government spent about eight times more on social services, i.e. education, medical and health, housing, social welfare and labour, than it did in 1967-68.[45] Probably more important than what the figures of expenditure illustrate is the intention of the Government to plan for a better quality of life in Hong Kong in the future. In the words of the Annual Report of Hong Kong for 1970, "the task that lies ahead now is to ensure that the efforts of both the community and the Government are used in the properly planned and common objective of raising the social benefits and standards of living for all and of making Hong Kong a better place in which to live."[46]

---

44 Hong Kong Hansard, 1971, p. 3.

45 The figures are as follows:

Government Expenditure on Social Services
(in Millions of HK dollars)

	1967-68	1976-77
Education	289.3	1,376.0
Medical & Health	166.9	630.7
Housing	41.5	396.1
Social Welfare	20.8	422.1
Labour	4.0	18.7
Total	356.5	2,733.3

Sources: Hong Kong 1969, Report for the Year 1968, Appendix 7, and Hong Kong 1977, Report for the Year 1976, Appendix 8.

46 Hong Kong 1971, Report for the Year 1970, p. 20.

It should be recalled that planning is an anomaly to a "borrowed place in borrowed time" and that the Government was formerly complacently satisfied with a policy that was laissez-faire in every aspect. The fact that the Government now has departed from the traditional free market model to a policy of planning and intervention has been deplored by some scholars.[47] It should be emphasized, however, that the public policy of the Hong Kong Government has become differentiated and cannot be fit into any analysis of an ideal type or model. It is only in the wide field of social services that the Government has started to plan and to intervene. The most alarming development to the admirers of laissez-faire policy lies with the labour legislation. There have been approximately 110 items dealing with labour legislation since 1967, of which the Labour Relations Ordinance may be the most important among them. This ordinance gives the Government the right to intervene in trade disputes so that efforts can be made to defuse potentially damaging situations.[48]

---

47 E.g. Alvin RABUSHKA, The Changing Face of Hong Kong, New Departures in Public Policy, Ch. 5, (Hoover Institution on War, Revolution and Peace, Stanford University), Stanford, Calif., 1973.

48 There is still no case of compulsory intervention. The Government prefers to convince the industrial establishments to set up joint consultation machinery to improve industrial relations and to mediate in industrial grievances brought to its attention. To accomplish the first task, a post of labour adviser on industrial relations was created in 1968. Despite these efforts, employers remain reluctant to buy the concept of joint consultation. On the other hand, the Labour Department has quite successfully played the role of mediator in the settlement of industrial grievances, as the following table illustrates:

Labour Grievances dealt with by the Labour Relations Service

Year	Major Grievances (claims of HK$ 1,500 or over)	Minor Grievances (claims of less then HK$ 1,500)
1964	233	1,748
1965-66	370	1,926
1966-67	388	2,200
1967-68	475	2,618
1968-69	488	2,783
1969-70	592	2,780
1970-71	615	3,580
1971-72	848	3,846
1972-73	842	3,593
1973-74	1,084	4,034
1974-75	1,712	4,973
1975+	1,759	4,992

In other policy areas, the Government has tried to provide compensatory services for those less privileged. The ten year housing programme announced in 1972 promises to provide public housing for an additional 1.5 million people by 1982, by which time about half of the population will live in low-rent homes built by public funds. The five year plan for social welfare development in Hong Kong 1973-78 (which accompanied the white paper on "Social Welfare - The Way Ahead" of 1973) seeks to facilitate the maximum expansion of services that are considered realistic and feasible in those priority areas. The ten year plan on medical and health services announced in December 1973 intends to raise the ratio of hospital beds per 1,000 persons from 3.5 in 1973 to 4.05 by 1982 through the construction of three new public hospitals and the subsidization of private clinics. The 10 year education programme of October 1974 proclaims to provide subsidized education to every child of school age for nine years. All these programmes form an impressive catalogue of Government efforts at compensatory social services which are second to none, at least in Asia, when due allowance is made for the persistent policy of keeping the standard salary tax at only 15 percent.

In addition to the development of a grass roots approach and a welfare orientation, the Government's attitude towards political participation has also changed. In the past, only social-economic elites were encouraged to play an active role in public affairs. Participation by the masses was regarded as dangerous to the political stability of Hong Kong due to the ideological fragmentation inherent in a society of immigrants. The events in 1966-67, however, demonstrated the rise of a new generation of people who regard Hong Kong as their home and possess increasing expectations with regard to the Government. Strong views were enunciated within the administration as to the necessity for a positive policy that would help people overcome the defeatist complex, resulting from the uncertain status of the Colony, and direct public energies into appropriate channels of participation in public affairs. In the words of the Secretary for Chinese Affairs: "The defeatist attitude to our

---

[+] Since 1975, computation covers the calender year instead of the financial year as in previous reports. (continued from page 161)

<u>Source</u>: Statistics and other information mentioned on previous page can be consulted from the Annual Departmental Reports of the Labour Department.

political status as a Colony is to say that since we cannot develop a Hong Kong nationalism or patriotism we can only fall back on promotion of materialistic progress and hope that this will act as a substitute. This attitude overlooks the great potential of emotional and altruistic energy that such a young population is bound to have. I believe the C.D.O. scheme can help to find channels through which this energy can be directed to the good of Hong Kong. I am not concerned so much with finding a label like civic pride to be a substitute for patriotism as to find ways in which people, particularly young people, can find an outlet for energy directed at improving the lot of those who live here."[49]

As a result thereof, activities were mounted to encourage participation in public affairs by local activists and youths. Of great significance was the development of a community involvement plan in 1972, with a view to mobilizing community participation in local affairs. Under the district officer scheme, area committees with approximately 45,000 people each were set up in every district in order to mobilize residents to participate in policy implementation campaigns, such as the Keep Hong Kong Clean campaign in November 1972. In June 1973, mutual aid committees were launched to organize residents in public estates to participate in the fight against violent crime. The committees proved themselves to be very useful and have subsequently become permanent grass roots organizations with a potential to extend their functions into other areas. (To gain a feeling of the seriousness of Government concern with the idea of community involvement, it is worthwhile to mention that the Department of Home Affairs devoted more than half of its staff to implement the Keep Hong Kong Clean campaign in 1972, this being the first mass campaign in Hong Kong's history).

---

[49] The City District Officer Scheme, Report by the Secretary for Chinese Affairs, Hong Kong, 24th January, 1969, p. 18. The Chinese version of the report speaks even of an intellectual exodus for the public based on the serving spirit of the young, p. 28. In another context, the Working Party on Local Administration had already urged in November 1966, that the uncertainty of the Colony's future "would not appear to constitute a valid argument against providing participation in local affairs". Report of the Working Party on Local Administration, November 1966, Acting Government Printer, Hong Kong, p. 6.

Citizens' participation in public policy since 1967 has primarily been confined to the implementation stage. At the input stage, however, a new system of Green Papers was devised in 1972 to invite public views on proposed Government policies.[50] Though the effectiveness of the system has not yet been subject to study, a warning has been issued that Government's stimulation of public views may create frustration and alienation in cases where the Government cannot afford to accommodate the public views thus endangering the basis of the entire colonial regime.[51]

Apart from the grass roots approach, the planned-welfare orientation, and the active interest in citizen participation, there has been an even more profound change in public policy since 1966-67, which is implied in the catchword "Quiet Revolution" used by the Governor in connection with a new anti-corruption policy. In his annual report to the Legislative Council in 1973, Sir MacLehose announced that "the Government is determined that the problem should now be tackled along lines very different to those of the past. The condition for success is nothing short of a quiet revolution in our society."[52]

In essence, this policy reflects the determination of the Government to eradicate corruption in Hong Kong with new ways and means. Following the enactment of a new Ordinance for the Prevention of Bribery in 1970, an Independent Commission Against Corruption was set up in 1973 in the midst of a social movement against corruption. The relevance of the corruption issue to political development in Hong Kong has been highlighted by the thesis that the basis of political legitimacy and integration is changing from a power-centered one to an authority-centered one.[53]

---

50 The first was on social welfare, followed by those on education and on medical services in 1973.

51 See N.J. MINERS, op. cit., p. 201.

52 Hong Kong Hansard, 1973, p. 151.

53 Peter N.S. LEE,"Police Corruption and Elite Mass Integration in Hong Kong: A Developmental Perspective,"paper presented to the 3rd meeting on "Bureaucratic Behaviour (Asia)" at Singapore, November 22-26, 1977.

The significance of the problem of corruption and its solution lies not with the Government's efforts to investigate, prosecute and prevent corruption (which is common to anti-corruption agencies in any other country), but with its long-term attempt to re-educate the society, in which corruption, such as the giving of tea-money and commercial kickbacks, has long been gracefully tolerated and widely practiced. The Government is now determined to clean up not only its own house but the society as well. It is striving to do so through efforts to re-mould public attitudes towards corruption in general and to convince the private sector to follow the same ethical standards as are promulgated within the public sector. The Government of Hong Kong has in fact assumed the positive role of an agent for change in social and political development. This constitutes a very fundamental departure in public policy from the style in previous years. The entreprise is formidable indeed and the prospect for success is fraught with innumerable difficulties. But there is at least an attempt.

V. Conclusions

This paper has given a brief account of the extent to which the political picture of Hong Kong has been changed within the entrenched legal-institutional framework of a Crown colony. The past preoccupation of the Government with the social-economic elites has been compensated for by a growing concern for the man in the street; the idea of a "minimal government", whose primary task is to provide an infrastructure for economic profits in a short time, has been supplemented by the idea of an active government which improves the quality of life for all. In sum, the traditional policy of laissez-faire has been skilfully changed to a policy of "discreet quidance".[54]

---

[54] The term is from Richard HUGHES, the author of "Hong Kong: Borrowed Place - Borrowed Time", who has timely recognized the changes that have taken place since the publication of his famous book. In a contribution to the annual report of Hong Kong 1976, he remarks: "To look back, there were once two ancient cliche references to Hong Kong: 'Laissez-faire' and 'resilience'. They have now been reduced to one. 'Laissez-faire' has been skilfully and pragmatically changed to 'discreet guidance'; it remains to be seen whether 'resilience' will endure. The odds are in favour." Hong Kong 1976, Report for the Year 1975, p. 9.

These changes were made possible by two fundamental facts: first, that Hong Kong was given much room for autonomous action by Chinese tolerance and British withdrawal; and second, that the society has, by means of the events in 1966-67, given the Government the impetus for a cognitive breakthrough. With these changes in progress, a new pattern of relationships between the Government and the people is bound to arise. Is it not time to think afresh of politics in Hong Kong?

RECENT TRENDS IN GOVERNMENT
AND INDUSTRY RELATIONSHIPS IN HONG KONG

Louis Nthenda

I. Introduction

The economic philosophy of the Hong Kong Government is said to be that of free enterprise and free trade. One consequence of this philosophy is that the Government is said to restrict itself to the provision of infrastructural facilities either directly or indirectly through cooperation with public utilities and autonomous organizations. Beyond such provision, there is a qualified and very much restricted presence of Government. This qualified presence seems to be felt in two ways. On the one hand, it is said that the Government does not protect or subsidize manufacturers; on the other, the Government is said to operate a "minimum" of internal and external controls on manufactures, imports, and exports. Again, the Government is reported to have no central planning machinery and no central plan and as a consequence of this, it has no voice in determining or influencing the pattern of industry and trade. It is, nevertheless, pointed out that the lack of centralized planning does not mean that the Government does not intervene; the Government certainly does but only in response to overriding economic and social events.[1]

Already, there are far too many qualifications to these statements. The Government is said to be pursuing a less doctrinaire policy in recent years. Departments have embarked on producing long term plans and the Government is applying an increasing number of regulatory measures.[2] The picture of a nineteenth century liberal political economy becomes blurred with so many qualifications that it is no longer possible to produce any meaningful generalizations

---

1 N.J. MINERS, The Government and Politics of Hong Kong, Oxford University Press, 1975, pp. 43-45, also N.C. OWEN, "Economic Policy in Hong Kong", in:Keith HOPKINS (ed.), Hong Kong, The Industrial Colony, Oxford University Press, 1975, pp. 155-156.

2 MINERS, op. cit., p. 45. The 1975-76 Budget Speech (Government Printer, Hong Kong), p. 1, note 1, has this to say about the organization of current estimates: "the ... year's revenue and

about Hong Kong's traditional economic philosophy.

This study starts from the point of view that free trade and free competition are not inconsistent with Government intervention. Instead of trying to establish the extent to which Government does or does not interfere with private enterprise, an approach which has severe limitations because it requires far too many qualifications, the present study is designed to show the extent of Government penetration into economic organizations, the kinds of controls and the type of organizational relationships associated with such controls. It should therefore be possible to empirically draw the parameters of the public sector in Hong Kong which will put the relationships between Government and Industry into proper perspective.

II. Public Bodies

The boundaries that describe the public sector are not clear cut. One can describe them in terms either of institutions or of methods of control. The institutional boundaries, though easier to describe, are, nevertheless, always in a state of flux.

A United Nations publication has described the institutional forms in which the public sector manifests itself as being the Government department, the public corporation, the mixed ownership corporation and the operating contract.[3]

To what extent are these forms of public enterprise manifest in Hong Kong? In drawing the institutional parameters of the public sector in Hong Kong one should perhaps begin by examining two ordinances in which an attempt has been made to define the term "public body". The difficulty of defining the term is compounded by the fact that the definition is purely declaratory and the lists under the two ordinances are not identical.

---

expenditure estimates, set in the context of a forecast of revenue and expenditure in the following three years, set in the context of an order of cost of projected capital works over a ten year period."

[3] United Nations, Some Problems in the Organization and Administration of Public Enterprises in the Industrial Field, New York, 1954, ch. 1.

In the Interpretation and General Clauses Ordinance the term "public body" is given as meaning

a) the Executive Council,
b) the Legislative Council,
c) the Urban Council,
d) any other urban, rural or municipal council,
e) any department of the Government,
f) any undertaking by or of the Government.[4]

At present, except for the Urban Council, there are no other urban, rural or municipal councils. There are in fact no local government institutions in Hong Kong. Administratively there is only one tier of government to deal with, and the public sector must therefore define the ramifications of this tier alone. The Executive, Legislative and Urban Councils are political institutions and their analysis is excluded from this study, whose emphasis is on the public sector as administrative machinery. This leaves two categories on the list: the Government department and the Government undertaking.

In the Prevention of Bribery Ordinance, the term "public body" is defined as

a) the Government,
b) the Executive Council,
c) the Legislative Council,
d) the Urban Council,
e) any board, commission, committee or other body, whether paid or unpaid, appointed by or on behalf of the Governor or the Governor-in-Council; and
f) any board, commission, committee or other body specified in the Schedule.[5]

Again, excluding the Executive, Legislative and Urban Councils, three categories relating to administrative agencies remain: the Government, appointed bodies, other bodies specified in the Schedule to the Ordinance. This list covers a wider area than that under the Interpretation and General Clauses Ordinance. But above all,

---

[4] The Interpretation and General Clauses Ordinance, ch. 1, sect. 2.

[5] The Prevention of Bribery Ordinance, ch. 201, sect. 2.

the most interesting category, from the point of view of drawing the institutional boundaries of the public sector in Hong Kong, is the Scheduled bodies. There are about forty of these bodies at present and the list is being added to from time to time.[6] Does this Schedule mark the institutional boundary of the public sector in Hong Kong?

The primary purpose of the schedule is to extend the application of the Prevention of Bribery Ordinance to the employees of the organizations mentioned on the grounds that such employees are "public servants". At first glance, there seems to be no rhyme or reason why employees of most of these organizations should be regarded as public servants. Most of the organizations do not fit into the United Nations types of public enterprise: none is a Government department, a few are public corporations, a couple are mixed ownership corporations, and none is an operating contract. Many of them are wholly privately owned, publicly quoted companies. Others are wholly privately operated charities. Yet there is a compelling reason why Government imposes public service ethics upon these enterprises.

There are enterprises in any country which may be described as natural monopolies; that even if such enterprises were run wholly privately, they would gravitate towards monopolistic or oligopolistic market forms. There are also enterprises whose activities cannot be conducted without necessarily interfering with citizens' property rights. Employees of such enterprises would require regular access to private premises; projects might involve the compulsory purchase of some citizen's property; it might be necessary to break up public highways in the course of carrying out work in furtherance of private interest. Such enterprises as gas supply, telephone services, railways, electricity supply, waterworks and sewage are natural monopolies and, in addition, would interfere with property rights and public highways. Pipes, cables, rails have to be laid or repaired. In most countries most of these utilities are operated either by local authorities or as public corporations. In Hong Kong,

---

[6] The Prevention of Bribery Ordinance, ch. 201, Schedule.

the Kowloon-Canton Railway and the Post Office are ordinary Government departments. All other utilities are private sector companies. This special characteristic means that such enterprises require Government backing when their operations necessarily interfere with citizens' legitimate property rights. In Hong Kong the Government has extended protection by conferring upon such enterprises _de jure_ monopoly status. Such monopolies come under various schemes of control, generally referred to in Hong Kong administration as franchises. They are concessionary companies. But even this generalization does not mean that the forms of control are uniform.

There are twelve concessionary companies in Hong Kong: China Light and Power Company, China Motor Bus Company, Hong Kong and China Gas Company, The Cross-Harbour Tunnel Company, Hong Kong and Yaumati Ferry Company, Hong Kong Electric Company, Hong Kong Telephone Company, Hong Kong Tramways Limited, Kowloon Motor Bus Company, Peak Tramways Limited, "Star" Ferry Company, Cable and Wireless Ltd. and Television Broadcasts Ltd.[7] Hong Kong Commercial Broadcasting Company and Taxicabs operate on a concessionary basis but are not listed as public bodies. These power, communications and transport utilities are _de jure_ monopolies established and operated by private entrepreneurs. In exchange for their _de jure_ monopoly status, the Government imposes four types of general restrictions.

There is generally a restriction on the level of dividends paid out to shareholders. There is no uniform percentage. It may be 13 1/2 % as in the case of China Light and Power Company,[8] or 15 % as in the case of China Motor Bus Company, or 16 % as in the case of Hong Kong Telephone Company.[9] Even the basis of calculating the level of dividends is not uniform. The Telephone Company's is calculated on the basis of 16 % of shareholders fund (i.e. the amount of capital actually subscribed). The percentage for the other companies is on the basis of average net fixed assets during the year. The Telephone Company's share profits are more like interest than dividend.

---

7 Ibid.

8 'Scheme of Control', _Fedacards_ (Far Eastern Data Service, Hong Kong).

9 'Profit Control Scheme', _Fedacards_ (Far Eastern Data Service, Hong Kong); _The Telephone Ordinance_, ch. 269.

The Government further imposes a restriction on the cost of services charged to the public: that is, Government approval is required before the Companies impose fares or other charges upon the consumer.

A third general restriction is that these Companies must maintain a Development Fund into which surplus funds are paid or, in the case of shortfalls, from which transfers can be made.

A fourth restriction is the payment of royalties, or permit fees to the Government in addition to ordinary taxes. Here again there is no uniformity. In the case of the Hong Kong and Yaumati Ferry Company, for instance, the amount of royalty was 25 % per annum of net operating profit. The Government waived the payment of royalties by the Hong Kong and Yaumati Ferry Company until 1979, the year the old concession was due to expire. Similar temporary waivers were applied to the "Star" Ferry Company, the Kowloon Motor Bus Company, the China Motor Bus Company and the Hong Kong Tramways in order to increase their profitability without raising fares.[10] The Cross Harbour Tunnel Company on the other hand pays 12 1/2 % of gross operating receipts.[11] Thus, not only the percentage but also the basis of calculation differs. The Hong Kong Tramways used to pay a royalty of 23 1/8 % of net profit[12] whereas the Peak Tramways still pays a permit fee for Crown land on an ascending scale calculated not on the basis of profit but on total amount of tolls; 5 % per annum on the first HK$ 700,000 of tolls; 10 % per annum on excess over HK$ 700,000.[13]

The Government has imposed additional restrictions on concessionary companies. In some cases, Government has placed restrictions on the Company's source of supply, as in the case of the Kowloon Motor Bus Company whose buses must be British made. Another type of restriction refers to Government representation on the Board of Directors. The Government is represented on the Board of the Hong Kong Telephone Company by a director appointed by the Governor. In other cases, the Government prescribes the nationality of the directorate, the management and administrative staff. In the case of the Hong Kong Telephone Company, all these three categories of staff must be

---

10 Hong Kong and Yaumati Ferry Company (Services) Ordinance, ch. 266.

11 The Cross-Harbour Tunnel Company Ordinance, ch. 203.

12 Tramway Ordinance, ch. 107.

British; in the case of the Hong Kong and Yaumati Ferry Company, "an effective majority" of staff in these three categories must be British.[14]

The Government promotes trade and industry through another group of public bodies which may be classified here as promotional agencies. One of these agencies was formed by Government jointly with a trade association, i.e. The Hong Kong Tourist Association.[15] The others are entirely Government promotional agencies which work closely with trade and manufacturing associations: the Hong Kong Productivity Council[16] and the Trade Development Council[17] are the two most active statutory bodies. The Tourist Association is a joint enterprise in finance, organization and operation, though the Government bears a major financial responsibility than the trade associations involved.

There are three public corporations as that term is understood in the British sense and in the sense in which it is used in the United Nations document referred to above: These are the Hong Kong Export Credit Insurance Corporation,[18] the Mass Transit Railway Corporation,[19] and the Hong Kong Industrial Estates Corporation. All these are statutory bodies, owned 100 % by Government, and carrying out commercial activities. This marks a definite departure from a laissez-faire policy and in the case of the last two corporations, the Government finds itself in something of a competitive market. The activities of the two corporations are bound to have an impact upon private entrepreneurs in the transport and property development sectors. In the words of the Financial Secretary, however, Government enters these and other activities because private entrepreneurs seem unwilling to take up the challenge. The grounds for this fear on the part of the private sector are not the same in every case although none of them has to do with profitability. As matters stand at present, there is no provision for future participation by the general public. This contrasts sharply with the following two mixed enterprise corporations.

---

[13] Peak Tramway Ordinance, ch. 265.

[14] See the relevant Ordinances quoted above.

[15] Tourist Association Ordinance, ch. 302.

[16] Productivity Council Ordinance, ch. 1116.

In 1964, on Government initiative, the Hong Kong Building and Loan Agency was formed to make mortgage finance at reasonable interest rates to prospective owner-occupiers of flats in the middle-income bracket. Government invited the Commonwealth Development Corporation - a British public corporation - the Hong Kong and Shanghai Banking Corporation, the Bank of East Asia, the Chartered Bank and the Hang Seng Bank to participate in the enterprise. In 1972, one million shares of $ 5 each were offered to the general public at $ 15 per share. Similarly in 1974, another mixed Government-private enterprise, the Cross-Harbour Tunnel Company, originally established in 1965 with Government, Wheelock Marden and Company, Hutchison International, Hong Kong and Shanghai Banking Corporation as major shareholders, offered 25 % of its issued capital to the public in accordance with its concession provisions.

Two sectors in which the Government has complete control are the local fishing industry through the Fish Marketing Organization,[20] and the local market gardening through the Vegetable Marketing Organization.[21] These two organizations have been the instruments of Government control since the War. The basic unit of commercial marketing enterprise in the two sectors is the Government-initiated co-operative, as the Government would like to preserve and foster the small-scale fisherman and the small-scale market gardener. These marketing organizations, therefore, run mainly by Government officials, own the wholesale markets and control the export and import of marine fish and agricultural products. With 75 % of the employees on Government payroll, these organizations should perhaps be classified quasi-departments of Government.

There are other organizations which are not listed in the Schedule but are important instruments of Government regulation of certain sectors of private enterprise. The organizations are entirely Government. Such organizations as the Office of the Commissioner for Securities and the Office of the Commissioner for Banking were set

---

[17] _Trade Development Council Ordinance_, ch. 1114.

[18] _Export Credit Insurance Ordinance_, ch. 1115.

[19] _Mass Transit Railway Ordinance_, ch. 270.

[20] _Marine Fish (Marketing) Ordinance_, ch. 291.

[21] _Agricultural Products (Marketing) Ordinance_, ch. 277.

up specifically for control[22] purposes unlike the 150 or so boards and commissions which are in the main advisory, consisting of nominated, part-time, mostly unpaid members. Most of these advisory bodies act as important bridges between the Government and certain sectors of industry, e.g. the Textiles Advisory Board which, *inter alia*, helps the Government in the negotiation and administration of international agreements.

This last point brings up certain external factors. A great deal of international trade is conducted within the framework of bilateral and international agreements and of a variety of export and import quotas and other restrictions. This necessarily increases Government activity in economic affairs in spite of a laissez-faire philosophy. The Government has to participate in the negotiation and administration of the Multi-Fibre Agreement, of export quotas into the European Economic Community, United States, Canada, Sweden and other countries. The Government has to attempt to secure markets for Hong Kong goods in as many countries as possible. The responsibility for securing these markets is becoming as much a Government responsibility as it is that of industry. No longer can the Government stand aside without abdicating the right to rule in the modern world. The realities dictate otherwise.

III. Government Controls

In his Budget Speech in 1977, the Financial Secretary said: "We do not believe that market forces will always operate efficiently without guidance and even the existence of legal constraints."[23] He went on to list five kinds of regulatory controls. These were controls of profits and charges of the non-competitive sector of the economy, controls of the banking sector, of other financial institutions, and of the securities market.

Most of these controls are carried out through specific institutions or through specific legal instruments. Other forms of control are non-specific: they are the consequences of general policies.

[22]See note 23.

[23]*The 1977-78 Budget Speech* (Government Printer, Hong Kong), p. 20.

The first group of controls relates to concessionary companies which have already been dealt with in the section on public bodies. As for the banking sector, these are administered by the Office of the Commissioner for Banking. Similarly, the securities market falls under the control of the Commissioner for Securities, the Insider Dealing Tribunal and self-regulating mechanisms called the Code on Takeovers and Mergers and Code on Unit Trusts and Mutual Funds.

In the same speech, the Financial Secretary pointed out that the philosophy of intervention was coupled with a view that Government had certain obligations; that, for example, Government budgetary and fiscal policies had monetary consequences linked to the foreign exchange of the Hong Kong dollar. Such consequences necessitated the Government having "a deliberate, if limited, policy" of intervention in the foreign exchange market.[24]

The Government also organized business services in default of the private sector. Such was the Government's rationale in establishing the Export Credit Insurance Corporation, the Productivitiy Council, the Trade Development Council. In addition, the Government subsidized many trade organizations established by private industry, e.g. the Shippers' Council, the Design and Packaging Council and the Management Association.[25]

But above all, Government's increasing influence on industry can be gauged from recent policy directions. These policies have two general effects. First, they have a discriminatory effect as between sectors and types of industry; and second, through these policies, the Government deliberately distorts factor prices, i.e. the cost of land, labour, capital and enterprise, which, in the particular circumstances in which such policies operate, do not reflect the free market demand-supply relationship.

There are five Government policies which have discriminatory and distorting effects on industry and on factor prices:

---

[24] Ibid.

[25] Ibid., p. 22.

A. Throughout the 1970's, Government's industrial dispersal policy has been gathering momentum and is now an accepted part of Hong Kong's economic life. The transfer of populations from the crowded areas of the Kowloon peninsula to the New Towns in the New Territories has also meant Government encouragement of industry to follow the labour force and locate in these areas, though other factors of production might not be competitive. Government incentives in promoting industrial location has in the main involved discriminatory land policies. Land is cheaper and therefore competitive in the New Territories, but the Government has from time to time thrown in such extras as selling land by private treaty to certain applicants instead of the usual sale by auction. This has been the case for a chemical plant and for shipyards.[26] The Hong Kong Industrial Estates Corporation, as a Government property development, has also operated as an instrument of industrial location policy. The Corporation's property development projects are located in the New Territories to facilitate industrial establishment in a hitherto rural agricultural environment.

B. The Corporation is also an instrument for the furtherance of another recent policy of significance: that of industrial diversification. This can be said to be the main thrust of the Corporation's work at present. Recent international market trends in textiles, which are the foundation of Hong Kong's prosperity, have exposed the fragility of this foundation. Textile import restrictions in the E.C., U.S.A., Canada and Sweden, have resulted in retrenchment in production and labour in Hong Kong. Electronics, and in particular, the watch industry, have had a temperamental market. This industry is also a foundation of Hong Kong's prosperity. The uncertainties which have been generated by these events have forced the Government in the direction of having an explicit industrial diversification policy. Although the details of the policy are still in the making, the Industrial Estates Corporation has adopted the policy as its cornerstone. Thus, the kind of industrial applicant who is likely to be successful is no longer one who is going to generate employment - since labour in general is becoming scarce -

[26] Annual Report 1978, p. 13.

but rather one who will introduce new sophisticated technology or one who will produce industrial goods.[27] Thus a machine parts industrial plant and a bottle-making factory are two of the recent successful applicants.

C. The Government has increasingly been using social and environmental policies in guiding and controlling industry. Legislation restricting the employment of women and children both as to type of industrial work and as to hours of employment has helped to reduce the exploitative image of Hong Kong industry. A greater awareness of industrial pollution has led the Government to restricting certain offensive trades - tanning and certain chemical plants - to locate on Tsing Yi island. This location is also a consequence of the industrial location policy and the industrial diversification policy. The statute book now has laws against air pollution and industrial noise.[28]

D. The Government is also moving in the direction of consumer protection and increased labour welfare policies. The Consumer Council which has hitherto been an advisory body is now a statutory body, and may soon be moving beyond investigation to the establishment and enforcement of standards.

There has always been price control of basic foodstuffs in Hong Kong since the War. The organization of the rice trade, for instance, the control of reserves and of retail prices by the Government have meant adequate regular supplies of the people's staple food over the years which have seen considerable fluctuations elsewhere in Asia.[29]

E. Similarly, the Government has never waivered in promoting industry. Besides maintaining trade missions abroad, the Government arranges industrial investment promotion visits[30] to Western Europe

---

27 Annual Report 1978, p. 13.

28 Annual Report 1978, pp. 192-193.

29 MINERS, op. cit., p. 44.

30 Annual Report 1978, pp. 13 and 19.

and North America and marketing promotion visits to Africa, Latin America and Eastern Europe.

In conclusion, both external and internal factors dictate a more active role in economic affairs by Government, irrespective of a philosophy of free trade and free competition. In order to preserve that freedom, it becomes necessary to limit it.

Appendix: Public Bodies in Hong Kong

1. Cable and Wireless Limited.
2. China Light and Power Company Limited.
3. China Motor Bus Company Limited.
4. Chinese University of Hong Kong.
5. Commercial Television Limited.
6. Cross-Harbour Tunnel Company Limited.
7. Fish Marketing Organization.
8. Hong Kong and China Gas Company Limited.
9. Hong Kong and Yaumati Ferry Company Limited.
10. Hong Kong Air Cargo Terminals Limited.
11. Hong Kong Building and Loan Agency.
12. Hong Kong Commercial Broadcasting Company Limited.
13. Hong Kong Electric Company Limited.
14. Hong Kong Export Credit Insurance Corporation.
15. Hong Kong Housing Authority.
16. Hong Kong Housing Society.
17. Hong Kong Model Housing Society.
18. Hong Kong Polytechnic.
19. Hong Kong Productivity Council.
20. Hong Kong Settlers Housing Corporation Limited.
21. Hong Kong Telephone Company Limited.
22. Hong Kong Tourist Association.
23. Hong Kong Trade Development Council.
24. Hong Kong Tramways Limited.
25. Kowloon Motor Bus Company (1933) Limited.
26. Mass Transit Railway Corporation.
27. Ocean Park Limited.
28. Peak Tramways Company Limited.
29. Rediffusion Television Limited.
30. Royal Hong Kong Jockey Club.
31. Royal Hong Kong Jockey Club (Charities) Limited.
32. "Star" Ferry Company Limited.
33. Television Broadcasts Limited.
34. The Community Chest of Hong Kong.
35. University of Hong Kong.
36. Vegetable Marketing Organization.
37. The Hong Kong Industrial Estates Corporation.
38. Hong Kong Examinations Authority.
39. The Consumer Council.
40. Silver Jubilee Sports Centre Board.

Source: Schedule to Prevention of Bribery Ordinance, ch. 201.

References:

Hong Kong Annual Reports, Government Printer, Hong Kong.

Budget Speeches, Government Printer, Hong Kong, (annual).

ENGLAND, J. and J. REAR, Chinese Labour under Colonial Rule, Oxford University Press, 1975.

Fedacards, Far Eastern Data Service, Hong Kong.

GEIGER, Th. and F., Tale of Two City-States: The Development Progress of Hong Kong and Singapore, National Planning Association, Washington, D.C., 1973.

HOPKINS, K. (ed.), Hong Kong: The Industrial Colony, Oxford University Press, 1975.

Laws of Hong Kong, Government Printer, Revised Edition 1974.

MINERS, N.J., The Government and Politics of Hong Kong, Oxford University Press, 2nd ed., 1977.

RABUSHKA, A., The Changing Face of Hong Kong, American Enterprise Institute, Washington, D.C., 1973.

United Nations, Some Problems in the Organization and Administration of Public Enterprises in the Industrial Field, New York, 1954.

HOUSING DEVELOPMENT AND HOUSING POLICY IN HONG KONG

C. Y. Choi and Y. K. Chan

I. Public Housing in Hong Kong

Hong Kong is an extremely crowded metropolis. Its land area of slightly over 1,000 square kilometres is hilly, and the formation of suitable building sites is difficult in many areas. Over 77 % of the population (4.5 million in 1977) reside on the built-up areas of Hong Kong Island, Kowloon Peninsula, and New Kowloon which together constitute only 11 % of the total area of Hong Kong. Development of the New Territories had been slow until the early 1970's when it became clear that the older urban areas would be unable to absorb further population increases and industrial development. For example, in 1971, Mongkok district already had a population density of over 150,000 persons per square kilometre.

This extreme overcrowdedness of Hong Kong is the result of very rapid population growth since the Second World War. Two large scale immigration waves, roughly during 1945-47 and 1949-52, brought over one million refugees into Hong Kong. When the first post-war census was taken in 1961, Hong Kong's population size had already reached the 3 million mark. The birthrate was high, reaching a peak in the mid-1960's when yearly births exceeded 100,000 and there was a continuation of in-migration from China. In the five years between 1961 and 1966, another 600,000 were added and the population rose to 3.7 million. Although fertility began to fall significantly after 1965, the rate of growth averaged around 2.0 percent per annum. The pressure of population continued to be high on all facilities and services, particularly housing, throughout the whole period.

Hong Kong has always had a problem of housing shortage. Before the Second World War, several commissions of inquiry recommended that low cost housing be made available by the government to alleviate severe housing shortage and to improve sanitary conditions (Pryor, 1973). Although these inquiries did not give rise to concrete policies regarding government low cost housing, they nevertheless indicate that the problem was well recognized.

The post-war situation differs from the pre-war one in one critical aspect. The post-war housing problem was of an overwhelming magnitude. The hundreds of thousands of refugees setting up sheds and huts on the hillsides and on roof tops presented a problem not only of accommodation, but also of health, of fire, and of other natural disasters, as well as of public order (Podmore, 1970). So immense was the housing problem that the government after the war discarded its policy of relying upon private estate developers to provide most or all of the housing units. A Resettlement Division under the Urban Services Department was created to look into the possibility of resettling the refugees. After two disastrous fires in 1954, a Resettlement Department was set up to provide temporary but immediate housing for the 50,000 fire victims. The massive programme of resettlement began initially to provide housing for victims of natural disasters and for occupants of dangerous dwellings but later also to resettle squatters.

In 1953, the government estimated the number of squatters at around 300,000 (Hong Kong, 1956); thereafter the number increased. By 1959 there were about 500,000 squatters; in 1964 they had increased to 550,000. After 1964 the number fell to 443,000 (Hopkins, 1970). In recent years, the squatter population has continued to drop, but only slowly (33 %, 1964-1976). The 1976 Squatter Control Survey revealed that there were still 274,427 squatters (Hong Kong, 1977).

At its peak in 1964-1965, the squatters formed about 20 per cent of the metropolitan population. These figures are of great significance in view of the effort the government has already put into resettlement. In 1956, two years after the fires of 1954, 69,000 persons were resettled in government multi-storied estates. By 1964, the number of resettled persons was 544,200, and in 1968 the number of persons residing in government housing estates increased to almost 1 million. With such a large number of persons resettled, the squatter population might be expected to have declined rapidly and that by 1964 almost all squatters would have been resettled. This did not happen, and it is clear that there were new additions to the squatter group.

Unlike the situation in many cities in Southeast Asia, the squatters in Hong Kong are not migrants from rural areas. According to surveys done in the 1950s (Johnson, 1966), roughly one half of all squatters consisted of families whose heads were born in Hong Kong or had been residents in Hong Kong since 1946 or before. The demand for housing was great. 20 % of urban housing had been destroyed in World War II and private development after the War was slow until the mid 1960s. This pushed the rentals up beyond the reach of many poor families (Munder, 1969), and "many of the new migrants since the war crowded older residents out of their accommodation in tenements and took their place" (Hopkins, 1970). A survey in 1968 showed that half of the squatters interviewed were living in private tenements before they became squatters, and 45 % of these reported that they chose squatting to gain accommodation either rent free or with a low rent (Hopkins, 1970).

In 1963, a "Working Party on Government Policies and Practices with regard to Squatters and Public Housing" estimated that potentially as many as 125,000 persons might be added to the squatter population each year from various sources including natural increase.

In view of the tremendous pressure, the government accelerated its building programme of public housing. The Resettlement Department established acquired a permanent status in 1958, and immediately raised the target of rehousing 50,000 persons a year to 100,000 and planned to build resettlement blocks of higher quality. The earliest buildings in the mid-1950s were seven-storied H-shaped blocks, with communal washing and toilet facilities on each floor. The rooms varied in size from 86 square feet to 152 square feet, but most of them had 120 square feet and were designed to house families of 4 to 5 persons. Children under 10 years of age were considered half an adult. These buildings, called Marks I and II, were meant to be temporary, and construction of more of this type was suspended in 1964. Since then, in later designs known as Marks III to VI, slightly better facilities were provided, including toilets and water taps in the units. Each unit also has a private balcony for laundries and for cooking. In 1964, following the 1963 Working Party report and a subsequent White Paper, a long-term resettlement building policy was formulated. The yearly target of resettlements was raised again, to 150,000 persons a year; and in 1966, the 24 square feet per person rule was raised to 35 square feet per person.

The number of persons resettled increased rapidly. In 1964, 10 years after the first resettlement estates had been built, about half a million persons were accommodated. By 1969, five years later, over 1 million were resettled, representing about one quarter of the total Hong Kong population.

There are three other important housing agencies apart from the Resettlement Department. The one with the longest history is the Housing Society, which was established in 1951 with a low-interest government loan. The Housing Society designed its self-contained flats on the basis of 35 square feet per adult, and these flats were primarily intended for families whose income was under HK$ 400 per month. This limit was subsequently increased to HK$ 1,250 per month in 1970 and has since been raised again. It now varies according to family size and type/location of the accommodation. Primarily a private effort, the Housing Society's building programme has been slow, relative to the two other housing agencies. Nevertheless, by 1967, over 110,000 persons were housed in Housing Society flats. The flats designed by the Society are of higher quality and contain private toilets, kitchens, and balconies. (This design later served as a model for the Resettlement, Housing Authority, and Low Cost Housing estates.)

The other important housing agency, the Housing Authority, was established in 1954 with a government loan on a similar basis as the Housing Society. The management of the Authority, however, was put under the control of the Urban Council, about half of whose members are appointed by government, and half elected. Again, similar to the programme of the Housing Society, self-contained flats were designed for lower to middle income families - those earning between HK$ 500 to HK$ 900 per month, subsequently raised to HK$ 1,250 in 1970 and to HK$ 1,800 for a family of three persons to a maximum HK$ 2,600 for a family of 10 or more in 1977. Other factors, such as the degree of overcrowding and sharing, were also taken into account as criteria for tenant selection. With a larger initial government loan, the Housing Authority had a more rapidly expanding building programme, and in 1969, the Authority estates housed a total of 164,000 persons. Both the Housing Authority and the Housing Society depended on government for the allocation of sites, and the lack of suitable sites was a constant deterrent to more rapid expansion.

The Authority won the confidence of the government, and in 1962 the government made more funds available to it. Since then its building rate has increased relative to that of the Housing Society. Also in 1962 the government decided to build another type of public housing - Government Low Cost Housing - and passed the management of these estates to the Housing Authority. The Low Cost Housing estate units were designed and built by the Public Works Department and were intended to be of similar quality as the Authority units. Different from the Resettlement estates, which were intended primarily for squatters and the homeless created by natural disasters, the Low Cost Housing estates were for the lower income groups in general. In this sense, the criteria for tenancy were similar to those of the Housing Society and the Housing Authority.

By 1977, nearly two million persons were housed in various types of public housing. This was approximately 45 per cent of Hong Kong's total population, and made the public housing project of Hong Kong one of the most ambitious in all non-socialist countries.

The existence, at least until 1973, of four different public housing bodies may be seen as an indication of the lack of coordination and long-term planning for housing provision in Hong Kong. Admittedly, the urgency of the problem made it necessary for the government to accept and encourage any private agency to build low-cost units on a large scale; but the initial reluctance of the government to become the landlord of a substantial proportion of the people is another factor which led to an inability to coordinate the various efforts in a more systematic way. A Housing Board was set up in 1968 as a liaison between the various bodies; only in 1973, however, was a new Housing Department established to centralize the activities of the Resettlement Department and the Housing Authority. Even then, the Housing Society still maintained its independence. A new Housing Authority, however, was created in 1973 which advises government on all aspects of housing, including the private sector. The Housing Department is established under the new Housing Authority.

II. Location Problems and the Concept of Industrial New Towns

Almost all public housing is built as estates, that is as a cluster of buildings, housing from a few thousand to tens of thousands of people. The largest single estate in Hong Kong houses more than 100,000 persons. In the newer public housing estates, the ground floor of each building is used for commercial purposes. Market places, schools, playgrounds, social welfare agencies, banks, post offices, and other community services are also located within the estates. Consequently, sites of considerable size are needed for their construction. As the built-up urban areas were already congested, most of the estates have been built on the fringes of the urban area, on the south side of Hong Kong Island, in New Kowloon, and, more recently, in the New Territories. Much of the redistribution of population towards these areas is thus the result of the location of public housing estates; and government policies on allocating sites for this purpose will more or less determine the pattern of population distribution in Hong Kong in the future.

While many of the earlier housing projects were developed primarily as an immediate relief to housing shortages and therefore had not taken proper consideration of other social and economic aspects, such as community facilities and employment location, later projects were designed with a view to establish integrated and partly self-sufficient industrial new towns. Not only are many community facilities provided within or adjacent to public housing estates, plans for these estates often include the provision of factory sites for industrial development. The availability of a large pool of labour force in nearby estates is an added attraction to industries in these new towns.

These developments offer certain solutions to the relief of residential overcrowding and to a more rationalized location of Hong Kong's rapidly developing industries. Many small-scale industries previously located in overcrowded residential areas have been assisted in relocating in new towns. Establishements of larger-scale enterprise are also assisted because suitable sites are now available. The earlier new towns, i.e. Kwun Tong and Tsuen Wan, have now become Hong Kong's main industrial centres.

In 1972, the Government announced a ten-year housing plan to house a further 1.5 million population which, according to the Hong Kong Housing Authority, would provide "permanent self-contained accommodation, in a reasonable environment, for virtually everyone in Hong Kong" (Annual Report, 1973-74). Although some of these new housing developments would be re-developments of older estates, a large portion of it would be further development of new towns in the New Territories. Tsuen Wan New Town is expected to house about 860,000 persons, Sha Tin New Town to house 524,000 persons and Tuen Mun New Town to house 486,000 persons. Concurrent with these major developments, expansion of the market towns of Tai Po, Fanling, Shek Wu Hui and Yuen Long will take place to meet an eventual population in the region of approximately 400,000 people (Hong Kong, 1977). The projected population for these developments in the New Territories is estimated to be over 2.1 million, or more than twice the population of 1976. This population target is expected to be achieved by 1985 (Hong Kong, 1976).

A system of industrial-residential new towns is rapidly becoming the mode of living in Hong Kong. The overcrowded and appalling conditions of many older built-up residential areas guarantee a continued demand for low cost public housing. While the rent and purchase price of private dwelling units are beyond the reach of many, public housing is often the only realistic answer.

The concept of industrial new towns has emerged over a considerably long period of time in which solutions to the dual problem of residential congestion and industrial land shortages were formulated and tested. Re-development of built-up areas would not have opened up enough land for the building of sizable new towns. The necessity to build fast for a large number of people left no choice but to open up new sites. When new sites are formed, it is possible to integrate industrial and residential development planning. It is in this context that Kwun Tong, as the first planned industrial new town, was developed and will, therefore, be analysed in greater detail.

III. Kwun Tong and the Role of Housing in Its Development

Proposals for the development of Kwun Tong were made in the 1950s when the government was attempting to provide more sites for booming industry. Available land at that time was already fully occupied and industrialists urged government to take early action (Kwun Tong Today, 1975). An Inter-departmental Committee was established in 1954 and this Committee recommended Kwun Tong as the site for the first planned industrial development. There were several reasons for this choice (Y.K. Chan, 1973):

- The Kwun Tong area was a refuse dump and the 1,000 squatters could be cleared without many difficulties.

- The geological structure facilitated site formation - the hills north of Kwun Tong were badly eroded and could be levelled easily; soil excavated could be used to reclaim land from the sea.

- Being adjacent to the built-up area of Kowloon, Kwun Tong had a big advantage regarding the degree of self-sufficiency.

- Kwun Tong could be easily linked to other parts of Kowloon by an improved road system and to Hong Kong Island by sea.

The recommendations of the Inter-departmental Committee were accepted and work began in late 1954. In 1956, the government published the "Kwun Tong Development Plan" which included the goal of housing approximately 120,000 persons. The plan also provided for a commercial centre with shops, offices, schools, cinemas, markets and other public amenities, four residential areas, a public park and a swimming pool.

As industrial growth has been rapid, sites released by government were keenly sought after by industrialists. Factories and high rise factory buildings were built quickly. As early as 1958, production in some factories had already started. Up to 1971, private investment in building cost alone was estimated to be over 1,000 million HK dollars, being several times the estimated amount which government spent on reclamation and site formation (C.K. Chan, 1973). In December 1975, factories operating in Kwun Tong were employing 105,000 persons, or 15.5 % of the total Hong Kong labour force (Hong Kong, 1976).

In addition to the provision of industrial land which led to the growth of industries, another important factor in the development of Kwun Tong is the provision of public housing which provided low cost residential units for more than half a million people in the area. The construction of public housing started in 1958-59. The first was "Garden Estate", a Hong Kong Housing Society project which completed its stage-one building programme in 1960 and stage-two programme in 1966. The former Resettlement department of the government also started its building programme in Jordan Valley and Tsui Ping Road in the late 1950s.

In 1961, the Kwun Tong area, comprising Ngau Tau Kok and Lei Yu Mun census districts, had a population of 81,000. By 1966, the population had grown to 252,000, and to 553,000 by 1971. The 1976 census counted 575,000 persons in Kwun Tong, the majority living in public housing estates. In a period of less than 20 years, Kwun Tong has become a major residential complex of more than half a million people.

Although public housing building programmes appear to have reached a certain saturation point, and further development appears to be restricted to the private sector, the importance of public housing in Kwun Tong is evident; over 80 per cent of Kwun Tong's residents now live in public housing.

IV. Population Movements in Kwun Tong

A. Movements into Kwun Tong

The residential movements into Kwun Tong's public housing estates have not been entirely voluntary. The Resettlement Estates (now called Group B Estates), by regulation, resettle those people who urgently need immediate housing. Under urgent circumstances, there is very little left for the individuals to choose from. Thus, government officials decide the location of their settlement depending on the availability of vacant units. A large proportion of Kwun Tong's residents moved to Kwun Tong through this process of allocation.

The other three types of public housing accept applications from eligible families. Eligibility criteria include monthly income, number of persons in the household, urgency of need for housing assistance, etc. Formerly, different criteria were applied to different types of housing, but these were standardized in 1973 after the new Housing Department assumed the responsibility of the former Resettlement Department and Housing Authority. Although in theory individual households can apply for particular types of units to suit their own requirements, the allotment of units to applicants is determined more by the availability of vacant units than by individual choice. It is possible for an individual household to reject an offer; but the waiting list is so long that if one rejects an offer for a relatively undesirable unit, one might have to wait for as long as four to five years before another offer is made again. The urgency of the housing situation has made it necessary for individual families to accept almost any offer.

The origin of Kwun Tong's residents is, therefore, very diverse. A 1975 survey (Choi, C.Y. and Chan, Y.K., 1977)[+] indicated that many (12 %) had moved to Kwun Tong from as far as Hong Kong Island, and many had moved many times previously before finally coming to Kwun Tong. The average frequency of residential movement since marriage was 2.2 times, but over 30 % had moved 3 times or more.

Among those who moved from other areas into Kwun Tong, a large majority had moved from a private dwelling outside of Kwun Tong to a public housing estate. Many also moved to a private estate (13 %). But again very few moved from public housing elsewhere to a private dwelling in Kwun Tong. Transfers within public housing sectors were also not frequent among those who had moved from outside of Kwun Tong.

Overall, public housing was the destination for 86 per cent, and private housing for only 14 per cent of all moves. The public-to-private movements were rare and insignificant in total movements. Much of the private housing in Kwun Tong was occupied by households which were previously in private housing as well.

The reasons for the above pattern of movement are not difficult to find. Public housing development is of a much larger scale than

---

[+] This is a survey of 1,293 households in Kwun Tong. The following discussions of residential movements utilize data from this survey.

private development and the rent in public housing is often only a fraction of the market rent. In spite of the still fairly small size of public housing units, they are often larger than the rooms and bed-spaces in private units. The reasons for moving to Kwun Tong are often stated as "space" and "demolition". In the private sector, 39 per cent of all those who moved into Kwun Tong said that "space" was the important factor for their moves and 20 per cent mentioned "demolition". This pattern does not vary between the district of last residence although the lack of "space" as a motivation to move appears to be strongest (53 %) among those from New Kowloon, and "demolition" the strongest (31 %) among those from Hong Kong Island. These differences, however, are slight. A large proportion (41 %) have moved to a self-contained flat in Kwun Tong from rooms or bedspaces elsewhere; this represents an important step in upward social mobility. Some have become owners of flats although their number is small. In the public sector, many more came from temporary structures, bedspaces, rooftops, and sheds, etc. This is necessarily so because public housing was designed to resettle persons in need of housing.

B. Movements within Kwun Tong

Many of those who moved frequently had moved within Kwun Tong, e.g. as squatters until public housing was available to them. This explains the large proportion of households who had Kwun Tong as their previous residence.

Movements within Kwun Tong are important as a component of total moves. Of all previous moves, 30 per cent of the households in public housing and 29 per cent of the households in private housing had moved from an address within Kwun Tong. The establishment of new households is also important, but more significant in the private sector. Single persons who live in public housing Group B (former Resettlement) estates can be granted, upon marriage, units in Group B estates for new households, but they are not eligible to apply for Group A estates.

Many of the movements within Kwun Tong are movements from the private to the public sector. Movements from public to private are much less frequent and indicate the stability of residents in public housing estates. Low rent would appear to be the main factor. There are also considerable movements within the public sector, and these represent the transfer from temporary government housing schemes (called Licensed Areas or Cottages) to the estates and the reallocation of suitable units within estates to households whose size had changed.

C. Movements out of Kwun Tong and/or out of Public Housing

In a community as new and as rapidly growing as Kwun Tong, one does not expect much out-migration from the community. Neither does one expect much out-migration from the public housing estates because public housing units are already a big improvement on private units of similar cost and rent. Nevertheless, the 1975 survey and incomplete data from public housing records (Choi and Chan, 1977) show the existence of some out-migration of individuals and households from Kwun Tong and from public housing estates.

Marriage migration appears to be the most important form of migration of single individuals, but they do not represent the total volume of individual migration. Other motivations for out-migration include work, overcrowding and transportation problems. Data from the 1975 survey show that apart from marriages, overcrowding is an important reason for members of households to move away. Thirteen percent of movements away from public housing estates are of this type.

Many of the movements away from the family of origin are movements to the private sector; this is true regardless of the original type of housing. Overall, 49 % moved to "rooms" and similar accommodations in the private sector. There is, however, an important proportion (38 %) among the public sector who moved within this sector.

This reflects some successful effort within public housing in the absorption of population growth. But the trend is clear; when sons/daughters grow up (regardless of whether these households are in the private or public sector), they move to the private sector and occupy poor housing. Only very few (particularly among public housing households), can afford to rent/buy a flat when they move away from their household of origin. This implies that a large proportion of the newly married who, because of unavailability of public housing and high rent in the private sector, have to be satisfied with just rooms or even less.

The choice of location is also very limited. A large proportion found rooms and other accommodations in Kwun Tong (33 %) and in nearby Kai Tak (13 %), while others moved back to older private residential areas (17 % to Kowloon Peninsula, 3 % to other, New Kowloon, etc.).

This pattern of out-migration of young adults suggests a migration cycle which is probably unique to urban environments in which housing dominates the housing scene. This migration cycle involves the following steps:

(1) Population growth creates an intense housing shortage, this shortage becomes more severe when old private units become unfit for dwelling.

(2) Government builds public housing on the periphery of built-up areas to provide low cost dwelling units for people affected by the housing shortage.

(3) Massive transfer of population and families from built-up areas to the periphery occurs as public housing programmes are completed.

(4) Families in public housing estates grow and their children reach marriage age and form independent households. Congestion in public housing units in most cases prevents the formation of joint families although the married sons/daughters as well as parents/parents-in-law might wish to reside together.

(5) The continued housing shortage makes it difficult for housing authorities to provide additional units for the newly married; the long waiting list of applicants from the private sector for public housing by far exceeds supply.

(6) For reasons of marriage, change of location of work or simply of the desire to live independently, young adults will need to move back to the private housing sector. Since rent is high, they will have to be satisfied with inferior accommodations.

(7) Meanwhile some of the older built-up areas which were vacated earlier when the population moved to public housing estates, will have been re-developed, new residential buildings been built. These new developments provide some housing for those who now move back to these areas from the public housing estates.

There is not enough evidence to measure the extent of this migration cycle, but there is no doubt that it exists and will become prevalent as more children grow into adulthood.

D. Commuting to and from Kwun Tong

It could well be expected that Kwun Tong residents would become a major source of supply of labour for local industries. This, however, is not entirely the case. A 1970 survey reported that only 48 per cent of all Kwun Tong employees actually lived there while the rest commuted from other areas. While 60 % of all "general" workers were recruited from within Kwun Tong, only 24 per cent of all clerical and managerial ones were recruited locally. (V. Mok, 1972).

Similarly, among the overall working population in Kwun Tong, only 54.4 per cent worked locally, the rest commuted to other localities for employment. This exchange shows that much of the work created in Kwun Tong was of the skilled and unskilled blue-collar type, and those who were not in these occupations have found it necessary to work outside of Kwun Tong. It also reflects the very rapid growth of Kwun Tong which has not provided enough time for adjustments.

Data from the 1975 survey (Choi and Chan, 1977) also show that, in both private and public dwelling units, some members of households spend several nights a week away from their family; many spend as many as four nights a week away from home. The stated reasons for staying away are, overwhelmingly, "close to work and school", and imply the acute problems involved in commuting; but the congested housing condition is certainly another reason, although it is not stated as such. Almost all those who stay out frequently stay with friends and very few stay with relatives. This is true among those in public housing as well as those in private housing.

A significant finding concerning living away from home is that many are the male heads of households. In total, 3 % of all households interviewed had their male heads living away from home for more than 3 nights a week. In the private housing sector, this is 33 % and in the public sector 22 % of all persons who frequently live away from home. The problems of adjustment which might arise when the head of the household is often away, have not been investigated thoroughly and should constitute an important topic of further social research in Hong Kong.

V. Conclusions

About 45 % of Hong Kong's present population live in public housing estates and a large proportion of public housing is constructed as part of the new town development in Kwun Tong, and Tsuen Wan. More new towns are being developed in the New Territories and their population alone will eventually be about 25 % of the total Hong Kong population. The present paper has concentrated on the effects of housing policy on the movement of population and its implications.

Public housing and new towns play an important role in the economic and social life of Hong Kong's population. The (future) distribution of population and industries is highly dependent upon the location of public housing and new towns, thus influencing transportation, land-use and other economic developments in the areas affected. Social and family life too are greatly influenced by the type of physical environment in these public housing estates and the facilities provided.

The Kwun Tong study gives us some clues as to what life in Hong Kong's new towns would be like if present housing policies continue. It is beyond doubt that public housing in Kwun Tong is a great improvement over the shabby squatter huts and congested tenement flats which many Hong Kong residents have to be contented with. Although critics can rank Hong Kong's public housing as "primitive" by most "objective" standards, there are nevertheless some indications of satisfaction on the side of Hong Kong's public housing residents. There are, however, several emerging problems:

A. With children growing into adulthood, extreme congestion and transportation problems cause many young people as well as family heads to frequently stay away from home. In many households, this has meant early separation of young people from the family before being married; and in other households, this has meant the regular absence of the father from the family. This, together with the increasing rate of entry into the labour force for young people and women, will have an important influence on the Hong Kong family.

B. Present housing policy accepts applications for public housing from families but not from individuals. Young people reaching marriage age will thus need to move away from public housing and "return" to private housing. This results in a migration cycle involving two generations - the parents' generation moving from the private housing sector to the public, usually from old built-up areas to newly developed areas, and the children making the return move, although private buildings in the old built-up areas may now be redeveloped.

C. As the standard of living slowly rises, there will also be a rise in the level of demand concerning space and quality of the dwelling units. What is being offered at present is perhaps adequate now, especially when compared with the past, but the level of tolerance among residents in regard to space and quality of their units may not continue for long. This problem will become acute if the private housing sector shows rapid improvements. In recent years, there has been a substantial upgrading of quality of private housing and this can be expected to continue. It is reasonable to expect those who become dissatisfied with public housing to move to the private sector if these are provided at tolerable cost. This could lead to the gradual stratification of the society into two layers - the wealthy living in private residential buildings and the poor in public housing. This is not yet the situation, and need not be so in the future. However, it is important to improve the quality of public housing now, even though this may imply an increase in rent. Given rising income and the low proportion of expenditure spent on public housing, it is reasonable to say that those living in public housing units are willing to pay slightly more for it.

D. Kwun Tong - which was taken as an example for studying the Hong Kong housing policy - is a city in itself, if only in terms of population size. If Kwun Tong were administered as a city, various economic and social policies could be better implemented. There is a strong case for Hong Kong to establish "regional" administration units (e.g. New Town administrations) in its governmental structure so that policies concerning housing, industry, transport, education, etc. can be co-ordinated for the benefit of the people. Even if Kwun Tong, being very near to the main built-up areas, would not be suitable for separate administration, other new towns could benefit from the experience of Kwun Tong.

Table 1: Authorized Population in Public Housing in Hong Kong, By Types of Housing, 1955-1977[+] (in thousands)

Year	Resettlement Estates	Government Low Cost Housing Estates	Housing Authority Estates	Housing Society Estates	Total	Per cent of Hong Kong Population
1955	85	-	-	6	91	4
1959	230	-	17	28	275	9
1961	360	-	39	31	430	14
1964	702	-	128	50	830	25
1965	740	67	133	77	1,017	28
1966	830	67	134	90	1,121	31
1967	944	83	138	96	1,261	34
1968	1,025	127	149	108	1,409	37
1969	1,071	161	167	108	1,507	39
1970	1,094	188	205	113	1,600	40
1971	1,148	258	218	122	1,746	43
1972	1,176	331	218	125	1,850	45
1973[++]	1,183	514		128	1,825	43
1974	1,181	565		131	1,877	44
1975	1,180	607		141	1,928	44
1976	1,165	662		145	1,972	44
1977	1,125	736		150	2,011	45

[+] Not including so-called "Cottage Areas" which had an estimated population of 40,126 in March, 1977.

[++] There is a break in the statistical series with the establishment of the new Housing Department which absorbed all activities formerly under the Resettlement Department and the Housing Authority. Since then, Government Low Cost Housing Estates and Housing Authority Estates have been combined and called Group A Estates and resettlement estates called Group B Estates.

Sources: Resettlement Department, Annual Report, 1955/56 - 1972/73; Hong Kong Housing Authority, Annual Report, 1959/60 - 1976/77; Hong Kong Housing Society, Annual Report, 1976.

Table 2: Authorized Public Housing Population in Kwun Tong, 1973-77

Estates	1971 census	1973[a]	1974[a]	1975[a]	1976[a]	1977[a]
Ping Shek	22,802	27,385	27,322	27,511	27,183	26,861
Wo Lok	12,204	12,283	12,173	12,149	11,910	11,715
Upper Ngau Tau Kok	35,780	37,477	37,154	36,891	36,428	35,812
Kwun Tong (L.Y.M.R.)	7,156	6,806	6,439	6,456	6,337	6,239
Ko Chiu Road	(b)	17,378	19,875	22,127	22,302	22,305
Garden Estate	20,641	21,110	22,230	22,230	22,230	22,230
Yau Tong	17,243	27,185	27,098	26,695	26,448	26,206
Lam Tin	51,432	67,985	76,177	86,504	91,867	91,831
Kwun Tong (T.P.R.)	44,446	55,405	54,289	53,893	52,091	80,867
Lower Ngau Tau Kok	48,863	54,930	55,058	55,515	55,294	54,862
Jordan Valley	15,589	19,456	18,953	18,760	17,604	16,566
Sau Mau Ping	81,300	116,501	123,659	125,501	129,069	128,464
All Estates	357,456	463,906	480,427	494,232	498,763	493,958

(a) Authorized population

(b) Established in 1972

Sources: 1971 Census, private communication; Housing Authority, *Annual Reports*, 1973/74, 1974/75, 1975/76 and 1976/77; Hong Kong Housing Society, *Annual Reports*, 1973-1976.

References:

Government Documents:

Census and Statistics Department, Monthly Digest of Statistics, various issues, Government Printer, Hong Kong.

Hong Kong Government, Hong Kong (Annual Reports), 1956, 1973, ... 1977, Government Printer, Hong Kong.

Hong Kong Housing Authority, Annual Report, 1959/60 - 1976/77. Government Printer, Hong Kong.

Other Publications:

CHAN, Y.K., "The Rise and Growth of Kwun Tong: A Study of Planned Urban Development", Social Research Centre, The Chinese University of Hong Kong, 1973.

CHOI, C.Y. and CHAN, Y.K., "Housing Policy and Internal Movement of Population: A Study of Kwun Tong, a Chinese New Town in Hong Kong", Social Research Centre, The Chinese University of Hong Kong, 1977.

Hong Kong Housing Society, Annual Report, 1976. Ye Olde Printeric, Ltd., Hong Kong.

HOPKINS, K., "Housing the Poor", in: K. HOPKINS (ed.), Hong Kong: The Industrial Colony, Oxford University Press, Hong Kong, 1970, pp. 271-335.

JOHNSON, S.K., "Hong Kong's Resettled Squatters: A Statistical Survey", Asian Survey, (6), 1966, pp. 643-650.

Kwun Tong District Kai Fong Welfare Association Ltd., Kwun Tong Today, Hong Kong, 1975.

MOK, V., "The Nature of Kwun Tong as an Industrial Community: An Analysis of Economic Organization", Social Research Centre, The Chinese University of Hong Kong, 1972.

MUNDER, W.F., Hong Kong's Urban Rent and Housing, Hong Kong University Press, Hong Kong, 1969.

PODMORE, D., "The Population of Hong Kong", in: K. HOPKINS (ed.), op. cit., pp. 21-54.

PRYOR, E.G., Housing in Hong Kong, Oxford University Press, Hong Kong, 1973.

ANALYSIS AND PROJECTION
OF HONG KONG's PUBLIC FINANCE

Tien-tung Hsueh and Koon-lam Shea

I. A Classical Model: The Case of Hong Kong's Public Finance

Economic theory has pointed out that the use of public finance as a compensatory policy is bound to be less effective in an open economy simply because of the leakage of imports which abates the multiplier effect.[1] Hong Kong, as an extremely small open economy[2] which adopts a laissez-faire doctrine, further narrows the scope of public activity. Throughout its recorded economic history, a fiscal conservatism has constituted the rule of law for the operation of the Hong Kong economy.

By and large, the Hong Kong economy can be best depicted as a type of economy belonging to the classical model in the contemporary world; in such a model the main tasks for the public sector are summarized in three ways:[3] First, to maintain law and order so that the residents are able to pursue their self-interest under the mechanism of the 'invisible hand'. In Hong Kong, several actions were taken by the government in order to attain the target, which include rent control on prewar premises, regulation of the banking system since the banking crisis in 1964 and 1965, and the founding of the independent Commission Against Corruption etc... Second, to create an environment which is conducive and attractive to capitalists and industrialists from all over the world. In so doing, limited government intervention and free entry principle have been the axioms for practical policy. In addition, a low tax burden, free mobility of capital, no custom duties on all but a few imported commodities are also implemented.[4] Third, to minimize the size of the government sector a wide range of activities pertaining to externalities

---

1 See JOHANSEN /11/ , chapter 3, and MUNDELL /13/.

2 See HSUEH (a) /9/.

3 See also RABUSHKA /18/, chapters 3, 4 & 5.

4 Hydrocarbon oils (motor spirit and light diesels), alcoholic liquors, tabacco, are the only commodities subject to the custom duty.

and social merits are left to the private sector to run. This includes land and sea transport (with the exception of the Kowloon-Canton Railway), electricity, telephone service, and the issuing of local currency by three private banks which acquire the purchase of certificates of indebtedness from the Government's Exchange Fund with pound sterling; there is no central bank in Hong Kong.

Four features describe Hong Kong's public finance. First, the public sector plays a supplementary role to the private sector. Hong Kong follows exactly the way of the classical model; it is believed that the activities of the public sector will damage the potential growth of the economy if it carries out tasks which can be performed by the private sector. Under this assumption public works are furnished only when they have the advantage of providing an investment outlet for industries which might otherwise be accomplished extravagantly by the private sector. Second, there is no intention that public activities should operate as a compensatory finance, for there is no planning technique available to make the forecast of the fluctuation of the economy possible, on the one hand; and the targets of full employment and capacity output are left to the private sector to achieve, on the other. It follows then that the adoption of a compensatory fiscal policy doesn't appear to be workable although it may not be unreasonable in some cases.[5] By and large, Hong Kong's public expenditures have increased in periods of economic prosperity, and slowed down when the economy was depressed. In effect, Hong Kong's public finance looks like a destabilizer in the strict sense of policy implication. Third, because of the limited scope of public activity, a low tax system can be practised. Broadly speaking, the tax system designed in Hong Kong is to keep the private economic structure unchanged in the sense that it plays a neutral role on the efficiency ground and takes little consideration of the redistribution of income. Under such circumstances, the private sector is presumed to be in an optimal condition so that little distortion should occur. Fourth, a balanced budget with slight surpluses has been adopted as a fiscal norm by the government. In past years, unless it was in an extraordinary situation due to public works, external loan and public debt were not practised. As a rule of thumb, the sources for public expenditures are sought from the taxes and collectable revenues imposed on local economic units which characterize the soundness of public finance in the traditional sense.[6]

The minor role of the public sector in Hong Kong can be fully verified from Table 1. Among the 12 Asian countries (except for Indonesia) the public expenditure ratio of Hong Kong has been towards the bottom of the list. Moreover, Hong Kong's external debt ratio was the lowest among the countries in the period under review. Furthermore, Hong Kong was lucky enough to assume a very low portion of national defense which reduced considerably the tax burden. Regarding the tax obligation of the average person, Hong Kong's tax burden has generally been light in comparison with other countries in the region.

II. Public Finance of Hong Kong, 1961 - 1975

The public expenditure of Hong Kong grew at a somewhat faster rate than that of gross domestic product (GDP) during the period under review.[7] Of all expenditures the growth rate of the economic services was the highest, replacing the position of social services which had the fastest rate of growth during the 50's and 60's.[8] The social services, however, still occupy more than half of the total expenditures (see Table 2), and rank among the highest rates when compared internationally (see Table 3).

One way to interpret this shift is that Hong Kong devoted itself to providing a favorable environment for domestic production activities during the early stage of development. The supply of low-cost housing due to the growth of population and the resettlement of slums,[9] the expenses on education and human investment, and the offer of free health care were all counted as indispensable tasks. However, as the economy was transformed from an entrepôt to one dominated by export,[10] government expenditures on the economic

---

5 Another view which is for the discretionary action of the public sector can be found in OWEN [17].

6 Cf. also BURKHEAD [3].

7 The average growth rate of GDP in the period 1962-'73 was 14.6 % in current prices. See [25], p. 23. For a discussion of the development of public finance during the earlier period see also STAMMER [20], and HO (a) [7].

Table 1: International Comparisons of Public Finance for Selected Asian Countries

		1966	'68	'70	'72	'74	Average '66 - '74	
SINGAPORE								
Government expenditure/GDP	(A)	20.4%	18.3%	21.6%	20.7%	20.4%	21.1%	
Taxes/GDP	(B)	12.5	12.0	13.7	14.1	12.8	13.4	
Taxes/Government revenue	(C)	71.4	64.6	63.0	65.8	71.4	66.2	
External public debt outstanding/GDP	(D)	4.7	13.8	15.9	17.7	11.5	21.1	
National defense/GDP	(E)	2.2	2.9	5.4	5.2	4.1	4.2	
HONG KONG	(A)	16.3%	13.9%	12.5%	14.8%	18.1%	14.6%	
	(B)	9.5	9.7	8.5	9.0	9.6	9.3	
	(C)	64.3	67.7	63.2	61.2	62.7	63.6	
	(D)	0.2	0.1	0.1	0.5	0.3	0.2	
	(E)	0.8	0.7	0.5	0.5	NA	0.6	(5)
TAIWAN	(A)	18.9%	19.3%	21.7%	20.5%	15.8%	19.9%	
	(B)	10.8	11.4	13.5	13.4	15.4	12.9	
	(C)	54.0	55.5	59.9	62.9	73.8	59.7	
	(D)	10.8	13.3	17.1	20.8	18.7	16.2	
	(E)	8.3	8.1	7.9	6.6	NA	7.5	(5)
MALAYSIA	(A)	NA	NA	24.3%	32.7%	29.7%	28.3%	(1)
	(B)	NA	NA	16.9	18.3	21.5	18.4	(1)
	(C)	80.5	81.1	83.3	82.0	90.8	84.0	
	(D)	NA	NA	14.4	21.0	25.1	19.0	(1)
	(E)	5.0	NA	4.3	4.5	3.7	4.3	(7)
KOREA	(A)	NA	17.8%	19.2%	21.2%	20.4%	19.2%	(2)
	(B)	NA	13.4	14.2	12.3	13.3	13.1	(2)
	(C)	NA	77.3	77.0	75.7	77.1	74.7	(2)
	(D)	18.1	29.1	30.9	37.1	28.0	30.4	
	(E)	4.0	4.2	3.9	4.4	3.1	4.0	
PHILIPPINES	(A)	13.0%	14.0%	11.4%	12.1%	15.1%	13.3%	
	(B)	6.4	7.1	6.6	7.7	9.1	7.5	
	(C)	83.6	84.5	87.2	89.3	83.9	85.7	
	(D)	6.8	5.6	11.6	14.0	14.2	9.7	
	(E)	1.1	1.2	1.1	1.1	1.3	1.2	
THAILAND	(A)	13.8%	16.7%	18.5%	17.7%	13.1%	16.3%	
	(B)	11.7	13.2	12.6	11.8	13.4	12.4	
	(C)	91.8	91.2	90.8	88.5	93.1	91.1	
	(D)	7.1	6.6	7.4	8.4	8.5	7.3	
	(E)	2.1	2.7	3.3	3.6	2.5	2.9	
INDONESIA	(A)	9.3%	8.8%	10.0%	11.9%	11.8%	10.7%	(3)
	(B)	3.9	6.9	7.2	8.7	9.3	7.5	(3)
	(C)	93.9	96.9	98.7	94.7	94.9	96.3	
	(D)	NA	41.2	39.7	47.4	36.6	42.0	(4)
	(D)	NA	NA	0.14	0.11	0.07	0.11	(1)

Table 1: continued

		1966	'68	'70	'72	'74	Average '66 - '74	
INDIA (10)	(A)	25.9%	21.0%	22.7%	26.3%	23.7%	24.1%	
	(B)	14.9	12.7	14.1	16.6	15.4	14.9	
	(C)	81.3	78.8	81.6	82.8	82.9	81.3	
	(D)	25.5	21.8	21.1	23.7	NA	22.8	(5)
	(E)	NA	NA	5.6	7.3	8.2	6.7	(8)
PAKISTAN	(A)	NA	NA	NA	21.1%	24.2%	22.3%	(6)
	(B)	NA	NA	NA	11.5	11.7	11.6	(6)
	(C)	NA	NA	NA	75.6	73.8	75.7	(6)
	(D)	NA	NA	40.8	96.3	63.6	63.9	(7)
	(E)	NA	NA	6.1	6.9	5.7	6.3	(1)
SRI LANKA	(A)	28.8%	26.8%	28.7%	39.6%	27.0%	29.8%	
	(B)	16.5	15.5	17.5	24.2	18.4	18.0	
	(C)	75.1	77.1	81.6	80.4	82.8	79.0	
	(D)	NA	20.0	23.4	26.1	26.0	24.4	(4)
	(E)	0.8	0.7	0.9	1.1	NA	0.8	(5)
BURMA	(A)	19.9%	16.5%	17.4%	17.5%	NA	17.8%	(5)
	(B)	22.8	14.1	14.3	12.5	NA	14.4	(5)
	(C)	90.4	84.7	87.2	80.2	NA	84.2	(5)
	(D)	19.9	16.5	17.4	17.5	NA	17.8	(5)
	(E)	6.5	5.3	5.7	5.5	NA	5.7	(9)

Sources: /28/ and /29/

Notes: (1) 1970-1974
(2) 1967-1974
(3) 1966-68, 1970-74 (excluding 1969)
(4) 1968-1974
(5) 1966-1973
(6) 1972-1974
(7) 1966-67, 1970-74
(8) 1969-1974
(9) 1966-1972
(10) For Fiscal Year

Table 2: Growth of Public Expenditures and Revenues in Hong Kong (at current prices)

		'62	'64	'67	'70	'73	'62-'73 average
A. Public Expenditures	Growth Rate	115.8	112.4	98.8	117.8	125.4	115.5
	% Share	100%	100%	100%	100%	100%	100%
I. General Services		106.6	116.2	104.3	114.1	126.4	114.3
		28.22%	27.11%	31.79%	31.51%	27.74%	29.55%
a. General administration		104.1	117.8	104.0	119.2	132.5	116.9
		13.17%	12.85%	16.91%	17.05%	16.82%	15.31%
b. Other general services		109.0	114.9	104.8	108.7	118.1	111.6
		15.06%	14.26%	14.89%	14.47%	10.93%	14.25%
II. Economic Services		117.5	114.7	88.6	125.6	117.9	113.7
		12.46%	12.09%	10.28%	10.35%	18.86%	12.48%
III. Social Services		121.3	110.3	98.3	118.6	128.0	114.8
		56.54%	58.40%	54.95%	55.05%	51.04%	55.11%
a. Education		114.9	116.8	108.6	123.2	136.2	117.4
		14.52%	14.57%	16.12%	20.11%	18.36%	16.57%
b. Housing & Resettlement		143.5	114.4	97.1	115.5	110.0	113.5
		8.57%	12.01%	8.83%	7.36%	5.09%	8.30%
c. Other social services		119.4	106.1	93.8	116.2	126.7	114.0
		33.46%	31.83%	30.00%	27.58%	27.60%	30.25%
IV. Unallocable Expenditures		106.3	109.5	93.7	118.7	121.1	114.3
		2.79%	2.42%	3.00%	3.09%	2.38%	2.89%
B. Public Revenues	Growth Rate	121.2	109.5	106.1	122.8	112.6	115.1
	% Share	100%	100%	100%	100%	100%	100%
I. Direct Tax		114.8	119.0	111.2	123.8	145.9	118.9
		19.52%	22.26%	26.45%	26.06%	30.56%	24.75%
a. Corporation & Business profit taxes		111.3	123.9	107.1	126.8	148.7	120.2
		11.27%	13.91%	15.31%	16.31%	20.34%	15.25%
b. Salaries & Estate taxes		129.0	110.5	122.6	125.9	142.7	119.5
		4.04%	4.44%	4.78%	4.76%	5.92%	4.62%

c. Property & Interest taxes and personal assessment	112.4 4-21%	112.6 4.32%	113.9 6.36%	113.1 4.99%	138.1 4.30%	114.7 4.91%	
II. Indirect Tax	112.1 37.83%	115.8 40.06%	106.3 41.03%	110.7 34.38%	106.2 34.47%	113.5 38.00%	
a. Rates	111.6 10.47%	115.1 10.89%	112.6 14.49%	106.2 11.32%	138.1 10.25%	114.2 11.74%	
b. Import & Excise duties	111.7 16.19%	113.1 16.66%	106.1 16.98%	110.5 13.79%	96.3 8.7%	108.4 14.69%	
c. Other indirect taxes	113.2 11.16%	120.4 12.51%	98.2 9.55%	117.3 9.27%	98.0 15.53%	120.7 11.58%	
III. Income from provisions of goods & services	134.4 42.65%	99.0 37.68%	102.3 28.60%	135.4 34.90%	103.9 33.80%	117.43 32.40%	(1) (2)
IV. Other revenues			99.5 4.00%	130.7 4.70%	40.4 1.20%	103.93 3.70%	(1) (2)
Surplus or deficit ratio (B-A)/GDP	1.80%	0.93%	1.63%	3.09%	0.70%	1.50%	

Sources: (1) Census and Statistics Department, Hong Kong Government
(2) /27/ , /24/ and /30/

Notes:
1. All in current prices because the price indicies for various items are not available.
2. Other indirect taxes include taxes on bets and sweeps, dance halls (abolished in 1970), entertainment, hotel accommodations, motor vehicles and government lotteries.
3. Other revenues are found as the residuals which include reimbursements, contributions, loan repayments, etc.
4. Economic services cover agriculture, fisheries and forestry, mining, railway and land transport, water transport, air transport, commerce and industry, reclamation and development.
5. Other general services include defense, justice, police, prisons and general information services.
6. Other social services include health, social welfare services, postal services, cooperatives and marketing, water supply, fire protection, sanitation.
7. (1) Average of the period 66-73
(2) Average of the period 65-73.

Table 3: International Comparison of Selected Public Expenditures and Revenues (at current prices)

			'66	'68	'70	'72	Average '66-'72		per capita GDP ('73)
UNITED STATES:			NA						$6,167
Education and Culture	% of GDP	(a)		7.53%	8.34%	8.57%	8.04%	(1)	
	US$/population	(b)		$323.64	$400.31	$476.52	$382.74	(1)	
Social Services		(a)		5.23	6.12	6.78	5.85	(1)	
		(b)		224.98	293.7	377.03	280.55	(1)	
Economic Services		(a)		3.84	3.92	3.67	3.85	(1)	
		(b)		164.94	187.93	204.07	181.71	(1)	
Taxes on Income		(a)		14.10	13.54	13.31	13.63	(1)	
Customs Duties		(a)		0.25	0.26	0.28	0.26	(1)	
Other Indirect Taxes		(a)		1.70	1.64	1.37	1.60	(1)	
AUSTRALIA:									$5,448
Education and Culture	% of GDP	(a)	2.54%	3.0%	3.46%	4.52%	3.39%		
	US$/population	(b)	$44.50	$54.20	$72.37	$94.20	$65.69		
Social Services		(a)	5.72	7.12	7.50	9.33	7.46		
		(b)	100.19	128.61	156.80	194.36	144.10		
Economic Services		(a)	0.52	0.60	0.82	0.86	0.71		
		(b)	9.09	10.93	17.20	17.82	73.30		
Taxes on Income		(a)	11.69	13.24	14.76	17.08	14.35		
Customs Duties		(a)	1.21	1.35	1.50	1.53	1.42		
Other Indirect Taxes		(a)	5.13	5.49	5.45	6.11	5.61		
SINGAPORE:									$1,890
Education and Culture	% of GDP	(a)	3.79%	3.47%	2.99%	2.49%	3.19%		
	US$/population	(b)	NA	$24.35	$27.40	$33.44	$27.14	(1)	
Social Services		(a)	3.59	2.75	2.26	1.84	2.58		
		(b)	NA	19.28	20.69	24.78	20.71	(1)	

Economic Services		(a)	1.28	1.14	1.15	0.98	1.16		
		(b)	NA	7.96	10.56	13.22	10.11	(1)	
Taxes on Income		(a)	3.32	3.65	4.20	4.95	3.95	(2)	
Customs Duties		(a)	NA	3.28	3.46	2.92	3.21	(2)	
Other Indirect Taxes		(a)	NA	5.09	5.47	5.53	5.49	(2)	
HONG KONG:									$1,416
Education and Culture	% of GDP	(a)	2.38%	2.49%	2.53%	2.76%	2.51%		
	US$/population	(b)	$12.72	$14.47	$19.67	$28.94	$18.27		
Social Services		(a)	7.65	6.24	5.33	6.47	6.22		
		(b)	40.95	36.18	41.48	67.85	44.12		
Economic Services		(a)	1.86	1.32	1.30	3.28	1.71		
		(b)	9.93	7.65	10.12	34.34	13.02		
Taxes on Income		(a)	2.91	3.00	3.18	3.66	3.16		
Customs Duties		(a)	2.71	2.49	2.16	1.93	2.33		
Other Indirect Taxes		(a)	3.83	3.54	3.22	5.01	2.73		
TAIWAN:								$574	
Education and Culture	% of GDP	(a)	2.97%	3.41%	3.89%	4.00%	3.58%		
	US$/population	(b)	$7.04	$10.71	$15.01	$20.08	$13.03		
Social Services		(a)	2.21	2.74	3.21	3.57	2.98		
		(b)	5.24	8.61	12.4	17.92	10.99		
Economic Services		(a)	1.96	2.11	2.34	2.00	2.13		
		(b)	4.64	6.65	9.05	10.06	7.57		
Taxes on Income		(a)	1.05	1.27	1.75	2.27	1.57		
Customs Duties		(a)	2.81	3.08	3.04	4.01	3.19		
Other Indirect Taxes		(a)	2.70	3.33	3.56	3.86	3.36		

Sources:
1. For United States, Australia and Singapore: /29/
2. For Singapore: /32/
3. For Hong Kong: /30/ and /27/

services began to grow at a rapid rate to avoid development bottlenecks. These services cover land reclamation for factory sites and residential use, water works, road construction, and the reconstruction of new towns. Other expenditures in the general services, particularly in general administration, also kept an impressive rate of growth, which seems to be a result of the government's desire not to deteriorate the quality of public services.

Except for a few extraordinary years when the government carried out enormous public works, which needed financial support from external sources, public revenues from the domestic sources have generally been sufficient to finance public expenditures. This is supported by the facts recorded throughout the fiscal years. Hong Kong encountered a deficit budget in only three fiscal years, 1959/'60, '65/'66 and '74/'75 with small deficit ratios (deficit/GDP) 0.98 %, 1.31 % and 1.36 % respectively, while the rest of the years starting from 1949/'50 up to 1973/'74 registered surpluses.[12] Among the public revenues, the ratio of direct taxes to indirect taxes has been in an upward trend since the sixties.[13]

The above two phenomena appear to be in consistency with the international tendency.[14] Attention should be paid, however, to the coverage of the direct and indirect taxes as defined by the government authorities. It is very doubtful whether corporation and business profit taxes and property tax should be wholly grouped into the category of direct tax.[15] In a more realistic treatment, assuming the shifting ratio of these two taxes is one half for each, we

---

[8] HO (a) /7/, pp. 20-21, 34-35 in which the community services are grouped into social services in our classification.

[9] Cf. SMITH /19/.

[10] See HSUEH (b) /10/.

[11] See THORN /22/, and MUSGRAVE (a) /14/, chapter 4.

[12] See /30/, Appendices p. 775; /25/, p. 23; GDP of 1959 is estimated. 1975 figure is not available.

[13] See HO (b), /8/, p. 79 & 82; although the coverage of direct and indirect taxes are not exactly the same as those of the Census & Statistics Department, the general trend seems to be quite clear.

[14] See THORN /22/, and MUSGRAVE (a) /14/.

[15] See also MUSGRAVE & MUSGRAVE /16/, chapters 18 & 19.

then have the ratio of indirect to direct tax in Hong Kong reaching 3:1, instead of 2:1 or less. Apart from that, it is interesting to note that the income tax in Hong Kong has always been extremely low, representing an average rate of 3 % of GDP, in contrast to 14 % in the United States and Australia (see Table 3). Summing up one can say that the Hong Kong tax system still relies mainly on the indirect tax.

III. Estimation of Public Revenues and Expenditures

A formula which characterizes a type of economy the income of which is propelled from the promotion of exports,[16] is designed for the estimation of the public revenues of Hong Kong. As a matter of fact, each item of public revenue comprises two components - the base for collection and the rate applied on it. Broadly speaking, the collection base in most cases is determined by the national income of the equivalent variable and the rate is, of course, set up by the government legislation. By taking these points into consideration, a revenue formula for the case of Hong Kong can then be specified.[17]

Assuming the response of the changes in tax yield (T) to the changes in the level of gross domestic product (Y) is designated by a form of arc elasticity

$$\varepsilon_{TY} = \frac{Y_o}{T_o}\frac{\Delta T}{\Delta Y} \qquad (1)$$

and the elasticity of the tax base (B) with respect to GDP is

$$\varepsilon_{BY} = \frac{Y_o}{B_o}\frac{\Delta B}{\Delta Y} \qquad (2)$$

Similarly, the elasticity of GDP with regard to exports is expressed by

$$\varepsilon_{YE} = \frac{E_o}{Y_o}\frac{\Delta Y}{\Delta E} \qquad (3)$$

From (1) we have[18]

---

16 See HSUEH (b) /10/.

17 A similar procedure is found in ANDO, BROWN and ADAMS /17/, TAUBMAN /21/, and BOLTON /2/.

18 See MUSGRAVE (b), /15/, p. 507.

$$\varepsilon_{TY} = \frac{t_o \Delta B + \Delta t\, B_1}{t_o B_o} \frac{Y_o}{\Delta Y} \tag{4}$$

where t stands for tax rate, $\Delta B = B_1 - B_o : \Delta Y = Y_1 - Y_o$, subscripts "O" and "1" represent the base year and any other period, respectively. It is easily derived from (2) that

$$\Delta B = \varepsilon_{BY} B_o \frac{\Delta Y}{Y_o} \quad \text{and so } B_1 = \varepsilon_{BY} B_o \frac{\Delta Y}{Y_o} + B_o \tag{5}$$

By substituting (5) into (4) we obtain

$$\varepsilon_{TY} = \frac{t_o B_o \varepsilon_{BY} \frac{\Delta Y}{Y_o} + \Delta t \left(\varepsilon_{BY} B_o \frac{\Delta Y}{Y_o} + B_o \right)}{t_o B_o} \frac{Y_o}{\Delta Y}$$

$$= \varepsilon_{BY} + \frac{\Delta t}{t_o} \left(\varepsilon_{BY} + \frac{Y_o}{Y} \right) \tag{6}$$

Rewrite (1) and take (6) and (3) into account, we obtain

$$T_1 = \varepsilon_{TY} T_o \frac{\Delta Y}{T_o} + T_o$$

$$= \left\{ \left[\varepsilon_{BY} + \frac{\Delta t}{t_o} \left(\varepsilon_{BY} + \frac{Y_o}{\Delta Y} \right) \right] \frac{\Delta Y}{Y_o} + 1 \right\} T_o$$

$$= \underbrace{\left(\varepsilon_{BY} \varepsilon_{YE} \frac{\Delta E}{E_o} + 1 \right)}_{\substack{\text{factors accounting for} \\ \text{the changes of tax} \\ \text{base}}} \underbrace{\left(\frac{\Delta t}{t_o} + 1 \right)}_{\substack{\text{factor accounting} \\ \text{for the changes} \\ \text{of tax rate}}} T_o \tag{7}$$

(7) is called the fundamental equation for estimating the public revenues.

Using the available data in Hong Kong, the estimates of the relevant parameters are shown in Table 4. For the purpose of projection, the average growth rates of the various kinds of tax yield for the period of 1974-1980 are also estimated.

For the estimation of public expenditure, allowance is made for the growth and size effects of the economy in a form of non-constant elasticity. In some cases, a specific ratio such as foreign capital ratio representing the extent of the available resources and a dummy variable indicating a structural change of the system in question will also be included. A general formulation appears to be[19]

---

[19] For a similar specification see CHENERY and TAYLOR /5/, and CHENERY and SYRQUIN /4/.

Table 4: Estimates of the Public Revenues of Hong Kong (at 1966 constant prices)

	Period	ε_{BY}	ε_{YE}	$\frac{\Delta E}{E_o}$	$\frac{\Delta t}{t_o}$	Average growth rate of T	
						1961-'73	'74-'80
I. Direct Tax							
a. Corporation and Business profit taxes	1971-1973	2.828	1.024	0.073	0.021	-	2.1%
b. Salaries and Estate taxes	1971-1973	1.231	1.024	0.073	0.117	-	11.7%
c. Property and Interest taxes and Personal assessment	1962-1967 1968-1973	1 1	1.015 0.814	0.109 0.102	0.046 -0.044	0.1%	0.1%
II. Indirect Tax							
a. Rates	1962-1967 1968-1973	1.272 0.066	1.015 0.814	0.109 0.102	0.007 0.0315	1.9%	1.9%
b. Import & Excise duties	1962-1967 1968-1973	0.487 0.35	1.015 0.814	0.109 0.102	0.027 -0.039	-0.6%	0.0%
c. Other indirect tax	1962-1967 1968-1973	0.742 0.982	1.015 0.814	0.109 0.102	-0.021 0.172	7.6%	7.6%
III. Others	1962-1967 1968-1973	1 1	1.015 0.814	0.109 0.102	-0.035 0.0398	0.2%	0.2%

Sources: 1. /25/
2. As for Table 2

Notes: 1. All the values above are obtained by finding the average of their annual values over the specified period.
2. Tax bases for I (a), I(b), II(a), II(b), II(c) are as follows:
II(b) : Alcoholic drink, imported & locally brewed, cigarettes & tobacco, imported & local made, and petrol & oil (Source 1, p.26)
II(a) : Rent & rates (Source 1, p. 26)
I(b) : Compensation to employees (Source 1, p. 32)
I(a) : Operation surplus (Source 1, p. 32)
II(c) : Purchase of motor cars, cinema entertainment, other entertainment & holiday expenses, betting, horse racing and others (Source 1, p. 27).

$$X_i = \alpha+\beta_1 \ln y + \beta_2(\ln y)^2+\gamma_1 \ln N+\gamma_2(\ln N)^2+\xi(F/GDP)+\eta D+u \quad (8)$$

or $$\ln X_i = \alpha+\beta_1 \ln y + \beta_2(\ln y)^2+\gamma_1 \ln N+\gamma_2(\ln N)^2+\xi(F/GDP) + \eta D + u \quad (8a)$$

where X_i: i^{th} public expenditure

y : GDP per capita in HK$ standing for the growth effect

N : population in millions designating the size effect

F : inflow of foreign capital

D : dummy variable

u : disturbance term

Both double logarithm and semi logarithm will be on trial. It is believed that (8) or (8a) is more suitable for explaining the patterns of public expenditure compared with the previous works in the same line.[20] The reason is that it takes into account the changeable elasticities in terms of both GDP per capita and population. (8) or (8a) is called the fundamental equation for estimating public expenditure.

After making a number of trials we are able to pick up these best estimated equations, in terms of better explanation in economic reasoning, higher coefficient of determination, and higher t - statistics, which are shown in Table 5.

IV. Projection of Public Revenues and Expenditures in 1980

The above analysis has formed the skeleton for our projection of government revenue and expenditure in 1980. In so doing, it is also necessary to project the income and population of Hong Kong in 1980. According to the data published in /28/ (April 1976), the population growth rate was 2 % for the period. Hence, in our projection, we assume that population will grow at a high rate of 2 % or a lower rate of 1.8 %, which gives the figures of 4.779 and 4.713 million, respectively, for 1980. The upper and lower limits for exports growth rate we propose are 10.5 % and 12 %,

20 Cf. also LEWIS and MARTIN /12/, WILLIAMSON /23/, HINRICHS /6/ and MUSGRAVE (a), /14/.

Table 5: Estimates of the Public Expenditures of Hong Kong

(at 1966 constant prices)

	Intercept	lny	$(\ln y)^2$	lnN	$(\ln N)^2$	$\frac{F}{GDP}$	D	R^2
General administration $\ln X_1$	8.076	2.089	-0.300	-18.389	7.443		-0.142	0.986
	(0.640)	(0.944)	(-0.309)	(-0.862)	(0.892)		(-1.989)	
Other general services $\ln X_2$	-2.998	1.617	-0.474	-0.413	0.560	0.203		0.990
	(-0.497)	(1.382)	(-0.960)	(-0.040)	(0.142)	(0.750)		
Economic services X_3	-6.608	-3.065	1.684	12.080	-4.574	1.442		0.850
	(-0.416)	(-0.997)	(1.297)	(0.450)	(-0.442)	(2.030)		
Education X_1	0.519	-1.181	0.588	-0.701	0.728	0.166		0.996
	(0.235)	(-2.757)	(3.251)	(-0.187)	(0.505)	(1.676)		
Housing & resettlement $\ln X_5$	-65.532	-6.103	2.337	97.605	-35.142	1.920	-0.178	0.950
	(-3.972)	(-1.889)	(1.758)	(3.494)	(-3.221)	(1.898)	(-1.367)	
Other social services $\ln X_6$	-16.381	2.623	1.436	23.079	-7.831	1.765	-0.141	0.972
	(-1.378)	(-1.127)	(1.499)	(1.146)	(-0.996)	(2.420)	(-1.505)	
Unallocable expenditure $\ln X_7$	16.464	8.427	-2.753	-36.527	13.034	1.275		0.937
	(0.835)	(2.206)	(-1.707)	(-1.094)	(1.013)	(1.445)		

Sources: [26] and [25]

Notes: 1. Dependent variables y & N are in thousand H.K. dollars & in million respectively
2. Figures in parentheses are t - Statistics

the former value being the average growth rate of exports from 1961 to 1973. Given the growth rate of exports, the export elasticity of income is estimated by

$$\ln Y = \underset{(6.31)}{1.845} + \underset{(25.7)}{0.811} \ln E \qquad R^2 = 0.9836 \qquad (9)$$

Direct calculation shows that the income for Hong Kong in 1980 corresponding to the 10.5 % and 12 % growth in exports are 34,832 and 37,918 million HK dollars (1966 constant prices), respectively. However, to do our projection, we still need to know the value of F/GDP in 1980. We assume that it takes the average value of F/GDP from 1967-1973, which is 0.019. The dummy variable assumes the value 1. Table 6 shows the results of our prediction.

To limit the number of possible cases, we have included cases where both export and population growth rates are high or low respectively. Compared with the values in 1973, we find that other social services and economic services will be tripled by 1980.

Table 6: Projection of Hong Kong's Public Expenditures in 1980 (at 1966 constant prices in million H.K. dollars)

	Projection A	Projection B
General administration	1523.0	1339.8
Other general services	385.1	386.5
Economic services	1999.4	1760.6
Education	1283.3	1175.5
Housing & resettlement	202.3	187.3
Other social services	3250.5	2633.7
Unallocated expenditure	44.5	51.2
Total	8688.1	7534.6

Notes: 1. Projection A:

annual growth rate of export 12 %
annual growth rate of population 2 %

2. Projection B:

annual growth rate of export 10.5 %
annual growth rate of population 1.8 %

To project the revenue of the government, we shall utilize the formula

$$T_{1980} = (\varepsilon_{BY}\varepsilon_{YE}\frac{\Delta E}{E} + 1)\ (\frac{\Delta t}{t} + 1)^7\ T_{1973} \qquad (10)$$

Thus what we have to estimate will be ε_{BY} of the different taxes and the change in tax rate over 1974-1980. For the change in tax rate, we shall use two different alternatives. The first one is that the change in tax rate will assume its past trend, as indicated in Table 4. The other is that the tax rate will remain the same as that in 1973, which means that $\frac{\Delta t}{t} = 0$. Regression analysis has been adopted to estimate the value of ε_{BY} of the different taxes. Table 7 presents our results.

Finally, to put the projected revenue and expenditure together and to predict the deficits or surpluses in 1980, we present Table 8. It is found that if government keeps the tax rate of 1973 with no change up to 1980, independent of the export growthrate we proposed, that the government will run a deficit. However, if the government changes the tax rates according to the past trend, it will run a surplus. In either of these cases, the deficit or surplus occupies less than 3.5 % of the GDP. Our conclusion is that given the fiscal conservatism of the Hong Kong government, it seems that the chances that government will keep the tax rate unchanged up to 1980 are rather slim, even though the resulting deficit is rather small by international standards. If the government is aiming at balancing the budget, the tax rate should increase less rapidly than in the past.

V. Concluding Remarks

Hong Kong's public finance is perhaps the only case of the classical model at the present time. There has been no difficulty in collecting enough revenues for public expenditures since the 50's. As a result, through the recorded years, Hong Kong has emerged with a balanced budget, with a slight surplus. Public debt and foreign loan were seldom incurred; if there were, the amount in terms of GDP was extremely low. The public sector of Hong Kong has been able to provide the minimal public goods and services required for the populace, with the least distortion on the private sector. The economy has achieved a prodigious growth of GDP, investment and consumption per capita since the 50's.

Table 7: Projection of Hong Kong's Public Revenues in 1980 (at 1966 constant prices in million H.K. dollars)

	ε_{BY}	ε_{YE} (8)	$\frac{\Delta t}{t}$ assuming past trend			$\frac{\Delta t}{t} = 0$	
			$1+\frac{\Delta t}{t}$ (9)	Revenue in 1980 (10) if exports grow at 10.5 % (A)	Revenue in 1980 if exports grow at 12 % (B)	(A)	(B)
(I) Direct Tax							
a. Corporation and Business Profit Taxes	2.828 (1)	0.811	1.021	2521.8	2868.3	2180.4	2480.0
b. Salaries and Estate Taxes	1.231 (2)	0.811	1.117	833.8	916.3	384.3	422.3
c. Property & Interest Taxes & Personal Assessment	1 (3)	0.811	1.001	254.3	276.8	252.5	274.9
(II) Indirect Tax							
a. Rates	0.79 (4)	0.811	1.019	622.1	670.3	545.3	587.6
b. Import & Excise Duties	0.454 (5)	0.811	1	385.3	405.9	385.3	405.9
c. Other Indirect Taxes	0.89 (6)	0.811	1.076	1448.6	1568.8	867.5	939.5
(III) Income from Provisions of Goods and Services and Other Revenues	1 (7)	0.811	1.002	2084.1	2268.7	2055.2	2237.2
TOTAL				8150	8975.1	6670.5	7347.4

Notes: (1) Obtained by finding the average of yearly values of ε_{BY} from 1971-1973

(2) Obtained by finding the average of yearly values of ε_{BY} from 1971-1973

(3) By assumption

(4) Obtained by regression analysis $\ln$ (Rate's base) $= -0.45 + 0.79 \ln y$ $\quad R^2 = 0.8566$
(0.51) (8.47)

(5) Obtained by regression analysis $\ln$ (Imports & excise duties base) $= 2.16 + 0.454 \ln y$ $\quad R^2 = 0.9628$
(8.57) (16.87)

(6) Obtained by regression analysis $\ln$ (Other indirect raxes base) $= -2.13 + 0.89 \ln y$ $\quad R^2 = 0.9666$
(4.56) (17.84)

(7) By assumption

(8) Obtained by regression (9)

(9) Obtained by finding their yearly averages

(10) $\frac{\Delta E}{E} = 1.012$ from 1973-1980 represents an annual growth rate of export = 10.5 %

$\frac{\Delta E}{E} = 1.211$ from 1973-1980 represents an annual growth rate of export = 12 %

The projection on different public revenue is obtained on formula (10)

Table 8: Summary of the Projection of Hong Kong's Public Revenues and Expenditures in 1980 (at 1966 constant prices in million H.K. dollars)

	$\frac{\Delta E}{E}$ = 10.5 % $\frac{\Delta N}{N}$ = 1.8 %		$\frac{\Delta E}{E}$ = 12 % $\frac{\Delta N}{N}$ = 2 %	
	$\frac{\Delta t}{t}$ takes past trend	$\frac{\Delta t}{t}$ = 0, i.e. tax rate remains the same as 1973	$\frac{\Delta t}{t}$ takes past trend	$\frac{\Delta t}{t}$ = 0, i.e. tax rate remains the same as 1973
Revenues	8150.0	6670.5	8975.1	7347.4
Expenditures	7534.6	7534.6	8688.1	8688.1
Revenues-Expenditures	615.4	-864.1	287.0	-1340.4
$\frac{\text{Surplus or Deficits}}{\text{GDP}}$	1.8 %	2.4 %	0.8 %	3.5 %

In this paper an attempt has been made to project Hong Kong's public finance in 1980 under the alternative assumptions that the tax rates follow the historical trend or are held constant up to 1980. The results show that the government will enjoy a surplus budget in the first case and will encounter a slight deficit in the second. It seems unreasonable to predict that the public expenditures will grow at a quick pace following the past patterns with tax rates left unchanged. If that is so, it is quite obvious that Hong Kong's public sector will also run well in the future.

For us it is interesting to note that a classical model like the case of Hong Kong's public finance has excellently carried out its job,[21] in contrast to many other countries facing great difficulties in balancing their budgets and in offering sufficient public goods and services.

[21] We have left the problem of income distribution untouched. A comparison of the effect of tax policy on the income distribution in Hong Kong with that of other countries should be an interesting topic for another research.

References:

ANDO A., E.C. BROWN and E.W. ADAMS Jr., "Government Revenues and Expenditures", in: J.S. DUESENBERRY, G. FROMM, L.R. KLEIN, and E. KUH (eds.), (a), The Brookings Quarterly Econometric Model of the United States, Chicago: Rand McNally, 1965, pp. 533-585.

BOLTON R.E., "Predictive Models for State and Local Government Purchases", in: J.S. DUESENBERRY, G. FROMM, L.R. KLEIN, and E. KUH (eds.), (b), The Brookings Models: Some Further Results, Amsterdam: North-Holland, 1969, pp. 223-267.

BURKHEAD J., "The Balanced Budget", in: A. SMITHIES and J.K. BUTTERS (eds.), Readings in Fiscal Policy, London: Allen & Unwin, 1955, p. 3-27.

CHENERY H.B. and M. SYRQUIN, Pattern of Development 1950-1970, published for the World Bank by Oxford University Press, 1975.

CHENERY, H.B. and L. TAYLOR, "Development Patterns: Among Countries and Over Time", Review of Economics and Statistics, Vol. 50, 4, 1968, pp. 391-416.

HINRICHS H.H., "Determinants of Government Revenue Shares among Less Developed Countries", Economic Journal, Vol. 75, 3, 1965, pp. 546-556.

HO, H.C.Y. (a), "Growth of Government Expenditure in Hong Kong", Hong Kong Economic Papers, 8, 1974, pp. 18-38.

__________, (b), "Growth of Government Revenue in Hong Kong", Hong Kong Economic Papers, 9, 1975, pp. 67-83.

HSUEH T.T. (a), "Development Features of A Mini-open Economy: The Cases of Singapore and Hong Kong", Journal of the Chinese Unisersity of Hong Kong, Vol. III, 1, 1976.

__________, (b), "The Transforming Economy of Hong Kong 1952-1973", Hong Kong Economic Papers, 10, 1976.

JOHANSEN L., Public Economics, Amsterdam: North-Holland, 1965.

LEWIS W.A. and A.M. MARTIN, "Patterns of Public Revenue and Expenditure", Manchester School of Economic and Social Studies, Vol. 24, 3, 1956, pp. 203-44.

MUNDELL R.A., "The Appropriate Use of Monetary and Fiscal Policy for Internal and External Stability", International Monetary Fund Staff Papers, Vol. IX, 1962, pp. 70-79.

MUSGRAVE R.A. (a), Fiscal System, New Haven: Yale University Press, 1969.

__________ (b), The Theory of Public Finance, New York: McGraw-Hill, 1959.

MUSGRAVE R.A. and P.B. MUSGRAVE, Public Finance In Theory And Practice, 2nd edition, New York:McGraw-Hill, 1976.

OWEN N.C., "Economic Policy", in: K. HOPKINS (ed.), Hong Kong: The Industrial Colony, Hong Kong: Oxford University Press, 1971, pp. 141-206.

RABUSHKA A., The Changing Face of Hong Kong. New Departures in Public Policy, Stanford, Calif.: Hoover Institute on War, Revolution and Peace, Stanford University, 1973.

SMITH H., _John Stuart Mill's Other Island. A Study of the Economic Development of Hong Kong_, London: Institute of Economic Affairs, 1966.

STAMMER, D.W., "The Public Finance of Hong Kong", _Malayan Economic Review_, Vol. 13, 1, 1966, pp.115-128.

TAUBMAN P., "Econometric Functions For Government Receipts", in: DUESENBERRG, FROMM, KLEIN and KUH (eds.), (b), op. cit.,189-222.

THORN R.S., "The Evolution of Public Finance During Economic Development", _Manchester School of Economic and Social Studies_, Vol. 35, 1967, pp. 19-51.

WILLIAMSON J.G., "Public Expenditure and Revenue: An International Comparison", _Manchester School of Economic and Social Studies_, Vol. 29, 1, 1961, pp. 43-56.

Annual Reports of the Accountant - General, Hong Kong Government, various issues.

Estimates of Gross Domestic Product 1961-74, Census and Statistics Department, Hong Kong, 1976.

Hong Kong Social and Economic Trends, 1968-72, Census and Statistics Department, Hong Kong, 1973.

Hong Kong Statistics 1947-67, Census and Statistics Department, Hong Kong, 1969.

Key Indicators of Developing Member Countries of ADB. Vol. VII, 1, 1976, Vol. VI, 1, 1975, Asian Development Bank, Economic Office.

Statistical Yearbook 1974 and 1971, New York: United Nations, 1975 and 1972.

Supporting Financial Statements and Statistical Appendices, Hong Kong Government, 1975.

Yearbook of Financial Statistics of the Republic of China, 1974, Department of Statistics, Ministry of Finance, Taipei, 1975.

Yearbook of Statistics, Singapore, 1973/74, Department of Statistics, Singapore, 1974.

IV. INTERNATIONAL RELATIONS

EXPORTS AND EMPLOYMENT IN HONG KONG

Tzong-biau Lin and Mei-chiang Lin

I. Introduction+

The purpose of this paper is (a) to break down the factors of export expansion and to gauge its effect on the growth of domestic manufactured production and (b) to measure the various employment effects of export expansion in Hong Kong. The factors of export expansion can be broken down into four categories, - the increase in world trade volume, the differential commodity composition, the differential area distribution, and the competitiveness of Hong Kong's exports. Among the four, we have found that export expansion in Hong Kong in the past two decades was mainly due to the increase in world trade and the changes in commodity composition. This result attests to the high degree of flexibility inherent in the Hong Kong economy. We have also found that export expansion has exerted the most significant effect on manufacturing industries in Hong Kong vis-à-vis the effects of home demand and import substitution.

By using the input-output analysis, not only the direct and indirect labour requirements of exports and imports but also their direct and indirect capital requirements are calculated. As a result of the empirical analysis, we have found that the linkage effect in employment creation of export is weak and the degree of industrial interdependence in Hong Kong is rather low.

II. The Changing Pattern of Hong Kong's Export Trade

Hong Kong is an extreme case of an outward-looking economy. In order to survive, it must import both consumer goods and raw materials, and the bulk of these must be paid for by exports. Historically, Hong Kong has always had a deficit in its balance of commodity trade which is financed by the net receipts from the invisible trade and capital accounts. Indeed, in the early 1960s, its merchandise trade deficit amounted to 50 % of its total exports. But due to the spectacular growth of its exports, this was lowered to less than 15 % in ten years time, and is still declining.

The degree of Hong Kong's reliance on trade and its success in export drive can be seen from its import/GDP and export/GDP ratios. Except for a few years, the former was well over 90 % during the period under study. The latter stood at 60 to 70 % in the early 1960s, and increased sharply after 1968 when the political situation began to stabilize again after the 1967 social upheaval, - a spillover from China's Cultural Revolution. By 1976, the ratio reached 88 %, a figure which has seldom been matched in other countries of the world.

Table 1 shows a brief account of Hong Kong's success record in the transformation from an entrepôt into an industrial city. This process started in the early 1950s during which Hong Kong's pattern of exports underwent such dramatic changes that there is little, if any, possibility that it will ever revert to what it was two decades ago. In a nutshell, there has been a complete turn around of the relative importance of its re-exports and domestic exports.

Re-exports: At the height of the Korean Boom in 1951, Hong Kong's total exports stood at HK$ 4,433 million (a figure that is higher than that of 1962). But domestic exports were estimated at only HK$ 550 million,[1] implying some 87 % of its exports were actually re-exports. Subsequent events led to its exports to fall to HK$ 2,899 million in 1952, a decrease of about 35 %, mainly due to the drastic curtailment of its re-exports to China.[2] Since then Hong Kong's exports to China have continued to dwindle, causing both its total exports and re-exports to decline to lower levels. In the meantime, its domestic exports have begun to gather momentum.

Starting in the early 1960s, Hong Kong's re-exports turned the corner and revived with amazing speed. By the early 1970s, they had surpassed the previous record set in 1951; in 1976, they amounted to HK$ 8,900, more than twice of that record. In other words, the loss of the Mainland Chinese market had been by far more than made up by increased re-exports to other markets. After long years of continuous decline, Hong Kong's re-exports seem to have stabilized at the level of 20 to 25 % of its total exports.

Traditionally, Asia was the principal market, and it remains very much so despite the dwindling importance of the Mainland Chinese market which at its peak took in some 30 % of Hong Kong's re-exports. But it is also worth noting that Asia's share has been declining, signifying that Hong Kong's re-exports have increasingly gone beyond the horizon of this region. On the other hand, China continues to be the leading supplier, accounting for approximately 25 %. It is interesting to note the increasing volume of Japanese and American exports channelled through Hong Kong. Of special significance is the progress made by Japan, for whose products Hong Kong finds major re-export markets in Singapore, Indonesia, the U.S. and Taiwan.[3]

In summary, even though we can hardly conceive of re-export trade recovering its pre-eminence in the Hong Kong economy it had in the early 1950s, developments in the last decade have indicated that there is every chance for it to flourish. With stability and development in the Asian and Pacific region, Hong Kong will have an extremely important role to play in entrepôt trade, mainly due to the following reasons:

A. It is endowed with an excellent natural harbour, which is situated at a strategic point in the Far East and is equipped with the most modern and efficient shipping facilities.

B. Its long history of trade has built up an excellent international network and financial infrastructure to facilitate re-export business.

C. Its traditional laissez-faire economic policy and free port arrangement have made it a unique entrepôt centre in the region.

Barring unexpected economic and political developments, these favorable factors will contribute to further re-export activities as well as domestic export and economic growth in Hong Kong.

<u>Domestic exports</u>: The growth and transformation of the Hong Kong economy is led by the phenomenal expansion of its export-oriented manufacturing industries. The relative importance of various manufacturing industries and their degree of export-orientation are shown in <u>Appendix 1</u>. The garment, knitwear, electrical and electronics,

Table 1: Pattern of Hong Kong's Export Trade, 1959-76

Year	1959	1960	1961	1962	1963	1964	1965	1966
Value: in Current HK$ Million								
Total Exports (T)	3,277	3,937	3,930	4,387	4,991	5,784	6,530	7,563
Re-exports (X_r)	995	1,070	991	1,070	1,160	1,356	1,503	1,833
Domestic Exports (X_d)	2,282	2,867	2,939	3,317	3,831	4,428	5,027	5,730
N. America and W. Europe (X'_d)	1,226	1,636	1,585	2,030	2,398	2,956	3,490	4,133
Rest of the World (X"d)	1,056	1,231	1,354	1,287	1,433	1,472	1,537	1,597
Manufacture Exports (X_m)[1]	2,019	2,571	2,635	3,038	3,506	4,087	4,694	5,406
Total Imports (M)	4,949	5,864	5,970	6,657	7,412	8,551	8,965	10,097
Total Merchandise Trade (T+M)	8,227	9,801	9,900	11,044	12,403	14,335	15,495	17,660
Merchandise Trade Balance (T-M)	-1,672	-1,927	-2,040	-2,270	-2,421	-2,767	-2,435	-2,534
Value: in Current HK$								
Per Capita Exports[2]	1,147	1,321	1,238	1,327	1,459	1,650	1,815	2,083
Proportion: in Percentages								
X_r/T	30.36	27.18	25.22	24.39	23.24	23.44	23.02	24.24
X_d/T	69.64	72.82	74.78	75.61	76.76	76.56	76.98	75.76
X_m/X_d	88.48	89.68	89.66	91.59	91.52	92.30	93.38	94.35
X'_d/X_d	53.72	57.06	53.93	61.20	62.59	66.76	69.43	72.13
X''_d/X_d	46.28	42.94	46.07	38.80	37.41	33.24	30.57	27.87
T/GDP[3]	--	--	64.96	63.75	62.43	65.03	62.10	68.19
M/GDP	--	--	98.68	96.73	92.72	96.14	85.25	91.04
(T+M)/GDP	--	--	163.64	160.48	155.15	161.17	147.35	159.23
(T-M)/T	-51.02	-48.95	-51.91	-51.74	-48.51	-47.84	-37.29	-33.51

Sources: For trade data: Census and Statistics Department, Hong Kong Trade Statistics (Hong Kong: Government Printer, various December issues). For GDP data: Census and Statistics Department, Estimates of Gross Domestic Product 1961-1975 (Hong Kong: Government Printer, 1977). For mid-year population data: Census and Statistics Department, Hong Kong Statistics, 1947-1967 (Hong Kong: Government Printer, 1969); and Hong Kong Monthly Digest of Statistics (Hong Kong: Government Printer, selected July issues).

Notes:

1. Manufacture exports refer to all commodities which fall into the SITC (Standard International Trade Classification) 512 to SITC 899.
2. Obtained by dividing the mid-year population from the annual values of total exports.
3. GDP estimate for 1975 is provisional and that for 1976 is preliminary. The 1976 estimate is from The 1977-78 Budget: Economic Background (Hong Kong: Government Printer, 1977), p. 3, Table 2.

1967	1968	1969	1970	1971	1972	1973	1974	1975	1976
8,781	10,570	13,197	15,239	17,164	19,399	25,999	30,035	29,832	41,557
2,081	2,142	2,679	2,892	3,414	4,154	6,525	7,124	6,973	8,928
6,700	8,428	10,518	12,347	13,750	15,245	19,474	22,911	22,859	32,629
4,830	6,240	7,897	9,156	10,408	11,723	14,068	15,799	16,431	24,142
1,870	2,188	2,621	3,191	3,342	3,522	5,406	7,112	6,428	8,487
6,366	8,046	10,071	11,839	13,252	14,719	18,822	22,108	22,168	31,656
10,499	12,472	14,893	17,607	20,256	21,764	29,005	34,120	33,472	43,293
19,230	23,042	28,090	32,846	37,420	41,163	55,004	64,156	63,304	84,850
-1,668	-1,902	-1,696	-2,368	-3,092	-2,365	-3,006	-4,085	-3,640	-1,736
2,359	2,779	3,415	3,849	4,243	4,757	6,250	7,069	6,832	9,482
23.70	20.26	20.30	18.98	18.89	21.41	25.10	23.72	23.37	21.48
76.30	79.74	79.70	81.02	80.11	78.59	74.90	76.28	76.63	78.52
95.01	95.47	95.75	95.89	96.38	96.55	96.65	96.50	96.98	97.02
72.09	74.04	75.08	74.16	75.69	76.90	72.24	68.96	71.88	73.99
27.91	25.96	24.92	25.84	24.31	23.10	27.76	31.04	28.12	26.01
70.75	79.14	83.57	81.62	81.83	80.31	84.90	85.20	79.70	88.21
84.19	93.38	94.31	94.31	96.57	90.10	94.72	96.79	89.43	91.89
154.94	172.52	177.88	175.93	178.40	170.41	179.62	181.99	169.13	180.10
-19.00	-17.99	-12.85	-15.54	-18.01	-12.19	-11.56	-13.60	-12.20	-4.18

toys and plastics industries are the most notable examples of export-orientation. They all have export/output ratios of over 80 % and carry substantial weights in the Hong Kong export basket.

Classified according to the SITC (Standard International Trade Classification) codes, the export composition of Hong Kong is indeed quite simple. There is very little to say about non-manufactures; their relative shares are insignificant and also decreasing. This pattern gives a clear picture of the nature of the Hong Kong economy - the lack of natural resources and concentration on non-resource based manufacturing. Manufactures (SITC 6 to 8) account for an overwhelming proportion of its domestic exports, which still continues to increase from around 90 % in the early 1960s to over 95 % in the mid-1970s. This must be the highest in the world.

Within the broad classification of manufactures, Miscellaneous Manufactured Articles (SITC 8) continued to occupy the dominant position. In fact, its share increased from 53 % in 1961 to 68 % in 1975. This is due to the sustained eminence of the clothing group and the rapid expansion of toys, watches and clocks, travel goods and jewellery in the Hong Kong export basket. On the other hand, Manufactured Goods Classified Chiefly by Material (SITC 6) have declined substantially, mainly because of the diminishing relative importance of textiles due to tariff and nontariff restrictions imposed thereon. With a modest start in the early 1960s, Machinery and Transport Equipment (SITC 7) climbed up to a respectable 15 % in the mid-1970s. This is mainly due to the fast development of the electrical and electronics industries.

Regarding the destinations of Hong Kong's domestic exports, the U.S. is by far the most important market. This started during the 1950s when the U.S. banned imports from China and turned to Hong Kong for Chinese-type products; at the same time, American restrictions on Japanese textiles also helped stimulate Hong Kong's development into an alternative source of supply. The mass American market also provided much room for products of other rapidly developing manufacturing industries. By 1959, it already accounted for 25 % of Hong Kong's domestic exports and reached its peak of 42 % in 1969. Although its share started to decline afterwards to about one-third in the mid-1970s, the American market is of about the combined size of that of the next four countries, namely, the U.K., F.R. Germany, Japan and Canada (or Australia).

For obvious historical and political reasons, Britain has been one of Hong Kong's most important trading partners. Its relative importance, however, has been diminishing. In 1959, its share still stood at 20 %, second only to the U.S.. At that time, the West German market had only a 3 % share, much less than a number of other countries. But its rapid and continuous expansion has enabled Germany to replace Britain and it became the second largest market in 1975, with a 12.5 % share, while the British market share dwindled to 12.2 %.

Over the years, Hong Kong has increasingly directed its exports to the developed countries (DCs). The diminishing importance of the less developed countries (LDCs market) is understandable. These countries generally have limited market size in terms of purchasing power. Moreover, many of them deliberately seek to build up their own infant industries through import protection. Thus, even though for some time in the early 1960s Malaysia and Singapore combined ranked as Hong Kong's third largest market, their shares have declined substantially. Only Taiwan, which is among the few LDCs having made certain trade liberalization efforts more recently, has increased its share of imports from Hong Kong.

Finally, the U.S.S.R. and the Eastern European countries, which potentially constitute a vast market for consumer non-durables, have come into the reach of Hong Kong at considerable speed. It is still too early, however, to say to what extent this market will open up and become significant, considering its low base and other non-economic factors.

III. Export Expansion - Causes and Effects

A. Factor Decomposition of Export Expansion

The extraordinary export expansion in the past two decades reviewed in the previous section is the conditio sine qua non for Hong Kong's miraculous economic growth. It is therefore appropriate to inquire as to the factors which have made the significant contributions to this phenomenal expansion in Hong Kong's domestic exports. To investigate these effects, we followed H. Tyszynski[4] in adopting the following formulae to compute the contributions of various factors in Hong Kong's export expansion during the decade 1964-74. For the sake of easier understanding, we first introduce the following notation:

x^{64}: domestic export receipts in 1964
x^{74}: domestic export receipts in 1974
p: growth rate of world exports during 1964-1974
i: this subscript (i = 1,2,....7) denotes seven different commodity groups[5]
j: this subscript (j = 1,2) denotes the two different markets, viz.: (1) DCs, and (2) LDCs[6]

The impact of export expansion can then be broken down into the following factors:

(1) The effect of the increase in total world trade on Hong Kong's exports by commodity classification[7]

$$\sum_i p x_i^{64} - \sum_i x_i^{64} = (p-1) \sum_i x_i^{64}$$

(2) The effect of the differential commodity composition of the increase in world trade on Hong Kong's exports, given the latter's 1964 commodity mix

$$\sum_i p_i x_i^{64} - \sum_i p\, x_i^{64}$$

(3) The effect of the differential area distribution of the increase in world trade on Hong Kong's exports, given the latter's 1964 geographic structure

$$\sum_{ij}\sum p_{ij} x_{ij}^{64} - \sum_i p_i x_i^{64}$$

(4) The effect of the increased competitiveness of Hong Kong's exports is defined to be equal to the residual:

$$\sum_{ij}\sum x_{ij}^{74} - \sum_{ij}\sum p_{ij} x_{ij}^{64}$$

It is easy to see that the sum of the four effects is:

$$\sum_{ij}\sum x_{ij}^{74} - \sum_i x_i^{64}$$

which is by definition equal to the total export increment from 1964 to 1974.

Table 2: Analysis of Changes in Hong Kong's Exports by Commodity Classes: 1964-1974[1]

	Clothing	Textile Yarn, Fabrics and Made-up Articles	Electrical Products	Metal Manufactures	Footwear	Miscellaneous Manufactured Articles	Others[3]	TOTAL
Exports in 1964	1,620	707	186	146	175	865	54	3,753
Exports in 1974	8,752	2,737	3,296	729	311	3,699	3,387	22,911
Changes in exports 1964-1974	7,132	2,030	3,110	583	136	2,834	3,333	19,158
a. Due to increase in world trade	3,483.00 (48.8)	1,520.05 (74.9)	399.90 (12.9)	313.90 (53.8)	376.25 (277.7)	1,859.75 (65.6)	116.10 (3.5)	8,068.95 (42.1)
b. Due to differential commodity composition	4,876.20 (68.4)	2,128.05 (104.9)	230.60 (7.4)	439.40 (75.4)	526.75 (387.3)	2,603.65 (91.9)	-122.60 (-3.7)	10,682.05 (55.8)
c. Due to differential market distribution	-299.88 (-4.1)	-166.68 (-5.6)	28.42 (0.9)	-73.48 (-12.6)	-268.05 (-197.1)	132.85 (4.7)	-7.57 (-0.2)	-595.39 (-3.1)
d. Due to increased competitiveness	-936.32 (-13.1)	-1,501.42 (-74.0)	2,451.08 (78.8)	-96.82 (-16.6)	-498.95 (-367.9)	-1,762.25 (-62.2)	3,347.07 (100.4)	1,002.39 (5.2)

Sources: Census and Statistics Department, Hong Kong Trade Statistics (Hong Kong: Government Printer, selected December issues); and United Nations, Monthly Bulletin of Statistics (New York: United Nations Publication, selected issues).

Notes: 1. Figures in parentheses are percentages of the total changes, they do not add to total because of rounding.
2. Including: plastic toys and dolls, artificial flowers, foliage, fruit, plastic coated rattan articles (except furniture), wigs, false beards, hair pads, and other manufactured products, not elsewhere classified.
3. Including food, beverage and tobacco, crude materials, animal and vegetable oils and fats, mineral fuels and related materials, chemicals, passengers road vehicles and their parts.

The four effects are listed in Table 2. During the decade 1964-74 exports increased more than 5 times. The increase was largely due to change in commodity composition (55.8 %) and expansion in world trade volume (42.1 %). The export expansion due to increased competitiveness was negligible, only 5.2 %, and the market distribution factor was unfavorable to Hong Kong as evidenced by the negative 3.1 %. This negative contribution implies that world demand grew less than proportionately in those markets to which Hong Kong's goods were traditionally exported. In this respect Hong Kong's export pattern was quite compatible with Taiwan's experience,[8] as from 1962 to 1972 the market distribution effect for Taiwan was -3.5 %. In terms of commodity composition effect, Hong Kong is better off since the latter experienced a -3.1 % for this effect. This is because Taiwan has a fairly high percentage of exports of primary products which have experienced an adverse trend of terms of trade in the past. The most striking difference between Taiwan and Hong Kong's export changes lies in the competitive effect. While in Taiwan this effect accounted for more than 80 % of the total export increase during 1962 to 1972, it accounted for only 5.2 % for Hong Kong during the period 1964-1974.

The high commodity composition effect reflects the high speed with which Hong Kong's economy has adjusted itself to changes in world demand. High degree of flexibility is indeed one of the most notable features of the Hong Kong economy.[9]

The world trade expansion effect is a result of the good international market network which Hong Kong has maintained ever since it became a big entrepôt in Asia and a result of effective export promotion.[10]

Among the four effects, the competitive effect may be the key factor in solving the trade problem in the future. If the Hong Kong economy is going to maintain its present level of high export expansion and economic growth, not only should new products be produced, but also more sophisticated production techniques and industrial management be introduced, so that both its labour productivity and capital efficiency can be increased. Only after all of these have been achieved, can its products be able to compete with those products from neighbouring developing countries in the international markets.

B. Factors Contributing to the Growth of Domestic Manufactured Production

Given the fact that Hong Kong's domestic exports have increased very rapidly, it is appropriate to ask the following question: To what extent has the export expansion contributed to the growth of the manufacturing industries in Hong Kong? Part of the answer can be found in the high proportion of those products which were produced for export. The higher the proportion is, the greater will be its impact on the domestic economy as a whole, especially on the manufactured production. To quantitatively evaluate the export expansion effect on manufactured production, the following modified version of Chenery's approach[11] was adopted.

Let

- Y: domestic production of manufactures
- S = Y + M; where M stands for imports, then S is the total supply of manufactured goods
- H: home demand for manufactures
- X: exports of manufactures
- μ = Y/S: the share of domestically produced manufactures in the total supply; is termed the degree of self-sufficiency, and (1-) the degree of import reliance

then the following identity holds

$$\Delta Y = (\mu_2 - \mu_1)S_2 + \mu_1 \Delta H + \mu_1 \Delta X$$

where ΔY, ΔH and ΔX stand, respectively, for increases in Y, H and X. Subscripts 1 and 2 refer, respectively, to the initial and terminal years of the period concerned. Thus the growth of manufactured production is broken down into import substitution effect $(\mu_2 - \mu_1)S_2$, home demand effect $\mu_1 \Delta H$, and export expansion effect $\mu_1 \Delta X$. The last two effects are arrived at by assuming that the μ, i.e., the degree of self-sufficiency, is kept at its initial level of the period, μ_1.

The various effects for the period 1961-74, and the three subperiods: 1961-64, 1965-67 and 1968-74 are listed in <u>Table 3</u>. Following are some of our major findings: For the whole period 1961-1974, the results for the total show that the export expansion effect (56.2 %) is the most important factor contributing to the expansion of domestic

Table 3: Relative Effects of Increased Home Demand, Export Expansion and Import Substitution on Manufactured Outputs of Selected Industry Groups in Hong Kong (in Percentages)[1]

	Effect of Home Demand	Effect of Export Expansion	Effect of Import Substitution
For 1961 - 1974			
Total Manufactured Output	39.32	56.22	4.46
Food	84.99	3.93	11.08
Beverage and Tobacco	145.58	4.15	-49.73
Clothing and Textiles	4.74	77.19	18.07
Machinery	15.80	20.15	64.05
Transport Equipment[2]	-7,298.65	-953.69	8,352.35
Furniture, Fixture and Household Equipment	87.69	12.04	0.27
For 1961-1964			
Total Manufactured Output	76.21	68.60	-44.81
Food	146.59	20.08	-66.67
Beverage and Tobacco	80.84	19.16	0.00
Clothing and Textiles	22.85	131.64	-54.49
Machinery	41.09	16.63	42.28
Furniture, Fixture and Household Equipment	102.69	10.05	-12.74
For 1965 - 1967			
Total Manufactured Output	19.62	99.57	-19.19
Food	-14.06	-2.97	117.03
Beverage and Tobacco	-200.23	248.29	51.94
Clothing and Textiles	3.69	74.43	21.88
Machinery	2.72	30.85	66.42
Transport Equipment	-7.69	12.82	94.87
Furniture, Fixture and Household Equipment	45.93	47.28	6.79
For 1968 - 1974			
Total Manufactured Output	38.01	50.98	11.01
Food	70.72	2.24	27.04
Beverage and Tobacco	109.88	3.38	-13.26
Clothing and Textiles	4.14	72.99	22.87
Machinery	29.42	35.31	35.27
Transport Equipment	-530.01	-22.22	652.23
Furniture, Fixture and Household Equipment	88.59	8.78	2.63

Source: Derived from Appendix Table 1.

Notes:
1. Save for the rounding discrepancies, the three relative effects add to 100.
2. These figures are large because their denominator is small, as the following calculation shows:

Since $\mu_{74} - \mu_{61} = -0.247$; $S_{74} = 655$; $\Delta Y = -1.937$.

And $\mu_{61}\Delta H = 141.375$; $\mu_{61}\Delta X = 18.473$; $(\mu_{74} - \mu_{61})S_{74} = -161.785$

Thus, $\frac{\mu_{61}\Delta H}{\Delta Y} = \frac{141.375}{-1.937} = -7,298.65$; $\frac{\mu_{61}\Delta X}{\Delta Y} = \frac{18.473}{-1.938} = -953.69$ and

$$\frac{(\mu_{74} - \mu_{61})S_{74}}{\Delta Y} = \frac{-161.785}{-1.937} = 8,352.35$$

production of manufactures. This reflects the fact that Hong Kong's industries are export-oriented. The home demand effect (39.3 %) is also a very important factor for Hong Kong's industrial growth. This is evidenced by the rapidly growing domestic market, which was brought about by the high growth rates of per capita income and population.

Unlike most developing countries for which import substitution has provided an important impetus, at least at the early stage of their industrialization,[12] this strategy of growth has played a negligible role in Hong Kong's industrialization process.[13] A comparison among the results for the 3 subperiods reveals that the import substitution effect appeared to be more pronounced at the later stage of economic development than at the early stage, even though it has never been significant. Although this result is in sharp contrast to what was observed in most LDCs, it reflects largely the fact that Hong Kong's industries were export-oriented from the very beginning.

The results of the aggregate conceal some salient features which emerge in those of the disaggregated data. While the totality of the products has indicated a dominant export expansion effect on output, some products which were produced mainly to meet the local needs have shown an extraordinarily strong home demand effect. These are the production of transport equipment, beverage and tobacco, food and furniture, fixtures and household equipment. The production of clothing and textiles is characteristically export-dependent as the import substitution effect is very small and the home demand effect is negligible.

The only industry which owed its expansion to the import substitution effect is the machinery industry,[14] 64 % for the period 1961-1974. The results for the 3 subperiods also clearly indicate its significant role in the development of machinery production.

IV. Measurement of Employment Effects of Export Expansion

The main theme of this paper is to evaluate the contribution of increased exports to employment in Hong Kong. In order to better understand the significance of the subject matter, it is important to review briefly what has been accomplished so far in this area of research. According to neo-classical trade theory, an increase in exports from those countries which have a relative abundance of labour and a scarcity of capital tends to favour labour-intensive industries and thus be particularly beneficial for employment. Recent studies have shown quite conclusively that the pattern of exports from the LDCs is strongly concentrated at the labour-intensive end of the spectrum of manufactured products, which is of course in line with the Heckscher-Ohlin relative factor endowment theory.[15]

A conceptual framework for analysing the likely effects on employment of an increase in exports is more or less shared by quite a number of economists, particularly by those of the International Labour Organization.[16] As far as domestic effects of the exporting country are concerned, there are four categories under which the likely employment effects of an increase in exports can be analysed, i.e., direct, indirect (linkage), multiplier, and balance of payments.[17] In the current paper, we have divided the effects into two categories, direct effect and secondary effect, with the latter consisting of linkage, multiplier and balance of payments effects.

One of the most recent empirical studies in this area is the one carried out for the International Labour Organization by Lydall. Confined to 12 selected manufactured and semi-manufactured products, Lydall's work tends to confirm the assumptions of the neo-classical approach. He finds that, in general, the lower the level of development is, the larger will be the number of jobs generated by a given increase in exports.

However, because of the different institutional and structural conditions under which exports are produced, conclusive empirical studies pertaining to the relationship between the aforesaid four categories of employment effects are still lacking, except that in most cases direct employment creation appears to play a relatively minor part of the total employment effects.[18] Although on theoretical grounds, it is frequently argued that export expansion creates significantly greater employment opportunities by linkage and multiplier effects than those by direct effects, we should not be too optimistic about such effects. The general structure of most underdeveloped economies suggests that the effectiveness and immediacy of these linkage and multiplier effects on employment are severely dampened by many constraining factors.[19] For example, the linkage employment-creating effects heavily depend on the assumption that the domestic economy is able to supply a significantly high proportion of necessary raw materials or semi-processed manufactures to the export industry in such a manner that some sort of balanced growth of various industries may be simultaneously maintained. Thus the expansion of a certain industry can lead to cumulative rounds of demand for the output of other industries, resulting in cumulative rounds of employment creation. Or there is a leading sector with strong backward linkages in the economy which is capable of spearheading other industries and generating employment as a consequence of its strong demand pull. Such arguments, in our view, can only be applicable to resource-rich economies. For most resource-poor economies, import leakages are likely to be large, indirect and multiplier employment-creation effects are thus likely to be considerably weaker than they are often supposed to be. Sometimes, even if the domestic economy can produce the necessary inputs for the export industry and employment can be generated, the opportunity cost of doing so must be carefully taken into account. In addition, export expansion of capital-intensive production, when accompanied by an adverse backwash effect, may fail to induce sufficient demand for labour. It it is found to be significant, it may well offset any likely linkage or multiplier effect of employment.[20]

In small resource-poor economies like Hong Kong (and Singapore) which rely heavily on imports of raw materials and intermediate inputs for the fabrication of domestic exportables, both linkage and multiplier effects would be very weak. In other words, the secondary employment effects are generally believed to be rather low in Hong Kong. Following is a detailed quantitative verification of this assertion.

A. Direct and Total Labour (or Capital) Inputs

If L_o and K_o denote the input coefficients vectors for labour and capital respectively (both have the order of 1 x 15 in our present case), then L_{oj} is the direct labour input coefficient for industry j and K_{oj} is the direct capital input coefficient for the same industry. The total labour and capital input coefficients are obtained by operating the whole system so as to produce a net output of one unit of j and zero net outputs elsewhere in the system. Specifically, the total labour requirement for industry j, denoted by L^+_{oj}, is given by

$$L^+_{oj} = L_o \cdot (I-A)^{-1}_j = \sum_i L_{oi} a^{ij}$$

where a^{ij} are the elements of $(I-A)^{-1}_j$, which is defined to be the jth column of $(I-A)^{-1}$.

Similarly, the total capital requirement for industry j, denoted by K^+_{oj}, is given by

$$K^+_{oj} = K_o \cdot (I-A)^{-1}_j = \sum_i K_{oi}\ a^{ij}.$$

Since $(I-A)^{-1} = I + A + A^2 + A^3 \ldots\ldots,$[21] and A is semi-positive and the diagonal terms of A^r (r = 1, 2, 3....) are non-negative and are, in fact, positive for some r[22], thus the diagonal terms of $(I-A)^{-1}$ must be greater than unity. Now in the expression of $\sum_i L_{oi}\ a^{ij}$, one of the terms is $L_{oj}\ a^{jj}$, where $a^{jj} > 1$, and the rest are certainly non-negative. So the sum is always greater than L_{oj}. In other words, the total labour requirement is greater than the direct labour requirement. The same conclusion holds for capital requirements.

B. The Direct Labour-Output and Capital-Output Ratios

As discussed above, the direct labour input coefficients or direct labour-output ratios are represented by the row vector L_o. L_{oj} then stands for the direct labour input coefficient of industry j. In order to compute the direct labour requirements of Hong Kong's exports, we have to determine the direct labour inputs coefficients for each industrial sector. The two industrial censuses conducted in 1971 and 1973 provide the data for these calculations. For simplicity, we have classified the manufacturing industries into 15 sectors.[23]

Since the trade statistics are classified according to the SITC (Standard International Trade Classification), and the census of industrial production is classified according to the ISIC (International Standard Industrial Classification), there is no way to guarantee that our trade classification will match completely with industrial classification. In 1971, the United Nations published a statistical paper listing the corresponding items between the SITC and ISIC.[24] It served as a guideline for our classifications. Granting that the trade and industrial production statistics published by the Census and Statistics Department of Hong Kong have adhered to the definitions and principles laid down in the CCIO (Classification of Commodities by Industrial Origin), then our classifications of trade and industries should largely dovetail each other.

Table 4 shows the coefficients of direct labour and capital requirements. For 1971, we have two definitions of labour inputs. One is the man-hour of operative workers (Definition I), the other is the man-hour of total employees, which include the non-operative personnel (Definition II). On the average, labour input by Definition II is larger than that of Definition I, by c.a. 10 %. Columns 1 and 2 in the table list the man-hour requirements per unit output corresponding to the Definitions I and II, respectively.

For 1973, only Definition I labour inputs are available. The results are displayed in column 3, which should be compared with those of column 1. One can easily discern that the 1973 labour requirements for each sector amounted to only about 60 % of the corresponding figure for 1971. The discrepancy is rather consistent, systematic and substantial. It may be attributed to the following two factors:

(1) In the 1973 survey, payments to outworkers/homeworkers were counted as part of "labour cost" and "value added", while the number of outworkers/homeworkers was excluded from "person engaged" (therefore, from the man-hours). As a result, measurements of productivity in terms of value added per person engaged (or per man-hour worked) take a higher value than it should be. In other words, its labour/output ratios tend to bias downward as compared with those of 1971.[25]

Table 4: Labour-Output and Capital-Output Ratios (Direct Labour and Capital Requirements Per Dollar Output)

Sector	Description	Man Hours of Operatives/Total Output (Hong Kong, 1971) (1)	Man Hours of Total Employees/ Total Output (Hong Kong, 1971) (2)	Man Hours of Operatives/Total Output (Hong Kong, 1973) (3)	Capital/Total Output (Singapore, 1970) (4)	Capital/Total Output (Hong Kong, 1973) (5)
1	Primary Products	0.0911 (7)	0.0986 (7)	0.0411 (9)	0.0192 (9)	0.0188 (8)
2	Food, Beverage and Tobacco	0.0325 (13)	0.0400 (13)	0.0200 (13)	0.0140 (13)	0.0328 (2)
3	Textiles	0.0565 (12)	0.0621 (12)	0.0328 (11)	0.0604 (1)	0.0271 (3)
4	Wearing Apparel and Footwear	0.0935 (5)	0.1019 (5)	0.0554 (4)	0.0184 (10)	0.0105 (13)
5	Furniture, Fixture and Wood Products	0.0915 (6)	0.0998 (6)	0.0463 (7)	0.0301 (3)	0.0114 (11)
6	Paper and Paper Products	0.0784 (9)	0.0943 (8)	0.0389 (10)	0.0414 (2)	0.0385 (1)
7	Leather	0.0756 (11)	0.0794 (11)	0.0416 (8)	0.0097 (15)	0.0108 (12)
8	Rubber and Chemical Products	0.1024 (4)	0.1152 (3)	0.0559 (3)	0.0105 (14)	0.0263 (4)
9	Basic Metals	0.0210 (14)	0.0240 (14)	0.0133 (14)	0.0297 (4)	0.0133 (10)
10	Metal Products	0.1038 (3)	0.1130 (4)	0.0659 (1)	0.0271 (5)	0.0242 (5)
11	Machinery	0.1139 (1)	0.1229 (1)	0.0528 (5)	0.0262 (6)	0.0239 (6)
12	Electrical Products	0.0821 (8)	0.0943 (9)	0.0474 (6)	0.0257 (7)	0.0179 (9)
13	Transport Equipment	0.1097 (2)	0.1217 (2)	0.0630 (2)	0.0149 (12)	0.0238 (7)
14	Miscellaneous Manufactures	0.0765 (10)	0.0849 (10)	0.0298 (12)	0.0217 (8)	0.0101 (14)
15	Other Services	Nil (15)	Nil (15)	Nil (15)	0.0152 (11)	Nil (15)

Sources: Census and Statistics Department, 1971 Census of Manufacturing Establishments (Hong Kong: Government Printer, 1973); Census Circular No. 1/75: 1973 Census of Industrial Production (Hong Kong, July 1975) (unpublished manuscript); and Kau Al Keng, 1970 Inter-Industry Table (Singapore: Economic Research Centre and Department of Business Administration of University of Singapore, 1974)(mimeo.)

Note: The numbers in parentheses indicate the sectoral ranking positions.

(2) In the 1973 survey, only a 10 % sample was used for the 20,000 odd small manufacturing establishments engaging 1 to 9 persons. Since the small firms tend to be more labour-intensive than their larger counterparts, the exclusion of the small firms from the statistics of the 1973 survey will make the results look less labour-intensive than they should be.

It is not possible to derive the direct capital requirements from the 1971 survey. The figures listed in column 4 were obtained from Singaporean data for reference. But the 1973 survey provides information on capital inputs and the direct capital-output ratios for 1973 are displayed in column 5. Comparing the last two columns of the table, we find that most of the sectors have similar relative ranking positions, with the apparent exceptions of sectors 2 (food, beverages and tobacco), 5 (furnitures, fixtures and wood products), 8 (rubber and chemical products), and 9 (basic metals). Sectors 2 and 8 are among the most relatively capital-intensive industries in Hong Kong, while sectors 5 and 9 are relatively more capital-intensive in Singapore than in Hong Kong.

In order to see the relationships between the various ratios we have computed Spearman rank correlation coefficients, R_{ij} (the subscripts i, j refer to the column numbers of the table). They are: $R_{1.2}= 0.99$, $R_{1.3}= 0.92$, and $R_{3.5}= 0.19$. The high value of $R_{1.2}$ suggests that there is a high degree of positive correlation between the number of operative workers and that of non-operative personnel engaged in each sector; while the high value of $R_{1.3}$ implies that the relative labour intensity in the various sectors does not change substantially between 1971 and 1973. The low value of $R_{3.5}$ reflects that a high labour-intensive sector has a low capital intensity and vice versa. Although this result is obtained from the 1973 survey only, there is no apparent ground to doubt that it would not apply to 1971.

The most labour-intensive sectors for 1971 are: machinery (11), transport equipment (13), metal products (10), rubber and chemical products (8), and wearing apparel and footwear (4). For 1973, the most labour-intensive ones are: metal products (10), transport equipment (13), rubber and chemical products (8), wearing apparel and footwear (4), and machinery (11). And the three most capital-intensive sectors (1973 figures) are: paper and paper products (6), food,

Table 5: Direct Labour Requirements of Hong Kong's Exports and Imports: Selected Years
(Unit: Million Man-Hour)

Sector	1964[1]		1970		1970[2]		1973		1974[4]	
	Exports	Imports	Exports	Imports	Exports	Imports	Exports[3]	Imports	Exports	Imports
1	10.86	146.20	24.97	297.11	27.04	321.70	14.42 (31.99)	219.08	18.02	299.99
2	6.32	42.25	7.10	63.82	8.73	78.48	6.03 (9.79)	67.15	6.27	77.98
3	40.59	111.16	72.79	215.17	80.04	236.61	77.76 (133.91)	199.46	90.71	192.46
4	167.68	20.61	433.50	30.89	472.84	33.69	427.53 (721.43)	39.42	501.93	34.96
5	13.80	15.09	27.16	21.22	29.60	23.12	20.49 (40.49)	23.06	22.89	24.03
6	0.95	16.08	2.95	34.43	3.55	41.39	3.14 (6.33)	28.01	4.98	35.00
7	0.12	2.46	0.48	6.43	0.51	6.75	0.63 (1.14)	9.44	0.61	10.64
8	5.39	75.51	11.06	153.61	12.43	172.71	9.98 (18.29)	128.74	11.82	168.48
9	0.89	9.32	1.70	15.39	1.94	17.60	1.18 (1.87)	14.52	1.89	20.45
10	15.14	12.25	35.78	21.13	38.97	23.01	34.31 (54.01)	23.71	42.26	28.19
11	2.78	48.34	10.60	110.38	11.44	119.14	11.32 (24.41)	76.81	16.72	91.74

12	15.30	33.61	106.14	123.85	121.83	142.17	124.40 (215.31)	129.83	156.34	157.32
13	1.63	20.89	7.56	45.99	8.40	51.05	3.86 (6.72)	46.19	3.90	35.88
14	71.48	54.19	273.07	162.37	302.95	180.13	132.76 (341.27)	99.63	147.93	121.42
TOTAL	352.90	607.95	1,014.86	1,301.79	1,120.26	1,447.56	867.81 (1,606.95)	1,105.01	1,026.25	1,298.54

Sources: Computed from Table 4 and Appendix Table 2.

Notes:
1. Based on the 1971's labour-output ratios (Definition I).
2. Definition II of labour input was used.
3. Figures in parentheses were based on the 1971's labour-output ratios (Definition I).
4. Based on the 1973's labour-output ratios.

beverage and tobacco (2), and textiles (3). These results are very much in line with our theoretical considerations.

C. Direct Labour Requirements of Hong Kong's Trade

The direct labour requirement coefficients given in Table 4 and the sectoral trade classification given in Appendix Table 2 enable us to compute the direct labour requirements of Hong Kong's exports and imports. The results are shown in Table 5. Our major findings are as follows:

At the early stage (1964)

In terms of absolute magnitude, the following sectors required most direct labour inputs or, in other words, created the greatest direct employment in Hong Kong. They were: wearing apparel and footwear (4), miscellaneous manufactured articles (14), textiles (3), electrical products (12), and metal products (10); on the other hand, the following sectors created least direct employment: leather (7), paper and paper products (6), transport equipment (13), and machinery (11).

At the later stage (1974)

The most employment-creating sectors of Hong Kong's exports are: wearing apparel and footwear (4), electrical products (12), miscellaneous manufactured articles (14), and furniture, fixture and wood products (5). The following sectors generated least employment: leather (7), basic metals (9), transport equipment (13), paper and paper products (6), and food, beverage and tobacco (2). In terms of employment creation, wearing apparel and footwear as a single sector turns out to be the most important exporting industry in Hong Kong. It has been maintaining its dominant position ever since the beginning of the sixties when the Hong Kong economy started to take off. In addition to sector 4, sectors 14, 12 and 10 are the most vital industries in Hong Kong. Now we turn to the import side.

In the early sixties, sectors 3 (textiles), 1 (primary products), 2 (food, beverage and tobacco), 8 (rubber and chemicals products), 12 (electrical products), and 14 (miscellaneous manufactures) took the largest trade shares (see Appendix Table 2). In terms of labour requirements, if they were produced in Hong Kong, these sectors are also the most significant ones. At the later stage (1973), although these sectors still maintained their significant positions, sectors 12 (electrical products), 11 (machinery), and 9 (basic metals) gained increasing importance, implying that in the course of industrialization, Hong Kong's imports of producer's goods became more and more important as compared with those of consumer goods.

D. Leontief's Paradox?

In order to determine whether Hong Kong's merchandise export structure is more labour-intensive than its import counterpart we have to compare the total labour requirements of exports and imports. Since Hong Kong's imports are always larger than its exports, we have to adjust the two sets of data to be on the same level so that meaningful comparisons can be drawn.

Column 4 of Table 6 shows that after exports were raised to the same level as imports, the direct labour requirements of exports are consistently greater than those of imports. The difference ranges from 12 % in 1964 to 18 % in 1974. The relative labour intensity of exports seems to have increased in the last decade.

Table 7 shows the direct and total labour requirements of Hong Kong's imports and exports with respect to both definitions of labour inputs for 1970. The figures in brackets refer to the total (direct and secondary) labour requirements, which will be discussed below.

From the labour requirement figures for imports and the augmented exports shown in the last row of Table 7, we can compute the relative labour intensity of Hong Kong's exports to imports for 1970. For the time being, our attention is confined to the relative direct labour intensities only. They are 1.11 and 1.10 by Definitions I and II of labour inputs, respectively.[26] One of the obvious reasons for Hong Kong's exports being more labour-intensive than its imports is that its export structure tends to be more labour-intensive than its import counterpart. This is evidenced by the relatively low rank correlation coefficients between the import and the augmented export. By Definition I of labour inputs, the coefficient

Table 6: Overall Direct Labour Requirements and Relative Labour Intensity of Hong Kong's Exports: Selected Years

Unit: Million Man-Hour

	Import/ Export Ratio λ (1)	Labour Requirements			Relative Labour Intensity of Exports (4)/(2) = (5)
		Imports (2)	Exports (3)	λ - augmented Labour Requirement of Exports (3) . λ = (4)	
1964	1.93	607.95	352.90	682.15	1.12
1970	1.43	1,301.79 (1,447.60)	1,014.86 (1,120.26)	1,448.21 (1,598.62)	1.11 (1.10)
1973	1.49	1,105.02	867.81	1,293.04	1.17
1974	1.49	1,298.54	1,026.25	1,529.11	1.18

Sources: Computed from Table 4 and Appendix Table 2.

Note: Figures in parentheses were based on the Definition II of labour inputs.

$R_{1.3}$ is 0.44, while by Definition II of labour inputs, it is 0.45 ($R_{4.6}$). These ratios apply to both the direct and total labour requirements. As can readily be seen from Table 7, the ranks are identical for both direct and total requirements of each sector. Through these sectoral rankings, an important conclusion can be drawn for Hong Kong's industrial structure, i.e., each sector's indirect labour requirements are highly compatible with its direct labour requirements, none of the sector's secondary labour requirements are large enough to upset its total labour requirements' ranking position.

E. Direct Capital Reqirements of Hong Kong's Trade

In addition to the labour requirements, the capital requirements of exports also concern the researchers very much. They are the two fundamental aspects of factor endowment and their state of relative abundance dictates a country's comparative advantage in international trade and thereby makes the international division of labour possible.

Table 7: Direct and Total Labour Requirements of Hong Kong's Imports and Exports for 1970 (Unit: Million Man-Hour)

Sector	Definition I of Labour Inputs			Definition II of Labour Inputs		
	Imports (1)	Exports (2)	Augmented Exports (3)	Imports (4)	Exports (5)	Augmented Exports (6)
1	297.10 (1) (315.44)	24.97 (26.51)	35.63 (7) (37.83)	321.70 (1) (342.13)	27.04 (28.75)	35.58 (7) (41.03)
2	63.82 (7) (85.88)	7.10 (9.55)	10.13 (11) (13.63)	78.48 (7) (103.28)	8.73 (11.48)	12.45 (10) (16.39)
3	215.17 (2) (262.32)	72.79 (88.74)	103.87 (4) (126.64)	236.61 (2) (289.44)	80.04 (97.92)	114.22 (4) (139.73)
4	30.89 (10) (33.58)	433.50 (471.19)	618.61 (1) (672.39)	33.69 (10) (36.65)	472.84 (514.29)	674.74 (1) (733.89)
5	21.22 (11) (25.44)	27.16 (32.56)	38.75 (6) (46.46)	23.12 (11) (27.76)	29.60 (35.53)	42.23 (6) (50.71)
6	34.43 (9) (38.48)	2.95 (3.30)	4.21 (12) (4.71)	41.39 (9) (46.14)	3.55 (3.96)	5.06 (12) (5.65)
7	6.43 (14) (9.42)	0.48 (0.71)	0.69 (14) (1.01)	6.75 (14) (10.00)	0.51 (0.75)	0.72 (14) (1.07)
8	153.61 (4) (158.30)	11.06 (11.40)	15.78 (8) (16.26)	172.71 (4) (177.90)	12.43 (12.81)	17.74 (8) (18.28)
9	15.39 (13) (18.50)	1.70 (2.04)	2.42 (13) (2.91)	17.56 (13) (21.12)	1.94 (2.33)	2.77 (13) (3.32)
10	21.13 (12) (22.88)	35.78 (38.74)	51.06 (5) (55.28)	23.01 (12) (24.94)	38.97 (42.24)	55.62 (5) (60.28)
11	110.38 (6) (116.59)	10.60 (11.20)	15.13 (9) (15.98)	119.13 (6) (126.04)	11.44 (12.11)	16.33 (9) (17.27)
12	123.85 (5) (138.87)	106.14 (119.01)	151.46 (3) (169.83)	142.17 (5) (159.03)	121.83 (136.29)	173.86 (3) (194.48)
13	45.99 (8) (58.16)	7.56 (9.57)	10.80 (10) (13.65)	51.05 (8) (64.60)	8.40 (10.63)	11.98 (11) (15.16)
14	162.37 (3) (178.55)	273.07 (300.28)	389.68 (2) (428.50)	180.13 (3) (198.18)	302.95 (333.30)	432.31 (2) (475.62)
TOTAL	1,301.79 (1,462.41)	1,014.86 (1,124.79)	1,448.21 (1,605.07)	1,447.56 (1,627.22)	1,120.26 (1,242.39)	1,598.62 (1,772.87)

Sources: Computed from Table 4 and Appendix Table 2.

Note: The figures in parentheses below each entry refer to the total labour requirements. The numbers in parentheses on the right hand side of labour requirement entries indicate their respective ranking positions.

In order to compare the overall relative capital intensity of Hong Kong's exports with that of its imports, we applied the same approach used in connection with the relative labour intensity, to determine the relative capital intensity of Hong Kong's trade structure.

Table 8: Overall Direct Capital Requirements of Exports and Imports and Relative Capital Intensity of Exports: Selected Years

Unit: HK$ Mn.

	Import/ Export Ratio λ	Capital Requirements			Relative Capital Intensity of Exports
		Imports	Exports	λ - augmented Capital Requirement of Exports (= λ · (3))	
	(1)	(2)	(3)	(4)	(4)/(2) = (5)
1964	1.93	249.60	118.04	228.18	0.91
1970	1.43	511.61	308.79	440.64	0.86
1973	1.49	637.39	286.96	427.57	0.67

Sources: Computed from Table and Appendix Table 2.

Note: Singaporean 1970 capital-output ratio was used for 1964 and 1970. For 1973, capital-output ratio from Hong Kong's 1973 Census of Industrial Production was used.

The last column of Table 8 presents the relative capital intensity of exports in comparison with that of imports. Hong Kong's export structure is less capital-intensive than that of its imports. The relative intensity index decreased from 0.91 in 1964 to 0.67 in 1973. These findings suggest that despite the remarkable capital accumulation in the last two decades, Hong Kong's export structure has increasingly shifted toward the less capital-intensive side when compared with its import structure. This result is in conformity with that of high relative labour intensity of Hong Kong's exports discussed in the preceding section.

F. Total Labour Requirements of Exports and Imports

In the previous two sections, we have briefly described the computation of the total capital and labour requirements after taking into account the interdependence among industrial sectors. One way of dealing with the problem is the application of the I-O table. We have made use of the Singaporean 1970 I-O table and grouped the industries into 15 sectors.[27] The input coefficients matrix is denoted by A; the Leontief inverse is then $(I-A)^{-1}$.

The total labour and capital requirements per unit output are defined, respectively, as

$$L_o \cdot (I-A)^{-1}, \text{ and } K_o \cdot (I-A)^{-1}$$

L_o represents the row vector of labour-output coefficients. This is the direct labour requirements per unit output. K_o stands for the row vector of capital-output ratios. Table 9 below shows the total (direct and secondary) labour and capital requirements per dollar output.

We have used these total labour and capital requirement coefficients to compute the total labour and capital requirements of Hong Kong's exports and imports for 1964, 1970, 1973 and 1974. The results are listed in Appendix Tables 3 and 4.

By merely scanning Appendix Table 3, we find that most entries have identical ranks both with respect to their direct and total labour requirements. And those entries which bear different ranks differ in only one position upward or downward on the ranking scale. This explains the high rank correlation coefficients between the sectoral direct and total labour requirements. For columns 3 to 8, as well as column 10 (Appendix Table 3), the coefficient is equal to unity, indicating a complete rank correlation between the direct and total labour requirements. However, this conclusion does not mean that the ratio of secondary labour requirements to its direct labour requirements remained the same for each sector. In fact, this ratio varies from one sector to another rather markedly. Their actual figures are shown in Tables 10 and 11.

Before going into the perspective major findings of the study, some notes pertaining to these two tables should be made, so that the algorithm which lies behind them can be better understood:

(1) It is a mathematical necessity that for any given year the secondary labour ratio (herafter termed as "linkage coefficient") of each sector is identical for imports and exports.[28]

Table 9: Total Labour and Capital Requirements Per Dollar Output

Sector	$L_o^{70}.(I-A)^{-1}$ (1)	$L_o^{70'}.(I-A)^{-1}$ (2)	$L_o^{73}.(I-A)^{-1}$ (3)	$K_o^{70}.(I-A)^{-1}$ (4)	$K_o^{73}.(I-A)^{-1}$ (5)
1	0.0967 (8)	0.1049 (10)	0.0439 (9)	0.0229 (9)	0.0207 (8)
2	0.0437 (13)	0.0526 (13)	0.0259 (13)	0.0206 (13)	0.0366 (2)
3	0.0689 (12)	0.0760 (12)	0.0395 (11)	0.0730 (1)	0.0321 (3)
4	0.1016 (7)	0.1109 (7)	0.0596 (3)	0.0223 (10)	0.0123 (13)
5	0.1098 (5)	0.1198 (4)	0.0557 (7)	0.0376 (3)	0.0144 (12)
6	0.0877 (10)	0.1051 (9)	0.0436 (10)	0.0470 (2)	0.0422 (1)
7	0.1107 (4)	0.1177 (6)	0.0587 (4)	0.0208 (12)	0.0185 (10)
8	0.1056 (6)	0.1186 (5)	0.0574 (5)	0.0118 (15)	0.0270 (5)
9	0.0252 (14)	0.0288 (14)	0.0158 (14)	0.0365 (4)	0.0156 (11)
10	0.1123 (3)	0.1225 (3)	0.0707 (2)	0.0327 (5)	0.0267 (6)
11	0.1203 (2)	0.1301 (2)	0.0563 (6)	0.0323 (6)	0.0258 (7)
12	0.0921 (9)	0.1054 (8)	0.0527 (8)	0.0318 (7)	0.0205 (9)
13	0.1387 (1)	0.1540 (1)	0.0789 (1)	0.0216 (11)	0.0305 (4)
14	0.0841 (11)	0.0934 (11)	0.0338 (12)	0.0287 (8)	0.0122 (14)
15	0.0076 (15)	0.0084 (15)	0.0039 (15)	0.0193 (14)	0.0019 (15)

Note: The columns of this table correspond to those of Table 4.
The numbers in parentheses refer to sectoral ranking positions.

(2) We have exactly the same linkage coefficients for 1964 and 1970 as their input matrix A is the same and the direct labour input vector L_o remains unchanged. The percentages listed in columns 3 and 5 of Table 10 are slightly different because direct input vectors of labour by Definitions I and II are different. The same explanation is applicable to the slight discrepancy existing between columns 4 and 6 of the table.

(3) For 1973's exports and imports, two percentage figures are listed for each sector which correspond to the two different direct labour input vectors, i.e. one from the 1973 survey and the other from the Definition I of 1971's labour input vector (the linkage coefficients with respect to the latter input vector are in brackets). An apparent result is that the linkage coefficients are

quite close to each other. This is because the two direct labour input vectors have quite similar structures among their components (see Table 4, column 1 and 3).

(4) Again, the 1974's linkage coefficients were based on the 1973's direct labour input vector. As a result, the percentages for each sector are identical to those of 1973.

Bearing these points in mind, we compared the sectoral ratio of secondary to direct labour requirements for 1964, 1970, 1973 and 1974 and found that in terms of this ratio, sectors 7 (leather), 2 (food, beverage and tobacco), 13 (transport equipment), 3 (textiles) and 9 (basic metals) have created the greatest secondary employment for Hong Kong in the past. Leather industry had the highest linkage coefficient simply because its intra-sectoral transaction is nil.

On the other hand, sectors 8 (rubber and chemical products), 11 (machinery), 1 (primary products), 10 (metal products), and 4 (wearing apparel and footwear) have generated the least secondary employment in Hong Kong.

G. Total Capital Requirements of Exports and Imports

The total and direct capital requirements for 1964, 1970 and 1973 are shown in Appendix Table 4 with the latter requirements in brackets. In terms of total capital requirements, the results are similar to those suggested by the direct capital requirements. Sectors 3 (textiles), 4 (wearing apparel), and 14 (miscellaneous manufactured articles) have been traditionally the most capital absorbing ones. In more recent years, sectors 12 (electrical products) and 10 (metal products) have gained their relative significance.

The secondary capital requirements as a percentage of the direct requirements are shown in Table 11. One salient point is sector 7 (leather), which has its secondary capital requirements greater than its direct capital requirements by 14 % for 1964 and 1970. It maintained its leading position in 1973, although the percentage dropped more than 40 points to the level of 71.6 %. So sector 7 has the highest secondary effects both in terms of labour and capital requirements. The reason for this is the zero intra-

Table 10: Secondary Labour Requirements (As Percentage of the Direct Requirements)[1]: Selected Years

Sector	1964[2]		1970		1970[3]		1973[4]		1974[5]	
	Exports	Imports	Exports	Imports	Exports	Imports	Exports	Imports	Exports	Imports
1	(12) 6.2	6.2	(12) 6.2	6.2	(12) 6.3	6.3	(12) 6.9 (12) (6.2)	6.9 (6.2)	(12) 6.9	6.9
2	(2) 34.6	34.6	(2) 34.6	34.6	(2) 31.6	31.6	(2) 29.5 (2) (39.6)	29.5 (39.6)	(2) 29.5	29.5
3	(4) 21.9	21.9	(4) 21.9	21.9	(4) 22.3	22.3	(4) 20.4 (4) (21.9)	20.4 (21.9)	(4) 20.4	20.4
4	(10) 8.7	8.7	(10) 8.7	8.7	(10) 8.8	8.8	(10) 7.7 (10) (8.7)	7.7 (8.7)	(10) 7.7	7.7
5	(6) 19.9	19.9	(6) 19.9	19.9	(5) 20.1	20.1	(5) 20.2 (6) (19.9)	20.2 (19.9)	(5) 20.2	20.2
6	(8) 11.8	11.8	(8) 11.8	11.8	(8) 11.5	11.5	(8) 12.2 (8) (11.8)	12.2 (11.8)	(8) 12.2	12.2
7	(1) 46.4	46.4	(1) 46.4	46.4	(1) 48.1	48.1	(1) 41.1 (1) (46.4)	41.1 (46.4)	(1) 41.1	41.1
8	(14) 3.0	3.0	(14) 3.0	3.0	(14) 3.0	3.0	(14) 2.8 (14) (3.0)	2.8 (3.0)	(14) 2.8	2.8
9	(5) 20.2	20.2	(5) 20.2	20.2	(6) 20.0	20.0	(6) 19.3 (5) (20.2)	19.3 (20.2)	(6) 19.3	19.3
10	(11) 8.3	8.3	(11) 8.3	8.3	(11) 8.4	8.4	(11) 7.3 (11) (8.3)	7.3 (8.3)	(11) 7.3	7.3
11	(13) 5.6	5.6	(13) 5.6	5.6	(13) 5.8	5.8	(13) 6.6 (13) (5.6)	6.6 (5.6)	(13) 6.6	6.6
12	(7) 12.1	12.1	(7) 12.1	12.1	(7) 11.9	11.9	(9) 11.1 (7) (12.1)	11.1 (12.1)	(7) 11.1	11.1

Table 10: continued

Sector	1964[2]		1970		1970[3]		1973[4]		1974[5]	
	Exports	Imports	Exports	Imports	Exports	Imports	Exports	Imports	Exports	Imports
13	(3) 26.5	26.5	(3) 26.5	26.5	(3) 26.5	26.5	(3) 25.3 (3) (26.5)	25.3 (26.5)	(3) 25.3	25.3
14	(9) 10.0	10.0	(9) 10.0	10.0	(9) 10.0	10.0	(7) 13.4 (9) (10.0)	13.4 (10.0)	(9) 13.4	13.4
TOTAL	11.4	13.0	10.8	12.3	10.9	12.4	10.7 (10.9)	13.0	10.6	12.2

Notes: 1. The sectoral percentage figures (degree of linkage) are the same for exports and imports. This is simply a mathematical necessity.
2. Based on the 1971's labour-output ratios (Definition I).
3. Definition II of labour inputs was used.
4. Figures in parentheses were obtained by using the 1971's labour-output ratios (Definition I).
5. Based on the 1973's labour-output ratios.

Table 11: Secondary Capital Requirements (As Percentage of the Direct Requirements): Selected Years

Sector	1964		1970		1973	
	Exports	Imports	Exports	Imports	Exports	Imports
1	(12) 18.9	18.9	(12) 18.9	18.9	(11) 10.0	10.0
2	(2) 47.7	47.7	(2) 47.7	47.7	(9) 11.8	11.8
3	(10) 20.9	20.9	(10) 20.9	20.9	(5) 18.4	18.4
4	(9) 21.6	21.6	(9) 21.6	21.6	(6) 17.7	17.7
5	(5) 24.9	24.9	(5) 24.9	24.9	(3) 26.3	26.3
6	(13) 13.6	13.6	(13) 13.6	13.6	(12) 9.7	9.7
7	(1) 114.9	114.9	(1) 114.9	114.9	(1) 71.6	71.6
8	(14) 12.8	12.8	(14) 12.8	12.8	(14) 2.9	2.9
9	(8) 22.9	22.9	(8) 22.9	22.9	(7) 17.1	17.1
10	(11) 20.5	20.5	(11) 20.5	20.5	(10) 10.4	10.4
11	(7) 23.3	23.3	(7) 23.3	23.3	(13) 8.1	8.1
12	(6) 24.1	24.1	(6) 24.1	24.1	(8) 14.8	14.8
13	(3) 45.1	45.1	(3) 45.1	45.1	(2) 28.5	28.5
14	(4) 32.3	32.3	(4) 32.3	32.3	(4) 20.8	20.8
TOTAL	23.9	23.6	24.7	23.5	16.9	13.8

Note: The sectoral percentage figures are the same for exports and imports. This is simply a mathematical necessity.

sectoral transaction within this sector. Other sectors which also have high secondary capital requirements are sectors 2 (food, beverage and tobacco), 13 (transport equipment), 14 (miscellaneous manufactured articles), and 5 (furniture, fixture and wood products). Among these, sectors 7, 2 and 13 also bear high secondary labour requirements.

In terms of aggregate data, the secondary effect of capital requirements is slightly higher for exports than that for imports. But the reverse is true with respect to the secondary effect of labour requirements.

H. Low Linkage Effect

From what we have discussed in the previous sections, we may conclude that the linkage effect with respect to employment creation of an export increment is rather low in Hong Kong. From Table 10 above, we see that the sectoral linkage coefficient (which is defined as the percentage ratio of secondary employment creation to direct labour requirements) in 1974 ranges from 2.8 % (sector 8) to 41 % (sector 7), with the average centering around 16 %, which is considerably lower than that of the average industrialized country. This phenomenon calls for some explanation.

The fact that Hong Kong is, perhaps, the most open and trade-dependent economy in the world implies that a very large portion of any increased expenditure "leaks" into the foreign markets through expanded demand for imports. These very substantial import leakages reflect the fact that the magnitudes of Hong Kong's foreign-trade multipliers are rather small,[29] and as a consequence of these "short-circuiting" effects, both the likely multiplier effects on employment generation and the backward linkages of labour requirements are expected to be small. In addition, the high proportion of Hong Kong's total export receipts accruing from profits, dividends, service payments and management charges also tends to weaken the magnitude of the domestic multiplier.

In the literature on inter-industry economics, a low degree of interdependence in production usually indicates a state of under-development with a primitive production structure so that a good proportion of output is either consumed after some initial stages of production, or exported in an unprocessed or semi-processed state. However, this generalization is not true with Hong Kong. Hong Kong appears to be in an intermediate position between the developed and the less developed economies.

According to two recent studies, although Hong Kong's domestic intermediate inputs account for only 23 % of total inputs, its total intermediate inputs, including both domestic and imported, stand for 43.9 % of total input.[30] This is a relatively high ratio when compared with those ratios for other industrialized countries. Therefore, the "effective" degree of indirectness in Hong Kong's production is relatively high and thus the production process long. Consider the textile sector as an example: It embraces all manufacturing stages, starting from spinning, to weaving and finally to clothing which are all well developed in Hong Kong. The industries in lower production stages are thus able to supply sufficient inputs for those in the higher stages. Unfortunately, this desirable situation is not generally held by other sectors. Most of them constitute only a certain stage in the entire production process. Therefore, they have to heavily rely on overseas markets for intermediate inputs.

Table 10, however, ignores one important factor which contributes greatly to the creation of secondary labour requirements in Hong Kong's economic structure. It can be expected that, other things being equal, export industries have a great demand for services in the fields of commerce, shipping and transportation because a lot of documentary paperwork, financial procedures and shipping arrangements need to be settled before goods can be sent abroad. Galenson is fairly optimistic about the employment-generating effects of the tertiary sector. He observes that, in most developing economies, the growth of the manufacturing sector plays a crucial role in employment generation. And based on his empirical findings, Galenson claims that "the more rapid the rise of manufacturing output (and of manufacturing employment, if output per worker remains at a relatively high level), the more employment can be afforded by the tertiary sector."[31]

Because of the small size of the domestic market, industrial development in Hong Kong has always been export-oriented. Unlike the situation in most developing economies, the experience of Hong Kong shows that export-oriented industrialization can have a large direct demand for employment;[32] and because of its high degree of commercialization, the secondary effects relating to tertiary activities are also expected to be significant. Hong Kong has no doubt made the best use of its comparative advantage by exporting relatively labour-intensive products to the markets of the developed economies. With its exports to the DCs expanding rapidly, Hong Kong's export expansion provided large job opportunities for its growing labour force, and made it possible to achieve the twin objectives of output and employment growth even in the very short run. So in Hong Kong the word "manufacturing" is a synonym for "industry". During the past one-and-a-half decades, Hong Kong's trade statistics reveal that approximately 95 % of its overall domestic exports are manufactured products. In view of the fact that Hong Kong's manufacturing sector produces predominantly for export, "domestic exports" in Hong Kong can also be used synonymously with "manufacturing output." Therefore, it should cause no difficulty to envisage that the path which maintains a rapid growth in exports is also the path that sustains a rapid growth in employment.

For the period 1959-73 under study, Hong Kong has achieved the compound annual real growth rates of 11.9 and 8.7 %, respectively, for manufactured exports and registered employment in manufacturing industries. These are high by any standard. Unlike the situation of most developing countries, the phenomenon that employment growth does not correspond closely with output growth is not a matter of concern in Hong Kong. In fact, we can hardly expect that they would move with the same rate, otherwise there would be no productivity increase. Hong Kong's employment growth rate was high enough to absorb the increase in total labour force and the backlog of those unemployed, and also a significant percentage of those underemployed. It is obvious that the rapid growth of manufacturing exports has provided the main thrust for employment-generation in Hong Kong, and growth in manufacturing employment in Hong Kong has been strongly correlated with growth in its domestic exports.[33]

One of the major features of the manufacturing sector of the economy of Hong Kong, as pointed out by England and Rear, is, however, instability.[34] Changes in consumer tastes, trade restrictions imposed by industrialized countries on Hong Kong's exports, penetration of its existing markets by relatively low wage Asian competitors, particularly South Korea, Taiwan, and Singapore, liquidation of firms or even the total decline of an industry, e.g. wig industry, are reasons for this phenomenon. However, unlike the experience of most developing countries, export industry in Hong Kong can easily switch from one line of production to another in a very short time span, due to the rare ingenuity and business flair of its average entrepreneur. Therefore, fluctuations in production and employment are a very common economic scene in the Hong Kong manufacturing industries.

Appendix Table 1: Production and Trade of Hong Kong's Manufacturing Industries for 1971

HK$ Mn.

ISIC Code No.	Industry Groups/Sectors	Total Output (1)		Exports (2)	Local Sales (3)	(2)/(1) %	(3)/(1) %
311-314	Food, Beverage and Tobacco	1,057.98	(5.86)	265.60	792.37	25.10	74.90
311-312	Food	652.20	(3.61)	198.88	453.32	30.49	69.51
313-314	Beverage and Tobacco	405.78	(2.25)	66.73	339.05	16.44	83.56
321, 325-329	Textiles	3,349.50	(18.56)	1,518.81	1,830.69	45.34	54.66
	Fabrics	2,811.99	(15.58)	1,199.43	1,612.56	42.65	57.35
	Made-up Articles	452.08	(2.50)	289.02	163.06	63.93	36.07
322	Wearing Apparel, Except Footwear	5,248.01	(29.08)	4,633.35	614.66	88.29	11.71
322.1	Garment	3,023.04	(16.75)	2,777.54	245.50	91.88	8.12
322.5	Knitwear from Yarn	1,418.44	(7.86)	1,244.50	173.94	87.74	12.26
	Others	806.53	(4.47)	611.31	195.21	75.80	24.20
323-324	Leather Products and Footwear	184.19	(1.02)	120.33	63.87	65.33	34.67
331-332	Wood Products, Furniture and Fixtures (Except Primarily of Metal)	379.36	(2.10)	172.39	206.98	45.44	54.56
341-342	Paper, Paper Products, Printing and Publishing	676.16	(3.75)	81.42	594.73	12.04	87.96
351-352 & 355-356	Chemical, Rubber and Plastic Products	2,201.23	(12.20)	1,697.87	503.37	77.13	22.87
356	Plastic Products	1,761.11	(9.76)	1,434.11	327.00	81.43	18.57
	Others	440.12	(2.44)	263.76	176.37	59.93	40.07
36	Non-Metallic Mineral Products, Except Petroleum and Coal	118.68	(0.65)	28.93	89.75	24.38	75.62
37	Basic Metals	336.98	(1.87)	56.82	280.16	16.86	83.14
381	Fabricated Metal Products	1,083.83	(6.01)	658.38	425.45	60.75	39.25

Appendix Table 1: continued

382	Machinery, Except Electrical	181.98	(1.01)	41.74	140.24	22.94	77.06
383	Electrical Machinery, Apparatus, Appliances and Supplies	1,512.97	(8.38)	1,264.86	248.11	83.60	16.40
384-385	Transport Equipment and Precision Instruments	577.73	(3.20)	246.23	331.50	42.62	57.38
39	Other Manufacturing	1,140.12	(6.31)	936.09	204.03	82.10	17.90
	ALL INDUSTRIES	18,048.72	(100.0)	11,722.82	6,325.90	64.95	35.05

Source: Census and Statistics Department, 1971 Census of Manufacturing Establishments (Hong Kong:Government Printer, 1973), pp. 34-39.

Note: Total output is the sum of the value of sales and of work done with reference to the calender year 1970 or to a period of 12 months close to it. Figures in parentheses are percentages of the total, they do not add to total because of rounding.

Appendix Table 2: Imports and Domestic Exports of Hong Kong by Sectoral Classification: Selected Years

HK$ Mn.

Sector	Description	1964		1970		1973		1974	
		Imports	Exports	Imports	Exports	Imports	Exports	Imports	Exports
1	Primary Products	1,605	119	3,262	274	5,334	351	7,304	439
2	Food, Beverage and Tobacco	1,300	194	1,964	218	3,353	301	3,893	313
3	Textiles	1,967	718	3,808	1,288	6,079	2,370	5,866	2,765
4	Wearing Apparel and Footwear	221	1,794	331	4,639	712	7,720	631	9,063
5	Furniture, Fixture and Wood Products	165	151	232	297	498	442	519	494
6	Paper and Paper Products	205	12	439	38	720	81	900	128
7	Leathers	33	2	85	6	227	15	256	15
8	Rubber and Chemical Products	737	53	1,500	108	2,303	179	3,014	212
9	Basic Metals	445	42	734	81	1,093	89	1,540	142
10	Metal Products	118	146	204	345	360	521	428	641
11	Machinery	424	24	969	93	1,455	214	1,738	317

12	Electrical Products	409	186	1,508	1,293	2,737	2,622	3,316	3,296
13	Transport Equipment	191	15	419	69	734	61	570	62
14	Miscellaneous Manufactures	708	954	2,122	3,570	3,348	4,461	4,080	4,971
15	Other Services	0	0	0	0	0	0	0	0
S_1	Overall Classified Merchandise	8,528	4,411	17,578	12,318	28,951	19,428	34,055	22,856
S_2	TOTAL MERCHANDISE	8,551	4,428	17,607	12,347	29,005	19,474	34,120	22,911
	S_1 / S_2 (%)	99.73	99.62	99.84	99.77	99.81	99.76	99.81	99.76

<u>Source</u>: Census and Statistics Department, <u>Hong Kong Trade Statistics</u> (Hong Kong: Government Printer, selected December issues).

<u>Note</u>: Since only merchandise trade is considered in the analysis, the sector "Other Services" is taken to be zero. Overall classified merchandise are the sum total of the 15 sectors listed in this table. Total merchandise are the sum total of the SITC Sections 0 to 9 (excluding gold and specie). The discrepancy between S_1 and S_2 is due to the omission of the SITC groups 911 (postal packages not classified according to kind), 912 (declarations of a value of HK$ 1,200 or less), 914 (firearms and ammunition), and 915 (coin, not current).

Appendix Table 3: Total and Direct Labour Requirements[1] of Hong Kong's Exports and Imports[2]: Selected Years

Sector	1964[3]		1970		1970[4]	
	Exports (1)	Imports (2)	Exports (3)	Imports (4)	Exports (5)	Imports (6)
1	(7) 11.53	(1) 155.22	(7) 26.51	(1) 315.44	(7) 28.75	(1) 342.13
	(7) (10.86)	(1) (146.20)	(7) (24.97)	(1) (297.11)	(7) (27.04)	(1) (321.70)
2	(8) 8.50	(5) 56.86	(11) 9.55	(7) 85.88	(10) 11.48	(7) 103.28
	(8) (6.32)	(6) (42.25)	(11) (7.10)	(7) (63.82)	(10) (8.73)	(7) (78.48)
3	(3) 49.47	(2) 135.53	(4) 88.74	(2) 262.32	(4) 97.92	(2) 289.44
	(3) (40.58)	(2) (111.16)	(4) (72.79)	(2) (215.17)	(4) (80.04)	(2) (236.61)
4	(1) 182.26	(9) 22.41	(1) 471.19	(10) 33.58	(1) 514.29	(10) 36.65
	(1) (167.68)	(9) (20.61)	(1) 433.50)	(10) (30.89)	(1) (472.84)	(10) (33.69)
5	(5) 16.54	(10) 18.09	(6) 32.56	(11) 25.44	(6) 35.53	(11) 27.76
	(6) (13.80)	(11) (15.09)	(6) (27.16)	(11) (21.22)	(6) (29.60)	(11) (23.12)
6	(13) 1.06	(11) 17.97	(12) 3.30	(9) 38.48	(12) 3.96	(9) 46.14
	(12) (0.95)	(10) (16.08)	(12) (2.95)	(9) (34.43)	(12) (3.55)	(9) (41.39)
7	(14) 0.17	(14) 3.61	(14) 0.71	(14) 9.42	(14) 0.75	(14) 10.00
	(14) (0.12)	(14) (2.46)	(14) (6.48)	(14) (6.43)	(14) (0.51)	(14) 6.75
8	(9) 5.55	(3) 77.81	(8) 11.40	(4) 158.30	(8) 12.81	(4) 177.90
	(9) (5.39)	(3) (75.51)	(8) (11.06)	(4) (153.61)	(8) (12.43)	(4) (172.71)
9	(12) 1.07	(13) 11.20	(13) 2.04	(13) 18.50	(13) 2.33	(13) 21.12
	(13) (0.89)	(13) (9.32)	(13) (1.70)	(13) (15.39)	(13) (1.94)	(13) (12.60)
10	(6) 16.39	(12) 13.26	(5) 38.74	(12) 22.88	(5) 42.24	(12) 24.94
	(5) (15.14)	(12) (12.25)	(5) (35.78)	(12) (21.13)	(5) (38.97)	(12) (23.01)
11	(10) 2.94	(6) 51.06	(9) 11.20	(6) 116.59	(9) 12.11	(6) 126.04
	(10) (2.78)	(5) (48.34)	(9) (10.60)	(6) (110.38)	(9) (11.44)	(6) (119.14)
12	(4) 17.15	(7) 37.69	(3) 119.01	(5) 138.87	(3) 136.29	(5) 159.03
	(4) (15.30)	(7) (33.61)	(3) (106.14)	(5) (123.85)	(3) (121.83)	(5) (142.17)
13	(11) 2.06	(8) 26.42	(10) 9.57	(8) 58.16	(11) 10.63	(8) 64.60
	(11) (1.63)	(8) (20.89)	(10) (7.56)	(8) (45.99)	(11) (8.40)	(8) (51.05)
14	(2) 78.60	(4) 59.59	(2) 300.28	(3) 178.55	(2) 333.30	(3) 198.18
	(2) (71.48)	(4) (54.19)	(2) (273.07)	(3) (162.37)	(2) (302.95)	(3) (180.13)
TOTAL	393.30	686.70	1,124.79	1,462.41	1,242.37	1,627.22
	(352.90)	(607.95)	(1,014.86)	(1,301.79)	(1,120.26)	(1,447.56)
Correlation Coefficient[8]	0.99	0.99	1.00	1.00	1.00	1.00

Sources: Computed from Tables 5 and 9 and Appendix Table 2.

Notes: 1. Figures in parentheses below each entry refer to direct labour requirements.

2. Numbers in parentheses on the left hand side of labour requirement entries indicate their respective ranking positions.

3. Based on the 1971's labour-output ratios (Definition I).

4. Definition II (including non-operative personnel) of labour inputs was used.

5. Arrived at by using the 1973's labour-output ratios.

6. Arrived at by using the 1971's labour-output ratios (Definition I).

Appendix Table 3: continued

Sector	1973						1974[7]			
	Exports				Imports		Exports		Imports	
	(7)	A[5]	(8)	B[6]	(9)		(10)		(11)	
1	(7)	15.42	(7)	33.96	(2)	234.28	(7)	19.27	(1)	320.80
	(7)	(14.42)	(7)	(31.99)	(1)	(219.08)	(7)	(18.02)	(1)	(299.99)
2	(10)	7.82	(10)	13.18	(6)	86.98	(10)	8.12	(6)	101.00
	(10)	(6.03)	(10)	(9.79)	(7)	(67.15)	(10)	(6.27)	(7)	(77.98)
3	(4)	93.65	(4)	163.26	(1)	240.22	(4)	109.25	(2)	231.79
	(4)	(77.76)	(4)	(133.91)	(2)	(199.46)	(4)	(90.71)	(2)	(192.46)
4	(1)	460.32	(1)	784.16	(9)	42.45	(1)	540.43	(10)	37.65
	(1)	(427.53)	(1)	(721.43)	(9)	(39.42)	(1)	(501.93)	(10)	(34.96)
5	(6)	24.64	(6)	48.55	(11)	27.72	(6)	27.52	(12)	28.90
	(6)	(20.49)	(6)	(40.49)	(12)	(23.01)	(6)	(22.89)	(12)	(24.03)
6	(12)	3.52	(12)	7.07	(10)	31.41	(11)	5.58	(9)	39.25
	(12)	(3.14)	(12)	(6.33)	(10)	(28.01)	(11)	(4.98)	(9)	(35.00)
7	(14)	0.89	(14)	1.67	(14)	13.31	(14)	0.86	(14)	15.01
	(14)	(0.63)	(14)	(1.14)	(14)	(9.43)	(14)	(0.61)	(14)	(10.64)
8	(9)	10.26	(9)	18.85	(4)	132.29	(9)	12.15	(4)	173.13
	(9)	(9.98)	(9)	(18.29)	(4)	(128.74)	(9)	(11.82)	(3)	(168.48)
9	(13)	1.41	(13)	2.25	(13)	17.31	(13)	2.25	(13)	24.39
	(12)	(1.18)	(13)	(1.87)	(13)	(14.52)	(13)	(1.89)	(13)	(20.45)
10	(5)	36.81	(5)	58.47	(12)	25.44	(5)	45.33	(11)	30.24
	(5)	(34.31)	(5)	(54.01)	(11)	(23.71)	(5)	(42.26)	(11)	(28.19)
11	(8)	12.07	(8)	25.76	(7)	81.89	(8)	17.82	(7)	97.82
	(8)	(11.32)	(8)	(24.41)	(6)	(76.81)	(8)	(16.72)	(6)	(91.74)
12	(3)	138.26	(3)	241.42	(3)	144.30	(2)	173.76	(3)	174.85
	(3)	(124.40)	(3)	(215.31)	(3)	(129.83)	(2)	(156.34)	(4)	(157.32)
13	(11)	4.84	(11)	8.50	(8)	57.88	(12)	4.89	(8)	44.96
	(11)	(3.86)	(11)	(6.72)	(8)	(46.19)	(12)	(3.90)	(8)	(35.88)
14	(2)	150.54	(2)	375.28	(5)	112.97	(3)	167.74	(5)	137.68
	(2)	(132.76)	(2)	(341.27)	(5)	(99.63)	(3)	(147.93)	(5)	(121.42)
TOTAL		960.44		1,782.37		1,248.45		1,134.96		1,457.47
		(867.81)		(1,606.95)		(1,105.02)		(1,026.25)		(1,298.54)
		1.00		1.00		0.99		1.00		0.99

Notes: continued

7. Based on the 1973's labour-output ratios.
8. Rank correlation coefficient between the direct and total labour requirements of each column.

Appendix Table 4: Total and Direct Capital Requirements[1] of Hong Kong's Exports and Imports[2]: Selected Years

HK$ Mn.

Sector	1964		1970		1973	
	Exports	Imports	Exports	Imports	Exports	Imports
1	2.73 (2.29)	36.71 (30.88)	6.27 (5.27)	74.61 (62.76)	7.28 (6.62)	110.56 (100.50)
2	4.01 (2.71)	26.80 (18.15)	4.50 (3.05)	40.48 (27.41)	11.04 (9.88)	122.82 (109.90)
3	52.41 (43.37)	143.58 (118.30)	94.02 (77.79)	277.92 (229.94)	76.17 (64.32)	195.37 (164.99)
4	40.05 (32.93)	4.92 (4.05)	103.55 (85.12)	7.38 (6.07)	95.01 (80.75)	8.76 (7.45)
5	5.67 (4.54)	6.20 (4.96)	11.16 (8.94)	8.72 (6.98)	6.38 (5.05)	7.18 (5.68)
6	0.57 (0.50)	9.64 (8.49)	1.77 (1.56)	20.64 (18.18)	3.40 (3.10)	30.40 (27.72)
7	0.03 (0.02)	0.68 (0.32)	0.13 (0.06)	1.77 (0.83)	0.28 (0.16)	4.20 (2.45)
8	0.62 (0.55)	8.72 (7.73)	1.28 (1.13)	17.73 (15.72)	4.82 (4.69)	62.21 (60.45)
9	1.55 (1.26)	16.21 (13.19)	2.95 (2.40)	26.78 (21.79)	1.39 (1.19)	17.07 (14.57)
10	4.77 (3.95)	3.86 (3.20)	11.26 (9.35)	6.65 (5.52)	13.91 (12.60)	9.62 (8.71)
11	0.79 (0.64)	13.71 (11.12)	3.01 (2.44)	31.31 (25.39)	5.53 (5.12)	37.57 (34.74)
12	5.93 (4.78)	13.03 (10.50)	41.15 (33.16)	48.01 (38.69)	53.78 (46.83)	56.13 (48.88)
13	0.32 (0.22)	4.12 (2.84)	1.49 (1.03)	9.07 (6.25)	1.87 (1.46)	22.40 (17.44)
14	26.85 (20.29)	20.35 (15.38)	102.56 (77.50)	60.98 (46.08)	54.58 (45.19)	40.96 (33.91)
TOTAL	146.29 (118.04)	308.53 (249.60)	385.10 (308.79)	632.06 (511.61)	335.46 (286.96)	725.25 (637.39)

Sources: Computed from Table 8 and Appendix Table 2.

Notes : 1. Figures in parentheses refer to direct capital requirements.

2. Singaporean 1970 capital-output ratios were applied to compute the capital requirements for 1964 and 1970. For 1973, the ratios used were derived from Hong Kong's 1973 Census of Industrial Production.

Notes:

+ The authors are indebted to Profs. M.H. HSING, Lawrence LAU and Dr. Victor MOK for their valuable comments. Thanks also go to Mr. Y.P. HO, K.W. WONG and Miss Julia HUI for their diligent work in compiling the data and computing the results. Finally, we appreciate the funding from the Council for Asian Manpower Studies Ltd., which has made the completion of the project possible.

1 See S.Y. CHUNG (1969), Appendix A.

2 Hong Kong's exports to China, consisting overwhelmingly of re-exports, fell from HK$ 1,604 million in 1951 to HK$ 520 million in 1952.

3 Hong Kong Review of Overseas Trade in 1975.

4 The following general procedure for separating the effect of export expansion was first suggested by H. TYSZYNSKI (1951). This approach has since been employed by, inter alia, J.M. FLEMING and S.C. TSIANG (1956), R.E. BALDWIN (1958), S. SPIEGELGLAS (1959), P.R. NARVEKAR (1960), A. ROMANIS (1961), A. LAMFALUSSY (1963), H.B. JUNZ and R.R. RHOMBERG (1965), M.E. KREININ (1967), R.M. STERN (1967), and F.G. ADAMS, H. EGUCHI and F. MEYER-ZU-SCHLOCHTERN (1969). For a penetrating discussion concerning the theoretical pitfalls of explaining export expansion by this approach, interested readers may refer to J.D. RICHARDSON (1971), pp. 227-39.

5 They are (1) clothing, (2) textile yarn, fabrics and made-up articles, (3) electrical products, (4) metal manufactures, (5) footwear, (6) miscellaneous manufactured articles, and (7) others.

6 The LDCs include those countries which are classified in the United Nations Monthly Bulletin of Statistics as "developing market economies, and the Communist countries". The rest is classified as developed area.

7 Here, world trade is assumed to have grown proportionately for all commodities and markets.

8 The four effects for Taiwan for the period 1962-1972 are 24.1 %, -3.1 %, -3.5 % and 82.5 %, respectively. Cf. K.S. LIANG and C.I.H. LIANG (1975), p. 20.

9 Cf. James RIEDEL (1974), p. 23.

10 The Hong Kong Trade Development Council, set up by statute in 1966, has been very effective in promoting Hong Kong's domestic exports.

11 H.B. CHENERY (1960), pp. 639-41; S.R. LEWIS (1969), pp. 20-21; and LIANG and LIANG (1975), pp. 21-23.

12 The importance of the import substitution effect for LDC's was stressed in various works such as CHENERY (1960), particularly pp. 639-41; and LEWIS (1969), pp. 20-21.

13 Similar results were also reached by T.T. HSUEH (1976, p. 48): "The negative sign of import substitution coefficient and of the growth factors ....., distinguishes an extremely small open economy from the other economies in that, in the former, it is the factors other than import substitution which are conducive to the growth". Similar experience was also observed in Taiwan (LIANG and LIANG, p. 23).

14 A similar situation was also confronted with in Taiwan (Cf. LIANG and LIANG, p. 24).

15 See, for instance, A.H.M. MAHFUZUR RAHMAN (1973).

16 See, inter alia, S. WATANABE (1972), pp. 495-526; H.F. LYDALL (1975); H.W. SINGER (1975), pp. 5-18; and Percy SELWYN (1975), pp. 19-27.

17 No doubt, this conceptual framework for analysing the likely employment implications of export expansion seems to form a sound methodological basis. However, there are many other factors which are not quantatively susceptible and thus have been ignored. As pointed out by Percy SELWYN (p. 22), "its weakness lies in the omission of social, political and institutional factors which profoundly affect the distribution of benefits from trade".

18 Cf. LYDALL (1975), p. 16; and SINGER (1975), p. 8.

19 For a detailed discussion of the issue, see Gunnar MYRDAL (1968), pp. 1184-1205.

20 As the pace of industrialization is pushing forward and new production activities are operated with the latest machinery and equipment and with relatively more efficient methods, those existing industrial firms with traditional labour-intensive methods of production will be either compelled to follow suit or driven out of the market by competition. Once that happens, technological unemployment is very likely to emerge. For a detailed discussion on backwash effects of industrialization, see MYRDAL (1968), Chap. 24, particularly pp. 1172-1202.

21 To prove this we formally evaluate the product: $(I-A)^{-1}.(I-A) = (I+A+A^2+....)(I-A)=I$, so the expression is valid (Cf. M.D. INTRILIGATOR, 1971, p. 488).

22 K. LANCASTER (1968), p. 310.

23 They are: (1) primary products, (2) food, beverage and tobacco, (3) textiles, (4) wearing apparel and footwear, (5) furniture, fixture and wood products, (6) paper and paper products, (7) leather, (8) rubber and chemical products, (9) basic metals, (10) metal products, (11) machinery (other than electric), (12) electrical products, (13) transport equipment, (14) miscellaneous manufactured articles, (15) other services.

24 United Nations, Classification of Commodities by Industrial Origin (1971).

25 Cf. STRATTON's covering note on Census Circular No. 1/75: 1973 Census of Industrial Production (1975).

26 In terms of total labour requirements, they are 1.10 and 1.09 by Definitions I and II of labour inputs, respectively.

27 An I-O table was compiled for Hong Kong for the year 1962 by R. HSIA, H. HO and E. LIM (1975). But since these data are really too old and the classification of sectors is not compatible with our present analysis, we decided not to use that table. The application of the Singaporean I-O table to the analysis of Hong Kong economy is a "second-best" choice. These two city-state economies have much in common, which may warrant our approach. The salient similarities between the two economies may be summarized as follows (Cf. T.T. HSUEH, 1975, pp. 257-78):

(a) Except for the industrious and intelligent population, both places are virtually endowed with no significant natural resources.
(b) Both economies are traditionally important entrepôts.
(c) Both economies are outward-looking and their industries are barely protected by trade policy against competition from imported goods.
(d) Both economies have considerable deficits with respect to their merchandise trade, which are, however, amply offset by net capital inflow and receipts from invisibles.
(e) The openness of these two economies makes the absorption of new technical know-how very easy. During the last two decades, both economies have successfully transformed from traditional entrepôt centres into highly industrialized economies.
(f) Through the highly successful industrialization, the manufacturing sector occupied a dominant position in the economy, while the agricultural sector played a negligible role with its share in GDP being less than 3 per cent in both places. Both economies are dualistic in the sense of services sector vs. industrial sector, which is distinctly different from the conventional one - namely industrial sector vs. agricultural sector.
(g) Both economies are small, the opportunities for realizing economies of scales in the production for the domestic market alone are limited. So both economies can be characterized as an extreme case of a "trade constrained economy", in the Chenery-Strout sense.

28 It can be easily shown that secondary labour ratio for both export and import of the i-th sector is: $\left[L_o.(I-A)^{-1}_i\right] / L_{oi} - 1$

29 Bruce GLASSBURNER and James RIEDEL (1972, p. 70 and note 24) based on the formula: $k = 1/(s+m-i)$, where k is the multiplier, s is the marginal propensity to save, m is the marginal propensity to import, and i is the marginal ratio of induced investment to income. And using data from LIM's thesis, m was calculated at 0.63, s at 0.19, and i at 0.08. Total net leakage is thus 0.74, and the multiplier, being the reciprocal of the leakage coefficient, is 1.35. These computed figures lead GLASSBURNER and RIEDEL to conjecture that an upper limit estimate of "the leakage" would fall in the range of 60 to 75 %, and "the multiplier" would be in the range of 1.3 to 1.7. In a macro-

economic study which purports to investigate the relationship between Hong Kong's economic growth and its growth in foreign trade for the period 1953-64, Patrick YEUNG (1971), using the constrained quadratic programming technique developed by G.G. JUDGE and T. TAKAYAMA (1966), has also found that, among other estimates, Hong Kong's "domestic-export multiplier" falls in the range of 1.24 to 1.33.

30 LIM (1969), p. 130, Table 5.2; and HSIA, HO and LIM (1975), p. 36.

31 Using data from a number of developed and some under-developed countries, GALENSON (1963, pp. 505-19) tried to establish a relationship through least squares technique between employment in manufacturing and that in tertiary activities. He found that a one percentage change in manufacturing was positively associated with 0.6 % of employment in tertiary activities.

32 The following five developing countries, namely, Singapore, South Korea, Taiwan, Israel, and Puerto Rico, have also experienced that export-oriented industrialization, having a great direct demand for employment. Of course, in comparison with Hong Kong's experience, their impact is still relatively small. This is evidenced by their figures of manufacturing labour force as a percentage of total labour force; see David MORAWETZ (1974), pp. 492-93, Table 1, for detailed figures.

33 Cf. K.R. CHOU (1969), p. 167.

34 See Joe ENGLAND and John REAR (1975), p. 36.

References:

ADAMS, F.G., H. EGUCHI and F. MEYER-ZU-SCHLOCHTERN (1969), An Econometric Analysis of International Trade: An Interrelated Explanation for Imports and Exports of OECD Countries. Paris: OECD Development Centre.

BALDWIN, R.E. (1958), "The Commodity Composition of Trade: Selected Industrial Countries, 1900-1954", Review of Economics and Statistics,XL, pp. 50-71.

CHENERY, H.B. (1960), "Patterns of Industrial Growth", American Economic Review, L (September), pp. 624-54.

CHOU, K.R. (1969), "Hong Kong's Changing Pattern of Trade and Economic Inter-dependence in Southeast Asia", in: T. MORGAN and N. SPOELSTRA (eds.), Economic Interdependence in Southeast Asia. Madison: University of Wisconsin Press.

CHUNG, S.Y. (1969), "The Role of Manufacturing Industry in the Economy of Hong Kong", in: J.W. ENGLAND (ed.), The Hong Kong Economic Scene. Hong Kong: University of Hong Kong.

ENGLAND, J. and J. REAR (1975), Chinese Labour under British Rule: A Critical Study of Labour Relations and Law in Hong Kong. Hong Kong: Oxford University Press.

FLEMING, J.M. and S.C. TSIANG (1956), "Changes in Competitive Strength and Export Shares of Major Industrial Countries", International Monetary Fund Staff Papers, V, pp. 218-48.

GALENSON, W. (1963), "Economic Development and the Sectoral Expansion of Employment", International Labour Review, LXXXVII (June), pp. 505-19.

GLASSBURNER, B. and J. RIEDEL (1972), "Government in the Economy of Hong Kong", Economic Record, XLVIII (March), pp. 58-75.

HSIA, R., H. HO and E. LIM (1975), The Structure and Growth of the Hong Kong Economy. Wiesbaden: Otto Harrassowitz.

HSUEH, T.T. (1975), "Development Features of a Mini Open Economy: The Cases of Singapore and Hong Kong", Journal of the Chinese University of Hong Kong, III (December), pp. 257-78.

HSUEH, T.T. (1976), "The Transforming Economy of Hong Kong, 1952-73", Hong Kong Economic Papers,(October), pp. 46-65.

INTRILIGATOR, M.D. (1971), Mathematical Optimization and Economic Theory. Englewood Cliffs, N.J.: Prentice-Hall.

JUNZ, H.B. and R.R. RHOMBERG (1965), "Price and Export Performance of Industrial Countries, 1953-63", International Monetary Fund Staff Papers, XII, pp. 224-69.

KREININ, M.E. (1967), "Price Elasticities in International Trade", Review of Economics and Statistics, XLIX, pp. 510-16.

LAMFALUSSY, A. (1963), The United Kingdom and the Six. Homewood, Illinois: Richard D. Irwin.

LANCASTER, K. (1968), Mathematical Economics, New York: Macmillan.

LEWIS, S.R. (1969), Economic Policy and Industrial Growth in Pakistan, London: George Allen & Unwin.

LIANG, K.S. and C.I.H. LIANG (1975), Exports and Employment in Taiwan, (mimeo.).

LIM, E.R. (1969), A General Equilibrium Model of an Export-Dependent Economy, (Unpublished Ph.D. thesis, Harvard University).

LYDALL, H.F. (1975), Trade and Employment: A Study of the Effects of Trade Expansion on Development in Developing and Developed Countries. Geneva: International Labour Office Publication.

MAHFUZUR RAHMAN, A.H.M. (1973), Exports of Manufactures from Developing Countries: A Study of Comparative Advantage. Rotterdam: Rotterdam University Press.

MORAWETZ, D. (1974), "Employment Implications of Industrialization in Developing Countries: A Survey", Economic Journal, LXXXIV (September), pp. 491-540.

MYRDAL, G. (1968), Asian Drama: An Inquiry into the Poverty of Nations, II. New York: Twentieth Century Fund.

NARVEKAR, P.R. (1960), "The Role of Competitiveness in Japan's Export Performance, 1954-58", International Monetary Fund Staff Papers, VIII, pp. 85-100.

RICHARDSON, J.D. (1971), "Constant-Market-Shares Analysis of Export Growth", Journal of International Economics, I, pp. 227-39.

RIEDEL, J. (1974), The Industrialization of Hong Kong. Tübingen: J.C.B. Mohr.

ROMANIS, A. (1961), "Relative Growth of Exports of Manufactures of United States and Other Industrial Countries", International Monetary Fund Staff Papers, VIII, pp. 241-73.

SELWYN, P. (1975), "Trade Expansion, Employment and Country Selectivity", Institute of Development Studies Bulletin, VI (March), pp. 19-27.

SINGER, H.W. (1975), "Trade Expansion, Employment and Income Distribution", Institute of Development Studies Bulletin, VI (March), pp. 5-18.

SPIEGELGLAS, S. (1959), "World Exports of Manufactures, 1956 vs. 1937", Manchester School of Economic and Social Studies, XXVII, pp. 111-39.

STERN, R.M. (1967), Foreign Trade and Economic Growth in Italy. New York: Frederick A. Praeger.

TYSZYNSKI, H. (1951), "World Trade in Manufactured Commodities, 1899-1950", Manchester School of Economic and Social Studies, XIX (September), pp. 272-304.

WATANABE, S. (1972), "Exports and Employment: The Case of the Republic of Korea", International Labour Review, LVI (December), pp. 495-526.

YEUNG, P. (1971), Exports, Re-exports and Economic Growth: The Case of Hong Kong. (Faculty Working Papers 28, University of Illinois), (mimeo.).

Census and Statistics Department, Hong Kong Trade Statistics. Hong Kong: Government Printer (various December issues).

Census and Statistics Department, *Hong Kong Monthly Digest of Statistics*. Hong Kong: Government Printer (selected issues).

______ (1969), *Hong Kong Statistics, 1947-1967*. Hong Kong: Government Printer.

______ (1973), *1971 Census of Manufacturing Establishments*. Hong Kong: Government Printer.

______ (1975), *Census Circular No. 1/75: 1973 Census of Industrial Production*, (unpublished manuscript).

______ (1976), *Hong Kong Review of Overseas Trade in 1975*. Hong Kong: Government Printer.

______ (1977), *Estimates of Gross Domestic Product 1961-1975*. Hong Kong: Government Printer.

Hong Kong Government (1977), *The 1977-78 Budget: Economic Background*. Hong Kong: Government Printer.

KAU, Al-Keng (1974), *1970 Inter-industry Table*. Singapore: Economic Research Centre and Department of Business Administration of the University of Singapore (mimeo.).

United Nations, *Monthly Bulletin of Statistics*. New York: United Nations Publication (selected issues).

______ (1971), *Classification of Commodities by Industrial Origin: Links Between the Standard International Trade Classification and the International Standard Industrial Classification*. New York: United Nations Publication.

FOREIGN INVESTMENT IN HONG KONG

Kin-chok Mun and Suk-ching Ho

I. Development of Foreign Investment in Hong Kong

In the early stages of industrial growth in Hong Kong in the 1950s, foreign investment in the manufacturing sector played an insignificant role. The then sources of capital were personal savings, company retained profits, borrowing from commercial banks and private lending. Additional capital came from British firms headquartered in Hong Kong and from overseas Chinese, but neither of these is, strictly speaking, "foreign capital." During this period, American and Japanese investments together comprised only a very small fraction of total industrial investments. However, in the 1960s, direct foreign investment began to increase in different manufacturing sectors. While the American investment was allocated to diversified industries, the Japanese investment concentrated primarily in the textile sector. Since 1970, foreign investment has increased at a rapid rate, nearly quadrupling its value in eight years. Table 1 shows foreign investment in Hong Kong in 1977, classified by countries of origin.

Nearly one half of all foreign investment in Hong Kong originates from the United States. Other leading sources of investment are Japan, the United Kingdom, the Netherlands and Australia. Foreign establishments account for approximately 1 % of the total number of manufacturing establishments in Hong Kong; they employ a work force of 75,000, which is nearly 10 % of the total work force in the manufacturing sector; of the total fixed capital formation, approximately 23 % is contributed by foreign investment.

The distribution of foreign investment in the Hong Kong manufacturing industry is shown in Table 2. It is obvious that the foreign investors seem to prefer labor- and skill-intensive industries. In 1977, about 26 % of foreign investment was in electronics, 16 % in textiles.

Foreign investment expenditures per employee can be used as a criterion for indicating whether more labor- or capital-intensive

Table 1: Sources of Foreign Investment in Hong Kong, Manufacturing Industry, 1977

Country	No. of Establish-ments	Investment (HK$ Million)	Percentage of Total Foreign Investment
U.S.A.	110	920.4	46.5
Japan	88	393.4	19.9
United Kingdom	31	148.6	7.5
Netherlands	7	102.8	5.2
Australia	23	90.3	4.6
Switzerland	12	64.8	3.3
Singapore	16	63.7	3.2
Thailand	16	52.4	2.6
West Germany	15	50.4	2.5
France	2	23.1	1.2
Taiwan	13	13.5	0.7
Philippines	3	11.0	0.6
Others	31	44.1	2.2
	367	1,978.5	100.0

Source: Commerce and Industry Department, Hong Kong

technology is used in the related industries. The production technology used in most manufacturing industries of Hong Kong is obviously labor-intensive. Investment per employee in the textiles industry, the leading export manufacturing sector in Hong Kong, was HK$ 18,206. Contrary to this, the chemicals industry has a much higher investment per employee: HK$ 402,215. This indicates the nature of production technology used in the chemical manufacturing industry as capital-intensive.

Recently, American firms have begun to invest in more capital-intensive and high technology industries in Hong Kong. For instance, Dow Chemical has developed manufacturing facilities for plastic raw materials. This was a direct result of Hong Kong being the largest plastic toy manufacturer in the world. The size of the domestic demand for the raw materials justified such an operation.

Table 2: Foreign Investment in Hong Kong by Industry, 1977

Industry	No. of Establish-ments	No. of Employees	Investment (HK$ Million)	Investment per Employee (HK $)	Distribution of Investment %
Electronics	64	29,620	$516.1	$17,424	26.1
Textiles	87	17,176	312.7	18,206	15.8
Watches/Clocks and accessories	25	4,894	135.2	27,626	6.8
Electrical products	21	4,918	201.5	40,972	10.2
Chemical products	13	587	236.1	402,215	11.9
Printing and publishing	9	1,777	140.3	78,953	7.1
Food Manufacturing	14	1,632	72.5	44,424	3.7
Toys	10	5,392	60.6	11,239	3.1
Building and construction	5	613	34.5	56,281	1.7
Metal products	26	2,215	95.1	42,935	4.8
Metal rolling, extrusion and fabrication	5	910	54.9	60,330	2.8
Miscellaneous	60	5,024	119.0	23,686	6.0
TOTAL	339+	74,758	$1978.5		100.0

\+ Figure is different from the one given in Exhibit 1. The discrepancy is because some establishments are joint ventures involving more than one overseas interest.

Source: Commerce and Industry Department, Hong Kong.

The success of Hong Kong's entry into a new era of its industrial development depends to a large extent on the operations of direct foreign investment, through which capital and especially technological know-how will be imported. In addition, an important psychological factor must be taken into consideration in the investment planning of local entrepreneurs, that is, the problem of Hong Kong's lease. Hong Kong's 99-year lease on the New Territories, in which most of the Colony's water, energy production, agricultural and industrial output are located, is due to expire in 1997. If the lease is not renewed or renegotiated, the return of the New Territories to China removes the economic basis for the continued survival of Hong Kong, Kowloon and Stonecutter's Island, even though these three territories have been ceded to the British in perpetuity. Under such circumstances, Chinese entrepreneurs are hesitant to plan long-term investment projects, but more interested in those which have the shortest payback period, say one to three years. However, whether the political environment of Hong Kong is really as "poor" as people think will be discussed in the following section. It is obvious that an increase in direct foreign investment can, directly or indirectly, help to rebuild and strengthen the confidence of the local entrepreneurs on the political future of Hong Kong. In this respect, direct foreign investment can play the role of catalyst in initiating local investments.

II. Investment Climate

In determining locations for foreign investment, the investment climate of the related countries should be carefully assessed. The environment for foreign investment in Hong Kong will be evaluated first on a basis which is more objective in nature, and then by a checklist of foreign executives' opinion which is a more subjective judgement but no less relevant.

In the following we use a rating scale adopted from the one described in Robert B. Stobaugh's article: "How to Analyze Foreign Investment Climates".[1] The rating scale consists of eight economic and political factors as the bases for screening the investment climate of a country. The maximum and minimum scores of this rating scale are 100 and 8, respectively. The higher the total score of a country, the more favorable its investment climate will be, and vice versa. Based on this rating scale, Hong Kong obtains a score of eighty-two. One can therefore say that Hong Kong has a favorable investment climate. (See Table 3).

A. Evaluating the Political Environment

Regarding the factor of "political stability," Hong Kong can be considered a stable area compared with other countries in the region. After the change in government of three countries in Indo-China (South Vietnam, Cambodia and Laos), unrest has begun to arise in Thailand, the front door of Malaysia and Singapore. Due to this political uncertainty in the future, a large number of wealthy people have transferred their money to Hong Kong which they consider to be one of the safest places in this region for foreign capital. As a result, capital inflow from Southeast Asia to Hong Kong has increased rapidly in the past few years. The political situation of Hong Kong is quite different from those of the neighbouring countries since the fate of Hong Kong is almost entirely decided upon by Peking. In fact, it is not a problem whether or not Hong Kong will be taken over by China, rather it is more of a time problem. As many people say, Hong Kong is just a "borrowed place with borrowed time." No one can predict when the day will come. One thing is certain, and that is that Hong Kong will maintain its present status as a British colony as long as the Taiwan problem has not been resolved. In addition, Peking may also need diplomatic support from the Western countries in its anti-Russia campaigns. To this regard a good relationship between China and the United Kingdom is of considerable value.

The Hong Kong government's attitude towards foreign investment is generally favorable, even though no specific investment incentives are offered to foreign companies. The basic principle of the government policy of Hong Kong is to maintain minimum intervention in economic and business affairs. This policy has been highly welcomed by both local and foreign investors. However, this policy seems to be changing in recent years. The increase in the company income

Table 3: Rating Scale for Evaluating a Country's Investment Climate

Screening Factor	Score		
	Individual Subcategory	Range for Category	Hong Kong
1. Capital repatriation:			
No restrictions	12	0-12	12
Restrictions based only on time	8		
Restriction on Capital	6		
Restriction on Capital and Income	4		
Heavy Restrictions	2		
No repatriation possible	0		
2. Foreign Ownership allowed:			
100 % allowed and welcomed	12	0-12	12
100 % allowed, not welcomed	10		
Majority allowed	8		
50 % maximum	6		
Minority only	4		
Less than 30 %	2		
No foreign ownership allowed	0		
3. Discrimination and controls, foreign versus domestic business:			
Foreign treated same as local	12	0-12	12
Minor restrictions on foreigners, no control	10		
No restrictions on foreigners, some control	8		
Restrictions and controls on foreigners	6		
Some restrictions and heavy controls on foreigners	4		
Severe restrictions and controls on foreigners	2		
Foreigners not allowed to invest	0		
4. Currency stability:			
Free convertible	20	4-20	20
Less than 10 % open/black market differential	18		
10 % to 40 % open/black market differential	14		
10 % to 100 % open/black market differential	8		
Over 100 % open/black market differential	4		

Table 3: continued

Screening Factor	Score		
	Individual Subcategory	Range for Category	Hong Kong
5. Political stability:			
Stable long term	12	0-12	
Stable, but dependent on key person	10		
Stable, but dependent on policy of neighbour country	8		8
Internal factions, but government in control	6		
Strong external and/ or internal pressures that affect policies	4		
Possibility of coup or other radical change	2		
Instability, real possibility of coup or change	0		
6. Willingness to grant tariff protection:			
Extensive protection granted	8	2-8	
Considerable protection	6		
Some protection	4		
Little or no protection	2		2
7. Availability of local capital:			
Developed capital market, open stock exchange	10	0-10	
Some local capital available, speculative stock market	8		8
Limited capital market	6		
Capital scarce, short term	4		
Rigid controls over capital	2		
Active capital flight	0		
8. Annual inflation for last 5 yr.:			
Less than 1 %	14	2-14	
1 % - 3 %	12		
3 % - 7 %	10		
7 % - 10 %	8		8
10 % - 15 %	6		
15 % - 35 %	4		
Over 35 %	2		
TOTAL		8-100	82

tax rate from 15 % to 16.5 % in 1975 is a case in point, and the business community may believe that the government policy is not as favourable as before. This could lead to a rise in uncertainty in business planning. The government, however, has no discrimination policy against foreign investment. On the contrary, the government always expresses its favourable attitude toward foreign investment, particularly for high technology and capital-intensive industries.

B. No Import Tariffs

Hong Kong is a traditional free-trade port; except for a few commodities, namely alcoholic liquors, tobacco and hydrocarbon oil, there is no import tariff. On the other hand, and contrary to Singapore whose economic structure is similar to Hong Kong, the government of Hong Kong has no incentive policy for encouraging foreign investment. The policy-makers of the Hong Kong government seem to be believers in economic liberalism and free trade. In fact, a protective tariff in a market with limited size would probably be less meaningful to foreign investors, particularly manufacturing industries, in Hong Kong who are strongly export-oriented. Therefore, Hong Kong obtains the lowest score under the screening factor "willingness to grant tariff protection" on the rating scale.

C. Capital Market and Speculation

Since 1969, the Hong Kong stock market has been developing rapidly. The level of speculation, however, has been very high so that the functions of a capital market could be seriously affected. The Hang Seng Index - the most well-known index for stock prices in Hong Kong - rose from 400, in 1972 to 1700, in 1973 and then fell back to 150, in 1974. In order to protect investors, the Government has appointed a commissioner for supervising the operations of the stock market. In spite of the high speculative element, the capital market in Hong Kong seems to be favorable for company financing. This assumption is based on two reasons. First, total bank deposits have shown an increase in recent years. At the end of 1977, total bank deposits increased to HK$ 53019 millions, representing a net increase of 20 % over the previous year. The continuing capital inflow from Southeast Asia has kept the interest rate at its lowest level, with 1.75 % and a 3 % for saving deposits and 12 months time deposits, respectively. Second, the Hong Kong people are changing their saving patterns from hoarding cash to investment in securities.

D. Inflation and Wage Flexibility

As with the rest of the world, Hong Kong has been affected by the inflation problem. However, prices have been stabilized since mid 1975. There are four primary reasons for the recent lowering of the inflation rate in Hong Kong. First, the lack of power of the labor unions enabled the nominal wage rate to remain unchanged; in some cases, the wage rate has even been reduced. This wage flexibility relieved the inflation pressure and made price stability possible. Second, people's willingness to accept a lower standard of living by cutting their consumption expenditures during the inflation period is another factor for stabilizing prices. Third, the development of the government's huge low-rent housing projects prevented the low income class from paying increasing rent in housing; this relieved the pressure of wage increases by the working class. Fourth, under the system of a floating exchange rate the Hong Kong dollar was revaluated against the US dollar and the pound sterling. This has contributed to the stabilization of import prices.

E. Foreign Investors' Opinion

The above rating scale method for evaluating Hong Kong's investment climate is primarily objective in nature. However, an investigation of the opinion of foreign investors in Hong Kong should be of equal value. One of the present authors[2] conducted a survey of this kind in 1976. The total number of respondent firms in the survey was 81, mainly with U.S., Japanese, and British interest. Respondents were asked to rate the relative influence of 20 factors on their decision to invest in Hong Kong. A rating scale ranging from 0 (no influence) to 3 (decisive influence) was employed. The responses of these four segments are summarized in Tables 4 - 6. It can be seen from the exhibits that apart from some minor variations, these investors were largely influenced by financial (low tax, freedom to

Table 4: Mean Scores of 20 Country-related Factors, American Investors

	Mean Scores
Factors with most influence (2.00 - 3.00)	
1. Peaceful industrial relations	2.355
2. Availability of efficient labor	2.323
3. Stability of Hong Kong government	2.323
4. Freedom to repatriate earnings	2.258
5. Freedom to transfer capital, assets	2.258
6. Low tax ceiling	2.032
7. Easy to serve export markets	2.000
Factors with moderate influence (1.00 - 1.99)	
8. Lower wage costs including fringe benefits	1.968
9. Strategic location of Hong Kong	1.839
10. Existence of adequate infrastructure	1.806
11. Existence of supporting industries	1.774
12. Relationship of Hong Kong with China	1.548
13. Access to specialized skills	1.290
14. Tax incentives	1.226
15. Conditions of living for expatriates	1.161
16. Lower cost of transportation	1.129
Factors with least influence (0.00 - 0.99)	
17. Government incentives	0.968
18. Greater depreciation allowances	0.903
19. Access to local sources of capital	0.806
20. Local market potential	0.806

manage their own assets) and labor (good industrial relations, availability of efficient workers) factors. Their low ratings on government-initiated incentives are reflective of the Hong Kong government's policy of minimum intervention.

F. A Comparative Profile of U.S. and Japanese Investors

Since American and Japanese investors have played the key role among all foreign investment in Hong Kong, a comparison of these two should be extremely meaningful. For simplicity purposes, the data in Tables 4-5 are rearranged into Figure 1.

Table 5: Mean Scores of 20 Country-related Factors, Japanese Investors

	Mean Scores
Factors with most influence (2.00 - 3.00)	
1. Low tax ceiling	2.312
Factors with moderate influence (1.00 - 1.99)	
2. Easy to serve export markets	1.937
3. Lower wage costs including fringe benefits	1.750
4. Availability of efficient labor	1.750
5. Freedom to repatriate earnings	1.687
6. Freedom to transfer capital, assets	1,625
7. Peaceful industrial relations	1.625
8. Local market potential	1.375
9. Stability of Hong Kong government	1.375
10. Existence of adequate infrastructure	1.375
11. Strategic location of Hong Kong	1.312
12. Lower cost of transportation	1.250
13. Existence of supporting industries	1.125
14. Greater depreciation allowances	1.000
Factors with least influence (0.00 - 0.99)	
15. Access to specialized skills	0.938
16. Access to local sources of capital	0.750
17. Tax incentives	0.750
18. Conditions of living for expatriates	0.563
19. Relationship of Hong Kong with China	0.375
20. Government incentives	0.313

For American firms, labor factors seem to be the most determining ones in their investment planning in Hong Kong. The electronics industry serves as a good example of this philosophy. Since the production technology of the electronics industry is more labor-intensive, Hong Kong enjoys the advantages of a comparatively low wage level and efficient, skilled labor for manufacturing and assembling electronic products, such as transistorized radios, calculators and computer parts. Despite the small size of the Hong Kong market for electronic products, American investment has not

Table 6: Mean Scores of 20 Country-related Factors, British Investors

	Mean Scores
Factors with most influence (2.00 - 3.00)	
1. Low tax ceiling	2.778
2. Freedom to transfer capital, assets	2.556
3. Freedom to repatriate earnings	2.444
4. Local market potential	2.333
5. Peaceful industrial relations	2.222
6. Availability of efficient labor	2.111
7. Easy to serve export markets	2.111
8. Existence of supporting industries	2.111
Factors with moderate influence (1.00 - 1.99)	
9. Existence of adequate infrastructure	1.889
10. Stability of Hong Kong government	1.778
11. Lower wage costs including fringe benefits	1.778
12. Access to local sources of capital	1.333
13. Lower cost of transportation	1.333
14. Strategic location of Hong Kong	1.333
15. Relationship of Hong Kong with China	1.222
16. Greater depreciation allowances	1.222
17. Conditions of living for expatriates	1.000
Factors with least influence (0.00 - 0.99)	
18. Access to specialized skills	0.889
19. Government incentives	0.444
20. Tax incentives	0.333

been deterred. This is due to the fact that the industry's target market is not Hong Kong, but the United States. As a result, a main investment objective in Hong Kong is apparently reduction in production costs rather than domestic sales.

Compared to American investors, the domestic market has played a more significant role for Japanese investors. In the past two decades, the industrial structure of Japan has undergone a gradual shift to manufacturing industries with emphasis on capital-intensive technology. One of the main reasons for such a structural change in Japan was due to the high wage rates which made the light industries,

Figure 1: Mean Scores of 20 Country-related Factors, American versus Japanese Investors

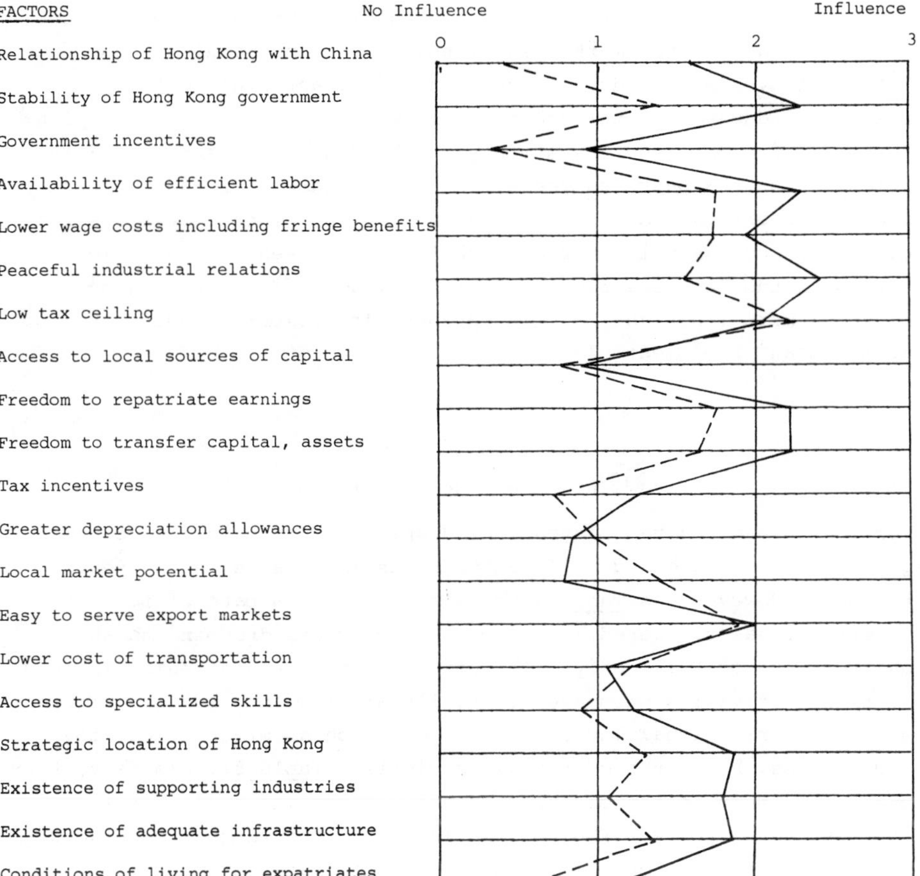

American investor

Japanese investor

particularly the textile industry, unprofitable in competition with similar products of the developing countries. However, the Japanese still possess high technology in textile manufacturing. Consequently, they continue to develop high quality products to meet the demand of the related market segments, on the one hand, and use the method of overseas production to reduce manufacturing costs and meet local demand, on the other. This would explain the underlying force for the Japanese investments in the Hong Kong textile industries during the past few years. Since the garment industry is the leading export manufacturing sector of Hong Kong, the materials for clothing, such as polyester and fabrics, have been the investment target of the Japanese firms. Obviously, domestic marketing has played a more important role in Japanese investment planning than in American investment planning.

III. Investment Opportunities

Foreign investment has played an indispensable role in the economic growth of Hong Kong and will maintain its importance in the years to come. However, as Table 7 reveals, the growth rate of foreign investment has slackened in the past three years dropping to an average rate of 6.1 % only. The effect of such a slackening in investment activities permeates virtually all industry sectors with the so-called traditional investment targets such as electronics, toys and watches, being the most obvious victims (Table 8). In fact, foreign investment in the electronics and watches industries fell in the last three years. The textile industry, the largest manufacturing sector in Hong Kong, only enjoyed a comparatively moderate increase, indicating that the potential of this industry may have reached the saturation level already. To what extent will Hong Kong attract foreign investment in the future? What will be the investment targets? A careful analysis is undoubtedly called for.

A. Input Contents of Manufacturing Output

An analysis of the input contents of manufacturing output will provide basic information regarding direct foreign investment activities

Table 7: Annual Growth Rate of Foreign Investment in Hong Kong, Manufacturing Industry

Year	Increase/Decrease
1971	+27.6 %
1972	+10.0 %
1973	+66.5 %
1974	+19.1 %
1975	+ 2.2 %
1976	+ 9.7 %
1977	+ 6.4 %

Notes: Mean value from 1971 - 1977 = 20.21 %
Mean value from 1975 - 1977 = 6.1 %

Source: Calculated from information prepared by Commerce and Industry Department, Hong Kong.

in Hong Kong. Table 9 shows the percentages of input contents of gross output for the manufacturing industry. Cost of materials and supplies constitutes the largest input content in production. Of every dollar of output, about 60 cents went to materials and supplies. Labor input was the second largest item of production costs, accounting for 19.3 % of gross output. The cost structure of the manufacturing industry indicates that production in Hong Kong is highly material- and labor-intensive in nature.

B. Value Added of Gross Output

Value added of gross output for manufacturing consisting of labor cost, rental and other payments, depreciation of fixed assets and net operating surplus is shown in Table 10. The value added ranged from 21.5 % to 59.4 %, with an average of 32.7 %. Compared with ratios in the developed countries, which range between 40 and 50 %, the ratio of Hong Kong appears to be low. When a high percentage of value added to output will make a positive contribution to the industrial growth as a whole, some government policies for encouraging foreign investments in "high value added industries," even in a liberal economic system, seem to be needed and well justified.

Table 8: Growth of Foreign Investment in Hong Kong, Manufacturing Industry

Industry	1970		1973		1975		1977		Annual Rate of Change for the Period 1971-1977	Annual Rate of Change for the Period 1975-1977
	Total Investment (HK$/Million)	Index	Total Investment (HK$/Million)	Index	Total Investment (HK$/Million)	Index	Total Investment (HK$/Million)	Index		
Electronics	243.0	100	243.0	125	587.5	241	516.1	212	15.0 %	-4.1 %
Textiles	106.6	100	306.5	288	253.1	237	312.7	293	20.5 %	11.2 %
Watches/Clocks and Accessories	8.7	100	184.0	2115	188.2	2163	135.2	1554	109.5 %	-7.7 %
Chemical Products	15.1	100	124.5	825	97.2	644	236.1	1564	160.7 %	48.0 %
Electrical Products and Accessories	9.7	100	49.8	513	96.5	995	201.5	208	63.2 %	35.6 %
Printing and Publishing	23.9	100	42.7	179	61.5	257	140.3	587	30.8 %	34.1 %
Food Manufacturing	5.3	100	58.5	1104	59.9	1130	72.5	1368	139.5 %	6.9 %
Toys	28.1	100	74.0	263	58.2	207	60.6	216	20.0	1.6 %
Building and Construction Materials	23.1	100	32.7	142	51.9	225	34.5	149	20.0	-11.2 %
Metal Rolling, Extrusion and Fabrication	11.4	100	43.0	377	46.8	411	54.9	482	31.4 %	6.4 %
Metal Products	12.9	100	24.9	193	49.7	385	95.1	737	37.7 %	27.6 %
Others	106.5	100	147.5	138	144.4	136	119.0	112	4.4 %	-5.0 %

Source: Calculated from information prepared by Commerce and Industry Department, Hong Kong.

Table 9: Input Contents as a Percentage of Gross Output of Overall Manufacturing Industry in Hong Kong, 1973

Input Contents	%
Consumption of materials/supplies	59.5
Labor cost	19.3
Industrial services	3.6
Non-industrial services	2.9
Rental & other payments	2.9
Depreciation of fixed assets	2.2
Fuel, water and electricity	1.3
Net operating surplus (before profit tax)	8.3
TOTAL	100.0

Source: Hong Kong Monthly Digest of Statistics, January, 1976.

C. Net Operating Surplus

The net operating surplus which is obtained by deducting all cost items from gross output was 8.3 % overall. Although net operating surplus is the income before profit tax of an industry, it can still be used as an indicator for showing the different profit opportunities of various industry groups. The industry groups with high net operating surplus are shown in Table 11.

D. Capital Productivity

Capital productivity of manufacturing industries can be expressed by their output-capital ratios as indicated in Table 12. The greater the output-capital ratio of an industry, the higher its capital productivity and vice versa. On the average, the output-capital ratio was 5.5. This means that fixed assets installed in manufacturing industries were capable of turning out goods and services 5.5 times their own value within the period of one year. Industries with high capital productivity were furniture and fixtures (13.1), footwear (13.0), leather products (13.0), wood and cork products (11.6), and wearing apparel (11.1). Production techniques used in the above

Table 10: Value Added as Percentage of Gross Output, Hong Kong Industries

	Labor Cost (1)	Rental and other payments (2)	Depreciation of fixed assets (3)	Net operation Surplus (4)	Value added (5) =(1)+(2)+(3)+(4)
Food	12.2 (20)	1.9 (18)	2.5 (8)	8.4 (9)	28.7 (19)
Beverage	16.8 (14)	3.3 (9)	4.8 (3)	30.7 (1)	55.6 (2)
Tobacco	6.3 (22)	1.0 (22)	6.3 (1)	22.8 (2)	36.3 (10)
Wearing apparel	21.1 (10)	2.9 (13)	1.0 (20)	5.3 (16)	30.5 (16)
Textiles	15.4 (16)	2.9 (14)	2.7 (6)	10.7 (6)	31.7 (13)
Leather and leather products	17.4 (13)	1.8 (19)	1.1 (19)	3.7 (22)	24.0 (20)
Footwear	29.1 (4)	3.5 (7)	1.1 (18)	6.9 (13)	40.7 (5)
Wood and cork products	16.5 (15)	2.9 (12)	1.0 (21)	10.3 (7)	30.8 (15)
Furniture and fixtures	30.3 (2)	4.2 (2)	1.2 (17)	7.3 (10)	43.0 (4)
Paper and paper products	15.2 (17)	4.1 (3)	2.1 (12)	6.1 (14)	27.5 (18)
Printing and publishing	23.5 (7)	4.0 (4)	5.0 (2)	13.7 (4)	46.1 (3)
Chemicals and chemical products	14.6 (18)	2.4 (16)	2.0 (13)	18.2 (3)	37.3 (9)
Rubber products	29.7 (3)	4.0 (6)	1.9 (14)	4.0 (21)	39.5 (7)
Plastic products	27.4 (5)	4.0 (5)	2.8 (5)	4.9 (18)	39.1 (8)
Non-metallic mineral products	18.9 (11)	2.5 (15)	2.9 (4)	7.2 (11)	31.5 (14)
Basic metal	7.1 (21)	1.2 (21)	1.3 (16)	13.2 (5)	22.8 (21)
Fabricated metal products	26.3 (6)	3.1 (11)	2.5 (9)	8.7 (8)	40.6 (6)
Machinery	22.1 (9)	3.1 (10)	2.2 (11)	4.8 (20)	32.2 (12)
Electrical machinery, apparatus and appliances including electronic pdts.	18.3 (12)	2.1 (17)	1.7 (15)	7.0 (12)	29.1 (17)
Transport equipment	45.2 (1)	6.9 (1)	2.5 (7)	4.8 (19)	59.4 (1)
Professional and scientific, measuring and controlling equipment, and photographic and optical goods	22.6 (8)	3.4 (8)	2.3 (10)	6.0 (15)	34.3 (11)
Other manufacturing industries	13.6 (19)	1.7 (20)	1.0 (22)	5.2 (17)	21.5 (22)
	M = 19.3	M = 2.9	M = 2.2	M = 8.3	M = 32.7

Figures in brackets are rankings.

Source: Hong Kong Monthly Digest of Statistics, January, 1976.

Table 11: Hong Kong Industries with High Net Operating Surplus

Industry Groups	Net Operating Surplus as % of Total Production	Local Sales as % of Total Production	Market Orientation
Transport equipment	30.7	99	Domestic market
Tobacco	22.8	73	Domestic market
Chemicals and Chemical Products	18.2	56	Domestic market Export market
Printing and Publishing	13.7	85	Domestic market
Basic metal products	13.2	83	Domestic market
Textiles	10.7	55	Domestic market Export market
Wood and cork products	10.3	51	Domestic and Export market

Source: Hong Kong Monthly Digest of Statistics, January, 1976.

manufacturing industries are obviously more labor-intensive and therefore make full utilization of the available capital stock, in this way increasing the capital productivity of these industries.

E. Payback Period

Investors are very much interested in the payback period of their investment; they want to know the time span of capital recovery. Due to the political shadow of the future, foreign companies usually take the length of payback period into their investment planning in Hong Kong. The shorter the payback period, the safer will be their invested capital. As stated earlier, net operating surplus has been used as an indicator for measuring gross income before profit tax of an industry. Therefore, the ratio of capital stock to net operating surplus can be used as an indicator for estimating the payback period of capital installed in an industry. After deducting profit tax, net operating surplus after tax or net cash flow should be smaller, so that capital-income ratios should also be greater than those ratios stated in Table 12. The ratio of capital

Table 12: Capital Productivity and its Payback Period

Industry group	Output-capital ratio	Ratio of capital stock to net operating surplus
Food	3.0 (19)	4.0
Beverage	2.4 (21)	1.4
Tobacco	2.3 (22)	2.0
Wearing apparel	11.1 (7)	1.7
Textiles	3.9 (18)	2.4
Leather and leather products	13.0 (4)	2.1
Footwear	13.0 (3)	1.1
Wood and cork products	12.6 (5)	0.8
Furniture and fixtures	13.1 (2)	1.1
Paper and paper products	6.1 (10)	2.7
Printing and publishing	2.8 (20)	2.6
Chemicals and chemical products	4.9 (14)	1.1
Rubber products	5.9 (11)	4.2
Plastic products	5.4 (13)	3.8
Non-metallic products	6.6 (9)	2.1
Basic metal	4.7 (16)	1.6
Fabricated metal products	4.7 (17)	2.5
Machinery	5.9 (12)	3.5
Electrical machinery and apparatus	11.6 (6)	1.2
Transport equipment	4.7 (15)	4.4
Photographic and optical goods	6.8 (8)	2.5
Other manufacturing industries	14.7 (1)	1.3
Figures in brackets are rankings.	M = 5.5	M = 2.3

Source: Hong Kong Monthly Digest of Statistics, January, 1976.

to net operating surplus was 2.3 overall. In other words, allowing profit tax liabilities, the payback period should approximately be 3; i.e. in Hong Kong it takes 3 years of production before capital outlays are recovered. (For details, see Table 12).

F. New Investment Targets

According to the suggestions from a recent survey[3] three manufacturing areas are to be seen as main targets for direct investment activities: raw materials (and supplies) industries; sophisticated products; capital-intensive industries.

Since Hong Kong's manufacturing industries are highly material-intensive, a development of various raw material and supply industries will meet the existing and rising demand of the related local manufacturers. Industries with a high import of materials and supplies were tobacco, paper products, beverage, printing and publishing, wood and cork products, transport equipment and chemical products.

Highly skilled labor in Hong Kong provides a good foundation for developing sophisticated products such as scientific instruments and equipment. However, a shortage of skilled labor will occur when the economy moves to an expansion phase. In addition, wage rates in Hong Kong are considerably higher compared with its neighboring countries. In order to react to these problems, one should devote attention to the development of more capital-using industries. Foreign investment, as mentioned earlier, could then play a significant and appropriate role in the future industrial development of Hong Kong.

Notes:

1 *Harvard Business Review*, September - October, 1969.

2 Suk-ching HO, "International Investors in Hong Kong - What did they look for?" *New Asia College Academic Annual*, Volume XIX, 1977, pp. 241 - 251.

3 H. SUTU and CHANG Chien-min, *The Industrial Structure in Hong Kong*, The Chinese University of Hong Kong, 1976.

TRADE BARRIERS AND EXPORT PROMOTION: THE HONG KONG EXAMPLE

Victor Mok

I. Introduction

Broadly speaking, the postwar world was characterized by a trend towards trade liberalization at least up to the early 1970s. Successive rounds of trade negotiations under GATT resulted in significant tariff concessions on broad groups of commodities, especially manufactures. The movement towards economic integration in Western Europe (EC) also opened up vast opportunities for trade and investment. Despite discriminatory effects inherent in regionalism, the impact of integration through its dynamic effects on income and development generated great potentials in the EC as a market for manufactures. The cumulative effect of these developments contributed to mark the 1960s as an era of rapid world trade expansion.

As a group confined by development and capacity to export, the less developed countries (LDCs) have rather limited participation in world trade. They were and are not satisfied with the traditional mode of trade. The convention of UNCTAD in 1964 was a reflection of this dissatisfaction and provided thereafter a continuing forum for the 'North-South' confrontation. It resulted in additional channels through which the LDCs could seek further trade expansion.

In the meantime, counteracting forces were at work. An increasing number of developed countries (DCs) have imposed import quotas on manufactures from the LDCs, in order to protect industries most vulnerable to competion, notably textiles, clothing and footwear. The notorious application of this form of trade regulation by some of these countries in the mid-1970s seems to render the talk about the establishment of a new international economic order purely academic.

Overall, trade opportunities do exist, and individual LDCs may well take advantage of their low cost of production to penetrate new markets. What is more, even a marginal increase in a vast market may mean an increase of substantial proportion for a 'small' exporting country. With the increasing capacity to produce and to export manufactures, the LDCs did make some progress. The increase, however, has not been evenly distributed.

Large proportions were taken up by Hong Kong, which traditionally thrived on free trade, and others like South Korea and Taiwan, which had switched from import substitution to export orientation in the 1960s. This suggests that, under given conditions, the performance of various LDCs depends much on their ability and willingness to trade. Indeed, recent studies (Balassa, 1, 2, 3; de Vries, 8; Morrison, 15; Mahfuzur Rahman, 14) have shown that it is positively related to their degree of 'openness', and the drive for export has in fact contributed much to the excellent economic performance of a number of LDCs.

The transformation of Hong Kong from an entrepôt into an industrial city is a typical example. Hong Kong is traditionally a free port, and tariffs are mainly for revenue purposes. With a small domestic market and an extreme lack of natural resources, its policy of free trade has guaranteed the import of goods and necessary materials at the lowest possible cost, a factor which has helped its export drive to become remarkably successful. Thus, manufacture for exports is Hong Kong's 'engine of growth'. What is more, with little room to indulge in import substitution, Hong Kong's manufacturing industries were oriented to export markets from the very beginning and therefore able to capitalize on favorable trading conditions existent at that time. As de Vries (8) has put it, where such a strategy of industrialization has been induced by the scarcity of natural resources, an initial obstacle to development has been turned into an economic advantage. At a time when competition has become intense and trade liberalization is grinding to a halt, Hong Kong has entrenched itself in the position as the leading exporter of manufactures[1] among the LDCs.

With this brief background, Section II will trace separate streams of development in tariffs on manufactures imported into the developed countries and analyse their impacts on Hong Kong's export trade. Section III deals with nontariff trade barriers. We shall concentrate on textile quotas which have become the major source of concern to Hong Kong's manufacturers. An analysis of their effects will also be given together with discussions on Hong Kong's 'voluntary restraint' programme. As trade performance depends on the ability to sell as much as on the ability to produce, we shall discuss in Section IV the institutional arrangements and activities of Hong Kong's export promotion. The last Section will summarize the issues and examine their implications on Hong Kong's future trade and development.

II. Tariffs as Barriers to Hong Kong's Exports

With respect to tariffs, there are three major developments which have not only provided great impetus to but also helped shape the pattern of Hong Kong's export trade in the postwar era. Chronologically, the Commonwealth Preference first came into existence in the 1930s but Hong Kong did not begin to feel its effects until after the war; negotiations and concessions under GATT were started in the late 1940s but major break-throughs came a decade later; and the GSPs under UNCTAD are mainly a matter of the 1970s.

At the outset, it is essential to point out that Hong Kong has only little bargaining power. It is neither a contracting party of GATT nor a member of UNCTAD. Circumscribed by its economic conditions, it has to rely on free trade. Therefore, it has little, if any, to offer in terms of concessions, and its market is too small for any threat of retaliation to be taken seriously.

A. The Commonwealth Preferences

The Commonwealth Preference Area (CPA) came into existence in 1932 when Britain undertook to keep her tariffs on imports from the Commonwealth at pre-1932 levels. This resulted in separate tariff rates, the Full (or MFN) and the CPA rate, on products imported into Britain due to subsequent changes in the former.[2] The ad valorem margin of preference enjoyed by CPA products is measured by the absolute difference between these rates. For an individual CPA country, the proportion of its exports enjoying preference and the average margin of preference depended on the pattern of its exports, since preference margins were quite different with respect to product groups. Manufactures were accorded higher preference and many of them were admitted free of duty. As part of the Commonwealth, Hong Kong was granted preference by Britain and a number of Commonwealth countries.

Like many LDCs, Hong Kong started its industrialization with cotton textiles and a variety of light manufactures. This dates back to the early 1950s when textile trade had not become an issue, and the fact that Hong Kong exported mostly manufactures placed it in a highly advantageous position. The Commonwealth rapidly became Hong Kong's largest market in textiles. It has been estimated by Green (12) that, in 1962, 97 % of its exports to the British market enjoyed preference at an average margin of 19 %, compared to 61 % of all CPA exports enjoying preferences at an average of 11.8 %. All but 4 % of its exports to the U.K. were free of duty, and the dutiable products were mainly textiles and clothing which had preference margins up to 25 % or more.

Because of the broad base built up in those early years, textiles maintained its importance in Hong Kong's trade with the Commonwealth. Table 1 lists the leading importers and their shares. Except for the U.S.A., they are all Commonwealth countries, and to the present time, textiles still occupy sizeable proportions in Hong Kong's exports to the Commonwealth, much higher than its exports to others.

Starting from the 1960s, signs of erosion began to appear in the Commonwealth Preference. Some countries partly removed while others abolished the Commonwealth Preference altogether. As a result, the value of Hong Kong's exports to the Commonwealth (other than Britain) covered by Commonwealth Preference Certificates never went back to the level it had reached in 1964/65.[3]

In the case of Britain, progressive reductions in the EFTA rate and the Full (MFN) rate continued to cut down the preference margin. In 1972, the CPA rate of cotton woven textiles was increased from nil to 85 % of the Full rate.[4] These developments, according to Bell (5), reduced the preference margin for manufactures and semi-manufactures from an average of 10.2 % in the Pre-Kennedy-Round era to an average of 6.1 % in the Post-Kennedy-Round era, which had very little advantage over the 5.1 % preference margin accorded to all non-CPA beneficiaries under the British GSP in 1972. Furthermore, when Britain joined the EC in 1974, she began to phase out

Table 1: Hong Kong's Export of Textiles

Destination	1960	1964	1968	1972	1973	1974	1975
	Shares of Leading Importers - Textiles (SITC 65)						
U.S.A.	15.4%	15.7%	24.2%	23.2%	18.7%	18.2%	17.1%
U.K.	35.3	28.7	26.4	23.5	16.5	16.2	19.0
Singapore		5.8	6.5	5.7	6.4	5.2	5.4
Australia	5.1	7.0	8.9	8.9	12.6	13.2	13.7
New Zealand	3.7	6.9	7.0	6.1	6.7	8.6	6.4
	Shares of Leading Importers - Cotton Fabrics (SITC 652)						
U.S.A.		20.0%	28.2%	33.4%	29.9%	28.4%	24.7%
U.K.		30.0	26.7	22.6	18.4	15.7	20.1
Australia		9.0	11.8	12.4	16.9	17.1	17.1
New Zealand		5.8	6.4	6.6	7.2	9.0	6.2
S. Africa		3.4	3.0	1.4	1.6	3.1	4.9
Singapore		6.9	5.9	4.9	5.4	4.6	4.8
	Share of Textiles in Hong Kong's Exports to:						
U.S.A.	11.9%	9.3%	7.3%	5.9%	6.5%	6.8%	5.1%
EEC	9.3	7.5	3.2	3.1	2.4	2.6	2.6
U.K.	34.1	21.2	20.6	16.7	13.9	16.2	14.8
Australia	35.9	47.5	39.4	32.1	39.6	28.5	29.1
Singapore		26.8	31.3	25.3	28.0	22.9	18.6
S. Africa	52.5	43.4	27.3	19.2	26.9	23.9	31.3
New Zealand	64.2	84.2	81.0	78.6	81.6	78.7	76.0

Source: Calculated from data given in Hong Kong Trade Statistics, Hong Kong Department of Commerce and Industry, and Department of Census and Statistics, various issues.

her Commonwealth Preference completely. Consequently, only 50 % of Hong Kong's exports to Britain were covered by Commonwealth Preference Certificates in 1974/75, compared to an average of well over 90 % in the 1950s and 1960s.[5] In other words, the Commonwealth Preference gradually passed into history. This resulted in decreasing shares of Hong Kong's principal manufactured exports in the British market, as seen in Table 2.

Table 2: Hong Kong's Share in Imports into U.K.

Commodity	1970	1971	1972	1973	1974	1975
Clothing	38.2%	41.8%	39.6%	37.0%	32.6%	32.6%
Textiles	8.1	8.9	7.5	6.6	6.2	5.9
Misc. Manufactures	10.1	8.2	6.9	7.6	7.1	5.7
Electrical Machinery	1.7	2.3	2.4	2.4	1.8	1.2
Manufactures of Metal	4.0	4.4	4.8	4.6	3.2	3.0
Footwear	24.9	22.3	17.6	13.9	9.2	7.7

Source: Hong Kong Review of Overseas Trade 1974, 1975, Hong Kong Department of Census and Statics.

B. Tariff Concessions under GATT

The fact that GATT was not originally intended to solve the trade and development problems of the LDCs has been the cause of much accusation. From Hong Kong's standpoint, however, these complaints are not relevant because its exports are almost exclusively manufactures and, being itself already a free port, any concession on the part of others is beneficial. For our purpose here, the effects of two major rounds of tariff concessions, namely the Dillon Round concluded in 1961 with 20 % and the Kennedy Round concluded in 1967 with 35 % tariff reductions, are of special importance. For they came at the time when Hong Kong looked beyond the Commonwealth for wider markets.

In a study of the effects of the Dillon Round on American imports from the LDCs, Finger (10) used the 'reduced group, non-reduced group' (tariff reduction) method and found that, for 1960-1965 and in manufactures, "..... on products which might be called atypical

LDCs exports (the DC basket) we observe not only a significant increase of supply from the LDCs, but also a significant response (especially in terms of quantity) to the marginal incentive of the tariff reduction". Among the LDCs which atypically exported manufactures of the DC basket to the U.S. during this period, Hong Kong had no doubt a very important role. The relative importance of textiles in its exports to the U.S. had already declined, while electrical machinery had increased from 1.0 % to 10.7 %, and toys from 6.1 % to 10.7 % in the basket from 1960 to 1965.

Effects of the Kennedy Round were more straight-forward. Comparing the imports of the U.S., the EEC and Japan of the 'big reduction' and 'small reduction' (tariff reduction) groups of manufactures from the LDCs in 1967 and 1970, Finger (11) concluded in very simple terms that (a) tariffs mattered and (b) the supply response on the part of the developing countries was substantial. In its continuous expansion, the American market at its peak accounted for well over 40 % of Hong Kong's export of manufactures.

Indeed, continuous tariff liberalization and income expansion in the developed countries had enabled Hong Kong's export of manufactures to advance on a broad front despite increasing competiton. In value terms, tremendous increases were recorded in all markets, but there were also changes in their relative importance. Declines were mainly found in the Commonwealth countries, especially the U.K., and the American market also started to soften after the early 1970s but still leading by far, compared to others.

The most notable feat of Hong Kong's performance is its successful penetration into newer markets. Economic integration, tariff liberalization, growth and the increasing international outlook of the EEC had generated tremendous trade potentials for Hong Kong's manufactured exports. The increase in the Federal Republic of Germany was spectacular, which by 1975 had replaced the U.K. as the second largest market for Hong Kong's manufactured exports. The most significant break-through was, however, in markets which were previously of negligible importance; Japan, Switzerland and Austria belonged to this group. In fact, their shares were larger than those of certain EC and Scandinavian countries.[6] Table 3 shows the development of various markets for Hong Kong's manufactured exports.

Table 3: Hong Kong's Export of Manufactures
(in million Hong Kong dollars)

Destination	1960	1964	1968	1972	1973	1974	1975
Developed Countries							
U.S.A.	715.7 (28.4)	1,196.6 (29.7)	3,441.6 (43.2)	6,063.2 (41.6)	6,743.8 (36.2)	7,316.7 (33.4)	7,227.1 (32.9)
Canada	72.3 (2.9)	109.7 (2.7)	275.0 (3.5)	486.0 (3.3)	492.0 (2.6)	600.1 (2.7)	752.1 (3.4)
U.K.	573.7 (22.8)	957.2 (23.7)	1,328.2 (16.7)	2,174.5 (14.9)	2,786.0 (14.9)	2,740.8 (12.5)	2,758.3 (12.6)
EEC - six	146.3 (5.8)	416.0 (10.3)	706.7 (8.9)	2,091.5 (14.3)	2,765.5 (14.8)	3,509.9 (16.0)	3,855.7 (17.5)
Nordic countries	58.6 (2.3)	144.7 (3.6)	255.5 (3.2)	464.1 (3.2)	614.7 (3.3)	743.2 (3.4)	894.4 (4.1)
Switzerland	3.5 (0.1)	23.4 (0.6)	64.0 (0.8)	163.1 (1.1)	265.0 (1.4)	356.5 (1.6)	408.7 (1.8)
Austria	0.4 ---	7.8 (0.2)	19.5 (0.2)	78.0 (0.5)	108.7 (0.6)	136.7 (0.6)	194.6 (0.9)
Rep. of Ireland	1.2 ---	6.3 (0.2)	5.9 (0.1)	13.7 (0.1)	23.6 (0.1)	41.5 (0.2)	24.0 (0.1)
Japan	5.4 (0.2)	36.5 (0.9)	111.4 (1.4)	303.2 (2.1)	839.5 (4.5)	798.3 (3.6)	715.6 (3.3)
S. Africa	37.7 (1.5)	54.6 (1.4)	81.5 (1.0)	97.9 (0.7)	169.0 (0.9)	264.4 (1.2)	220.2 (1.0)
Australia	78.8 (3.1)	104.7 (2.6)	234.6 (2.9)	430.3 (2.9)	750.2 (4.0)	1,271.3 (5.8)	1,012.7 (4.6)
New Zealand	30.7 (1.2)	57.1 (1.4)	87.5 (1.1)	118.0 (0.8)	188.3 (1.0)	294.5 (1.3)	176.6 (0.8)
Rest of the World	794.7 (31.5)	919.9 (22.8)	1,355.4 (17.0)	2,104.2 (14.4)	2,904.7 (15.6)	3,832.8 (17.5)	3,735.4 (17.0)
Total	2,519.0 (100.0)	4,034.5 (100.0)	7,966.9 (100.0)	14,587.7 (100.0)	18,651.0 (100.0)	21,906.7 (100.0)	21,975.4 (100.0)

Source: Hong Kong Trade Statistics, Hong Kong Department of Commerce and Industry, and Department of Census and Statistics, various issues.
Figures in parentheses are percentages of totals.

C. GSPs under UNCTAD

Resulting from the North-South confrontation, the most important change in trade policies on the part of the developed countries relevant to Hong Kong is tariff preference on imports of manufactures from the LDCs. When the major GSPs were announced one after another in the early 1970s, there was quite a relief to Hong Kong that it was not excluded.[7] In most cases, its textiles and footwear are not qualified for preference. However, these restrictions also apply to most of its serious competitors.[8]

As the LDCs were already having increasing shares of manufactured exports to the developed countries under the impact of the Kennedy Round concessions, it is difficult to estimate how much additional incentive the GSPs could provide. Based on the structure of the EC scheme and 1968 trade figures, Cooper (6) estimated that only 22 % of manufactures (excluding textiles) imported into the Community from the LDCs would not have been subject to quota ceilings in the second year of operation of the GSP. The faster the LDCs increased their manufactured exports, the sooner they faced the full duty. (If the U.K. had been included in the calculation, only 17 % of manufactures imported into the enlarged Community would have had unused quotas.) As might have been expected, the more advanced LDCs benefited more from the GSPs upon implementation. But soon after, there was little additional incentive due to the inherently discriminatory nature of these schemes.

The EC scheme is an example. Some beneficiaries have been named 'more competitive' with respect to certain textiles. Their exports are limited by maximum participation shares (butoirs) within the Community quota, and each Member State also has its internal ceiling for imports. Hong Kong has been named 'more competitive' in 5 items.[9] As for other manufactures, products are classified as 'non-sensitive', 'semi-sensitive', 'sensitive' and 'super-competitive', with increasing stringency of control in that order. Hong Kong has been named 'super-competitive' in 8 products and, therefore, is limited to a 'butoir' of 15 % each.[10] In general, a beneficiary will soon lose its entitlement to the GSP if its exports are substantial and have a high rate of growth, and even sooner if it is named 'more competitive' or 'super-competitive'. Considering Hong Kong's remarkable performance in the EC market in subsequent years, there must have been little additional incentive provided by the GSP. (The American scheme is somewhat different but has similar effects, since a beneficiary is denied preference in products in which it accounts for more than half of U.S. imports, or its sales amount to more than U.S. $ 25 million.)[11]

Therefore, it was pointed out by Baldwin and Murray (4) that the more advanced LDCs, like Hong Kong, would benefit more from further MFN tariff reductions than from maintaining the existing GSP margins. It is doubtful, however, that much further reductions can result from the Tokyo Round. In any case, due to existing low levels, tariffs have become much less significant as trade barriers.

III. Import Quotas as Barriers to Hong Kong's Exports

The attempt to remove non-tariff trade barriers has a long history under GATT, but success has been limited. This is why non-tariff trade barriers have become the focal point of trade discussion in the 1970s. Ironically, it was with GATT's sanction that the most comprehensive system of quantitative restrictions ever came into existence. The reason is that the flow of textiles from the LDCs has created 'market disruptions' in the developed countries.

A. Hong Kong's Encounter with Textile Quotas

It was pointed out earlier that Hong Kong's initial development had benefited much from the Commonwealth Preference under which its cotton textiles entered the British market with a substantial preference margin. Towards the end of the 1950s, imports of large volume of textiles from Hong Kong began to cause concern and protest in Britain, especially among cotton textile manufacturers in Lancashire. This resulted in an agreement between Hong Kong and Britain, the so-called Lancashire Pact, according to which Hong Kong undertook to restrain its export of cotton garments and piece-goods in three years. This was known as the Undertaking which was extended a few times until 1972, with revisions in its details. The annual quota limit was raised from time to time, but finer categorization was incorporated into the scheme with sub-quotas for separate groups of cotton textiles to make sure that shipments would not be made entirely in the so-called 'sensitive' items. There were also certain flexibility provisions, such as a limited 'swing' between quotas of different groups, over-fulfilment of an annual quota in anticipation of next year's quota, and 'carry-over' of an unfulfilled quota into the following year. In October 1972, a new agreement was enacted for Hong Kong to limit its export of woven cotton and polyester/cotton fabrics, garments and made-up articles for fifteen months. This Undertaking, which had gone beyond cotton textiles, was Hong Kong's last with Britain, for bilateral agreements would no longer be made after the latter's entry into the EC.

Initiated by the U.S., GATT started its discussion on textile trade.[12] A Short Term Arrangement Regarding International Trade in Cotton Textiles (STA) was first reached for 1961-62, according to which the importing countries were given the right to call upon the exporting countries for restraint. This was later replaced by a Long Term Arrangement Regarding International Trade in Cotton Textiles (LTA) for five years up to September 1967, and another Arrangement Regarding International Trade in Cotton Textiles (CTA) for three years, and later extended until 1973. By this time, requests for restraint had actually gone beyond the scope of cotton textiles; a Multi-Fibre Arrangement (MFA) came into effect in early 1974 until the end of 1977.

From the brief account given above, it can be readily seen that, historically, quotas on textiles started with cotton textiles and ended up on all textiles. Indeed, 'textiles' is a catch-all term covering not only cotton, non-cotton and man-made fibre 'Textile yarn, fabrics, made-up articles and related products' (SITC 65), but also 'Clothing except fur clothing' (SITC 841). When the MFA came into effect, all Hong Kong textiles were under restraint with detailed categorization, and sub-quotas were imposed on certain specific groups.

Inasmuch as Hong Kong exercises 'voluntary restraint', it retains the right to allocate quotas internally. This has a definite advantage over the situation in which quotas are allocated at the importing end. As quota imposition necessarily causes the price of the restricted product to rise, an allocation carries with it an economic rent.[13] This is seen in the transfer price of an export quota allocation or import license. Thus, when quota allocations are controlled at the exporting end, the exporting country can push the price as high as the market can bear and the economic rent accrues to the export quota holders.

In more recent years, some importing countries, or rather the importers, are trying to take over the control of quotas; Australia has succeeded, while others are hinting to replace bilateral quotas with a system of global quotas to be allocated by their authorities.

B. Hong Kong's Voluntary Restraint Programme

Since Hong Kong undertakes voluntary restraint, all textile exports covered by Arrangements must be authorized by the Department of Commerce and Industry. All categories subject to 'specific' quotas must have quota allocations and export permits issued by the Department, while categories not subject to 'specific' quotas (the 'basket' categories) are required to have Export Authorizations so that the Department can make sure that the sum of 'specific' and 'basket' categories within the same broader group will not exceed the group quota, and the sum of all groups will not exceed the total quota. To maximize quota utilization, the Department has developed a mechanism with basic features as follows.

(1) Allocation of Quota by Performance: At the beginning of a quota-year after actual shipments of the previous year are verified, quotas are allocated to firms on the basis of their performance according to the following formula: Those with performance of 95 % or more against their quotas will have the same allocation as in the previous year plus a certain percentage growth depending on overall quota availability; those with performance between 50 and 95 % will receive allocations equal to their actual shipment; and those with less than 50 % performance will have no allocation at all. After allocations have been made, a Free Quota Scheme will be in operation for categories where quotas are not exhausted. Applications are open to all, and allocations are made on a 'first come first served' basis upon evidence of export document. These allocations

are not transferable and holders are penalized if quotas are not used within a stipulated period, but performance against these quotas will qualify for allocations in the following year. Any further unused quota is allocated under the Year-End Special Shipment Scheme, with similar details.

(2) Freedom of Transfer: Allocation according to past performance has its shortcomings. Performance may differ from year to year and in various categories for various reasons. Thus, firms will find themselves not only having over- or under-allocations, but also their allocations in various categories not matching their needs. To facilitate better utilization, a transfer of quotas is permitted after final allocations have been made. Therefore, an open market has come into existence in which quotas are traded at a price depending on demand and supply conditions. Despite allegations, the freedom of transfer does serve one economic purpose; given the existing method of quota allocation, it is an efficient way to maximize overall utilization.

(3) Flexibility Provisions: Subject to conditions in Hong Kong's Bilateral Agreements with importing countries, flexibility is provided to improve quota utilization. For example, firms can increase their allocations by a certain percentage or an absolute amount when unused quotas are still available. They can 'swing' their quota holdings from 'specific' to 'basket' categories if they want to change their line of exports. Furthermore, they can also over-fulfill their quotas in anticipation of future quotas.

The existing method of quota allocation and freedom of transfer has been the cause of much complaint in Hong Kong and abroad. As long as quotas must be allocated in some way, the issue of 'fairness' inevitably rises. Allocation based on historical performance naturally favors the well-established firms; but it can be argued that it provides some certainty which long term investments require. Even if allocations are made on a 'first come first served' basis, the well-established firms will still be in a better position because they can line up orders ahead of time.

Table 4: Performance Against STA, LTA and CTA Quotas, in percent

Country and Coverage	1961/62	62/63	63/64	64/65	65/66	66/67	67/68	68/69
U.S.A.								
30 categories	105.9	98.3						
36 categories			96.9					
37 categories				99.5				
all					108.2	94.3	102.2	100.4
F.R. Germany								
woven nightwear			88.3	89.3	100.0			
7 groups						93.6	98.7	100.9
Sweden								
5 garment categories								83.6

Source: Calculated from data given in Annual Report, Hong Kong Department of Commerce and Industry, various issues.

Table 5: Performance Against British Cotton Textile Quotas, in percent

Textile Group	1962	1963	1964	1965	1966	1967	1968
Yarn		100.0	99.1	98.8	97.6	97.2	94.1
Loomstate Fabrics } Finished Fabrics }	100.9	99.1	99.9	127.9 }	101.8	100.0	101.3
Garments & Made-ups	105.1	99.5	99.9	66.6 }			
Miscellaneous					69.0	82.4	89.5

Source: Calculated from data given in Annual Report, Hong Kong Department of Commerce and Industry, various issues.

† A supplementary quota was given this year.

C. Performance against Quotas

From reports of the Department of Commerce and Industry, Hong Kong's performance in textile exports against quotas was highly satisfactory in the 1960s. This is seen in Tables 4 and 5 in which performance is defined as the ratio between actual shipment to the restraint limit. Such remarkable performance continued in the early 1970s, but there is evidence that it has become poorer recently. Since Hong Kong has been working with more or less the same restraint programme throughout the years, explanations for this change must be found elsewhere.

First, whether a quota limit is really effective is determined by overall demand and supply conditions. This depends not only on the general economic condition of the importing countries but also on comparative cost-price relationships. The mid-1970s have been characterized by a world recession and intensified competition in textile exports.

Second, the coverage of quota arrangements is also important. If only certain groups are subject to restraint, performance would be high because these usually are the 'hot' items. But, when coverage is extended to include all categories, the overall average performance is bound to become lower.

And third, the categorization of textiles into groups and categories each with sub-quotas is a great hindrance to full utilization of the overall quota. There is little question that quotas on 'hot' items will be utilized to the full extent, and the only allowance is found in the permissible 'swing' which usually amounts to a few percentage points, if any, while there may be substantial unused quotas in other items. Generally speaking, the more detailed the categorization of products and the more concentrated the demand for the 'hot' items, the more difficult it becomes to utilize fully the overall quota.

The effects of these factors can be seen in Hong Kong's performance against quotas in the American market which has extended its coverage on restrained items repeatedly and in the process developed a highly structured scheme of product categorization. For 1973/74, performance was poor as shown in Table 6, where only high-performance categories are listed. They tend to concentrate in 'specific'

Table 6: Performance Against U.S. Textile Quotas, 1973/74

Products	Performance in Percentage		
1. Textile Yarns & Fabrics			80.5
Cotton with			
6 specific categories, of which			
twill & sateen	97.6		
16 basket categories			
Man-made Fibre with			
14 basket categories			
Wool with			
10 basket categories			
2. Textile Garments			61.0
Cotton with		75.0	
15 specific categories, of which			
knit shirts & blouses	96.9		
men's & boys' dress shirts	113.9		
men's & boys' sport & work shirts	110.7		
all other coats, not knit	103.1		
9 basket categories			
Man-made Fibre with		50.0	
9 specific categories, of which			
knit shirts & blouses	95.7		
Sweaters & cardigans, knit	102.6		
18 basket categories			
Wool with		40.9	
1 specific category			
14 basket categories			
3. Textile Made-ups & Misc. Articles			83.8
Cotton with			
4 specific categories, of which			
shop towels	99.7		
6 basket categories			
Man-made Fibre with			
3 basket categories			
Wool with			
4 basket categories			
4. Corduroy Used in Cotton Apparel with 8 basket categories			65.6

Source: Calculated from data given in *Annual Statistical Review 1974-75*, Hong Kong Department of Commerce and Industry.

categories (the 'hot' items) with some having more than 100 % performance, made possible by flexibility provisions. But overall performance was far from satisfactory due to large amounts of unused quotas in the 'basket' categories.

The same pattern can be found in Hong Kong's export of cotton textiles to the EC. There were 6 'specific' and 16 'basket' categories (1974). Only 2 'specific' categories, namely 'woven trousers for men and boys' and 'woven outergarments for women, girls and infants' had full utilization. As a result, overall performance stood at only 86.3 %.[14] 'Burden sharing' among the EC countries had similar effects, as initially Hong Kong's exports were concentrated in the German market.

D. Effects of Quota Restrictions

For an exporting country, adjustments in response to quota restrictions are quite different from those in response to tariffs. Unless tariffs are prohibitively high, the quantity of exports can still be increased by cutting cost or lowering the profit margin. In the face of quota restrictions, it can only increase the unit value of the controlled items or diversify into exports which are not subject to control. Hong Kong has adjusted its export pattern along both these lines.

Table 7 shows clearly the effects of quotas on 'textiles' (proper) and 'footwear' (which is also subject to control in certain developed countries). Even though in value terms these exports have increased substantially over the years, their relative importance in the export basket has declined. In the meantime, new lines of exports have come into prominence, most notably electrical machinery which has replaced textiles as Hong Kong's second largest source of export earnings. Interestingly, 'clothing' does not seem to have been affected. In fact, it bounced back in the 1970s after some initial decline.

The difference in performance between textiles and clothing, both subject to quotas, calls for explanations. In comparing the average growth rates of exports, Hsia (13) pointed out that "... the shift to synthetic yarn and fabrics requires substantial reinvestment on the part of the spinners and weavers, inasmuch as the

Table 7: Hong Kong's Export of Selected Manufactures to the Developed Countries (in million Hong Kong dollars)

SITC Code	Description	1960	1964	1968	1972	1973	1974	1975
65	Textile Yarn, fabrics etc.	368.1 (21.3)	497.9 (16.0)	781.0 (11.8)	1,117.9 (9.0)	1,612.8 (1o.2)	1,827.9 (10.1)	1,517.3 (8.3)
69	Manufactures of metal		54.0 (1.7)	125.5 (1.9)	282.0 (2.3)	360.9 (2.3)	432.6 (2.3)	397.2 (2.2)
71	Machinery other than electrical	1.7 (0.1)	2.8 (0.1)	6.7 (0.1)	28.6 (0.2)	107.8 (0.7)	185.0 (1.0)	355.3 (1.9)
72	Electrical machinery	20.9 (1.2)	140.8 (4.5)	684.4 (10.4)	1,721.0 (13.8)	2,237.9 (14.2)	2,764.6 (15.3)	2,320.7 (12.7)
812	Sanitary etc. fixtures & fittings		49.0 (1.6)	86.4 (1.3)	127.1 (1.0)	160.1 (1.0)	173.7 (1.0)	119.9 (0.7)
831	Travel goods, hand-bags etc.	7.9 (0.5)	24.6 (0.8)	92.3 (1.4)	252.4 (2.0)	346.8 (2.2)	356.4 (2.0)	361.8 (2.0)
841	Clothing	801.4 (46.5)	1,371.3 (44.0)	2,662.9 (40.3)	5,612.4 (45.0)	6,864.4 (43.6)	7,934.3 (43.9)	9,140.6 (50.1)
851	Footwear	83.6 (4.8)	135.0 (4.3)	231.9 (3.5)	268.0 (2.1)	240.4 (1.5)	271.8 (1.5)	215.3 (1.2)
861	Scientific etc. instruments		10.0 (0.3)	53.3 (0.8)	85.1 (0.7)	119.9 (0.8)	195.2 (1.1)	177.5 (1.0)
864	Watches & clocks	3.2 (0.2)	2.9 (0.1)	36.3 (0.5)	105.3 (0.8)	152.3 (1.0)	264.4 (1.5)	375.0 (2.1)
893	Plastic products	4.9 (0.3)	17.2 (0.6)	40.3 (0.6)	133.1 (1.0)	206.5 (1.3)	236.8 (1.3)	190.1 (1.0)
894	Perambulators, toys etc.	103.7 (6.0)	281.4 (9.0)	765.3 (11.6)	1,323.6 (10.6)	1,567.7 (10.0)	1,717.0 (9.5)	1,483.4 (8.1)
897	Jewellery		42.7 (1.4)	71.8 (1.1)	179.2 (1.4)	303.9 (1.9)	345.1 (1.9)	359.6 (2.0)
899 (pt.)	Wigs & related hair products		8.6 (0.3)	311.9 (4.7)	210.9 (1.7)	99.6 (0.6)	41.2 (0.2)	32.8 (0.2)
6-8	All manufactures	1,724.3 (100.0)	3,114.6 (100.0)	6,611.4 (100.0)	12,483.5 (100.0)	15,746.3 (100.0)	18,073.9 (100.0)	18,240.0 (100.0)

Source: Hong Kong Trade Statistics, Hong Kong Department of Commerce and Industry, and Department of Census and Statistics, various issues. Figures in parentheses are percentages of respective totals.

machinery and equipment used in manufacturing cotton yarn and fabrics are unsuitable for synthetic products... In the garment sector, on the other hand, the existing machinery and equipment can be used for processing synthetic inputs with minor modifications". That is, the textile industry technically has less feasibility in internal diversification.

A somewhat related explanation is that the textile industry is fairly capital-intensive. The core of this industry is in the mass-production of comparatively homogeneous products with a longer period of capital turnover. This makes it less flexible in adaptation and more vulnerable to competition from other LDCs which also have access to modern technology. The clothing industry, however, is highly labor-intensive.[15] It requires a great deal of skilled or semi-skilled labor, the supply and quality of which Hong Kong is well-renowned. The nature of this industry also allows more product differentiation. Not only is there a wide range of garments, but also its varieties change swiftly over time. Consequently, manufacturers can switch quickly from product to product and from market to market in response to changing demand conditions. In other words, the vast possibility for internal diversification and a comparatively shorter period for capital turnover have provided the clothing industry with the necessary flexibility to sustain its prominence.

Product differentiation has yet another dimension. It expresses itself in quality and design catering to a special group of customers. There are indications that Hong Kong is moving in this direction, and this may well explain the resurgence of the relative importance of clothing exports in the 1970s. Despite quota restrictions, higher unit values have helped maintain a high rate of growth in terms of total export value. Furthermore, the production of quality clothing for segmented markets does not depend so much on economies of scale. Manufacturers of moderate or even modest size can do just as well as larger producers. With a good supply of skilled labor and independent-minded entrepreneurs, Hong Kong is excellent in this respect.

As a result, the clothing industry has remained the backbone of Hong Kong's manufacturing. In 1975, Hong Kong was by far the leading garment exporter to the U.S. and the U.K., accounting for 23.3 and 32.6 % of their imports, respectively, and had replaced France and become second only to Italy in the German market, with a 13.8 % market share.[16]

Table 8 shows the quantum and unit value indices of the export of Hong Kong's selected manufactures. Effects of quota restrictions on textile fabrics, made-ups and footwear are clearly seen in the quantum indices.[17] In contrast, exports of transistorized radios, electronics components, watches and clocks have increased remarkably in quantity, and the clothing industry is somewhere in between. As for unit value indices they have in general risen faster in products which are under quota restrictions.

Considering the recent poor performance of Hong Kong's export against quotas, it suggests that even under present quota limits, there is still room for diversification within product and country groups given better demand conditions.

So far, Hong Kong has been allowed to exercise voluntary restraint, but importers in some countries are trying to take over the control of quotas. This constitutes a major threat to the future of Hong Kong's textile and clothing industry.

IV. Export Promotion

As Hong Kong must survive on trade, the need for trade expansion increases with every step of its industrial development. To understand Hong Kong's export promotion, we must emphasize that it is not just a matter of simple 'salesmanship'. Since the bulk of its exports are oriented to markets abroad, it cannot produce first and sell later; for, an export-led economy can continue to develop only in so far as it can adjust its pattern of production in response to changing demand conditions.

A. Export Promotion before 1966

As early as 1952, the Economic Division of the Department of Commerce and Industry had set up a Trade Promotion Office, signifying the official recognition of the importance of trade promotion. A Trade Development Division was established in 1953. But at that stage its

Table 8: Export Unit Value and Quantum Indices of Hong Kong's Selected Manufactures

Product	1968	1969	1970	1971	1972	1973	1974	1975
Clothing								
V	100	108	114	121	129	156	192	188
Q	100	118	126	150	157	159	150	178
Textile Fabrics								
V	100	104	105	115	124	166	215	165
Q	100	105	118	116	122	139	123	130
Tex. Yarn & Thread								
V	100	106	108	112	119	161	220	152
Q	100	123	149	159	180	293	250	224
Textile Made-ups								
V	100	102	101	111	122	134	214	175
Q	100	97	104	110	98	80	65	67
Footwear								
V	100	109	119	129	137	155	187	180
Q	100	100	93	100	82	63	61	53
Transistorized Radios								
V	100	110	121	133	126	140	163	154
Q	100	131	138	163	122	249	245	256
Electronic Components								
V	100	81	88	91	84	81	70	101
Q	100	200	308	348	413	604	257	462
Watches & Clocks								
V	100	96	108	105	110	128	163	196
Q	100	165	183	243	268	335	455	480

Source: Hong Kong Review of Overseas Trade, Hong Kong Department of Census and Statistics, various issues.

Note: V - unit value index
Q - quantum index

work included a host of administrative duties including export certification. Routine matters were later taken out of the Development Division, but still the situation was far from satisfactory.

Export Promotion was elevated to Division status in 1965, with one Trade Development Branch responsible for executing trade promotion programmes undertaken with public funds, one Trade Publications Branch and one Hong Kong Products Display Centre. The Development Division, on the other hand, was charged with trade relations, information collection, market research and trade inquiries. The Department also had three overseas offices in London, Brussels and Sydney, which, as overseas arms, helped the work in all aspects including trade promotion.

The Department started publication of a monthly Trade Enquiries Bulletin in 1952, which was changed to the Trade Bulletin in the following year, giving information on Hong Kong's industries, legislation, trade statistics and economic conditions in general. Trade inquiries were also listed so that local manufacturers and overseas buyers could seek out contacts. Another publication, the annual Commerce, Industry and Finance Directory came out in 1955 mainly for overseas circulation. For similar purposes, the Information Services Department published a number of pamphlets such as the Hong Kong for the Businessman, Opportunity Hong Kong, Hong Kong Products, Joint Venture Hong Kong etc. for distribution through various channels.

In the meantime, written inquiries from overseas were dealt with by the Department. This work was extended to an increasing number of visiting business people when a permanent Display Centre was opened in 1963. The staff there also helped make introductions and appointments for visitors to meet with local manufacturers.

From 1955 to 1965, the Department undertook a series of major export promotion activities including five outward trade missions to some forty countries (Central America 1958, West Africa 1960, Australia 1961, Middle East 1962 and the EEC 1963), and the organization of firms to participate in some twenty-four international fairs, mainly in the developed countries.

In the private sector, the Chinese Manufacturers' Association was the pioneer in overseas promotion when it participated in the first postwar British Industries Fair of 1948. Selling tours were later organized to visit the U.S., Australia and Southeast Asia. For the interest of incoming buyers, the Association opened a Display Centre in 1964 to show products of particular manufacturers. Moreover, The Hong Kong General Chamber of Commerce organized its members for participation in a number of trade fairs abroad in cooperation with the Department of Commerce and Industry.

After 1962, the Hong Kong General Chamber of Commerce and the Federation of Hong Kong Industries obtained subvention from public funds for trade promotion jointly through their Public Relations Joint Committee, which engaged in promotional activities through its resident representatives in Europe, North America and East Africa, with chief executives operation in Hong Kong.

With no central planning, let alone execution, of activities of such a diverse nature, it is understandable that there was considerable confusion of work and duplication of efforts. As public funds were involved in financing the Public Relations Joint Committee, it was recognized that steps should be taken to ensure that resources would not be wasted through the lack of coordination. Thus, a Commercial Public Relations Co-ordinating Committee was appointed by the Government in 1962, under the Chairmanship of the Director of Commerce and Industry and composed of the Chairmen and chief executives of the trade-promoting agencies receiving public funds, to coordinate their efforts and recommend to the Government the amount, source and distribution of public funds provided for this purpose. It was responsible for the examination and evaluation of reports on the use of funds on various projects, and perhaps most significantly of all, to recommend, after a period of two years, whether an organization should be formed to advise on matters concerning commercial public relations and trade promotion in general.

In its report of September 1964, the Co-ordinating Committee pointed out the various difficulties in effecting coordination of all trade-promoting activities, and then called for a radical reorganization under which there would be a quasi-independent body with resources pooled at its disposal to plan and execute one single coordinated programme.

B. The Hong Kong Trade Development Council

A Working Committee on Export Promotion Organization was appointed in March 1965, working under new terms of reference.[18] After reviewing the local situation and studying the experience of some other countries, the Working Committee's conclusion was straight-forward. It pointed out that "... the present organizational structure tends to cause confusion of purpose and duplication of effort which would be avoided through the direction of all export promotion activities ... by a policy making council widely representative of all agencies interested in trade promotion, including commercial and industrial associations, the banks and Government,"[19] and went on to make detailed recommendations concerning the creation of a 'Hong Kong Export Promotion Council' to assist the development of Hong Kong's overseas trade and the creation of a favourable image of Hong Kong as a trading partner and manufacturing centre.

The Hong Kong Trade Development Council, instead of the recommended Hong Kong Export Promotion Council, was created in 1966 largely in line with the recommendations of the Working Committee. It is a statutory body under an independent Chairman appointed by the Government from among prominent figures of the commercial and industrial community with 7 ex officio members, 3 nominated members, and 4 appointed members.

The Council itself is a policy-making body. It formulates the general policy and programme as well as the budget for trade promotion thus superseding the Commercial Public Relations Coordinating Committee. It is serviced by a permanent Secretariat headed by an Executive Director with its initial staff coming from the Department of Commerce and Industry and the Public Relations Joint Committee who were previously engaged in trade promotion. It is financed by government subvention from general revenue and an ad valorem levy on imports and exports.

Upon formation, the Council had five overseas offices located in London, New York, Brussels, Sydney and Nairobi taken over from other agencies. In day-to-day work, these offices acted like feelers and were in the front-line of trade promotion. Over the years, many new offices were opened and strategically located in key cities of Hong Kong's major trading partners, each charged with the responsibility of trade promotion in a certain country or region. By 1975, there were altogether fifteen offices and subsidiary offices in London, Manchester, Frankfurt, Hamburg, Stockholm, Zurich, Amsterdam, Vienna, Milan, New York, Chicago, Los Angeles, Toronto, Tokyo and Sydney.[20]

The increasing scope and dimension of the Council's work naturally called for more manpower and financial resources. During its first year of operation, total expenditure stood at about HK$ 12 million almost entirely financed by subvention. By 1975/76, it had reached HK$ 35 million with only around HK$ 5 million coming from the Government and the rest mainly from the ad valorem levy.[21] In other words, trade expansion has generated sufficient financial resources for the bulk of the Council's expenditure. Currently, it is organized into five Departments, Design, Publicity Services, Trade Services, Administration and Accounts with a total staff of around 300.[22]

C. Work of the Trade Development Council (TDC)

The TDC specifies its own task as the provision not only of support for current export endeavours but also of guidance to Hong Kong traders and manufacturers in the production of new and improved products to be sold through new and improved channels and methods.[23] Thus, its emphasis is on export promotion which includes not only marketing in the ordinary sense of the word but also guidance of production to meet market demand. This involves a comprehensive network of activities with the following major aspects.

(1) Trade information: The collection and dissemination of trade information constitute the basis of trade promotion. Since its creation, the TDC has started building up a data bank which includes general information on world economic development, market conditions, business practices and commercial policies, trade statistics as well as reports and feedbacks from overseas offices on its own activities. It has also commissioned market surveys and retained consultants.

Publication is the major channel to make trade information available. Under the TDC, the former Trade Bulletin was changed into the Hong Kong Enterprise which is a monthly pictorial introducing Hong Kong's products and manufacturers with a list of trade inquiries. Japanese,

French and German inserts are regularly included for circulation in respective areas. The need for specialized information has prompted the TDC to issue two more periodicals since 1969, namely the annual Hong Kong Toys and the bi-annual Hong Kong Apparel. Another new monthly journal, the Hong Kong Trader, was introduced in 1976. In addition to these regular publications, there has been a whole range of occasional publicity material. Currently, annual circulation of these periodicals, booklets, product pamphlets and brochures amounts to well over a million copies.

Publicity is important in keeping Hong Kong in the lime-light. A Press Section was set up in 1967 to provide a comprehensive press service. To obtain more international publicity, the Overseas Press Service was established in 1970, especially for preparing and placing materials on Hong Kong's trade opportunities in international trade and economic magazines.

The handling of inquiries is an important part of the TDCs daily work. It has been reported that a daily average of some 200 inquiries are handled by its head and overseas offices.[24] By virtue of being on the spot, the TDCs overseas offices are vital in doing public relations work and creating a favorable image of Hong Kong. They have also assisted in arranging inward trade groups, handling complaints, settling disputes and dealing with adverse publicity.

(2) Trade Missions: Hong Kong's location and long history of trade have attracted many overseas firms and independent agents to set up purchasing offices, and there is much traffic of business people on an individual basis. But much is to be done in bringing broad groups of officials and business people together for exploration of trade possibilities. This is fulfilled by trade missions, which may be general in nature aimed at exchanging information and establishing contacts, or more specific such as in conjunction with trade fairs.

Under the TDC, Hong Kong's outward trade missions have visited every continent with increasing frequency. In the mid-1970s, the average was about ten missions per year. Needless to say, the majority of them went to North America and Western Europe, but recent developments have caused Hong Kong to look beyond. Exploratory missions have been sent to the Middle East and some African countries, while Japan has also become another point of thrust. And the Eastern

European countries, which potentially constitute a vast market for consumer non-durables, have also come into reach.

(3) Trade Exhibitions: In addition to publicity and trade contacts, participation in international trade fairs and exhibitions has the advantage of appealing directly to consumers. By the mid-1970s, Hong Kong's participation in international fairs and exhibitions averages over twenty a year. Special effort has been made to participate in international fairs and exhibitions held in the EC countries; another development is the penetration into Eastern European countries.

Locally, Hong Kong's first attempt to hold an exhibition for international buyers was made in 1967 when the Federation of Hong Kong Industries organized the 1st Hong Kong Festival of Fashions; the 9th Festival in 1976 was attended by 3,000 buyers representing 30 countries.[25] Similar developments took place with the Toys Fair which attracts thousands of buyers every year.

(4) Promotion of Foreign Investments: As a free port, Hong Kong is open to overseas investment with virtually no restrictions. Much direct investment has been attracted to Hong Kong by its liberal trading atmosphere and excellent location as an offshore base for labor-intensive and "foot-loose" manufacturing industries, the products of which can either be intermediate goods for use by parent firms or final goods for export. Therefore, the promotion of foreign investments in Hong Kong, among other things, is also a means to promote export.

The emerging position of Taiwan and South Korea in manufacturing, and especially in attracting foreign investments, has prompted Hong Kong to take more positive action. In addition to providing more information, the TDC sent missions to various countries seeking direct discussion with top management of pre-selected companies in choosing Hong Kong as a manufacturing base. As a result, a number of companies have already established or are seriously considering setting up manufacturing operations in Hong Kong.

To strengthen activities in this field, a Co-ordinating Committee on Industrial Investment Promotion was formed in October 1975 to coordinate the efforts of the TDC, the Department of Commerce and Industry, and the Hong Kong General Chamber of Commerce.

In view of the need for more industrial diversification, much work will have to be done in the near future. To overcome the difficulties resulting from rising protectionism in the developed countries and increasing competition from the developing countries, Hong Kong must continue to seek new markets and manufacture new products which are subject to less restriction. Whether the existing framework of export promotion is adequate for this task is a matter for further discussion.

V. Concluding Remarks

Being a small economy and extremely poor in natural resources, Hong Kong has to survive on trade. In fact, it had been a trade-dependent economy long before its manufacturing sector came into prominence. Industrialization has only changed its position from an entrepôt, which derives its existence from rendering trading services to others, to an industrial city, which earns its living from trading its own manufactures.

From the very beginning, the development of Hong Kong's manufacturing sector has been geared to export markets. Confined by the nature of its economy, Hong Kong had little alternative; and after some twenty years of development in this direction, there is virtually no room for retreat. To sustain economic growth and support its millions, it must continue to expand its manufactured exports and be ever competitive, alert and adaptable to changing market conditions. It has little influence on its destiny, let alone control. Trade barriers are examples of this harsh reality.

With respect to tariffs, developments have been favorable. The Commonwealth Preference provided the first stimulus to Hong Kong's industrialization in the early 1950s. This was the time when it had few opponents among its peers and its emerging capacity in manufacturing was too small to cause concern among the importing countries. By the time the Commonwealth Preference started to erode, in the mid-1960s, Hong Kong had built up a wide range of manufactures and penetrated deep into other markets, due to the trend towards tariff liberalization under GATT.

But more recent developments are less favorable. On the one hand, because of its more advanced status and large volume of manufactured exports, Hong Kong can obtain little additional incentive from the GSPs. In fact, it is discriminated against in the major scheme. On the other hand, the rest of the world is not standing still. An increasing number of LDCs have built up their manufacturing industries for exports and pose as serious contenders in fields Hong Kong used to dominate. Even though in the short run the general picture is blurred by the recent world recession and slow recovery, these developments do have far-reaching implications as they involve the fundamental issue of changing comparative advantage.

Currently, tariffs on manufactures imported into the developed countries have been reduced to such low levels that any further reduction is bound to come across intense resistence, especially in these years of retarded economic growth. What is more, any benefit resulting from further reduction will most likely be shared by more competitors.

Approximately half of Hong Kong's manufactured exports are under quota restrictions which concentrate on textiles and clothing. In analysing the extra-ordinary burden of nontariff trade barriers on the LDCs, Walter (19) came to the conclusion that this was mainly due to: (a) the coincidence of manufactured and semi-manufactured product groups subject to such obstacles and the export interest of the LDCs in these products, and (b) the disproportionate impact of certain nontariff trade barriers on the emerging supplier. For Hong Kong, point (a) goes without saying, but as a well-established supplier, it is less vulnerable to point (b) because it can stabilize its export volume by virtue of its 'voluntary restraint' programme. In our analysis, textiles have clearly felt the pinch. But clothing, the most important group of Hong Kong's manufactured exports, has shown no sign of decline due to its ability to adjust to changing market conditions. In fact, quota restrictions have promoted quality improvement and product differentiation in this industry and resulted in a tremendous growth of exports in value terms, so much so that its share in Hong Kong's total exports has increased in recent years. Meanwhile, Hong Kong has also successfully diversified into new manufactures for exports, most notably electrical machinery and toys.

Overall, Hong Kong has increasingly oriented towards manufactured exports for the developed countries. Table 9 summarizes this trend and presents the concentration ratios of its exports with respect to the top three markets and four commodity groups.

Since the 1960s, the top three markets continue to account for over half of Hong Kong's exports. But there has been a process of re-orientation, first from the traditional markets in Asia and the Commonwealth to the U.S. in the 1960s, and then to the EC and other Western European countries in the 1970s. Being an export-oriented economy, Hong Kong simply has to go where the markets are. There are already some signs of further regional diversification at the present time.

Table 9: Concentration of Hong Kong's Exports, in percent

	1960	1964	1968	1972	1973	1974	1975
Markets							
U.S.A.	26.0	27.7	41.4	40.2	35.0	32.4	32.2
U.K.	20.4	21.9	15.9	14.4	14.5	12.1	12.2
F.R. Germany	3.7	6.6	5.9	10.0	9.8	10.7	12.5
Top Three	50.1	56.2	63.2	64.6	59.3	55.2	56.8
Commodity Groups							
Textiles	22.0	17.5	13.0	10.6	12.6	12.5	9.8
Clothing	20.1	40.1	37.7	41.9	39.8	39.6	45.9
Toys & Games	4.6	7.4	9.9	9.6	8.9	8.3	7.3
Footwear	4.5						
Elec. Machinery		4.6	9.7	13.5	14.1	15.0	12.7
Top Four	71.2	69.6	70.3	75.6	75.4	75.4	75.7

Source: Calculated from data given in Hong Kong Trade Statistics, Hong Kong Department of Commerce and Industry, and Department of Census and Statistics, various issues.

With respect to commodity composition, Hong Kong's exports are highly concentrated in four major groups. There are even indications of more concentration despite changes in the relative importance of individual commodity groups. It seems that this pattern will continue for some time since toys and electrical machinery are Hong Kong's fast growing industries.

There has been much discussion on the need for more export diversification, both geographically and in commodity composition. The argument that one should not put all his eggs in one basket does have its appeal. But the unfortunate fact is that a small open economy has to live with a certain degree of export concentration; one might go further to point out that even this degree of export concentration is externally determined. It was the sheer force of market gravitation which shaped Hong Kong's export pattern.

The simple fact is that the world trading condition has undergone substantial changes since the 1960s. Hong Kong is facing gathering protectionism in the form of more restrictive controls on textiles and increasing competition from other LDCs. It is difficult to conjecture how much diversification Hong Kong can achieve with respect to markets, because there is an obvious limit to new markets, and one has to admit that the existing ones are those with greatest potentials. But there is more room to maneuver with respect to manufactures. To sustain its economic growth, Hong Kong must move into more skill-intensive, sophisticated and high-technology manufactures which are not subject to controls (and the other LDCs have yet to acquire that knowledge and capacity), as required by comparative advantage and the change to it.

Notes:

1 Manufactures are here defined to cover SITC Sections 6-8 since Hong Kong exports only a negligible amount of chemicals, and the developed countries comprise North America, Western Europe (including the Scandinavian countries but excluding Spain and Portugal), South Africa, Australia, New Zealand and Japan.

2 A third one, the EFTA rate, came into effect in 1960.

3 The value for 1964/65 was 228.5 million Hong Kong dollars. For 1968/69, 1972/73 and 1974/75, it was 175.7, 126.9 and 197.9 million Hong Kong dollars, respectively. See Annual Reports and Statistical Reviews, Hong Kong Department of Commerce and Industry, various issues.

4 It was originally announced to replace quota restrictions but turned out to be additional to them.

5 These percentages are derived from information given in Annual Reports and Statistical Reviews of the Hong Kong Department of Commerce and Industry.

6 For 1975, the share intake of Netherlands and Sweden was approximately 2.2 % each, whereas those of France, Belgium, Italy, Norway and Denmark were all somewhat below 1 %.

7 At first, Hong Kong was not included in the American scheme because it granted 'reverse preference' to the Commonwealth. This was changed after it undertook to abolish its Commonwealth Preference in respect of liquor, manufactured tobacco and motor vehicles.

8 In the EEC scheme, South Korea and Singapore were included for preference in respect of textiles and footwear. But later Hong Kong was also included for non-leather footwear and some 80 items of textiles.

9 They are: cotton yarn, certain woven and knitted fabrics, non-cotton gloves, mittens, etc.

10 They are: imitation jewellery, portable electric battery and magneto lamps, retracting telescopes, gramophones and various sound recording and reproducing equipment, and dolls.

11 Based on 1971 data, Erb (9) estimated that only 10 % of American dutiable imports would have been qualified for the GSP after the rule to deny preference was applied, instead of 40 % before its application. In fact, the American scheme was implemented in 1976.

12 Hong Kong's Undertakings with Britain were outside the ambit of GATT.

13 For a theoretical discussion on this point, see Corden (7), pp. 202-15.

14 These percentages are calculated from data given in the Hong Kong Department of Commerce and Industry's Annual Statistical Review 1974-75.

15 According to statistics from Hong Kong's 1973 Census of Industrial Production (Census and Statistics Department, 1975), the clothing industry ranks second in labor intensity according to the value-added-per-worker definition and third according to the stock-of-fixed-assets-per-worker definition, while the textile industry ranks sixteenth and eighteenth, respectively, in twenty-two industries.

16 See Hong Kong Review of Overseas Trade 1975, Hong Kong Department of Census and Statistics.

17 Textile fabrics account for approximately 75 % of Hong Kong's export of textiles, while textile yarn and thread are not subject to control in certain markets.

18 Report of the Working Committee on Export Promotion Organization, Hong Kong Government, 1965, Introduction.

19 Ibid., Introduction.

20 The Nairobi office was closed down in 1971, and preparations were underway for an office in Paris and a couple more in the U.S.A.

21 Annual Report 1967/68, and 1975/76, Hong Kong Trade Development Council.

22 Annual Report 1975/76, Hong Kong Trade Development Council.

23 Hong Kong 1966, Hong Kong Government, 1967, p. 57.

24 Annual Report 1974/75, Hong Kong Trade Development Council.

25 Hong Kong 1977, Hong Kong Government, 1977, p. 20.

References:

(1) BALASSA, B., "Growth Strategies in Semi-Industrial Countries", Quarterly Journal of Economics, 1970, pp. 24-47.

(2) ________, "Industrial Policies in Taiwan and Korea", Weltwirtschaftliches Archiv, 1, 1971, pp. 55-77.

(3) ________, "Trade Policies in Developing Countries", American Economic Review, 1971, pp. 178-87.

(4) BALDWIN, R.E. and MURRAY, T., "MFN Tariff Reductions and Developing Country Trade Benefits under the GSP", Economic Journal, 1977, pp. 30-46.

(5) BELL, H.H., "Trade Relations with the Third World: Preference Aspects of Protective Structures", in: R.G. HAWKINS and I. WALTER (eds.), The U.S. and International Markets: Commercial Policy Options in An Age of Controls, Lexington, Mass.: Lexington Books, 1972, pp. 299-334.

(6) COOPER, R.N., "The European Community's System of Generalized Tariff Preferences: A Critique", Journal of Developmental Studies, 1972, pp. 379-94.

(7) CORDEN, W.M., The Theory of Protection, Oxford: Clarendon Press, 1971.

(8) de VRIES, B.A., The Export Experience of Developing Countries, Baltimore: John Hopkins Press, 1967.

(9) ERB, G.F., "The Developing Countries in the Tokyo Round", in: J.W. HOWE, et al., The U.S. and the Developing World: Agenda for Action 1974, New York: Praeger Publishers, 1974, pp. 85-94.

(10) FINGER, J.M., "GATT Tariff Concessions and the Exports of Developing Countries: United States Concession at the Dillon Round", Economic Journal, 1974, pp. 566-75.

(11) ________, "Effects of the Kennedy Round Tariff Concessions on the Exports of Developing Countries", Economic Journal, 1976, pp. 87-95.

(12) GREEN, R.W., "Commonwealth Preference: United Kingdom Customs Duties and Tariff Preferences on Imports from the Preference Area", Board of Trade Journal, December 31, 1965, pp. 1551-8.

(13) HSIA, R., "Hong Kong Textile Exports. A Case Study of Voluntary Restraints", in: H.E. ENGLISH and K.A.J. HAY (eds.), Obstacles to Trade in the Pacific Area: Proceedings of the Fourth Pacific Trade and Development Conference, Ottawa: School of International Affairs, Carleton University, 1972, pp. 167-85.

(14) MAHFUZUR RAHMAN, A.H.M., Exports of Manufactures from Developing Countries: A Study of Comparative Advantage, Rotterdam: Rotterdam University Press, 1973.

(15) MORRISON, T.K., "Manufactured Exports and Protection in Developing Countries: A Cross-Country Analysis", Economic Development and Cultural Change, 1976, pp. 151-58.

(16) MURRAY, T., "How Helpful is the Generalized System of Preferences to Developing Countries", Economic Journal, 1973, pp. 449-55.

(17) ________, "Preferential Tariffs for the LDCs", Southern Economic Journal, 1973, pp. 35-46.

(18) ________, "E.E.C. Enlargement and Preference for the Developing Countries", Economic Journal, 1973, pp. 853-57.

(19) WALTER, I., "Nontariff Barriers and the Export Performance of Developing Economies", American Economic Review, 1971, pp. 195-205.

V. BIBLIOGRAPHY

ECONOMIC, SOCIAL AND POLITICAL STUDIES ON HONG KONG

Tzong-biau Lin, Rance P. L. Lee and Udo-Ernst Simonis

Scientific interest in Hong Kong has been fairly strong in the last few decades and has been increasing rapidly in the last few years. To some extent this may be attributed to Hong Kong's extraordinary economic growth and rapid social change, but also to its special political relationships to the Peoples' Republic of China. This interest has led to the publication of a great number of books and articles on Hong Kong.

The present bibliography grew out of an extensive literature search, and concentrates on English and German publications, written within the last three decades, primarily in the years after 1966. It was necessary here to accentuate selected topics and for the most part to include only those publications which give account of economic, social and political developments. We especially tried to include works which not only describe recent developments but which critically examine the side-effects of such developments as well. While it is not a complete list of all the materials available in western languages, it is, probably, the most comprehensive bibliography on Hong Kong to date.

The purpose of this bibliography is, first, to bring together both published and unpublished materials related to Hong Kong and thus illustrate the extent to which it has been possible to cover and analyse its development. Second, it is hoped that the bibliography will prove to be a tool for those with more specialized interests. Many of the scientific journals cited give current information on Hong Kong and may be used as a help for further research, as well as providing a good opportunity for getting acquainted with works on Hong Kong which have not been documented here.

The bibliography, which was completed in October, 1978, is arranged in two parts, the first of which names books, monographs, articles and degree theses, while the second one contains official publications on Hong Kong.

I. BOOKS, MONOGRAPHS, ARTICLES AND DEGREE THESES

AGASSI, J.: Hong Kong's Housing Problems, Far Eastern Economic Review, 36, 1962, pp. 515-522

--: Housing the Needy, in I.C. Jarvie (ed.): Hong Kong: A Society in Transition, London 1969

--: Social Structure and Social Stratification in Hong Kong, in I.C. Jarvie (ed.): Hong Kong: A Society in Transition, London 1969

AGASSI, J. and JARVIE, I.C.: A Study in Westernization, in I.C. Jarvie (ed.): Hong Kong: A Society in Transition, London 1969

AIJIMER, L.G.: Expansion and Extension in Hakka Society, Journal of the Hong Kong Branch of the Royal Asiatic Society, 7, 1967, pp. 42-79

ANDERSON, Jr., E.N.: Changing Patterns of Land Use in Rural Hong Kong, Pacific Viewpoint, 9, 1968, pp. 33-50

--: Prejudice and Ethnic Stereotypes in Rural Hong Kong, Kroeber Anthropological Society Papers, 37, 1967, pp. 90-107

--: Some Chinese Methods of Dealing with Crowding, Urban Anthropology, 1, 1972, pp. 141-150

Asia Yearbook: Far Eastern Economic Review, Hong Kong

ASTON, A.: Water Resources and Consumption in Hong Kong, Urban Ecology, Amsterdam, 2, 1977, pp. 327-353

BAILEY, S.F.: Some Problems of Higher Education in Hong Kong, Chung Chi Journal, 11, No. 1, 1972, pp. 166-171

BAKER, H.: The Five Great Clans of the New Territories, Journal of the Hong Kong Branch of the Royal Asiatic Society, 6, 1966, pp. 25-48

BARNETT, A.D.: Hong Kong and China Trade, American Universities Fieldstaff Reports, 3, No. 2, 1954, pp. 1-34

BARNETT, K.M.A.: Hong Kong Before the Chinese, Journal of the Hong Kong Branch of the Royal Asiatic Society, 4, 1964, pp. 42-67

Basic Data on the Economy of Hong Kong: Overseas Business Reports, U.S. Department of Commerce, Washington, D.C., 1968

BEAZER, W.F.: The Commercial Future of Hong Kong, New York 1978

BENHAM, F.: The Growth of Manufacturing in Hong Kong, International Affairs, 32, 1956, pp. 456-643

BENZENBERG, W.: Wachstum und Planung in Tsuen Wan und Kwun Tong. Zwei neue Städte in der Kronkolonie Hong Kong, Ph.D. Dissertation, Köln 1977

BERKOWITZ, M.I. and POON, E.K.K.: Hong Kong Studies: A Bibliography, Hong Kong 1969

--: Political Disintegration of Hakka Village: A Study of Drastic Social Change in the New Territories of Hong Kong, Chung Chi Journal, 8, 2, 1969, pp. 16-31

BISSING, W.M.F. von: Ostasiatische Studien zu Wirtschaft und Gesellschaft in Thailand, Hong Kong und Japan, Berlin: Duncker & Humblot, 1962

BLACK, Sir Robert: Hong Kong and its Position in the Pacific, Royal Central Asian Society Journal, 53, 1966, pp. 16-22

BLOOM, A.H.: A Cognitive Dimension of Social Control. The Hong Kong Chinese in Cross-cultural Perspective, in: Deviance and Social Control in Chinese Society, New York, London: F.A. Praeger, 1977, pp. 67-81

BOLDRICK, M. S.: Social Welfare in Hong Kong. A Review of Welfare Services in the Past Twenty Years, Chung Chi Journal, 11, 1, 1972, pp. 188-195

BOXER, B.: Space, Change and "feng-shui" in Tsuen Wan's Urbanization, Journal of Asian and African Studies, 3, 1969, pp. 226-240

--: Ocean Shipping in the Evolution of Hong Kong, University of Chicago, Department of Geography, Research Paper No. 72, Chicago 1961

BRACHON, P.: Hong Kong à l'heure de l'évolution extrême-orientale, Société d'Etudes et d'Expansion, Revue Bimestrielle, Liège, No. 250, Année 71, 1972, pp. 219-238

BRAGA, J.M.: A Hong Kong Bibliography, Hong Kong 1965

BROWN, E.H.P.: The Hong Kong Economy: Achievements and Prospects, in: K. Hopkins (ed.), Hong Kong: The Industrial Colony, Hong Kong 1971

BRUGGER, W.: Democracy and Organization in the Chinese Industrial Enterprise, (1948-1953), Cambridge: University Press, 1976

BUCHHOLZ, H.J.: Bevölkerungsmobilität und Wohnverhalten im sozialgeographischen Gefüge Hong Kongs, Paderborn 1978

BUCHHOLZ, F.J.: Die chinesische Zuwanderung nach Hong Kong. Ein Beitrag zur Analyse einer ungewöhnlichen Bevölkerungsentwicklung, Geographische Zeitschrift, Wiesbaden, 61, 1973, pp. 295-318

BUCK, S.: Chinese Temples in Hong Kong, The Orient, 2, 7, 1952, pp. 27-29

BURKHARDT, V.R.: Chinese Creeds and Customs, 3 vols., Hong Kong: South China Morning Post Ltd., 1954

BURTON, R.A.: Self-Help, Chinese Style (Rotating-Credit Societies), American Universities Field-staff Reports, 6, No. 9, 1958, pp. 1-10

CANSDALE, J.S.: Cultural Problems of Chinese Students in a Western-Type University, in: I.C. Jarvie (ed.), Hong Kong: A Society in Transition? London 1969

Caritas, Hong Kong and Hong Kong Christian Service: Care for Old Age in Hong Kong, Hong Kong 1972

CARR, N.: Employee Attitude Survey in a Hong Kong Engineering Company, Journal of Industrial Relations, 1973, pp. 108-111

CATRON, G.W.: China and Hong Kong, 1945-1967, Ph.D. thesis, Harvard University, 1971

--: Hong Kong and Chinese Foreign Policy, 1955-1960, The China Quarterly, 51, 1972, pp. 405-424

CHADWICK, O.: Report on the Sanitary Conditions of Hong Kong, Hong Kong 1882

CHALKLEY, A.: A Lion at the Gates of China: The Hong Kong and Shanghai Banking Corporation, Insight, Sept. 1972, pp. 18-23

CHAN, K.C.: Hong Kong Oral Contraceptive Fellow-Up Study, Studies in Family Planning, 2, No. 3, 1971, pp. 70-74

--: Hong Kong: Report on the IUD Reassurance Project, Studies in Family Planning, 2, No. 11, 1971, pp. 225-233

CHAN, K.M.: The Trend of Governmental Activity in Hong Kong since 1947, in: Social and Economic Studies, Economics Society, Chinese University of Hong Kong, 1974, pp. 45-58

CHAN, K.S.: The Role of the Family Planning Association in Hong Kong's Fertility Decline, Studies in Family Planning, 7, 1976, pp. 284-289

CHAN, Y.K.: The Growth Patterns of Organisations in Kwun Tong, Social Research Centre, Chinese University of Hong Kong, 1972

--: The Rise and Growth of Kwun Tong: A Study of Planned Urban Development, Social Research Centre, Chinese University of Hong Kong, 1973

CHAN, Y.K. and LAU, R.: Biosocial Survey: Report on Sampling. Social Research Centre, Chinese University of Hong Kong, 1974

CHANDLER, G.: Libraries in the East. An International and Comparative Study, London, New York: Seminar Press, 1971

CHANEY, D.C.: Job Satisfaction and Unionization: The Case of Shopworks, in: K. Hopkins (ed.), Hong Kong: The Industrial Colony, Hong Kong 1971

CHANEY, D.C. and PODMORE, D.B.L.: Young Adults in Hong Kong: Attitudes in a Modernizing Society, Hong Kong: University of Hong Kong, 1973

CHANG, H.K.: The Hong Kong Toy Industry, with Special Emphasis on Export Marketing Analysis, M. Com. thesis, Chinese University of Hong Kong, 1968

CHAU, C.K.Y.: Hong Kong Women and Society: A Study, Philippine Educational Forum, 16, No. 3, 1967, pp. 32-38

CHAU, L.C.: Estimates of Hong Kong's Gross Domestic Product, 1959-69, Hong Kong Economic Papers, Sept. 1972, pp. 13-15

CHAU, L.C. and HSIA, R.: An Anatomy of Income Distribution in Hong Kong, 1971, in Income Distribution, Employment and Economic Development in Southeast and East Asia, II (Tokoyo/Manila: Japan Economic Research Centre/Council for Asian Manpower Studies, July 1975), pp. 600-631

CHEN, E.E.K.: Economies of Scale and Capital-Labour Substitution in Hong Kong Manufacturing, Hong Kong Economic Papers, 11, 1977, pp. 42-49

CHEN, E.K.Y.: The Electronics Industry of Hong Kong, M. Soc. Sc. thesis, University of Hong Kong, 1971

CHEN, P.: Tea Trade in Hong Kong, Journal of Economics Society, Chinese University of Hong Kong, 1957, pp. 60-64

CHENG, I.: Clara Ho Tung: A Hong Kong Lady, Her Family and Her Times, Hong Kong: Oxford University Press, 1973

CHENG, T.C.: Chinese Unofficial Members of the Legislative and Executive Councils in Hong Kong up to 1941, Journal of the Hong Kong Branch of the Royal Asiatic Society, 9, 1969, pp. 7-30

CHENG, T.Y.: Hong Kong, a Classical Growth Model. A Survey of Hong Kong's Industrialization 1948-68, Weltwirtschaftliches Archiv, 104, 1970, pp. 138-158

--: Landownership and Housing Problems in Hong Kong, New Asia College Academic Annual, 14, 1972, pp. 113-125

--: The Economy of Hong Kong, Hong Kong: Far East Publications, 1977

--: The Impact of Industrialization upon Consumption With Special Reference to Hong Kong and Singapore, Hong Kong 1971

CHEUNG, S.N.S.: Roofs and Stars: The Stated Intents and Actual Effects of a Rents Ordinance, Economic Inquiry, 13, 1975, pp. 1-21

CHEUNG, Y.W., TSUI, W.Y.: A Preliminary List of Social Science Publications on Hong Kong, Social Research Centre, Chinese University of Hong Kong, 1977

CHIN, A.L.: Hong Kong Managerial Styles: Chinese and Western Approaches to Conflict Management, Social Research Centre, Chinese University of Hong Kong, 1972

CHIU, T.N.: Hong Kong: A Study in Port Development, Ph.D. thesis, University of London, 1963

--: The Port of Hong Kong: A Survey of Its Development, Hong Kong: Hong Kong University Press, 1973

CHO, K.: Kaifong Welfare Associations in Hong Kong, Hemisphere, 12, No. 7, 1968, pp. 28-31

CHOI, C.Y.: Population Movement in Hong Kong, 1961-1971, United College Journal, II, 1973, pp. 147-154

--: The Impact of Industrialization on Fertility in Hong Kong. Some Psychological Aspects, Social Research Centre, Chinese University of Hong Kong, 1976

--: Urbanization and Redistribution of Population. Hong Kong - A Case Study, Patterns of Urbanization, Vol. 1, Dolhain 1977, pp. 239-287

CHOI, C.Y. and CHAN, Y.K.: Housing Policy and Internal Movement of Population: A Study of Kwun Tong, A Chinese New Town in Hong Kong, Social Research Centre, Chinese University of Hong Kong, 1977

CHOI, C.Y. and CHAN, K.C.: The Impact of Industrialization on Fertility in Hong Kong. A Demographic, Social and Economic Analysis, Social Research Centre, Chinese University of Hong Kong, 1973

CHOI, H.: Production Functions of the Manufacturing Industries in Hong Kong, unpublished M.Phil. thesis, Chinese University of Hong Kong, 1978

CHONG, S.D.: The Distribution and Occupations of Overseas Chinese, Geographical Review, 58, No. 1, 1968, pp. 89-107

CHOU, K.R.: Hong Kong's Changing Pattern of Trade and Economic Interdependence in Southeast Asia, in: T. Morgan and N. Spolestra (Eds.), Economic Interdependence in Southeast Asia, Madison, London 1969

--: Hong Kong's Growth Rates, I, II, in: Far Eastern Economic Review, Jan. 1966, pp. 31-34 and pp. 67-69

--: The Hong Kong Economy. A Miracle of Growth, Hong Kong: Academic Publications, 1966

CHOUGH, S.: The Growth of Exports and Economic Development in Labor Surplus Economies. With Particular Reference to Korea, Taiwan and Hong Kong, The Japan Economic Research Center, Center Paper No. 21, Tokyo 1974

CHOW, C.Y.: Hong Kong's Trade Promotion Policy and the Impact of Trade Barriers on Her Exports, unpublished M. Phil. thesis, Chinese University of Hong Kong, 1978

CHOW, T.L.: An Economic Study of Hong Kong's Imports, 1959-1972, unpublished M.A. thesis, Thammasat University, 1974

CHUN, W.C.: Hong Kong: The Family Planning Association, Eastern World, 18, No. 2, 1964, pp. 13-14

CHUNG, B.J. and KWOK, Z.K.: Methodological Problems in Data Collection and Questionnaire Construction in the Social Context of Hong Kong. A Sub-study of the Impact of Industrialization on Fertility in Hong Kong, Social Research Centre, Chinese University of Hong Kong, 1974

COLLAR, H.J.: China and Hong Kong, Asian Review, 50, No. 181, 1954, pp. 64-66

COLLIS, M.: Wayfoong: The Hong Kong and Shanghai Banking Corporation, London: Faber & Faber, 1965

Commercial and Industrial Hong Kong: 1841-1935, Hong Kong, 1935

COOPER, J.: Colony in Conflict. The Hong Kong Disturbances May 1967 - Jan. 1968, Hong Kong: Swindon Book, 1970

DAVIS, J.G., SMART, T., FOX, P.: Hong Kong Through the Looking Glass, 4th ed., Hong Kong: Kelly & Walsh, 1975

DAVIS, S.G.: Hong Kong Banking After the Crisis, The Banker, 1965, pp. 243-251

--: Hong Kong in its Geographical Setting, London: Collins, 1949

--: The Rural-Urban Migration in Hong Kong and Its New Territories, Geographical Journal, 128, No. 3, 1962, pp. 328-333

DAVIS, S.G. (ed.): Land Use Problems in Hong Kong. A Symposium, Hong Kong: Hong Kong University Press, 1964

DAWSON, J.L.M. and W.W.C. NG: Effect of Parental Attitudes and Modern Exposure on Chinese Traditional-Modern Attitude Formation, Journal of Cross-Cultural Psychology, 3, No. 2, 1972, pp. 201-207

Department of Architecture, University of Hong Kong: Appraisal of Hong Kong Housing, Hong Kong 1964

DEVOY, J.: Hong Kong's Runaway Girls: Some Reflections on the Problem, Hong Kong Journal of Social Work, 1, 1972, pp. 35-37

DINGLER, W.B. (ed.): Youth and Religion: A Religious Attitude Study of Hong Kong Secondary School Students, Hong Kong: Lutheran World Federation Broadcasting Service, 1969

DORNHEIM, A.R. and M.A. KELLEHER: Establishing a Business in Hong Kong, in: Overseas Business Reports, U.S. Department of Commerce, Washington, D.C., 1972

DRAKAKIS-SMITH, D.W.: Housing Needs and Policies for Cities in Developing Countries with Special Reference to Hong Kong, Ph.D. thesis, Hong Kong University, 1973

--: Housing Needs and Planning Policies for the Asian City: The Lessons from Hong Kong, The International Journal of Environmental Studies, 1, 1971, pp. 115-128

--: Housing Provision in Metropolitan Hong Kong, Centre of Asian Studies Publication, Hong Kong University, 1973

--: Tenement Slum Renewal. Hong Kong, Pacific Viewpoint, Wellington, 13, 1972, pp. 155-168

DRAKAKIS-SMITH, D.W.: Traditional and Modern Aspects of Urban Systems in the Third World, Pacific Viewpoint, Wellington, 12, 1971, pp. 21-40

--: Urban Renewal in an Asian Context. A Case Study in Hong Kong, Urban Studies, Chicago, 13, 1976, pp. 295-305

DWYER, D.J. (ed.): Asian Urbanization: A Hong Kong Casebook, Hong Kong: Hong Kong University Press, 1971

--: The Changing Face of Hong Kong, Hong Kong 1971

--: The City as a Centre of Change in Asia, Hong Kong: Oxford University Press, 1972

DWYER, D.J.: The Problem of In-Migration and Squatter Settlement in Hong Kong and Manila, Asian Studies, Vol. II, No. 2, 1964

--: Urban Squatters. The Relevance of the Hong Kong Experience, Asian Survey, 10, 1970, pp. 607-613

DWYER, D.J. and LAI, C.Y.: The Small Industrial Unit in Hong Kong. Patterns and Policies, Hull: University of Hull Publications, 1967

EATON, Ch.D. van: Adaptation of a Land-scarce Economy. The Economic Growth and Trade of Hong Kong, 1950-1966, Ph.D. dissertation, Tulane University, 1974

Economic Research Centre, The Chinese University: Long-term Economic and Agriculture Commodity Projections for Hong Kong, 1969

Economist Intelligence Unit Ltd.: Industry in Hong Kong, Hong Kong 1962

Editorial Staff: Hong Kong's National Income, Far Eastern Economic Review, 1966, pp. 424-426

--: The Hong Kong and Shanghai Banking Corporation: A Brief History, Far Eastern Economic Review, 1965, pp. 397-402

EITEL, E.J.: Europe in China. The History of Hong Kong, London: Luzac & Co., 1895

ELEGANT, R. and BRAKE, B.: Hong Kong, Amsterdam: Time-Life International, 1977

EMERY, R.E.: The Financial Institutions of Southeast Asia, New York: F.A. Praeger, 1970

ENDACOTT, G.B.: A Bibliographical Sketchbook of Early Hong Kong, Singapore: Eastern Universities Press, 1962

--: A History of Hong Kong, London: Oxford University Press, rev. ed., 1973

--: An Eastern Entrepôt, London: Her Majesty's Stationary Office, 1964

--: Government and People in Hong Kong 1841-1962, Hong Kong: Hong Kong University Press, 1964

--: Proposals for Municipal Government in Early Hong Kong, Journal of Oriental Studies, 3, 1957-58, pp. 75-82

--: The Hong Kong Mint and the Colony's Currency Problems, Far Eastern Economic Review, 1956, pp. 744-746 and pp. 794-795

ENDACOTT, G.B. and HINTON, A.: Fragrant Harbour. A Short History of Hong Kong, Hong Kong: Oxford University Press, 1962

ENGLAND, J.: Hong Kong: Britain's Responsibility, Hong Kong: Fabian Society Publications, 1976

--: Industrial Relations in Hong Kong, in: K. Hopkins (ed.): Hong Kong: The Industrial Colony, Hong Kong 1971

ENGLAND, J., (ed.): The Hong Kong Economic Scene, Hong Kong: Hong Kong University Press, 1969

ENGLAND, J. and REAR, J.: Chinese Labour under British Rule: A Critical Study of Labour Relations and Law in Hong Kong, Hong Kong: Oxford University Press, 1975

ESPY, J.L.: Hong Kong as an Environment for Industry, Chung Chi Journal, 10, 1971, pp. 27-38

--: The Strategies of Chinese Industrial Enterprises in Hong Kong, Ph.D. dissertation, School of Business Administration, Harvard University, 1970

--: Some Notes on Business and Industry in Hong Kong, Chung Chi Journal, 11, No. 1, 1972, pp. 172-181

EVAN, E.: Problems of Bilingual Milieu in Hong Kong: Strain of the Two-Language System, in: I.C. Jarvie (ed.): Hong Kong: A Society in Transition, London 1969

EVANS, D.M.E.: Chinatown in Hong Kong: The Beginnings of Taipingshan, Journal of the Hong Kong Branch of the Royal Asiatic Society, 10, 1970, pp. 69-78

--: Some Legal Aspects of Urbanization in Hong Kong, in:D.J. Dwyer (ed.): Asian Urbanization. A Hong Kong Casebook, Hong Kong 1971

FAN, S.C.: Hong Kong Urban Rents and Housing. Journal of Oriental Studies, 8, 1970, pp. 230-232

--: The Population of Hong Kong, Hong Kong: Swindon Book Co., 1974

--: The Population of Hong Kong, 1961 and 1971, Demographic India, Delhi, 4, 1975, pp. 393-406

Financial Centres of the World: Hong Kong, The Banker, 1970, pp. 725-770

FIRTH, J.R. The Work of the Hong Kong Housing Authority, Journal of Royal Society of Arts, 113, 1965, pp. 175-195

FISCHER, G.: La Problème des Enclaves Territoriales, Hong Kong, Revue Française de Science Politique, 18, 1968, 2, pp. 315-332

FISCHER-SHORT, W.: Some Thoughts on Educational Testing in Hong Kong, Journal of Education (Hong Kong University) 23, 1966, pp. 40-50

FONTAINE, J.P.: Hong Kong. Une économie florissante, Industrie, Bruxelles, 23, 1969, pp. 402-403

FORBES, G.I.: Occupational Deaths in Hong Kong - 1969, Far East Medical Journal, 7, 1971, pp. 117-121

--: Plague in Hong Kong, 1896-1929, Far East Medical Journal, 5, 1969, pp. 398-405

FREEDMAN, M.: Shifts of Power in the Hong Kong New Territories, Journal of Asian and African Studies, V. 1, No. 1 (Jan. 1966) pp. 3-12

--: Sociology in and of China, British Journal of Sociology, 13, 1962, pp. 106-116

--: The Chinese in Southeast Asia: A Longer View, Asian Review, 3, No. 1, 1966, pp. 24-38

FREEDMAN, R.: Hong Kong: The Continuing Fertility Decline, 1967, Studies in Family Planning, No. 44, 1969, pp. 8-15

FREEDMAN, R. and ADLAKHE, A.L.: Recent Fertility Decline in Hong Kong, Population Studies, 1968, pp. 181-188

FREEDMAN, R., NAMBOOTHIRI, D.N., ADLAKHA, A. and CHAN, K.C.: Hong Kong's Fertility Decline, 1961-68, Population Index, 36, 1970, pp. 3-18

FREEMAN, F., SMITH, W. and Associates: Hong Kong Mass Transport Study, Report Prepared for the Hong Kong Government, Hong Kong: Government Printer, 1968

FRIEDRICH, J.: Hong Kong heute, Deutsche Außenpolitik, Berlin, 13, 1968, pp. 1488-1492

FRY, R.: A Financial Entrepôt for East Asia, The Banker, 1970, pp. 728-32

--: Hong Kong. Aftermath and Prospect, The Banker, 1973, pp. 557-560

FUNG, Y.F.: A Brief Analysis of Some Economic Problems in Hong Kong, New Asia College Academic Annual, 10, 1971, pp. 95-99

--: The Problem of Air Pollution in Hong Kong, Journal of Economics Society, Chinese University of Hong Kong, 1975, pp. 24-37

FUNG, H.: Land and Housing, Journal of Economics Society, Chinese University of Hong Kong, 1975, pp. 69-80

FUNG, Y.W.: Some Contributory Factors to Student Movements in Hong Kong, Asia Quarterly, Bruxelles, 1973, pp. 287-311

GEIGER, T. and GEIGER, F.M.: Tales of Two City-States. The Development Process of Hong Kong and Singapore, Washington, D.C.: National Planning Association, 1973

GILES, E.M.: New Industries for Hong Kong, Far Eastern Economic Review, 36, 1962, pp. 429-431

GITTINGS, J.: China-Watching in Hong Kong, Journal of Contemporary Asia, 2, No. 4, 1972, pp. 415-430

GOH, K.L.: Factors Influencing U.S. International Firms in Locating Export-oriented Manufacturing Facilities in Singapore, Taiwan, and Hong Kong, Ph. D. dissertation, Indiana University, 1973

GLASSBURNER, B. and RIEDEL, J.: Economic Development Lessons from Hong Kong. A Reply, The Economic Record, 49, 1973, pp. 637-643

--: Government in the Economy of Hong Kong, The Economic Record, XLVIII, March 1972, pp. 58-75

GLEASON, G.: Hong Kong, New York: Day, 1963

GOLGER, O.J.: An Environmental Study of Squatter and Resettlement Housing in Hong Kong, Ph.D. thesis, Hong Kong University, 1968

--: Bauen und Wohnen in Hong Kong. Ein Beispiel für die urbanen Probleme in Entwicklungsländern, Graz 1975

--: Hong Kong oder das Hausen von Massen, Werk, Schweizer Monatszeitschrift für Architektur, Vol. 12, Dez. 1966

--: Resettlement Estates in Hong Kong. Das größte städtische Wohnbauprogramm der Welt, Werk, Vol. 3, März 1967

--: Squatters and Resettlement. Symptoms of an Urban Crisis. Environmental Conditions of Low-standard Housing in Hong Kong, Wiesbaden: Harrassowitz, 1972

GOODSTADT, L.: Hong Kong's Dilemma, Far Eastern Economic Review, 7, 1973, pp. 58-59

--: Urban Housing in Hong Kong, in: I.C. Jarvie (ed.): Hong Kong: A Society in Transition, London 1969

GRAHAM, P.A.: Hong Kong's Banks and Financial Institutions, The Banker, 1970, pp. 747-53

GRANTHAM, A.: Hong Kong: History and Future Problems, Royal Central Asian Journal, 1959, pp. 119-129

--: Conditions and Problems Including Relations with China, Journal of Royal Commonwealth Society, 1959, pp. 11-14

--: Housing 600,000 Homeless, Geographical Magazine, 1959, pp. 573-586

--: Via Port. From Hong Kong to Hong Kong, Hong Kong: Hong Kong University Press, 1965

GRAVEREAU, J.: Hong Kong, Analyse d'un Boom, Paris: Ed. Cujas, 1975

GREENFIELD, D.E.: Marriage by Chinese Law and Customs in Hong Kong, International and Comparative Law Quarterly, 7, 1958, pp. 437-451

GREGORY, W.G.: An Architect's Comments on Land Use in Hong Kong, in: Davis, S.G. (ed.): Symposium on Land Use and Mineral Deposits in Hong Kong, Southern China and Southeast Asia, Hong Kong: Hong Kong University Press, 1964, pp. 20-39

HADDON-CAVE, C.P.: Government and the Financial Services Sector (paper read to the Hong Kong Society of Accountants on Nov. 4, 1977) (mimeo.)

--: The Future of Hong Kong (paper read at the Financial Times Asian Business Conference held at the Hong Kong Convention Centre, Oct. 21-23, 1975) (mimeo.)

--: The Hong Kong Economy: The Adjustment Process, 1973-76 (paper read to the Hong Kong Society of Security Analysts on Sept. 3, 1976) (mimeo.)

--: The Hong Kong Economy: The Later Phase of the Recovery (paper read to the Hong Kong Management Association on Sept. 9, 1977) (mimeo.)

--: Hong Kong Dollar and Sterling, International Currency Review, London, 5, 1973, pp. 7-17

HÄNISCH, A. von: Jebsen & Co, Hong Kong. China-Handel im Wechsel der Zeiten, 1895-1945, Apenrade: Selbstverlag, 1970

HALPERN, E. and JONES, P.H.M.: Hong Kong, in: G. Reimann and Wigglesworth, E.F. (eds.), The Challenge of International Finance, London 1966, pp. 337-51

HAMBRO, E.I.: Chinese Refugees in Hong Kong, Phylon Quarterly, 18, 1957, pp. 69-81

HANNA, W.A.: Japan - Hong Kong - Indonesia Relationships, American Universities Fieldstaff Reports, 1956, pp. 1-14

HARING, J.F.: Trade and Development: The Structure of Export Industrialism, Hong Kong Economic Papers, March 1963, pp. 1-7

HARRIS, P.B.: Representative Politics in a British Dependency. Some Reflections on Problems of Representation in Hong Kong, Parliamentary Affairs, London, 28, 1975, pp. 180-198

HARRIS, P.B.: The Frozen Politics of Hong Kong, The World Today, London, 30, 1974, pp. 259-267

--: The International Future of Hong Kong, International Affairs, 48, 1972, pp. 60-71

HARRISON, B. (ed.): University of Hong Kong. The First 50 Years, 1911-1961, Hong Kong: Hong Kong University Press, 1962

HAYASE, T. Overseas Chinese in Southeast Asia, Oriental Economist, 3, 1965, pp. 580-584

HAYDON, E.S.: The Choice of Chinese Customary Law in Hong Kong, International and Comparative Law Quarterly, 11, 1962, pp. 231-250

HAYES, J.W.: Movement of Villages on Lantau Island for Fung Shui Reasons, Journal of the Hong Kong Branch of the Royal Asiatic Society, 3, 1963, pp. 143-144

--: Old Ways of Life in Kowloon: The Cheung Sha Wan Villages, Journal of Oriental Studies, 8, No. 1, 1970, pp. 154-188

--: A Short History of Military Volunteers in Hong Kong, Journal of the Hong Kong Branch of the Royal Asiatic Society, 11, 1971, pp. 151-171

--: The Hong Kong Region. Its Place in Traditional Chinese Historiography and Principal Events since the Establishment of Hsin-an Courts in 1573, Journal of the Hong Kong Branch of the Royal Asiatic Society, 14, 1974, pp. 108-135

HAYWOOD, S.: Poverty in Hong Kong: Some Reflections, Chung Chi Journal, 11, No. 1, 1972, pp. 138-149

HEATON, W.: Maoist Revolutionary Strategy and Modern Colonialism. The Cultural Revolution in Hong Kong, Asian Survey, 10, 1970, pp. 840-857

HENDERSON, N.K.: Education for Enlightened Leaderships and Community Awareness: An Analysis of one of Hong Kong's Future Needs, Journal of Education (Hong Kong University), 23, 1966, pp. 34-43

--: Educational Problems and Research: A Hong Kong Introduction, Hong Kong: University of Hong Kong, Department of Education Research Unit, 1973

HEPPELL, T.S.: Social Security and Social Welfare. A 'New Look' from Hong Kong, Journal of Social Policy, London, 2, 1973, pp. 225-238; 3, 1974, pp. 113-126

HERMAN, Th.: The Role of Cottage and Small-Scale Industries in Asian Economic Development, Economic Development and Cultural Change, 4, 1955-56, pp. 356-370

HERMANN, M.: Hong Kong versus Singapore: Ein Erklärungsversuch divergierender Entwicklungsverläufe, Stuttgart: Gustav Fischer, 1974

HETHERINGTON, R.M.: Industrial Labour in Hong Kong, Hong Kong Economic Papers, 2, March 1963, pp. 29-41

HICKS, U.K.: The Finance of the City State, Malayan Economic Review, 5, 1960, pp. 1-9

HINTO, A. Education and Social Problems in Hong Kong, Journal of Education (Hong Kong University) 24, 1967, pp. 29-35

Historical and Statistical Abstract of the Colony of Hong Kong 1841-1920, Hong Kong, 1922

HO, C.Y.: Cotton Supply and Demand in Hong Kong, Textile Asia, Jan. 1971, pp. 18-29

HO, H.C.Y.: A Comparative Study of Postwar Industrial Development in Singapore and Hong Kong, M.Sc. thesis, University of London, 1962

--: A Measurement of Fiscal Performance in Hong Kong, Malayan Economic Review, 19, 1974, pp. 94-108

--: Developmental Effects of Earnings and Profit Tax in Hong Kong, Hong Kong Economic Papers, 10, 1976, pp. 33-45

--: Growth of Government Expenditure in Hong Kong, Hong Kong Economic Papers, No. 8, March 1974, pp. 18-38

--: Growth of Government Revenue in Hong Kong, Hong Kong Economic Papers, No. 9, June 1975, pp. 67-83

HO, K.F.: Some Consideration on Social Policy in Hong Kong, United College Journal, 10, 1972, pp. 248-252

HO, S.C.: Women into Management in Hong Kong? New Asia College Academic Annual, 18, 1976, pp. 273-282

HO, S.C.: International Investors in Hong Kong - What did they look for? New Asia College Academic Annual, Volume XIX, 1977, pp. 241-251

HO, Y.P.: Export Earnings Instabilities and Employment Fluctuations in a Trade-Dependent Economy: Hong Kong as a Case Study, M. Phil. thesis, Chinese University of Hong Kong, 1977

--: Foreign Trade and Economic Development of Hong Kong, in: Social and Economic Studies, Economics Society, Chinese University of Hong Kong, 1974, pp. 17-44

--: The Demand for Money in Hong Kong, 1961-1973, New Asia College Academic Annual, 17, 1975, pp. 285-305

HOADLEY, J.S.: Hong Kong is the Life Boat. Notes on Political Culture and Socialization, Journal of Oriental Studies, Vol. VIII, 1970, pp. 206-218

--: Political Participation of Hong Kong Chinese. Patterns and Trends, Asian Survey, 13, 1973, pp. 604-616

HOOKER, M.B.: The Relationship Between Chinese Law and Common Law in Malaysia, Singapore and Hong Kong, The Journal of Asian Studies, 28, 1969, pp. 723-742

HODGE, P.: Community Development and Mental Health, Hong Kong Journal of Mental Health, 2, No. 1, 1973, pp. 2-7

--: Urban Community Development in Hong Kong, Community Development Journal, Manchester, 7, 1972, pp. 154-164

HONG, L.K.: A Profile Analysis of The Chinese Family in an Urban Industrialized Setting, International Journal of Sociology of the Family, 3, No. 1, 1973, pp. 1-9

--: The Association of Religion and Family Structure: The Case of Hong Kong Family, Sociological Analysis, 33, 1972, pp. 50-57

--: The Chinese Family in a Modern Industrial Setting: Its Structure and Functions, Ph.D. dissertation, University of Notre Dame, 1970

Hong Kong. A Case to Answer. By a Group at the Hong Kong Research Project, Nottingham: Spokesman Books, 1974

Hong Kong. A Survey by the Economist, The Economist, London, Oct. 19, 1968

Hong Kong. An Industrial Power in Asia, Current Notes on International Affairs, Canberra, 30, 1959, pp. 103-106

Hong Kong and Western Germany. Five Years of Trade with the Federal Republic, Trade Bulletin, Hong Kong, 1958, pp. 103-106

Hong Kong Baptist College Department of Sociology and Social Work: A Study of the Leisure Activities of Youth Labourers in Hong Kong, Hong Kong 1971

Hong Kong Development and Perspective of a Clothing Colony, Research Project. Industrial Re-adjustment and the International Division of Labour, Development Research Institute, Tilburg, Progress Report No. 6, Tilburg 1977

Hong Kong in Africa, African Development, London, 9, 1975, 8, pp. 54-59

Hong Kong. La Documentation Française. Notes et Etudes Documentaires, No. 3047, Paris 1963

Hong Kong Research Project: Hong Kong. A Case to Answer, London: Spokesman Books, 1974

HOPKINS, K. (ed.): Hong Kong. The Industrial Colony. A Political, Social and Economic Survey, Hong Kong: Oxford University Press, 1971

HOPKINS, K.: Public and Private Housing in Hong Kong, in: Dwyer, D.J. (ed.): The City as a Centre of Change in Asia, Hong Kong: Oxford University Press, 1971

--: Public Housing Policy in Hong Kong (An Inaugural Lecture from the Chair of Sociology). University of Hong Kong, Supplement to the Gazette, Vol. XVI, No. 5, May 1969

HSIA, R.: Effects of Industrial Growth on Hong Kong Trade, Pakistan Development Review, 2, 1962, pp. 559-586

--: Hong Kong Textile Exports: A Case Study of Voluntary Restraints, in: English, H.E. and Hay, K.A.J. (eds.), Obstacles to Trade in the Pacific Area, Ottawa, 1972, pp. 167-185

HSIA, R. and CHAN, L.: Industrialization, Employment and Income Distribution of Hong Kong, London: Croom & Helm, 1978

HSIA, R. and CHEN, E.K.Y.: Mutamento tecnologico, sostituzione dei fattori e crestica industriale ad Hong Kong, Giomale degli Economisti e Annali di Economia, Milano, 37, 1978, pp. 141-166

HSIA, R.: Technological Change in the Industrial Growth of Hong Kong, in: Williams, B.R. (ed.): Science and Technology in Economic Growth, London: Macmillan, 1973, pp. 335-359

HSIA, R., HO, H., and LIM, E.: The Structure and Growth of the Hong Kong Economy, Wiesbaden: Otto Harrassowitz, 1975

HSING, M.H.: A Critical Evaluation of the Existing NI/GDP Estimates in Hong Kong, Hong Kong: Economic Research Centre, Chinese University of Hong Kong, 1977

HSU, F.L.K.: Americans and Chinese, New York 1972

HSUEH, S.S.: Government and Administration of Hong Kong, Hong Kong: University Book Store, 1962

HSUEH, T.T.: Development Alternatives for the Hong Kong Economy: An Aggregate Analysis, Malayian Economic Review, Vol. XX, No. 1, 1975, pp. 83-104

--: Development Features of a Mini Open Economy: The Cases of Singapore and Hong Kong, Journal of the Chinese University of Hong Kong, Vol. III, No. 1, 1975, pp. 255-278

--: Growth Pattern and Structure Change of the Hong Kong Economy 1959-1970, United College Journal, Vols. 12-13, Feb. 1975, pp. 293-326

--: International Comparisons of Development Features of the Asian Countries 1960-1972, in: Internationales Asienforum, Vol. 8, 1977, pp. 124-145

--: The Transforming Economy of Hong Kong 1952-1973, in: Hong Kong Economic Papers, 10, 1976, pp. 46-65

HSUEH, T.T. and SHEA, K.L.: Economic Growth with an Emphasis on Fiscal Policy: A Comparison of Hong Kong, Taiwan and Japan, Academic Economic Papers, Vol. V, 1977, pp. 35-61

HSUEH, T.T. and WONG, Y.L.: Growth and Liquidity in a Small Open Economy, Hong Kong, Chinese University of Hong Kong, 1977 (mimeo.)

HU, Y.: The Problem of the Hong Kong Refugees, Asian Survey, 2, 1962, pp. 28-37

HUANG, S.S.C.: The Chinese University of Hong Kong, Journal of the Hong Kong Branch of the Royal Asiatic Society, 5, 1965, pp. 86-94

HUCK, A.: Hong Kong, Macao and China, Europa-Archiv, Bonn, 23, 1968, 13, pp. 485-494

HÜRLIMANN, M.: Hong Kong, Zürich: Atlantis, 1962

HUGHES, R.: Hong Kong. Borrowed Place - Borrowed Time, London: Andre Deutsch, 2d ed., 1968

--: Hong Kong. Brückenkopf auf Abruf, Wien: Molden, 1967

HUGHES, R.H.: Hong Kong: An Urban Study, Geographical Journal, 117, No. 1, 1961, pp. 1-23

--: Hong Kong: Far Eastern Meeting Point, Geographical Journal, 129, No. 4, 1963, pp. 450-465

HUGO-BRUNT, M.: Hong Kong Housing, in: Taming Megalopolis, Vol. 1, New York 1967, pp. 477-493

HUNG, C.L.: An Analysis of Mainland China's Exports to Hong Kong Since 1950, M.A. thesis, University of Hong Kong, 1968

IP, I.P.: Flatted Factories: Hong Kong, M.Arch. thesis, University of Melbourne, 1967

JAO, Y.C.: A Commission on Money and Finance For Hong Kong, Hong Kong Economic Papers, Nov. 1968, pp. 50-56

--: Banking and Currency in Hong Kong, London: Macmillan, 1974

--: Commercial Banking in Hong Kong: An Analysis of Its Growth, Structure and Strains, 1954-1968, Ph.D. thesis, University of Hong Kong, 1971

--: Financing Hong Kong's Textile Growth, Textile Asia, Dec. 1970, pp. 23-25

--: Hong Kong's Export-propelled Growth, Intereconomics, 1974, 9, pp. 288-291

JAO, Y.C.: Linear Programming and Banking in Hong Kong, Hong Kong Economic Papers, Oct. 1971, pp. 28-32

--: Money Supply in Hong Kong 1954-1968, Hong Kong Economic Papers, Apr. 1970, pp. 24-48

--: Proximate Determinants of Money Supply in Hong Kong, Hong Kong Economic Papers, 8, 1974, pp. 1-17

--: Recent Changes and Trends in Hong Kong's Taxation, Bulletin for International Fiscal Documentation, Vol. XXVI, July 1972, pp. 267-273

--: Recent Developments in Hong Kong Banking, The Bankers' Magazine, 1970, pp. 263-268

--: Streamlining Hong Kong's Tax System, Bulletin for International Fiscal Documentation, Amsterdam, 28, 1974, pp. 236-241

--: Tax Reform and Fiscal Policy in Hong Kong, Bulletin for International Fiscal Documentation, Amsterdam, 31, 1977, pp. 17 and 186

JAP, K.S. und HINTZEN, L.: Die Besteuerung von Kapitalgesellschaften und Personengesellschaften in Hong Kong, Recht der Internationalen Wirtschaft, Heidelberg, 21, 1975, pp. 26-29

JARVIE, I.C. and AGASSY, J. (eds.): Hong Kong: A Society in Transition, London: Routledge & Kegan Paul, 1969

JEPHCOTT, A.P.: Hong Kong. A Quick Look, Contemporary Review, London, Vol. 221, 1972, pp. 82-87

JOHNSON, G.E.: Leaders and Leadership in an Expanding New Territories Town, The China Quarterly, 69, 1977, pp. 109-125

JOHNSON, G.F.: From Rural Committee to Spirit Medium Cult: Voluntary Association in the Development of a Chinese Town, Journal of Asian and African Studies, 1972, pp. 123-145

JOHNSON, S.K.: Hong Kong's Resettled Squatters: A Statistical Analysis, Asian Survey, 6, 1966, pp. 643-656

JONES, P.H.M.: Hong Kong Stills its Rioters. The Need for More Than Riches, The Round Table, London, No. 228, 1967, pp. 391-398

KALMA, J.S. and NEWCOMBE, K.: Energy Use in Two Large Cities. A Comparison of Hong Kong and Sydney, The International Journal of Environmental Studies, New York, 9, 1976, pp. 53-64

KAM, C.C.M.: Credit Union for Small Manufacturers in Hong Kong, M.Com. thesis, Chinese University of Hong Kong, 1969

KAN, A.W.S.: A Study of Neighborly Interaction in Public Housing: The Case of Hong Kong, Social Research Centre, Chinese University of Hong Kong, 1974

--: Implications of Concentrated Utilization of Local Facilities and Services in Public Housing Estates in Hong Kong, Social Research Centre, Chinese University of Hong Kong, 1975

KAN, L.B.: Libraries in Hong Kong: A Directory, Hong Kong: Library Association, 1963

KANI, H.: The Boat People in Shatin, N.T., Hong Kong - The Settlement Patterns in 1967 and 1968, Chung Chi Journal, 11, No. 2, 1972, pp. 57-65

KANN, E.: The Strength of the Hong Kong Dollar, Far Eastern Economic Review, 1956, pp. 391-394

KAO, C. and LIN, T.B.: Logistics of Natural Resources in Hong Kong. A Case Study of Urban Ecological Problems in a Locality with High Density Population, Internationales Asienforum, Vol. 6, 1975, pp. 202-208

KENDRICK, D.M.: Price Control and its Practice in Hong Kong, Hong Kong: K. Weiss, 1954

KING, A.Y.C.: Administrative Absorption of Politics in Hong Kong. Emphasis on the Grass Roots Level, Asian Survey, 15, 1975, pp. 422-439

--: The Administrative Absorption of Politics in Hong Kong, With Special Emphasis on City District Officer Scheme, Social Research Centre, Chinese University of Hong Kong, 1973

--: The Political Culture of Kwun Tong: A Chinese Community in Hong Kong, Social Research Centre, Chinese University of Hong Kong, 1972

KING, A.Y.C. and CHAN, P.K.: A Theoretical and Operational Definition of Community: The Case of Kwun Tong, Social Research Centre, Chinese University of Hong Kong, 1972

KING, A.Y.C. and LEUNG, D.: The Chinese Touch in Small Industrial Organizations, Social Research Centre, Chinese University of Hong Kong, 1976

KING, A.Y.C. and MAN, P.J.L.: The Role of Small Factory in Economic Development: The Case of Hong Kong, Social Research Centre, Chinese University of Hong Kong, 1974

KING, F.H.H.: Credit and Speculation in Hong Kong, Far Eastern Economic Review, 1955, pp. 729-730

--: Money and Monetary Policy in China, Cambridge, Mass., 1965

--: The Monetary System of Hong Kong, Hong Kong: Weiss, 1953

KING, F.H.H. and CLARKE, P.: A Research Guide to China Coast Newspapers, 1822-1911, Cambridge, Mass.: Harvard University Press, 1965

KIRBY, E.S. Developing Small Industries in Hong Kong, Far Eastern Economic Review, 32, 1961, pp. 216-219

--: Economic Development in East Asia, New York: F.A. Praeger, 1967

--: Hong Kong and the British Position in China, Far Eastern Economic Review, 1951, pp. 613-616

--: Money, Banking and the Stock Exchange in Hong Kong, Far Eastern Economic Review, 1955, pp. 740-742

KIRBY, E.S. (ed.): Report of the Hong Kong Working Party on the European Common Market, Hong Kong, 1963

KIRKUP, J.: Hong Kong and Macao, London: Dent & Sons, 1969

KNÜBEL, H.: Probleme Hong Kongs, Geographische Rundschau, Braunschweig, 25, 1973, pp. 232-238

KOO, S.E.: The Role of Export Expansion in Hong Kong's Economic Growth, Asian Survey, 8, 1968, pp. 499-515

Kowloon Disturbances 1966, Report of Commission of Inquiry, Hong Kong: Government Printer, 1967

KÜCHLER, J. und SUM, K.S.: Das räumliche Ungleichgewicht Hong Kongs. Resultat einer liberalistischen Wirtschafts- und Raumpolitik, Die Erde, Berlin, Vol. 102, 1971, pp. 141-179

KWONG, S.C.: The Role of Trade Unions in Labor Movement in Hong Kong, in: New Asian Management Journal, 1974, pp. 96-105

Kwun Tong District Kai Fong Welfare Association: Kwun Tong Today, Hong Kong 1975

LAI, C.W.: Computerization in Hong Kong, Social and Economic Studies, Economics Society, New Asia College, Chinese University of Hong Kong, 1971, pp. 73-77

LAI, C.Y.: Small Industries in Hong Kong, Problems of Relocation Associated with Urban Renewal, Town Planning Review, Liverpool, 44, 1973, pp. 135-146

LAI, D.C.Y.: Some Geographical Aspects of the Industrial Development of Hong Kong Since 1841, M.A. thesis, University of Hong Kong, 1963

LAI, C.Y. and DWYER, D.J.: Tsuen-Wan. A New Industrial Town in Hong Kong, Geographical Review, 54, 1964, pp. 151-169

--: Kwun Tong, Hong Kong: A Study of Industrial Planning, Town Planning Review, 35, No. 4, 1965, pp. 299-310

LAM, M.J.: Facing Changing Social Values in Hong Kong upon Returning from Graduate Study in the United States, Journal of Social Work Process, Philadelphia, 16, 1967, pp. 107-124

LANG, O.: Chinese Family and Society, New Haven: Yale University Press, 1946

LAU, S.K.: Utilitarianistic Families: An Inquiry into the Political Stability in Hong Kong, Social Research Centre, Chinese University of Hong Kong, 1977

LAURENS, H.: Hong Kong. Une économie florissante, France-Asie, Paris, No. 196, Vol. 23, 1969, pp. 29-42

LAW, C.K.: Wage Differentials: A Case Study of Hong Kong, 1964-1973, unpublished M.A. thesis, Thammasat University, 1974

LAWRENCE, M.J.: The Wool Manufacturing Industries in Hong Kong, Quarterly Review of Agricultural Economics, Canberra, 19, 1966, pp. 152-162

LEE, C.M.: Why a Regular Labour Force Sample Survey for Hong Kong. The Hague 1973

LEE, K.Y.: Singapore-Hong Kong: A Tale of Two Cities, Far Eastern Economic Review, Vol. 67, 1970, No. 10, pp. 49-51

LEE, P.N.S.: Police Corruption and Elite Mass Integration in Hong Kong: A Development Perspective, Paper Presented to the 3rd Meeting on "Bureaucratic Behaviour" (Asia) at Singapore, Nov. 22-26, 1977

LEE, R.P.L.: Growth and Limitations of Social Science Research Institutions in Asia: The Hong Kong Experience, Social Research Centre, Chinese University of Hong Kong, 1975

--: Health Services System in Hong Kong: Professional Stratification in a Modernizing Society, Inquiry, Supplement to V, XII, 1975, pp. 51-62

--: Interaction between Chinese and Western Medicine in Hong Kong: Modernization and Professional Inequality, in: A. Kleinman et al. (eds.), Medicine in Chinese Cultures: Comparative Studies of Health Care in Chinese and other Societies, U.S. Dept. of Health, Education, and Welfare, 1975, pp. 219-240

--: Organizational Complexity and Industrial Health Services: A Study of Kwun Tong, Social Research Centre, Chinese University of Hong Kong, 1972

--: Organizational Size, Structural Differentiation and the Man at the Top in Hong Kong, Social Research Centre, Chinese University of Hong Kong, 1972

--: Perceptions and Uses of Chinese and Western Medical Care in Hong Kong, Social Research Centre, Chinese University of Hong Kong, 1977

--: Population, Housing and the Availability of Medical and Health Services in an Industrializing Chinese Community, in: Journal of the Chinese University of Hong Kong, Vol. 1, 1973, pp. 191-210

LEE, R.P.L.: Problems of Integrating Chinese and Western Health Services in Hong Kong: Topia and Utopia, Social Research Centre, Chinese University of Hong Kong, 1974

--: The Stratification Between Modern and Traditional Professions: A Study of Health Services in Hong Kong, Social Research Centre, Chinese University of Hong Kong, 1974

--: Toward a Convergence of Modern Western and Traditional Chinese Medical Services in Hong Kong, in: S.R. Ingman and A.E. Thomas (eds.), Topias and Utopias in Health, The Hague: Mouton, 1975, pp. 393-412

LEE, T.C.: The Economy of Hong Kong Since World War II, in: E.F. Szczepanik (ed.), Symposium on Economic and Social Problems in the Far East, Hong Kong, 1962, pp. 166-179

LEE, W.Y.: Youth and the Media: A Mass Media Study of Hong Kong Secondary School Students Hong Kong: Lutheran World Federation Broadcasting Service, 1969

LEEDS, P.F.: Housing in Hong Kong. Post-war Problems, Journal of Administration Overseas, 5, 1966, pp. 184-193

--: Public Transport in Hong Kong, Journal of Administration Overseas, 9, No. 4, 1970, pp. 255-261

LEEMING, F.: The Earlier Industrialization of Hong Kong, Modern Asian Studies, London, 9, 1975, pp. 337-342

--: Street Studies in Hong Kong. Localities in a Chinese City, Hong Kong, London: Oxford University Press, 1977

LEGGE, J.: The Colony of Hong Kong, Journal of the Hong Kong Branch of the Royal Asiatic Society, Vol. 11, 1971, pp. 172-193

LENT, J.A. (ed.): The Asian Newspapers' Reluctant Revolution, Ames, Iowa: State University Press, 1971

LETHBRIDGE, H.J.: A Chinese Association in Hong Kong: the Tung Wah, Contributions to Asian Studies, 1, 1971, pp. 144-158

LETHBRIDGE, H.J.: Condition of the European Working Class in Nineteenth Century Hong Kong, Journal of the Hong Kong Branch of the Royal Asiatic Society, 15, 1975, pp. 88-112

--: Hong Kong under Japanese Occupation: Changes in Social Structure, in: I.C. Jarvie (ed.), Hong Kong: A Society in Transition, London 1969

--: The District Watch Committee: The Chinese Executive Council of Hong Kong, Journal of the Hong Kong Branch of the Royal Asiatic Society, 11, 1971, pp. 116-141

--: The Emergence of Bureaucratic Corruption as a Social Problem in Hong Kong, Journal of Oriental Studies, XII, Nos. 1 and 2, 1974, pp. 17-29

--: The Evolution of a Chinese Voluntary Association in Hong Kong: The Po Leung Kuk, Journal of Oriental Studies, 10, No. 1, 1972, pp. 33-50

LEUNG, C.K.: The Growth of Public Passenger Transport, in: D.J. Dwyer (ed.), Asian Urbanization: A Hong Kong Casebook, Hong Kong 1971

--: Mass Transport in Hong Kong, in: D.J. Dwyer (ed.), Asian Urbanization: A Hong Kong Casebook, Hong Kong 1971

LEUNG, C.L.: Internal Public Passenger Transport in Hong Kong, M.A. thesis, University of Hong Kong, 1969

LEUNG, H.K.: Residential Housing in Hong Kong: An Economic Analysis of Housing Policies, unpublished M.Phil. thesis, Chinese University of Hong Kong, 1977

LI, C.H.: An Analysis of the Chinese Refugees in Hong Kong, Issues and Studies, Institute of International Relations, Taipei, 8, 1972, pp. 44-53

LI, R.: Financing of Hong Kong's Building Industry, Hong Kong Manager, April 1970, pp. 11-15

LIANG, C.S. Urban Land Use Analysis. A Case Study on Hong Kong, Hong Kong: Ernest Publications, 1973

--: Urban Land Use in Hong Kong and Kowloon - Part I: Tsim-sha-tsui District, Chung Chi Journal, 6, No. 1, 1966, pp. 1-24

LIANG, C.S.: Urban Land Use in Hong Kong and Kowloon - Part II: The Central Business District: Its Structure and Development Trend, Chung Chi Journal, Vol. 8, No. 1, 1968, pp. 107-132

LIANG, L.S.: Die Textilindustrie Hong Kongs, Zeitschrift für Allgemeine und Textile Marktwirtschaft, Münster, 1969, pp. 306-320

LIAO, S.K.: An Analysis of Export Growth and Trade Flows of Hong Kong, unpublished M.Phil. thesis, Chinese University of Hong Kong, 1977

LIM, E.R.: A General Equilibrium Model of an Export-Dependent Economy, Ph.D. dissertation, Harvard University, 1969

--: Consumer Demand in Hong Kong: An Econometric Analysis, Hong Kong Economic Papers, 4, 1968, pp. 26-44

LIN, T.B. Das monetäre System und das Verhalten des Angebotes an und der Nachfrage nach Geld in Hong Kong, Freiburg i. Br.: Eberhard Albert, 1969

--: Determinants and Projections of Hong Kong's Import, Academia Economic Papers, IV, Sept. 1976, pp. 21-58

--: Monetary Behaviour under the Sterling Exchange Standard. Hong Kong as a Case Study, Economic Research Centre, Chinese University of Hong Kong, 1971

--: Monetary System and Monetary Behaviour in Hong Kong, New Asia College Academic Annual, 13, 1971, pp. 183-201

--: Problems of Hong Kong's Monetary System, in: Internationales Asienforum, Vol. 5, 1974, pp. 43-52

LIN, T.B. and HO, Y.P.: Exports and Employment in Hong Kong, Hong Kong: Chinese University of Hong Kong, 1978 (mimeo.)

--: Export Variabilities and Employment Fluctuations in Hong Kong's Manufacturing Industries, Hong Kong: Chinese University of Hong Kong, 1978 (mimeo.)

LIN, T.B. and MOK, V.: Employment Implications of Exports: A Case Study of Hong Kong, Council for Asian Manpower Studies, 1977 (mimeo.)

LIU, W.T.: Chinese Value Orientations in Hong Kong, Sociological Analysis, V. 27, No. 2, 1966, pp. 53-66

--: Family Interactions among Local and Refugee Chinese Families in Hong Kong, Journal of Marriage and the Family, 28, No. 3, 1966, pp. 314-323

LLEWELLYN, B.: Overcrowded Hong Kong, Eastern World, 12, No. 2, 1958, pp. 24-25

LO, C.P.: A Typology of Hong Kong Census Districts. A Study in Urban Structure, in: Changing South-East Asian Cities, Singapore, London 1976, pp. 224-233

--: Changes in the Ecological Structure of Hong Kong 1961-1971. A Comparative Analysis, in: Environment and Planning, 7, 1975, pp. 941-963

--: Changing Population Distribution in the Hong Kong New Territories, Annals of The Association of American Geographers, 58, No. 2, 1968, pp. 273-284

LO, H.L.: The Role of Hong Kong in the Cultural Interchange between East and West, East Asian Cultural Studies Series, No. 6 and 7, Tokyo 1963

LO, K.L.: Hong Kong's Small-scale Industries, Hong Kong Manager, Jan/Feb 1967, pp. 19-25

LORENZO, M.: The Attitude of Communist China Towards Hong Kong, M.A. thesis, University of Chicago, 1959

LUEY, P.: Interindustry Specialization in International Trade: The Hong Kong Case, Hong Kong Economic Papers, 11, 1977, pp. 20-41

LUTZ, H. and SNOW, R.: Hong Kong. Hard Labour for Life, Far Eastern Economic Review, 71, 1971, 3, pp. 17-19

LYCZAK, R., FU, G.S. and HO, A.: Attitudes of Hong Kong Bilinguals Toward English and Chinese Speakers, Journal of Cross-Cultural Psychology, 7, No. 4, 1976, pp. 425-438

MA, R.A. and SZCZEPANIK, E.F.: The National Income of Hong Kong 1947-50, Hong Kong: Hong Kong University Press, 1955

MA, W.Y.: The Development of Kwun Tong, Journal of Geological, Geographical and Archaeological Society, 1960/61, pp. 49-52

McCOY, A.W. et al.: The Politics of Heroin in Southeast Asia, New York, London: Harper & Row, 1972

McGEE, T.G.: Hawkers in Hong Kong: An Outline of Research Project and Fieldwork, Unpublished mimeographed copy, Centre of Asian Studies, University of Hong Kong, 1969

MÄDING, K.: Wirtschaftswachstum und Kulturwandel in Hong Kong, Köln, Opladen: Westdt. Verlag, 1964

MARK, K.C.: The Banks in Hong Kong and Their Possible Improvements, Chung Chi Journal, May 1963, pp. 113-127

MAUNDER, W.F.: An Examination of Demand Conditions for Rice and Related Cereals in Hong Kong, Hong Kong Economic Papers, 2, 1963, pp. 49-78

--: Hong Kong Urban Rents and Housing, Hong Kong 1969

--: Rents and Housing Standards for Poorer Households on Hong Kong Island, Hong Kong Economic Papers, 4, 1968, pp. 12-25

MAUNDER, W.F. and SZCZEPANIK, E.F.: Hong Kong Housing Survey 1957, in: The Final Report of the Special Committee on Housing 1956-1958, Hong Kong: University of Hong Kong, 1958

MENARD, W.: The Boat People of Hong Kong, Michigan Quarterly Review, 8, No. 3, 1969, pp. 189-193

Merkblatt für Kapitalanlagen im Ausland: Hong Kong, BfA-Mitteilungen, Köln, 22, 1972, pp. 1-16

MILLS, L.A.: British Rule in Eastern Asia. A Study of Contemporary Government and Economic Development in British Malaya and Hong Kong, Oxford: Oxford University Press; London: Humphrey Milford, 1942

--: British Rule in Eastern Asia. A Study of Contemporary Government and Economic Development in British Malaya and Hong Kong, New York 1970

MINERS, N.J.: The Government and Politics of Hong Kong, Hong Kong: Oxford University Press, 1975

--: Hong Kong. A Case Study in Political Stability, The Journal of Commonwealth and Comparative Politics, 13, 1975, pp. 26-39

MITCHELL, R.E.: Chinese Fertility Rates and Family Size in Response to Changes in Age at Marriage, the Trend away from Arranged Marriages, and Increasing Urbanization, Population Studies, 25, No. 3, 1971, pp. 481-489

--: Family Life in Urban Hong Kong, Vols. I-II, Unpublished Project Report of the Urban Family Life Survey, 1969

--: How Hong Kong Newspapers Have Responded to 15 Years of Rapid Social Change, Asian Survey, 9, 1969, pp. 669-681

--: Husband-Wife Relations and Family Planning Practices in Urban Hong Kong, Journal of Marriage and the Family, 34, No. 1, 1972, pp. 139-146

--: Research Centers: The Social Science Research Centre of The Chinese University of Hong Kong, Social Sciences Information, 5, No. 4, 1966, pp. 117-118

--: Some Implications of High Density Housing, American Sociological Review, 36, 1971, pp. 18-29

MITCHELL, R.E. and LO, I.: Implications of Changes in Family Authority Relations for the Development of Independence and Assertiveness in Hong Kong Children, Asian Survey, 8, No. 4, 1968, pp. 309-322

MOK, B.N.H.: A Study of the Population of Hong Kong, Bombay 1959

MOK, M.C.H.: The Development of Cotton Spinning and Weaving Industries in Hong Kong, M.A. thesis, University of Hong Kong, 1969

MOK, V.: The Nature of Kwun Tong as an Industrial Community: An Analysis of Economic Organization, Social Research Centre, Chinese University of Hong Kong, 1972

--: The Organization and Management of Factories in Kwun Tong, Social Research Centre, Chinese University of Hong Kong, 1973

--: The Small Factories in Kwun Tong: Problems and Strategies for Development, Social Research Centre, Chinese University of Hong Kong, 1974

MOONITZ, M.: Financial Reporting in Hong Kong, Hong Kong Economic Papers, 4, 1968, pp. 1-11

MORGAN, W.P.: Triad Societies in Hong Kong: Government Printer, 1960

MORLAND, J.K.: Race Awareness among American and Hong Kong Chinese Children, American Journal of Sociology, 75, 1969, pp. 360-374

MORKRE, M.R.: The Construction and Appraisal of Unit Value and Quantity Indexes of Imports and Domestic Exports in Hong Kong, Hong Kong: Hong Kong University, 1974 (mimeo.)

MORRISON, T.K.: Manufactured Exports and Protection in Developing Countries: A Cross-Country Analysis, Economic Development and Cultural Change, Oct. 1976, pp. 151-158

MUN, K.C.: Die Wirtschaftliche Entwicklung Hong Kongs, Ph.D. thesis, Freiburg i.Br.: Albert-Ludwigs-Universität, 1966

MUNDER, W.F.: Hong Kong's Urban Rent and Housing, Hong Kong: Hong Kong University Press, 1969

MYERS, J.T.: Hong Kong Spirit-Medium Temple, Journal of the Hong Kong Branch of the Royal Asiatic Society, 15, 1975, pp. 16-27

--: Traditional Chinese Religious Practices in an Urban-Industrial Setting: The Example of Kwun Tong, in: Internationales Asienforum, Vol. 7, 1976, pp. 355-377

MYERS, J.T. and LEUNG, D.: A Chinese Spirit-Medium Temple in Kwun Tong. A Preliminary Report, Social Research Centre, Chinese University of Hong Kong, 1974

MYERS, R.H.: Education, Technology, and Economic Development in Hong Kong, Chung Chi Journal, May 1964, pp. 190-201

MYRDAL, G.: Asian Drama: An Inquiry into the Poverty of Nations, New York: Twentieth Century Fund, 1968

NELSON, H.G.H.: Ancestor Worship and Burial Practices, in: A.P. Wolf (ed.), Religion and Ritual in Chinese Society, California: Stanford University Press, 1974

NEWCOMBE, K.: Energy Use in Hong Kong, Urban Ecology, 1, 1975, 1 and 1, 1975, 2

NG, A.: Social Causes of Violent Crimes Among Young Offenders in Hong Kong, Social Research Centre, Chinese University of Hong Kong, 1975

NG, P.P.T.: Access to Educational Opportunity: The Case of Kwun Tong, Social Research Centre, Chinese University of Hong Kong, 1975

--: The Family and Family Planning in Kwun Tong: An Overview of the Findings, Social Research Centre, Chinese University of Hong Kong, 1976

NG, R.: Culture and Society of a Hakka Community on Lantau Island, Hong Kong, in: I.C. Jarvie (ed.), Hong Kong: A Society in Transition, London 1969

NORTON-KYSHE, J.W.: History of the Laws and Courts of Hong Kong, Reprinted Version, Hong Kong: Vetch & Lee, 1971

NUTTALL, T.: Trade Unions in Hong Kong, The Journal of Industrial Relations, Sydney, 17, 1975, 2, pp. 207-209

OBERHUMMER, E.: Hong Kong, Mitteilungen der Geographischen Gesellschaft in Wien, Bd. 71, 1928, pp. 368-380

OSGOOD, C.: A Study of a Hong Kong Community, Tucson: University of Arizona Press, 1975

OWEN, N.C.: Economic Policy in Hong Kong, in: Hopkins, K. (ed.), Hong Kong. The Industrial Colony. A Political, Social and Economic Survey, Hong Kong: Oxford University Press, 1971, pp. 141-196

--: Manpower Deficiencies and Industrial Training, Hong Kong Economic Papers, Sept. 1972, pp. 45-59

--: The Decline of Competition with Industrial Maturity: The Implications for Income Distribution in Hong Kong, Hong Kong: Centre of Asian Studies, Hong Kong University, 1971 (mimeo.)

PAPINEAU, A.J.G.: A Guide to Hong Kong, Singapore: André Publications, 1976

PODMORE, D.: Localisation in the Hong Kong Government Service, 1948-1968, Journal of Commonwealth Political Studies, 9, 1971, pp. 36-51

PODMORE, D.: The Population of Hong Kong, in: Hopkins, K. (ed.), Hong Kong. The Industrial Colony, Hong Kong, 1971, pp. 21-54

POON, P.W.T.: Bibliographical Control in Hong Kong, 1965-1973, New Asia College Academic Annual, 17, 1975, pp. 241-257

POPE-HENNESSY, J.: Half-Crown Colony, London: Jonathan Cape, 1969

PORTER, R.: Child Labour in Hong Kong, Publ. by the Bertrand Russell Peace Foundation for the Hong Kong Research Project and "The Spokesman", Nottingham 1975

--: Child Labour in Hong Kong and Related Problems. A Brief Review, International Labour Review, 111, 1975, pp. 427-439

POTTER, J.M.: Capitalism and the Chinese Peasant: Social and Economic Changes in a Hong Kong Village, Berkeley, Los Angeles: University of California Press, 1968

--: P'ing Shan: The Changing Economy of a Chinese Village in Hong Kong. Ph.D. thesis, Berkeley, University of California, 1964

--: The Structure of Rural Chinese Society in the New Territories, in: I.C. Jarvie (ed.), Hong Kong: A Society in Transition, London 1969

PRESSNELL, L.A.: A Glimpse of Banking in Hong Kong, Three Banks Review, Sept. 1961, pp. 22-33

PRESCOTT, J.A.: Hong Kong: the Form and Significance of a High-Density Urban Development, in: D.J. Dwyer (ed.), Asian Urbanization: A Hong Kong Casebook, Hong Kong 1971

PRIESTLEY, K.E. and WRIGHT, B.R.: Mental Health and Education in Hong Kong, Hong Kong: Hong Kong University Press; London: Oxford University Press, 1956

PRIESTLEY, K.E.: The University of Hong Kong, Civilizations, 5, No. 3, 1955, pp. 353-361

PRYOR, E.G.: Historical Review of Housing Conditions in Hong Kong, Journal of the Hong Kong Branch of the Royal Asiatic Society, 12, 1972, pp. 89-129

PRYOR, E.G.: An Assessment of the Need and Scope for Urban Renewal in Hong Kong, Ph.D. thesis, Department of Geography and Geology, University of Hong Kong, 1971

--: Housing in Hong Kong, Hong Kong, London: Oxford University Press, 1973

--: Environmental Quality and Housing Policy in Hong Kong, Pacific Viewpoint, Wellington, 16, 1975, pp. 195-206

--: Population Changes in Hong Kong Between 1961 and 1966, Australian Planning Institute Journal, 5, No. 4, 1967, pp. 99-102

--: The Delineation of Blighted Areas in Urban Hong Kong, in: D.J. Dwyer (ed.), Asian Urbanization: A Hong Kong Casebook, Hong Kong 1971

--: The Great Plague of Hong Kong, Journal of the Hong Kong Branch of the Royal Asiatic Society, 15, 1975, pp. 61-70

--: Workshops in Domestic Premises. A Hong Kong Case Study, Pacific Viewpoint, Wellington, 13, 1972, pp. 167-186

RABUSHKA, A.: The Changing Face of Hong Kong. New Departures in Public Policy, Washington, D.C., Stanford, Calif., 1973

--: Value for Money. The Hong Kong Budgetary Process, Stanford: Hoover Institution Press, 1976

RANGANATHAN, V.K.: Hong Kong's External Reserves: Tinsel in Sombre Guise, Far Eastern Economic Review, 1972, pp. 48-52

REAR, J.: British Labour Law in a Colonial Environment. The Hong Kong Experience, Industrial Law Journal, 3, 1974, 3, pp. 138-151

--: One Brand of Politics, in: K. Hopkins (ed.), Hong Kong: The Industrial Colony, Hong Kong 1971

--: The Law of the Constitution, in: K. Hopkins (ed.), Hong Kong. The Industrial Colony, Hong Kong: Oxford University Press, 1971

Report of the 1963 Working Party on Government Policies and Practices with Regard to Squatters, Resettlement and Government Low Cost Housing, Hong Kong 1963 (mimeo.)

RICHES, G.: Framework for Community Development in Hong Kong, Community Development Journal, 4, 1969, pp. 83-87

RIEDEL, J.: The Hong Kong Model of Industrialization, Kieler Diskussionsbeiträge, 29, Kiel: Institut für Weltwirtschaft, 1973

--: The Industrialization of Hong Kong, Tübingen: J.C.B. Mohr, 1974

RIFBEIN, Susan Imperial Relic, in: New Internationalist, March 1974, pp. 22-24

ROBERTS, D.: Foreign Investment in Hong Kong, in: Legal Aspects of Doing Business in East Asia, New York, 1977, pp. 91-112

ROBERTS, P.J.: Valuation of Development Land in Hong Kong, Hong Kong: Hong Kong University Press, 1975

ROBERTSON, F.: Refugees and Troop Moves - A Report from Hong Kong, China Quarterly, 11, 1962, pp. 111-115

ROLL, Chr.: Hong Kong, vor dem Bambusvorhang, Außenpolitik, 18, 1973, pp. 180-188

RONALL, J.O.: Hong Kong's New Banking Legislation, The Bankers' Magazine, 1965, pp. 187-191

ROSENBERG, W.: Economic Development Lessons from Hong Kong. A Rejoinder, The Economic Record, 49, 1973, pp. 644-645

--: Hong Kong. Model for Development?, The Economic Record, 49, 1973, pp. 629-636

ROSERBERG, G.: Population Densities in Relation to Social Behavior, Ekistics, 25, 1968, pp. 425-427

ROUCEK, J.S.: The Geopolitics of Hong Kong, Revue du Sud-Est Asiatique, Bruxelles, 1967, pp. 155-189

RUSCOE, N.: Hong Kong Register 1962, Hong Kong 1962

SALAFF, J.W.: The Status of Unmarried Hong Kong Women and the Social Factors Contributing to their Delayed Marriage, Population Studies, 30, 1976, pp. 391-412

--: Working Daughters in the Hong Kong Chinese Family: Female Filial Piety or a Transformation in the Family Power Structure? Journal of Social History, 9, 1976, pp. 439-465

SALAFF, J.W. and WONG, A.K.: Chinese Women at Work. Work Commitment and Fertility in the Asian Setting, in: The Fertility of Working Women, New York, London: F.A. Praeger, 1977, pp. 81-145

SAUNDERS, J.A.H.: The Hong Kong and Shanghai Banking Corporation, The Banker, 1970, pp. 755-759

SAVIDGE, J. (ed.): Hong Kong 1976. Report for the Year 1975, Hong Kong: Hong Kong Government Press, 1976

SAYER, G.R.: Hong Kong, London: Oxford University Press, 1937

SCHMITT, R.C.: Implications of Density in Hong Kong, Journal of the American Institute of Planners, 29, 1963, pp. 210-217

SCHÖLLER, P.: Hong Kong. Weltstadt und "Drittes China", Geographische Zeitschrift, Wiesbaden, 55, 1967, pp. 110-141

SHEN, J.C.Y.: The Law and Mass Media in Hong Kong, Chung Chi Journal, 11, No. 1, 1972, pp. 60-125

SHIVELY, A.M. and SHIVELY, S.: Value Changes During a Period of Modernization: The Case of Hong Kong, Social Research Centre, Chinese University of Hong Kong, 1972

SHIVELY, S.: Political Orientations in Hong Kong - A Socio-Psychological Approach, Social Research Centre, Chinese University of Hong Kong, 1972

SILBERBERG, D.: Refugees. Miracle-makers Missing Out, Far Eastern Economic Review, 67, 1970, pp. 28-30

SILIN, R.H.: Marketing and Credit in a Hong Kong Wholesale Market, in: Willmott W.E. (ed.), Economic Organization in Chinese Society, Stanford, Calif., 1972, pp. 327-352

SIMONIS, U.E.: The Dynamics of German Foreign Trade, Economic Research Centre, Chinese University of Hong Kong, 1976

SIMPSON, R.F.: I.Q. in Hong Kong - Some Views on Intelligence and its Measurement in Hong Kong, Journal of Education (Hong Kong University), 14, 1956, pp. 48-53

SIMPSON, R.F.: Population Projection, Economic Resources and Educational Enrolments, Hong Kong 1966

--: Some Economic Aspects of Educational Planning in Hong Kong, Journal of Education (Hong Kong University), No. 21, 1963, pp. 22-30

SINGH, P.H., HUANG, S.C. and THOMPSON, G.C.: A Comparative Study of Selected Attitudes, Values and Personality Characteristics of American, Chinese and Indian Students, Journal of Social Psychology, 57, 1962, pp. 123-132

SMITH, A.H.: Trade with Hong Kong, Law and Politics in China's Foreign Trade, Seattle, London (Asian Law Series, No. 4), 1977, pp. 189-219

SMITH, C.T.: The Emergence of a Chinese Elite in Hong Kong, Journal of the Hong Kong Branch of the Royal Asiatic Society, 11, 1971, pp. 74-115

SMITH, H.: John Stuart Mill's Other Island: A Study of the Economic Development of Hong Kong, London: The Institute of Economic Affairs, 1966

SMYLY, W.J.: Tsuen Wan Township, Far Eastern Economic Review, 33, 1961, pp. 395-421

SORBY, T.D.: The Economy of Hong Kong - Reminiscences and Reminiscences, Chung Chi Journal, 11, No. 1, 1972, pp. 182-187

STAMMER, D.W.: Money and Finance in Hong Kong, Ph.D. thesis, Australian National University, 1968

--: The Public Finance of Hong Kong, Malayan Economic Review, Vol. 13, 1966, pp. 115-128

STAMP, L.D.: Land Utilization Map of Hong Kong, Journal of Oriental Studies, 2, 1955, pp. 377-379

STOODLEY, B.H.: Normative Family Orientations of Chinese College Students in Hong Kong, Journal of Marriage and the Family, 29, No. 4, 1967, pp. 773-782

STRINGER, H.R.: Marketing in Hong Kong, Overseas Business Reports, Washington, D.C., 1975, 21

STYLER, W.E.: Adult Education in Hong Kong, Overseas Education, 34, No. 3, 1962, pp. 112-118

SU, Ch.J.: China's Assimilation of Western Cultures Through Hong Kong, East Asian Cultural Studies, 6, Nos. 1-4, 1967, pp. 73-81

SAW, S.H.: Errors in Chinese Age-Statistics, Demography, 4, 1967, pp. 859-875

SUN, M.J.D.: The Prospects of Science of Managing and its Further Application in Hong Kong, New Asia College Academic Annual, 18, 1976, pp. 251-257

SUNG, K.: Hong Kong's World Markets, Far Eastern Economic Review, 51, 1966, pp. 359-364

--: The Role of the Hong Kong Textile Industry, Textile Asia, Nov. 1970, pp. 22-26

SUTU, H.: Free Trade and Hong Kong's Economy, Far Eastern Economic Review, 36, 1962, pp. 609-615

--: Helping the Small Man, Far Eastern Economic Review, 49, 1965, pp. 511-513

--: Industrialization in Hong Kong, California Management Review, 11, 1968, 1, pp. 85-90

SUTU, H. et al.: A Study of Government Financial Assistance to Small Industries, With Special Reference to Hong Kong, The Lingnan Institute of Business Administration, Chinese University of Hong Kong, 1973

SUTU, H. and CHANG, C.M.: The Industrial Structure in Hong Kong, Hong Kong, Chinese University of Hong Kong, 1976

SUTU, H. and DAVIES, D.: Finance for Industry, Far Eastern Economic Review, 1963, pp. 439-443

SZCZEPANIK, E.: Economic System of Hong Kong, Far Eastern Economic Review, 1964, pp. 545-548

--: The Economic Role of the Government of Hong Kong, Far Eastern Economic Review, 17, 1954, pp. 609-613

--: The Gains of Entrepôt Trade, Far Eastern Economic Review, 1954, pp. 771-775

--: The Cost of Living in Hong Kong, Hong Kong: Hong Kong University Press, 1956

--: The Economic Growth of Hong Kong, London: Oxford University Press, 1958

SZCZEPANIK, E.F.: The Embargo Effect on China's Trade with Hong Kong, Contemporary China, Vol. 2, 1958, pp. 85-93

--: External Trade of Hong Kong: Trends and Problems, Hong Kong Exporter and Far Eastern Importer, 1960-61, pp. 13-33

--: Financing the Post-war Economic Growth of Hong Kong, Far Eastern Economic Review, 1956, pp. 781-783

--: Hong Kong's National Income, Far Eastern Economic Review, 1959, pp. 1004-1005

--: Hong Kong's Trade with Mainland China, Hong Kong Economic Papers, No. 1, 1961, pp. 65-74

--: Problems of Macro-Economic Programming in Hong Kong, in: I.C. Jarvie (ed.), Hong Kong: A Society in Transition, London 1969

--: Pros and Cons of a Central Bank for Hong Kong, Far Eastern Economic Review, Aug. 1961

SZCZEPANIK, E.F. (ed.): Symposium of Economic and Social Problems in the Far East, Hong Kong 1962

TAEUBER, J.B.: Chinese Population in Transition. The City-states, Population Index, 38, 1972, pp. 3-34

--: Hong Kong. Migrants and Metropolis, Population Index, 29, 1963, pp. 3-25

TAM, S.M.: A Case Study. Sample Design of the Hong Kong 1976 By-Census, The Statistician, 26, 1977, pp. 29-39

TANG, A.M.: Hong Kong's Devaluation and Revaluation, Hong Kong Economic Papers, Nov. 1968, pp. 45-49

TANG, D. and DWYER, D.J.: The Port of Hong Kong, in: S.G. Davis (ed.): Symposium on Land Use and Mineral Deposits in Hong Kong, Southern China and South-East Asia, Hong Kong, 1964, pp. 122-132

TCHANG, P.K.: Demographische und Flüchtlingsfragen in China, New Asia College Academic Annual, 4, 1962, pp. 3-11

TO, Ch.Y.: The Development of Higher Education in Hong Kong, Comparative Education Review, 9, 1965, pp. 74-80

TOM, C.F.J.: Monetary Standard, Entrepôt Trade, and Prices, Hong Kong Economic Papers, 3, 1964, pp. 1-52

--: The Entrepôt Trade and the Monetary Standards of Hong Kong, 1842-1941, Hong Kong 1964

TOMKINS, H.J.: Report on the Hong Kong Banking System and Recommendations for the Replacement of the Banking Ordinance, Hong Kong 1962

TOPLEY, M.: Capital, Saving and Credit among Indigenous Rice Farmers and Immigrant Vegetable Farmers in Hong Kong's New Territories, in: Firth, R. and Yamey, B.S. (eds.), Capital, Saving and Credit in Peasant Societies, London, 1964, pp. 157-187

--: Chinese Traditional Ideas and The Treatment of Disease: Two Examples from Hong Kong, Man, 5, No. 3, 1970, pp. 421-437

--: Published and Unpublished Materials on Hong Kong by Overseas Affiliated Scholars, Journal of Oriental Studies, 8, 1970, pp. 219-225

--: The Role of Savings and Wealth among Hong Kong Chinese, in: I.C. Jarvie (ed.), Hong Kong: A Society in Transition, London 1969

The Government and the People, Hong Kong: Government Printer, 1962

TREGEAR, T.R.: Hong Kong and the New Territories. A Survey of Land Use in Hong Kong and the New Territories, Hong Kong: Hong Kong University Press, 1958

--: Land Utilization in Hong Kong, Hong Kong: Hong Kong University Press, London: Macmillan, 1955

TREGEAR, T.R. and BERRY, L.: The Development of Hong Kong and Kowloon as told in Maps, Hong Kong: Hong Kong University Press, 1959

TRENERY, D.: Tourism in Hong Kong, Far Eastern Economic Review, 36, 1962, pp. 332-337

TRESSIDER, J.O.: Hong Kong Traffic Survey 1960, Hammondsworth, 1961

TSE, F.Y.: Street Trading in Hong Kong, I-III, Social Research Centre, Chinese University of Hong Kong, 1974

--: Market and Street Trading: A Conceptual Framework, Social Research Centre, Chinese University of Hong Kong, 1974

TSE, N.Q.: Industrialization and Social Adjustment in Hong Kong, Sociology and Social Research, 52, 1968, pp. 237-251

TURNER, J.C.: Barriers and Channels for Housing Development in Modernizing Countries, Journal of the American Institute of Planners, May 1967, Vol. XXXIII, No. 3

VAUGHAN, T.D. and DWYER, D.J.: Some Aspects of Post-War Population Growth in Hong Kong, Economic Geography, 42, 1966, pp. 37-51

WARD, B.E.: A Hong Kong Fishing Village, Journal of Oriental Studies, 1, No. 1, 1954, pp. 195-214

--: Floating Villages: Chinese Fishermen in Hong Kong, Man, 59, 1959, pp. 44-55

--: A Small Factory in Hong Kong: Some Aspects of Its Internal Organization, in: Willmot, W.E. (ed.), Economic Organization in Chinese Society, Stanford, Calif., 1972, pp. 353-386

--: Chinese Fishermen in Hong Kong. Their Post-peasant Economy, in: Freedman (ed.), Social Organization, London, 1967, pp. 271-288

WAT, S.Y. and HODGE, R.W.: Social and Economic Factors in Hong Kong's Fertility Decline, Population Index, 26, No. 3, 1972, pp. 455-464

WATSON, K.A.: Housing in Hong Kong, South China Morning Post, 29th May, 1964

WEAKLAND, J.H.: Real and Reel Life in Hong Kong: Film Studies of Cultural Adaptation, Journal of Asian and African Studies, 6, Nos. 3/4, 1971, pp. 238-243

WEISS, K.: Hong Kong from A to Z. Guide Book, Hong Kong 1955

WELLINGTON, A.R.: Public Health in Hong Kong, Hong Kong 1930

WHATMORE, R.: Land in Hong Kong, Far Eastern Economic Review, July 1962, pp. 29-32

WIGGLESWORTH, J.M.: The Development of New Towns, in: Dwyer, D.J. (ed.), Asian Urbanization: A Hong Kong Casebook, Hong Kong, 1971, pp. 48-69

WILLIAMS, D.: Hong Kong, in: Crick, W. (ed.), Commonwealth Banking Systems, London, 1965, pp. 170-185

WILSON, B.D.: Chinese Burial Customs in Hong Kong, Journal of the Hong Kong Branch of the Royal Asiatic Society,, 1960/61, pp. 115-123

WILSON, R.W.: The Moral State. A Study of the Political Socialization of Chinese and American Children, New York: Free Press, 1974

WILSON, D.: New Thoughts on the Future of Hong Kong, Pacific Community, Tokyo, 8, 1977, pp. 588-599

WILTSHIRE, T.: Hong Kong. An Impossible Journey through History, Hong Kong: Seresia, 1971

WOLF, A. (ed.): Religion and Ritual in Chinese Society, Stanford, Calif., 1975

WONG, A.: Higher Non-Expatriate Civil Servants in Hong Kong, Social Research Centre, Chinese University of Hong Kong, 1972

WONG, A.K.: Chinese Community Leadership in a Colonial Setting. The Hong Kong Neighbourhood Associations, Asian Survey, 12, 1972, pp. 587-601

--: Chinese Voluntary Associations in Southeast Asian Cities and the Kaifongs in Hong Kong, Journal of the Hong Kong Branch of the Royal Asiatic Society, 11, 1971, pp. 62-73

--: Political Apathy and the Political System in Hong Kong, United College Journal, 8, 1970-71, pp. 1-20

--: Rising Social Status and Economic Participation of Women in Hong Kong - Review of a Decade, Southeast Asian Journal of Social Science, 1, No. 2, 1973, pp. 11-28

WONG, C.H.: Walled and Moated. A Hong Kong Village, Arts of Asia, 1971, pp. 20-26

WONG, D.O.Y.: The Future of the Hong Kong Habitat. Land Use Planning in the New Territories, Los Angeles: University Archives, 1975

--: Urban Analysis with Computers. The Case of Hong Kong, Geographic Society, United College, Chinese University of Hong Kong, 1974

WONG, F.M.: Industrialization and Family Structure in Hong Kong, Journal of Marriage and the Family, Nov. 1975, pp. 958-1000

--: Maternal Employment and Family Task-Power Differentiation among Lower Income Chinese Families, Social Research Centre, Chinese University of Hong Kong, 1972

--: Modern Ideology, Industrialization and the Middle-class Chinese Family in Hong Kong, Ph.D. thesis, University of California, Santa Barbara 1969

--: Modern Ideology, Industrialization, and Conjugalism: The Hong Kong Case, International Journal of Sociology of the Family, 2, Sept. 1972, pp. 139-150

WONG, K.A.: On the Stock Market Efficiency and Corporate Capital in Hong Kong, New Asia College Academic Annual, 17, 1975, pp. 313-330

WONG, L.S.K.: A Geographical Study of Squatter Areas in the Victoria - Kowloon Urban Areas, M.A. thesis, University of Hong Kong, 1969

WONG, P.S.: The Influx of Chinese Capital into Hong Kong since 1937, Hong Kong: Kai Ming Press, 1958

WONG, S.K.: Squatters in Pre-War Hong Kong, Journal of Oriental Studies, 8, 1970, pp. 189-205

--: The Aplichau Squatter Area: A Case Study, in: D.J. Dwyer (ed.), Asian Urbanization: A Hong Kong Casebook, Hong Kong 1971

WONG, S.L.: Probleme des Lehrens der Soziologie in Hong Kong, Kölner Zeitschrift für Soziologie und Sozialpsychologie, 18, 1966, pp. 753-762

--: Social Change and Parent-Child Relations in Hong Kong, in: R. Hill and R. Konig (eds.), Families in East and West, The Hague: Mouton, 1970

WOO, T.O.: Imports from China: Its Impact on Hong Kong's Manufactured Export Performance, 1962-1973, unpublished M.Phil. thesis, Chinese University of Hong Kong, 1977

WOOD, W.A.: A Brief History of Hong Kong, Hong Kong: South China Morning Post Ltd., 1940

WOODRUFF, A.M. and BROWN, J.R. (eds.): Land for the Cities in Asia, Hartford, Conn., 1971

WOODWARD, R.: The Shipbuilding and Repair Facilities of Hong Kong, Trade Bulletin, Hong Kong, April 1960, pp. 114-116

WORTH, R.M.: Urbanization and Squatter Resettlement as Related to Child Health in Hong Kong, American Journal of Hygiene, 78, 1963, pp. 338-348

WRIGHT, B.R.: Student Guidance and Counselling in Hong Kong, Journal of Education (Hong Kong University), 19, 1961, pp. 78-81

--: Social Aspects of Change in the Chinese Family Pattern in Hong Kong, Journal of Social Psychology, 63, No. 1, 1964, pp. 31-39

WU, C.T.: Policy-making over Land Rent in Hong Kong: A Case Study of the Bureaucracy and the Pressure Groups, Centre of Asian Studies, University of Hong Kong, 1973 (mimeo.)

WÜLKER, G.: Ist Hong Kong noch ein Entwicklungsland? Europa-Archiv, 20, 1965, pp. 349-358

YANG, C.K.: Religion in Chinese Society, Berkeley and Los Angeles: University of California Press, 1967

YAP, P.M.: Suicide in Hong Kong, Hong Kong: Hong Kong University Press, 1958

--: Suicide in Hong Kong, Journal of Mental Science, 104, 1958, pp. 266-301

YEUNG, P.: Hong Kong's Foreign Trade Multiplier, Journal of Economic Society, University of Hong Kong, 1969, pp. 6-10

--: Trade Ties Between Hong Kong and Mainland China, Asian Survey, Vol. X, 1970, pp. 820-839

--: Exports, Re-exports and Economic Growth: The Case of Hong Kong. Faculty Working Papers 28, University of Illinois, 1971 (mimeo.)

YEUNG, Y.M. and DRAKAKIS-SMITH, D.W.: Comparative Perspectives on Public Housing in Singapore and Hong Kong, Asian Survey, 14, 1974, pp. 763-775

YOUNG, S.C.: The GATT's Long-Term Textile Arrangement and Hong Kong's Textile Trade, Ph.D. thesis, Washington State University, 1969

YU, T.W.C.L.: Die Industrialisierung Hong Kongs von 1949 bis 1964, Ph.D. Dissertation, Köln 1967

YUEH, H.: The Problem of the Hong Kong Refugees, Asian Survey, 2, No. 1, 1962, pp. 28-37

YUEN, K.M.: Export Performances and Structures of Hong Kong and South Korea, unpublished M.Phil. thesis, Chinese University of Hong Kong, 1978

II. OFFICIAL PUBLICATIONS

Abkommen zwischen der Europäischen Wirtschaftsgemeinschaft und Hong Kong über den Handel mit Textilwaren, Amtsblatt der Europäischen Gemeinschaften. Rechtsvorschriften, Luxemburg, 19, 1976. L 108, pp. 2-16

Annual Departmental Report by the Registrar of Trade Unions, Hong Kong

Annual Report of the Commissioner of Police, Hong Kong

Annual Report of the Family Planning Association of Hong Kong, Hong Kong

Bibliography of Social Science Periodicals and Monograph Series, Hong Kong, 1950-1961, by Foreign Manpower Research Office, Bureau of the Census, Washington, D.C.: Government Printing Office, 1962

Building Reconstruction, Advisory Committee, Final Report, Hong Kong 1946

Census and Statistics Department: Hong Kong: Government Printer, Report on the 1961 Census, 1962

--: Report on the 1966 By-Census, 1967

--: Population Projections for Hong Kong 1966-1981, 1968

--: Hong Kong Statistics, 1947-1967, 1969

--: Special Review: Labour Supply Projections for Hong Kong, Monthly Digest of Statistics, Oct. 1972, pp. 64-67

--: Estimates of Gross Domestic Product 1966-1971, 1973; 1961-1973, 1975

--: Special Review: Overcrowding and Sharing of Housing Accommodation, Monthly Digest of Statistics, Jan. 1973, pp. 64-71

--: 1971 Census of Manufacturing Establishments, 1973

--: Hong Kong Life Tables 1971-1991, 1973

--: Hong Kong Population Projections 1971-1991, 1973

--: Hong Kong Monthly Digest of Statistics

--: Census Circular No. 1/75: 1973 Census of Industrial Production, 1975

Census and Statistics Department: Census of Manufacturing Establishments, 1973

--: Estimates of Gross Domestic Product 1961-1975, 1977

--: The Household Expenditure Survey 1973-1974, and the Consumer Price Indexes, 1976

--: Hong Kong Population and Housing Census: Main Report, 1973

--: Hong Kong Review of Overseas Trade

--: Hong Kong Social and Economic Trends, 1973, 1976

--: Hong Kong Statistics, 1947-1967, 1969

--: Hong Kong Trade Statistics

CHANG, E.R.: Report on the National Income Survey of Hong Kong, Hong Kong: Government Printer, 1969

City of Victoria, Hong Kong. Central Area Redevelopment. Report by the Director of Public Works, Hong Kong: Government Printer, 1961

Commissioner of Labour: Annual Departmental Report, Hong Kong: Government Printer

Commissioner of Rating and Valuation: Property Review 1971, Hong Kong: Government Printer, 1972

Department of Commerce and Industry: Hong Kong Trade Statistics

--: Textile Hong Kong, Hong Kong 1966

--: Industry Survey Reports (various numbers)

--: Trade Bulletin

--: Commerce, Industry and Finance in Hong Kong, Hong Kong 1955

--: Review of Overseas Trade

Drug Addiction Research Programme 1969. Hong Kong Prisons Department, Hong Kong: Government Printer, 1971

Financial Secretary, Budget Speech, Hong Kong: Government Printer, various years

Focus on Hong Kong: World Development, Oxford, 1, 1973, pp. 65-71

Focus on Hong Kong: Changing Roles in the East and West, A Special Report, International Herald Tribune, Paris, Sept. 1978

Government Publications Directory, Hong Kong

HETHERINGTON, R.M., et al.: The Final Report of the Industrial Training Advisory Committee, Hong Kong: Government Printer, 1971

Hong Kong. A Survey, The Banker, 1974, pp. 773-811

Hong Kong and Cyprus. Third Report from the Expenditure Committee, Defence and External Affairs Sub-Committee, London: Stat. Office, 1976

Hong Kong for the Businessman, Hong Kong Government Office, London 1963

Hong Kong General Chamber of Commerce: Classified Directory of Members, Hong Kong 1957 ff.

Hong Kong Government: The Budget: Economic Background, Hong Kong: Government Printer, various years

--: Economic Report, Hong Kong: Government Printer, various issues

--: Report of the Working Committee on Export Promotion Organization, Hong Kong: Government Printer, 1965

Hong Kong Productivity Centre: Industry Data Sheet (for various industries), 1972 (mimeo.)

Hong Kong Legislative Council: Hong Kong Hansard, Hong Kong: Government Printer, various years

Hong Kong Trade Development Council: Hong Kong Trade Review, Hong Kong, various years

Hong Kong Government: Annual Departmental Reports 1965-66, 1966-67, 1967-68, 1968-69, Department for Resettlement, Government Printer

--: Report of the Housing Commission, Hong Kong 1923

--: Report of the Housing Commission 1935, Hong Kong, 1938

Hong Kong Housing Authority: Annual Report, 1959/60, 1976/77, Hong Kong: Government Printer, 1977

Hong Kong 1975, Far Eastern Economic Review, 87, 1975, 13

Information Services Department: Hong Kong For the Businessman

Inland Revenue Department: Synopsis of Taxation in Hong Kong, 5th edition, Hong Kong: Government Printer, 1972

International Bank for Reconstruction and Development: Report on Hong Kong, 1967 (mimeo.)

International Labour Office: Report to the Government of Hong Kong on Manpower Assessment, Geneva 1967

Labour Department: Some Facts about Employment in Hong Kong, Hong Kong: Government Printer, 1973

List of Government Publications, Hong Kong: Government Printer, 1975

Opportunity Hong Kong. A Review of Industry, Commerce, Achievements and Opportunities in the British Crown Colony, Hong Kong: Government Printer, 1964

OWEN, N.: Competition and Structural Change in Unconcentrated Industries, The Journal of Industrial Economics, Oxford, 19, 1971, pp. 133-147

Registrar of Trade Unions: Annual Departmental Report, Hong Kong: Government Printer, various years

Report of the Administrator of German Enemy Property, Hong Kong. Distribution of German Enemy Property Ordinance, No. 34 of 1956, Hong Kong: Government Printer, 1957

Report of the Fulton Commission: Commission to Advise on The Creation of a Federal-type Chinese University in Hong Kong, Minerva, London, 1, 1963, pp. 493-507

Report of the Housing Board 1972, Hong Kong: Government Printer, 1972

Report of the Committee on Air Pollution, Hong Kong 1970

Report of the Committee on Government Policies and Practices with regard to Squatters, Resettlement and Government Low-cost Housing, Hong Kong 1963

Report of the Finance of Home Ownership Committee, Hong Kong 1964

Report of the Industrial Bank Committee, Hong Kong 1960

Report of the Industrial Training Advisory Committee, Hong Kong 1971

Report of the Inter-Departmental Working Party on the Proposed Crossharbour Tunnel, Hong Kong: Government Printer, 1956

Report of the Loans for Small Industry Committee to the Trade and Industry Advisory Board, 1970

Report of the Working Committee on Productivity, Hong Kong 1964

Report of the Working Party on Export Credit Insurance, Hong Kong 1963

Review of Policies for Squatter Control, Resettlement and Government Low Cost Housing 1964, Hong Kong 1964

SCHREIBER, M.: Offshore. A Survey of Hong Kong, The Economist, London, No. 6882, Vol. 256, 1975

Scientific Directory of Hong Kong. Compiled by the Committee for Scientific Coordination, Hong Kong 1969

Special Committee on Higher Education, 2, Interim Report, Hong Kong: Government Printer, 1968

Statistisches Bundesamt, Wiesbaden: Allgemeine Statistik des Auslandes, Länderkurzberichte: Hong Kong 1976, Stuttgart, Mainz: Kohlhammer, 1976

--: Fachserie G. Außenhandel, Reihe 8, Außenhandel des Auslandes: Hong Kong, Stuttgart, Mainz: Kohlhammer, 1967

The Chinese University of Hong Kong: Calendar 1977-1978, Hong Kong 1977

The 1976-1977 Budget: Economic Background, Hong Kong: Government Printer, 1976

Trade Development Council: Hong Kong Enterprise

--: Industrial Investment Hong Kong 1971-72, Hong Kong 1971

TSUEN, W.: District Outline Development Plan, Town Planning Board, Hong Kong 1961

United Kingdom Colonial Office: Hong Kong Currency, London 1931

United Kingdom Treasury: The Basle Facility and the Sterling Area, London 1968

United Nations: Economic Commission for Asia and Far East: Industrial Development in Asia and Far East, Bangkok, 1966 (sections on Hong Kong)

United Nations: Economic Survey of Asia and the Far East, New York, various years

United Nations: Office of the High Commission for Refugees: The Problem of Chinese Refugees in Hong Kong, Leyden 1955 (Hambro Report)

United States Bureau of Foreign and Domestic Commerce: Hong Kong under Japanese Occupation, Washington 1943

United States Congress: Refugee Problem in Hong Kong, Report of a Special Sub-Committee, Washington 1962

Urban Council: Annual Departmental Report, Hong Kong

VI. APPENDICES

Hong Kong's Major Economic Indicators
(HK$ Mn.)

	1950	1951	1952	1953	1954	1955	1956
Mid-year Population (million)	2.24	2.02	2.13	2.24	2.36	2.49	2.61
Gross Domestic Product (at market prices)							
Per Capita GDP (HK$)							
Total Imports	3,788	4,870	3,779	3,873	3,435	3,719	4,566
Total Exports	3,716	4,433	2,899	2,734	2,417	2,534	3,210
Domestic Exports							
Re-exports							
Total Trade	7,503	9,303	6,678	6,606	5,852	6,253	7,776
Visible Trade Balance	-72	-437	-880	-1,139	-1,018	-1,185	-1,356
Total Deposits					1,069	1,137	1,267
Demand					829	852	928
Time					139	152	173
Savings					101	133	166
Money Supply (M_1)						1,480	1,615
Money Supply (M_2)						1,765	1,954
Bank Loans and Advances					510	632	769
Gov't Revenue (Fiscal Year)	292	309	385	397	434	455	510
Gov't Expenditure (Fiscal Year)	252	276	312	355	373	402	470
Fiscal Surplus/ Deficit (Fiscal Year)	40	33	73	42	61	53	40

Sources: Hong Kong Government, Annual Report (Hong Kong: Government Printer, various years); Gazette, Special Supplement, No. 4 (Hong Kong: Government Printer, various issues); The 1978-79 Budget: Economic Background (Hong Kong: Government Printer, 1978); Census and Statistics Department, Hong Kong Statistics, 1947-1967 (Hong Kong: Government Printer, 1969); Hong Kong Monthly Digest of Statistics (Hong Kong: Government Printer, from January 1970 onwards); Hong Kong Social & Economic Trends, 1964-1974 (Hong Kong: Government Printer, 1976); and Estimates of Gross Domestic Product (Hong Kong: Government Printer, 1977 and 1978 issues).

Hong Kong's Major Economic Indicators
(HK$ Mn.)

1957	1958	1959	1960	1961	1962	1963	1964	1965	1966	1967
2.74	2.85	2.97	2.98	3.17	3.31	3.42	3.51	3.60	3.63	3.72
				6,050	6,882	7,994	8,894	10,516	11,091	12,411
				1,910	2,082	2,337	2,538	2,923	3,055	3,334
5,149	4,594	4,949	5,864	5,970	6,657	7,412	8,551	8,965	10,097	10,449
3,016	2,989	3,278	3,938	3,930	4,387	4,991	5,784	6,530	7,563	8,781
		2,282	2,867	2,939	3,317	3,831	4,428	5,027	5,730	6,700
		995	1,070	991	1,070	1,160	1,356	1,503	1,833	2,081
8,166	7,583	8,227	9,801	9,900	11,045	12,403	14,334	15,494	17,660	19,230
-2,133	-1,605	-1,671	-1,926	-2,040	-2,270	-2,421	-2,767	-2,435	-2,534	-1,668
1,412	1,582	2,055	2,681	3,367	4,311	5,425	6,491	7,250	8,405	8,162
955	988	1,205	1,392	1,470	1,664	1,997	2,337	2,532	2,681	2,658
267	350	482	752	1,234	1,768	2,283	2,639	3,098	3,742	3,324
190	244	368	537	663	879	1,145	1,515	1,620	1,982	2,180
1,649	1,732	2,015	2,240	2,353	2,626	3,026	3,537	4,052	4,301	4,632
2,106	2,326	2,865	3,529	4,250	5,273	6,454	7,691	8,770	10,025	10,136
865	919	1,373	1,720	2,334	2,849	3,642	4,612	5,038	5,380	5,343
584	629	665	859	1,030	1,253	1,394	1,518	1,632	1,818	1,900
533	590	710	845	953	1,113	1,295	1,440	1,769	1,806	1,766
51	39	-45	14	77	140	99	78	-137	12	134

Sources: see page 388

Hong Kong's Major Economic Indicators
(HK$ Mn.)

1968	1969	1970	1971	1972	1973	1974	1975	1976	1977
3.80	3.86	3.96	4.05	4.12	4.21	4.32	4.40	4.44	4.51
13,356	15,791	18,670	20,976	24,156	30,736	35,252	37,268	47,329	54,444
3,512	4,087	4,716	5,185	5,869	7,296	8,161	8,478	10,651	12,072
12,472	14,893	17,607	20,256	21,764	29,005	34,120	33,472	43,293	48,701
10,570	13,197	15,238	17,164	19,400	25,999	30,036	29,832	41,557	44,833
8,428	10,518	12,347	13,750	15,245	19,474	22,911	22,859	32,629	35,004
2,142	2,679	2,892	3,414	4,154	6,525	7,124	6,973	8,928	9,829
23,042	28,090	32,845	37,420	41,164	55,004	64,156	63,304	84,849	93,534
-1,902	-1,696	-2,369	-3,092	-2,364	3,006	-4,084	-3,640	-1,736	-3,868
10,367	12,297	14,955	18,785	24,613	26,191	30,998	36,343	44,030	53,019
3,144	3,714	4,326	5,317	8,500	8,623	8,161	9,911	9,667	12,650
4,432	5,216	6,407	7,395	7,807	9,958	14,200	13,629	18,423	19,616
2,791	3,367	4,222	6,073	8,306	7,610	8,637	12,803	15,940	20,753
4,965	5,642	6,548	7,891	11,412	11,761	11,370	13,563	14,050	18,081
12,188	14,225	17,177	21,359	27,525	29,329	34,207	39,995	48,413	58,450
6,038	7,884	9,669	11,836	17,726	23,263	29,549	35,075	42,735	55,649
2,081	2,481	3,071	3,541	4,991	5,241	5,875	6,520	7,494	10,233
1,873	2,032	2,452	2,901	4,385	5,169	6,255	6,032	6,591	8,997
208	449	619	640	606	72	-380	488	903	1,236

Sources: see page 388

HONG KONG FACT SHEET

D e s c r i p t i o n [+]

Hong Kong is a British Crown Colony. It consists of 236 islands and islets, many of them waterless and uninhabited, and a portion of the Chinese mainland east of the Pearl River estuary adjoining the province of Kwangtung. Its total land area is 404 square miles (1,046 square kilometres), including recent reclamations.

The most important island is Hong Kong Island, which together with adjacent islets has an area of 29.2 square miles (75.6 square kilometres). Victoria, the capital and centre of commerce, is situated on the north side. It is 91 miles (146 kilometres) southeast of Canton, 40 miles (64 kilometres) east of Portugese Macau and 70 nautical miles south of the Tropic of Cancer.

Hong Kong Island was ceded to Britain in 1842. This was followed in 1860 by Kowloon on the mainland opposite and Stonecutters Island which together total 4.3 square miles (11.1 square kilometres).

The New Territories, totalling 370.5 square miles (959 square kilometres) were leased from China on June 9, 1898 for 99 years and comprise the area north of Kowloon up to the Shum Chun River along with 235 islands.

Between Hong Kong Island and the mainland lies Victoria Harbour, which ranks with San Francisco and Rio de Janeiro as one of the three most perfect natural harbours in the world. It varies in width from one to six miles (1.6 to 9.66 kilometres) and has a total area of 23 square miles (59.5 square kilometres).

The greater part of the territory consists of steep, unproductive hillsides. In the New Territories almost all flat, lowlying land is intensively cultivated, while hanging valleys and plateaux also contain villages with small areas of farm land. The highest point is Tai Mo Shan, 3,142 feet (958 metres), situated in the centre of the New Territories. Victoria Peak, which dominates Hong Kong Island is 1,817 feet (554 metres) high.

Despite the island's steep and rugged terrain, postwar building development has been spectacular. Great blocks of flats, many of them erected by the government for low-salaried workers, cling to almost perpendicular hillsides. Many sidestreets are so steep they must be stepped. Banks, merchant houses, and warehouses that have helped to make Hong Kong prosperous as a trading port, tower above narrow streets on reclaimed land beside the harbour.

In Kowloon, blocks of shops built before the war have been demolished to make way for blocks of air-conditioned offices and flats and, on both sides of the harbour, hotels up to 35 storeys high accommodate the more than 1.7 million tourists who now visit Hong Kong each year.

[+] A Hong Kong Government Information Services Publication. Printed by the Government Printer, Hong Kong, February 1978.

To cope with Hong Kong's industrial and population growth, three new towns are being developed in the New Territories as part of a 10-year housing programme launched in 1973. One, at Tsuen Wan, is already more than half complete, housing 500,000 of its planned population of about 900,000. A second, at Tuen Mun (Castle Peak), which in 1973 had only 40,000 inhabitants, is being expanded to an ultimate capacity of 486,000. The third, at Sha Tin, where 25,000 people lived in 1973, is intended to house about 530,000 when fully developed.

These three new towns will provide homes for about one million of the additional 1.5 million people who are to be accommodated under the housing programme. The towns are being developed as balanced self-sufficient entities with a comprehensive range of community facilities to go in hand with the provision of housing and the promotion of industry.

Similarly, the market towns of Tai Po, Yuen Long, Fanling and Shek Wu Hui, which in 1973 had a combined population of 80,000 are being planned for development to an ultimate capacity of about 370,000.

Population

1931 Census	840,473
1945 Estimate	600,000
1947 Estimate	1,800,000
1957 Estimate	2,796,800
1961 Census	3,133,131
1966 By-census	3,716,400
1971 Census (March 9)	3,948,179
1972 Estimate (Dec 31)	4,165,500
1975 Estimate (Dec 31)	4,429,200
1976 Estimate (Dec 31)	4,477,600
1977 Estimate (June 30)	4,513,900

The natural increase has long been among the highest per capita in the world, but over the past 10 years has shown a steady decline. Live births registered in 1975 were 78,200, compared with 102,195 in 1965. More than 1,000,000 people have crossed the border from China since 1950, but this immigration has decreased in recent years. More than 98 per cent of the population are Chinese and 59 per cent were born in Hong Kong.

Climate: Sub-tropical and monsoonal. Winter is cool and dry, summer hot and humid. The mean daily temperature ranges from 15°C in February to 28°C in July. The average annual rainfall is 85 inches (2,168.8 mm).

Languages: Both English and Chinese are given equal status and, as far as possible, equal use in government business. English is widely used in commerce. Cantonese is the spoken language of the majority of people, but several other Chinese dialects are spoken.

Main religions: Christian, Buddhist, Moslem.

Government

Status: Crown colony.

Constitution: Hong Kong is administered under letters patent of 1917 by a Governor, an Executive Council and a Legislative Council.

The Executive Council, which is presided over by the Governor, consists of five ex-officio and nine nominated members. Of these, one is an official and eight are unofficial members.

The Legislative Council at present consists of four ex-officio members, 17 nominated officials and 24 nominated unofficials. The council is presided over by the Governor.

There is also an Urban Council consisting of 24 members (12 appointed by the Governor and 12 elected). The council receives the bulk of its revenue from rates. Its statutory responsibilities, which are confined to the urban areas, cover abattoirs, hawkers and markets, environmental sanitation and hygiene, cultural services, public health, recreation and amenities.

The administration of the New Territories is in the hands of the Secretary for the New Territories, who is assisted by district officers.

Justice

English common law and the rules of equity are in force in Hong Kong, so far as they may be applicable to local circumstances. They have been extended and modified by the application of certain subsequent enactments and by Hong Kong ordinances. The locally enacted laws are consolidated and revised periodically. The courts in Hong Kong include the Supreme Court, consisting of the Court of Appeal and the High Court, the District Court, magistrates courts and the tenancy, labour and small claims tribunals.

Economy

Many factors have contributed to give Hong Kong its international reputation as both a leading manufacturing complex and major commerical centre within Asia. This success stems from an economic policy of free enterprise and free trade, an industrious work force, a sophisticated commercial infrastructure, one of the finest ports in the world, a strategically located airport, and excellent worldwide communications.

By June 1977 there were 23,459 registered industrial undertakings in Hong Kong employing 687,352 workers.

According to the results of the 1976 By-Census, employment in the major occupations are: Manufacturing 845,920; services 284,970;

commerce 423,770; construction 104,040; farming and fishing 48,500; communications 136,180.

Wages have continued to rise. The overall nominal increase in wage rates among the selected industries and services during 1976 was estimated to be 15 per cent over the previous year. As the consumer price indexes have increased by about three per cent during the same period, the level of real wages in 1976 had increased by 12 per cent when compared with that in 1975. The Factories and Industrial Undertakings Ordinance is the basis for controlling hours and conditions of work. Standard working hours for women and young people are eight hours a day and 48 hours a week. The employment of women on overtime is limited to 200 hours a year since January 1, 1976.

Finance

Currency: Hong Kong dollar. HK$ 1 = about US 21 cents and 11p sterling (at the end of January 1978).

Coins of HK$ 5, $ 2, $ 1, and 50, 20, 10, and five cents are issued by the Hong Kong Government. A legal tender note of one cent is also issued. Notes of denominations from HK$ 10 upwards are issued by the Hong Kong and Shanghai Banking Corporation and the Chartered Bank.

Budget:

			HK$ (million)
	1956-7	1966-7	1976-7
Revenue	509.7	1,817.8	7,493.5
Expenditure	469.5	1,806.1	6,590.9

The main sources of revenue for the year 1976-7 were: internal revenue (47.3 per cent), duties (9.1 per cent), general rates (8.3 per cent), revenue from properties and investments (4.3 per cent), and land sales (7.4 per cent).

Major items of expenditure were: social services 40.2 per cent - including education (21.3 per cent), medical and health (9.8 per cent), housing (3.3 per cent) and social welfare (5.5 per cent) - community services (21.7 per cent) - including transport, roads and civil engineering (11.2 per cent) and water (7.2 per cent) - general services (19.8 per cent) - including law and order (11.6 per cent) and economic services (8.5 per cent).

Banking: At the end of 1977 there were 74 licensed banks and deposits totalled HK$ 55,646 million (£ 6,252 million; US $ 12,09 million). There were also 100 bank representative offices and 201 registered deposit-taking companies.

T r a d e

The value of merchandise imported, exported and re-exported in 1977 was HK$ 93,534 million (£ 10,509 million; US$ 20,333 million) an increase of 10 per cent over 1976.

The main imports are raw materials and semi-manufactures (42 per cent), consumer goods (23 per cent), foodstuffs (15 per cent) and capital goods (13 per cent).

The main domestic exports are clothing (40 per cent), miscellaneous manufactured articles such as plastic ware, toys and dolls (17 per cent), electrical machinery, apparatus and appliances (15 per cent), textiles (9.8 per cent), professional, scientific and controlling instruments, photographic and optical goods (1.2 per cent), watches and clocks (4.8 per cent) and manufactures of metal (2.8 per cent).

In 1977 the principal market was the United States, which took 38.7 per cent of all Hong Kong's domestic exports, followed by West Germany (10.5 per cent), Britain (8.7 per cent), Japan (4.0 per cent), Canada (3.3 per cent) and Australia (3.6 per cent).

The main sources of imports are Japan (23.7 per cent), China (16.6 per cent), the United States (12.5 per cent), Taiwan (6.7 per cent), Singapore (5.9 per cent) and Britain (4.5 per cent).

(HK$ Million)

	1971	1972	1973	1974	1975	1976	1977
Imports	20,256	21,764	29,005	34,120	33,472	43,293	48,701
Exports (Including re-exports)	17,164	19,399	25,999	30,036	29,832	41,557	44,833

R e s o u r c e s

Hong Kong has little more than 40 square miles (103 square kilometres) of agricultural land and therefore most food must be imported. Despite the scarcity of land, however, Hong Kong produces 43 per cent of its own vegetables, as well as considerable quantities of poultry and pigs. The fishing fleet is one of the biggest in the Commonwealth with 5,500 vessels, of which 93 per cent are mechanised.

C o m m u n i c a t i o n s

Sea: There are regular sailings from Hong Kong to all parts of the world. Major shipyards are able to build tankers, dry cargo, or passenger vessels up to 500 feet (152 metres) in length, but although their work is increasingly directed towards ship repairing and major modifications, a large shipbuilding and repair yard is planned for Tsing Yi Island to handle even the largest vessels now afloat. The Ocean Terminal, opened in 1966, accommodates the world's largest ocean liners as well as conventional cargo ships. Hong Kong also boasts one of the most modern container terminals in the world. Situated at Kwai Chung, it began operations in 1972 and now ranks third in the world.

Ferries: Two companies operate ferries between Kowloon and Hong Kong and the outlying islands. In 1976-7 a total of 183,433,000 passengers and 3,487,662 vehicles were transported. The ferry organisations are among the largest in the world. An international ferry service operates between Hong Kong and Portugese Macau utilising conventional vessels, hydrofoils and the recently developed jetfoils. In 1977 5.1 million passengers were carried.

Roads: At the end of 1977 there were 677 miles (1,092 kilometres) of road and 207,521 vehicles, giving a density of 281 vehicles per mile (175 per kilometre). A mile-long (1.61 kilometre) cross-harbour tunnel links Hong Kong Island to mainland Kowloon.

Kowloon-Canton Railway: The British Section of the Kowloon-Canton Railway runs for 21 miles (33.7 kilometres) from Hong Kong on the Kowloon peninsula to Lo Wu on the border with China. It is currently a single tracked railway of standard gauge with passing points at six intermediate stations. The current volume of traffic is 44 passenger trains per day in addition to a maximum of 20 freight trains. An investment programme amounting to HK$ 1,500 million (£ 168 million; US$ 326 million) for the period 1976-7 to 1985-6 is under review to expand and modernise the railway including double tracking the main line from Hung Hom to Lo Wu, including a new signalling system, electrification, constructing a new double-tracked tunnel 1.2 miles (two kilometres) long through Beacon Hill, building new branch lines and remodelling stations. These plans will enable the railway to improve its service to the public, play a more significant role in the transport needs of Hong Kong and substantially improve its ability to carry freight traffic from China.

Mass Transit Railway: Construction of the Modified Initial System, a 9.6 mile (15.6 kilometre) underground railway connecting Central District on Hong Kong Island with Kwun Tong in northeast Kowloon, is now about 30 per cent complete. Costing HK$ 5,800 million (£ 651.6 million; US$ 1,260 million) the Modified Initial System will begin partial operation in September 1979 and become fully operational in March 1980. In July 1977, approval was given to extend the railway from North Nathan Road to Tsuen Wan in the New Territories, a distance of 6.6 miles (10.7 kilometres).

Air: Hong Kong International Airport is linked to all parts of the world by 30 international airlines which provide more than 900 scheduled passenger services to and from Hong Kong each week. In addition, there are many scheduled cargo flights and non-scheduled passenger and cargo charter flights. The 11,130 feet (3,390 metre) single runway lies along a promontory built on reclaimed land extending into Kowloon Bay. The Passenger Terminal, with its new extension, is capable of handling up to 4,500 passengers an hour.

Telecommunications: Overseas communications include telephone and telegraph circuits by submarine cable, HF radio, satellite and troposheric scatter systems. Two satellite earth stations give round-the-world coverage via the Indian Ocean and Pacific Ocean satellites. The fully automatic internal telephone system serves over 964,000 subscribers with more than 1,207,600 telephone stations and has an installed equipment capacity of 1,181,000 lines.

Postal Services: The Post Office Department operates postal services within Hong Kong and conducts a worldwide exchange of mail by both air and surface, with direct mail services to some 266 different mail offices throughout the world. About one million items are posted or delivered each day and there are more than 80 post offices in Hong Kong. Normally there are two deliveries a day in urban areas and one in rural districts.

Power: There are three electric supply companies. Electricity consumption in 1977 totalled 29,792 million megajoules compared with 26,190 million megajoules in 1976. The number of consumers in 1977 was 1,044,300.

H o u s i n g

By June 1977 more than two million people, 46 per cent of the population of Hong Kong, were housed under government or government-assisted programmes.

The Housing Authority supplies low-cost homes and it is aiming to provide low-rent housing for another 1.5 million people by 1986. By the end of September 1977, the authority had rehoused 334,440 people since its establishment in April 1973.

It is anticipated that the authority will be able to offer self-contained homes to 200,000 people a year from 1979-80.

At the end of June 1977, 1,863,351 people were accommodated in the Authority's 62 public housing estates scattered throughout urban areas and in the New Territories. Another 148,600 people, in September 1977, were living in housing provided by the Housing Society, a non-profit organisaiton which in previous years received the majority of its funds from the government but which now finances its own construction work. The society obtains building sites from the government at one third of the current market value of the land.

Rents for public housing under the management of the Housing Authority vary from HK$ 24 (£ 2.6) a month for one of the smallest domestic flats in the older estates to HK$ 557 (£62; US$ 121) a month for a large two bedroom flat in the newest estates.

In the private sector HK$ 2,435 million (£ 273.5 million; US$ 529.3 million) was spent on private development during 1977, the bulk of this being new housing and commercial projects.

H e a l t h

Full medical facilities are available throughout Hong Kong and charges are according to means. Starting at HK$ 5 (56p; US$ 1.) a day for hospital care. Fees can be waived altogether. There is a doctor to every 1,140 people, and the ratio of hospital beds to head of population is 4.4 per 1,000.

	No.	Beds
Government hospitals	28	8,788
Aided hospitals	21	8,788
Private hospitals	11	2,289
Government maternity homes	22	393
Private maternity and nursing homes	25	110
	107	19,779

Government expenditure on medical services:

1966-7	$ 173.4 million	1971-2	$ 304.4 million
1967-8	$ 174.3 million	1972-3	$ 397.3 million
1968-9	$ 194.5 million	1973-4	$ 469.7 million
1969-70	$ 217.4 million	1974-5	$ 575.2 million
1970-1	$ 252.2 million	1975-6	$ 570.6 million
		1976-7	$ 665.8 million

Birth rate	17.7 per 1,000
Death rate	5.2 per 1,000
Infant mortality rate	13.9 per 1,000 live births
Maternal mortality rate	0.16 per 1,000 total births

S o c i a l W e l f a r e

Development in social welfare services continues to be carried out under the Five Year Plan adopted in 1973. The plan includes the development of social security on the basis of cash benefits and emergency relief for victims of natural disasters; programmes on community services with emphasis on young people; social rehabilitation of young offenders and probationers; welfare services for individuals and families with problems; facilities for the physically and mentally disabled to enable them to become independent and productive members of the community; and improvements in services for the elderly.

Social security is a government responsibility and is at present mainly provided by the Public Assistance Scheme and the Disability and Infirmity Allowances Scheme. Public assistance is given in the form of cash payments based on need, with the aim of ensuring that in all reasonable circumstances incomes are maintained above the subsistence level. The scheme is means-tested and, subject to their registering for and not refusing suitable employment, has recently been extended to all able-bodied adults of working age. At the end of March 1977, the public assistance caseload was 48,917. Disability and infirmity allowances are not subject to proof of financial needs. They are intended to provide a small pension, on top of any public assistance payment, to help the disabled and the elderly to live in the community and reduce the burden on their families. At the end of March 1977, the total disability and infirmity allowance caseload was 72,437.

E d u c a t i o n

Nearly a third of Hong Kong's population is enrolled in local schools, colleges and education centres. In 1977 primary school enrolment was 621,276 and for secondary schools it was 452,899.

March 1977

Schools	No.	Enrolment
Government	119	62,958
Aided	834	581,414
Private	1,889	655,827
Special education	35	3,338
Technical institutes	3	17,920
Total:	2,880	1,321,457

The government's aim is to make available free and compulsory education for every child for nine years, i.e. six years in a primary school followed by three years in a secondary school. The government will provide enough subsidised Form One places for all Primary Six leavers in September 1978.

The Hong Kong Polytechnic has 15 departments and 24,524 full-time and part-time students. There are two universities in Hong Kong - the University of Hong Kong, with an enrolment of 4,710 and the Chinese University of Hong Kong, with 4,715 students.

W a t e r

Providing an adequate water supply for Hong Kong has always been difficult because the territory has no natural lakes or rivers or substantial underground water sources. Nevertheless, apart from a brief period in 1974 and the latter half of 1977 when its rainfall was exceptionally low, Hong Kong has enjoyed a virtually uninterrupted 24-hour supply since 1968, when its first "reservoir-in-the-sea" was completed at Plover Cove. This reservoir - created by dredging, damming and draining an inlet of Tolo Harbour on the east coast of the New Territories - had an initial storage capacity of 170 million cubic metres which was increased to 230 million cubic metres by extensions completed in 1973. The reservoir then represented more than 75 per cent of Hong Kong's total storage capacity.

The success of Plover Cove led to plans for the High Island Reservoir. Work began in 1972 on damming both ends of the sea channel separating High Island from the Sai Kung peninsula. Impounding began in the summer of 1977 and when major works are finished in 1979, the reservoir will be able to hold 273 million cubic metres and will raise Hong Kong's total storage capacity to 579 million cubic metres.

Hong Kong has installed the world's largest desalination plant, with a capacity of 181,800 cubic metres a day; the first unit began producing fresh water from the sea in early 1975 and by mid-1977 all six evaporator units were operational. The territory also continues to buy water from China, by arrangement with the People's Council of Kwangtung Province. An agreement reached in mid-1977 increased the supply from this source from 109 million cubic metres to 136 million cubic metres a year.

Law and Order

Hong Kong claims the distinction of having one of the oldest, yet most modern, police forces in the world.

Formed 136 years ago, the Royal Hong Kong Police Force has grown from a mere handful of men to a highly efficient establishment of more than 21,500 all ranks (including auxiliaries) who have at their disposal a wide range of the latest and most sophisticated equipment.

During 1977, 24 new police reporting centres were opened in urban areas and there are now 87 in all - 30 of them operating as Neighbourhood Police Units. A new police division has been established at Hong Kong International Airport, new police stations are being built in the new towns and improved rural policing is being introduced. The total number of crimes reported decreased by 5,260 in 1977 and in particular there were reductions in crimes of robbery, blackmail, trafficking in dangerous drugs, burglary, and fraud. The overall crime detection rate was 60.6 per cent in 1977, compared with 59.7 per cent in the previous year.

The Independent Commission Against Corruption, set up by law in February 1974, investigates suspected corruption offences, prevents corruption and promotes higher social ethics. The commissioner is directly responsible to the Governor and his staff are not subject to the purview of the Public Services Commission.

Besides the police and the ICAC important contributions towards the safety and well-being of the community are made by the Customs and Excise Service, the Prisons Department and the Fire Services Department.

Press, Broadcasting and Television

Hong Kong has a large and active press. At the end of 1977 there were 388 publications registered, of which 121 were newspapers, including four English dailies, 107 Chinese language newspapers, eight other English newspapers, one bi-lingual and three Japanese newspapers. Besides 34 concerned with general news, other Chinese dailies are solely entertainment orientated.

Radio Television Hong Kong is financed by the government from general revenue and produces in FM stereo, almost 600 hours of programmes a week on four separate channels, two in Chinese and two in English.

In addition, the station has introduced Radio 5 an FM relay of the BBC World Service from 5 pm to 2:30 am daily. The same channel also relays the Chinese Service from 6 am to 5 pm.

Commercial Radio broadcasts three services on AM, two in Chinese and one in English.

There are three commercial television stations in Hong Kong all using the UHF 625-line PAL colour system. Rediffusion Television Ltd. (RTV) and Television Broadcasts Ltd. (HK-TVB) both operate English and Chinese channels whereas Commercial Television Ltd. (CTV), a new station set up in 1975, operates a single Chinese channel.

HONG KONG KOWLOON AND THE NEW TERRITORIES

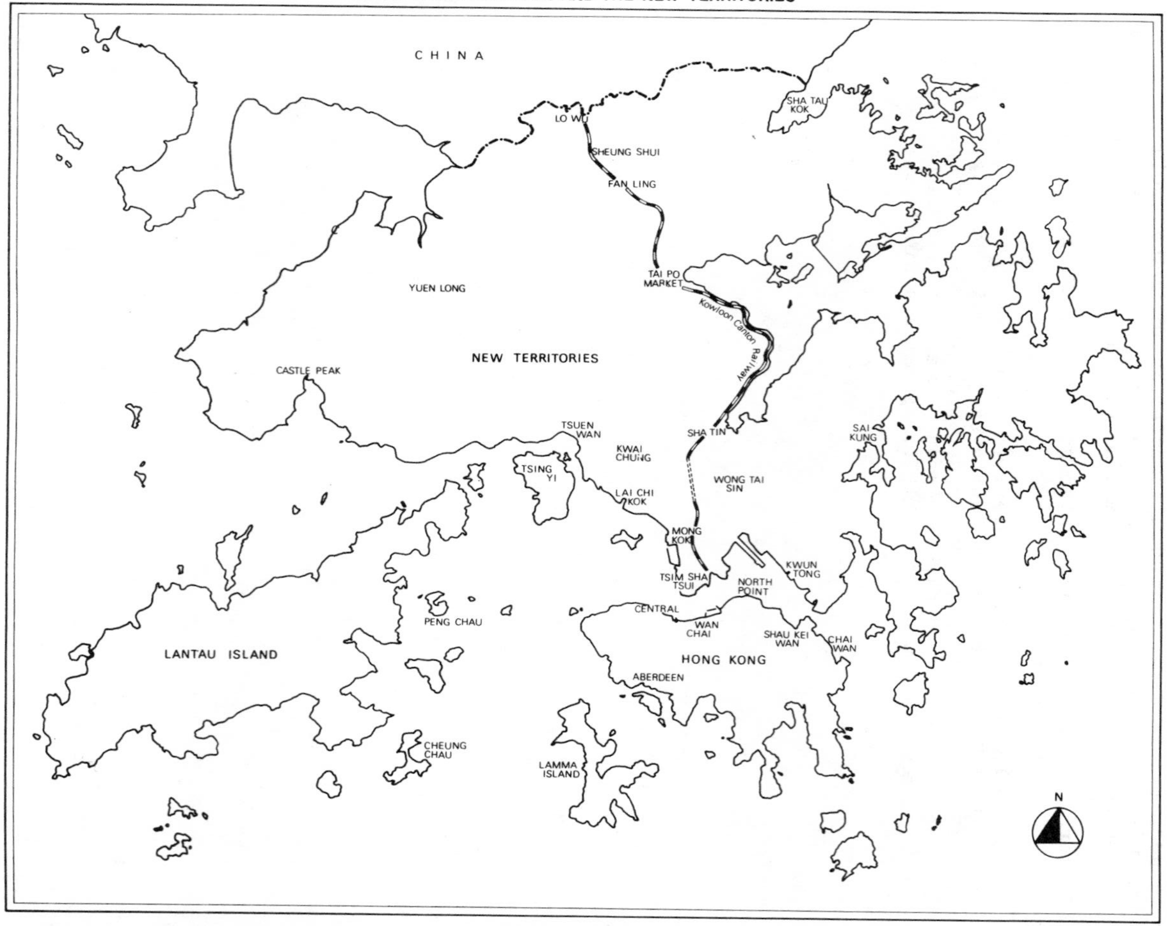

VII. ABOUT THE AUTHORS

Ying-Keung CHAN graduated in Geography from The Chinese University of Hong Kong in 1967 and received his Doctorat d'Université (Très Honorable) in Human Geography from the Université de Bordeaux, France in 1970. From 1971 to 1975 he worked as Research Specialist for the Social Research Centre, The Chinese University of Hong Kong and currently he is Lecturer in Sociology, United College, The Chinese University of Hong Kong. He is particularly interested in population and urban environment studies and has several publications in English and in Chinese.

Tak-Sing CHEUNG graduated from The Chinese University of Hong Kong in 1972 and received his Ph.D. in Sociology from State University of New York at Buffalo in 1978. Since 1976 he has been teaching Sociology at The Chinese University of Hong Kong. His research interest is in social psychology in general and the self-concept in particular.

Yuet-Wah CHEUNG graduated in Sociology from Chung Chi College, The Chinese University of Hong Kong, in 1975 and received his M.A. in Sociology from the University of McMaster in 1968. He was a teaching assistant in the Sociology Department of The Chinese University of Hong Kong from 1975 to 1977. Presently, he is a graduate student in Sociology at the University of Toronto. His major research interests are health services in China and in overseas Chinese communities in North America.

Ching-Yan CHOI received his B.A. in Sociology from the International Christian University in Japan in 1965, M.A. in Sociology from the Western Reserve University, U.S.A., in 1967 and his Ph.D. in Demography from the Australian National University in 1970. He was formerly a Lecturer in Sociology, United College, The Chinese University of Hong Kong and is currently on the staff of the Australian Bureau of Statistics. His major interests are fertility and migration studies.

Suk-Ching HO is Lecturer in Marketing and International Business at The Chinese University of Hong Kong. She has studied at the University of Indiana where she received her MBA in 1974. Her main interests are in consumer behaviour and international marketing.

Tien-Tung HSUEH received his Ph.D. in Economics from the University of Colorado (U.S.A.) and was research fellow at Harvard-Yenching Institute, Harvard University in 1977-78. Before he joined The Chinese University of Hong Kong in 1971, he was Associate Professor at National Taiwan University (1969-1971). His main publications include: An Econometric Model for Taiwan Economic Development, 1971; "Development Alternatives for the Hong Kong Economy: An Aggregate Analysis," Malayan Economic Review, 1975; "Sectoral Value Added Projections for Singapore. Based on the 1970 and 1967 Input-Output Tables," Ibid., 1976; "International Comparisons of the Development Features of the Asian Countries, 1960-1972," Internationales Asienforum, 1977 and "The Impact of Collectivisation on Chinese Grain Production, 1952-1957" (with Pak-Wai LIU) in Political Economy.

Ambrose Yeo-Chi KING graduated in Law from the National Taiwan University in 1957. In 1970, he received his Ph.D. in Public and International Affairs from the University of Pittsburgh. He is now Senior Lecturer and Chairman of the Department of Sociology, and Head of New Asia College, The Chinese University of Hong Kong. In the academic year 1975-76, he was visiting fellow at both the University of Cambridge, U.K., and M.I.T. He has published works in various international journals among them the British Journal of Sociology, Asian Survey, the Journal of Social and Political Affairs, Modern Asian Studies. He has also published books in Chinese such as "From Tradition to Modernity - an Analysis of Chinese Society and its Change", and "The Modernization of China and the Intellectuals". A monograph on the historical development of Sociology in China is forthcoming.

Hsin-Chi KUAN, born in 1940, is Lecturer in Government and Public Administration at The Chinese University of Hong Kong. He graduated from the National Chengchi University, Taipei, in 1963. He received his Diplom in Politologie from the Freie Universitaet Berlin in 1967 and his Ph.D. in Political Science from the University of Munich in 1972. He is author of "The Nonproliferation Treaty and the Federal Republic of Germany" (1973).

Siu-Kai LAU graduated from the University of Hong Kong with a B.S.Sc. in Economics and Sociology in 1971. In 1975 he received his Ph.D. in Sociology from the University of Minnesota. At present, he is Lecturer in Sociology at The Chinese University of Hong Kong, as well as Associate Director of its Social Research Centre. His major interests are in the social and political development of Hong Kong, and the diffusion of agricultural technology in China.

Rance Pui-Leung LEE received his Ph.D. in Sociology from the University of Pittsburgh in 1968. Presently he is Senior Lecturer in Sociology and Director of the Social Research Centre, The Chinese University of Hong Kong. He is also Associate Editor of the International Review of Modern Sociology, and International Advisory Editor of the Southeast Asian Journal of Social Science. His main publications include: "Population, Housing and the Availability of Medical and Health Services in an Industrializing Chinese Community" (1973); "Toward the Utopia of Integrating Western and Chinese Medical Systems in Hong Kong" (1975); "The Interaction between Chinese and Western Medicine in Hong Kong: Modernization and Professional Inequality" (1976); "The Causal Priority between Socio-economic Status and Psychiatric Disorder: A Prospective Study" (1976), and many other internationally published articles.

Mei-Chiang LIN received her B.A. degree in Economics from the National Taiwan University in 1960. Between 1973-76 she studied at the University of Freiburg and from 1973-74 she did research at Pittsburgh. She is currently Associate Professor of Economics at Chu Hai College and concurrently a part-time teacher at the Hong Kong Baptist College. Her main research interest is in the field of development and trade.

Tzong-Biau LIN obtained his Ph.D. from the University of Freiburg in 1969. Between 1973-74 he was a visiting scholar at Stanford University and the University of Pittsburgh. He is now Chairman of the Department of Economics and concurrently Dean of the Social Science Faculty, The Chinese University of Hong Kong. His field of specialization is in econometrics and applied economics. But his publications cover various aspects of economics, including three books about money, trade and employment, and numerous internationally published papers on topics ranging from pure econometric methods to practical development and trade problems of the Hong Kong economy.

Peter Jic-leung MAN graduated in Sociology from the Chinese University of Hong Kong in 1972. He was research assistant at the Social Research Centre of the Chinese University of Hong Kong from 1972 to 1973. Currently he is a Ph.D. candidate at the University of Portland, U.S.A.

Victor MOK graduated in Economics from The Chinese University of Hong Kong in 1959 and received his Ph.D. in Economics from the Michigan State University in 1964. He was Assistant Professor in the Economics Department of Saint Mary's College of California, from 1964 to 1969. Since 1970 he has been teaching Economics at The Chinese University of Hong Kong. During 1978-79, he was visiting scholar at the University of Cambridge, England. His main publications include: "The Nature of Kwun Tong as an Industrial Community: An Analysis of Economic Organizations", 1972; "The Small Factories in Kwun Tong: Problems and Strategy for Development", 1974; "Capital Mobility and the Effectiveness of Fiscal Policy under the Foreign Exchange Standard: The Case of Hong Kong", 1976.

Kin-Chok MUN is Senior Lecturer in Marketing and International Business at The Chinese University of Hong Kong. He obtained his Diplom-Volkswirt degree in 1965 and his Ph.D. in 1967 from the University of Freiburg. He has taught at Nanyang University in Singapore and was Visiting Senior Research Fellow at the London Business School. He has published numerous articles, particularly in the fields of marketing and international business.

Louis NTHENDA, B.Sc. Econ. (London), D.Phil. (Oxon); b. Malawi, East Africa; Lecturer, United College, The Chinese University of Hong Kong; formerly taught public administration at Ahmadu Bello University, Zaria, Nigeria; Sometime Scholar, St. Antony's College, Oxford; currently writing a book on the role of government in the industrial development of Hong Kong since 1945. Other interests: public sector management, staff relations, administrative theories.

Koon-Lam SHEA earned his Bachelor of Social Science from The University of Hong Kong and his Ph.D. from Washington University, St. Louis. He has been teaching at The Chinese University of Hong Kong since 1974. His contributions have appeared in Southern Economic Journal, Economia Internazionale, Weltwirtschaftliches Archiv and Academic Economic Papers.

Udo-Ernst SIMONIS is Professor of Economics at the Technical University of Berlin. He received his M.A. from the University of Freiburg (1963) and Ph.D. from Kiel University (1967). Between 1967-68 he was Personal Advisor to the President of the Republic of Zambia; from 1970-72 Fellow of the Japan Society for the Promotion of Science at the University of Tokyo; in 1976 he was Visiting Professor at The Chinese University of Hong Kong. He is author or editor of ten books and many chapters and articles in scholarly journals and collections. The most recent books include "Japan. Economic and Social Studies in Development"; "Infrastruktur. Theorie und Politik"; "Quality of Life. Methods and Measurement".

Fai-Ming WONG, Senior Lecturer of Sociology at The Chinese University of Hong Kong, received his B.A. (1961) from the University of Redlands, M.A. (1963) from the University of California at Los Angeles, and Ph.D. (1969) from the University of California at Santa Barbara. He has taught Sociology at The Chinese University since 1963. He had also served as Senior Research Fellow at the Department of Sociology, Yale University in 1974-75. His main publications include: "Modern Ideology, Industrialization, and Conjugalism," International Journal of Sociology of the Family, 1972; "Industrialization and Family Structure" (1974) and "Family Change and the Agrarian Commune in China" (1977).